LOW-WAGE WORK IN THE NETHERLANDS

LOW-WAGE WORK IN THE NETHERLANDS

Wiemer Salverda, Maarten van Klaveren, and Marc van der Meer, Editors

The Russell Sage Foundation Case Studies of Job Quality in Advanced Economies

Russell Sage Foundation • New York

The Russell Sage Foundation

The Russell Sage Foundation, one of the oldest of America's general purpose foundations, was established in 1907 by Mrs. Margaret Olivia Sage for "the improvement of social and living conditions in the United States." The Foundation seeks to fulfill this mandate by fostering the development and dissemination of knowledge about the country's political, social, and economic problems. While the Foundation endeavors to assure the accuracy and objectivity of each book it publishes, the conclusions and interpretations in Russell Sage Foundation publications are those of the authors and not of the Foundation, its Trustees, or its staff. Publication by Russell Sage, therefore, does not imply Foundation endorsement.

Library of Congress Cataloging-in-Publication Data
Low-wage work in the Netherlands / Wiemer Salverda, Maarten van Klaveren and Marc van der Meer, editors.
    p.   cm. — (The Russell Sage Foundation case studies of job quality in advanced economies)
  ISBN 978-0-87154-770-5
  1. Unskilled labor—Netherlands. 2. Wages—Netherlands. 3. Minimum wage—Netherlands. 4. Labor market—Netherlands. I. Salverda, Wiemer.
II. Klaveren, Maarten van. III. Meer, Marc van der.
  HD8516.5.L69 2008
  331.7'9809492—dc22   2007045944

Text design by Suzanne Nichols.

RUSSELL SAGE FOUNDATION
112 East 64th Street, New York, New York 10021

10 9 8 7 6 5 4 3 2 1

Contents

About the Authors   vii

Acknowledgments   ix

Introduction   The Dutch Story   1
               Robert Solow

Chapter 1   The Debate in the Netherlands on Low Pay   16
               Wiemer Salverda, Maarten van Klaveren, and
               Marc van der Meer

Chapter 2   Low-Wage Work and the Economy   32
               Wiemer Salverda

Chapter 3   Labor Market Institutions, Low-Wage Work, and   63
               Job Quality
               Wiemer Salverda

Chapter 4   The Position, Design, and Methodology of the   132
               Industry Studies
               Maarten van Klaveren

Chapter 5   The Retail Industry: The Contrast of Supermarkets   148
               and Consumer Electronics
               Maarten van Klaveren

Chapter 6   Hotels: Industry Restructuring and Room   177
               Attendants' Jobs
               Ria Hermanussen

Chapter 7   Health Care: Integrated Quality Care Sheltered   206
               from Cost Control?
               Marc van der Meer

Chapter 8   Call Center Employment: Diverging Jobs and   237
Wages
Maarten van Klaveren and Wim Sprenger

Chapter 9   The Food Industry: Meat Processing and   267
Confectionary
Arjen van Halem

Chapter 10   Labor Market Institutions and Firm Strategies that   297
Matter for the Low-Paid
*Wiemer Salverda, Maarten van Klaveren, Marc van
der Meer, Wim Sprenger, Kea Tijdens, Arjen van
Halem, and Ria Hermanussen*

Index   317

About the Authors

WIEMER SALVERDA is director of the Amsterdam Institute for Advanced Labour Studies (AIAS) of the University of Amsterdam, and coordinator of the European Low-Wage Employment Research Network (LoWER).

MAARTEN VAN KLAVEREN is senior consultant and researcher in the field of technology, work organization, and industrial relations at STZ consultancy and research, Eindhoven, the Netherlands.

MARC VAN DER MEER is associate professor and director of studies at the Amsterdam Institute for Advanced Labour Studies (AIAS) of the University of Amsterdam.

RIA HERMANUSSEN is senior consultant and researcher in the field of labor-market related issues at STZ consultancy and research, Eindhoven, the Netherlands.

ROBERT SOLOW is Institute Professor Emeritus at the Massachusetts Institute of Technology and a Nobel laureate in economics.

WIM SPRENGER is researcher on work organization and trade union innovation at STZ consultancy and research, Eindhoven, the Netherlands.

KEA TIJDENS is research coordinator of the Amsterdam Institute for Advanced Labour Studies (AIAS) of the University of Amsterdam, professor of sociology at Erasmus University, Rotterdam, and scientific coordinator of the worldwide WageIndicator web survey.

ARJEN VAN HALEM is researcher and consultant in the field of technology, work organization and industrial relations at STZ consultancy and research, Eindhoven, the Netherlands.

Acknowledgments

The research project was a joint undertaking of two teams, Amsterdam Institute for Advanced Labour Studies (AIAS) of the University of Amsterdam and STZ Consultancy and Research, coordinated by Wiemer Salverda and Maarten van Klaveren, respectively, under the final responsibility of AIAS. Jointly with Marc van der Meer, they have acted as editors of this volume.

We are grateful to the members of the joint team and other individuals for the following contributions to the research and reporting in this volume: Maite Blázquez Cuesta researched earnings mobility for chapter 2 (see Blázquez Cuesta and Salverda 2007), and Yvette Berghuijs, Ernest Berkhout, Daniella Brals, Matthijs Kooiman, and Vid Štimac helped with data treatment for this chapter. Maarten van Klaveren made many contributions to chapter 3, especially with respect to the Polder model, health and safety, works councils, and equal treatment, as did Kea Tijdens, with her research on temp agency work (see Tijdens et al. 2006), and Suzan Leydesdorff, who contributed research on education and training to this chapter and lent support to the work reported in chapter 7. His coeditors acknowledge Marc van der Meer's work on firm strategies in chapter 4. In chapters 5 and 6, Anja van de Westelaken helped with interviews and case studies. Marieke van Essen helped with the interviews and case studies reported in chapter 7. Theo Bouwman helped with the research and case studies reported in chapter 9.

In addition, Kea Tijdens and Maarten van Klaveren made important contributions to the international guidelines for the interviews and the templates for the industry reports.

We gratefully acknowledge the comments and suggestions made by the special discussants of the Russell Sage Foundation, Robert Solow and Eileen Appelbaum; by two anonymous referees of the foundation; by the other country teams of the research project, particularly Gerhard Bosch and Thorsten Kalina (Gelsenkirchen), Eve Caroli and Jérôme Gautié (Paris), Geoff Mason (London), and Niels Westergaard-Nielsen (Aarhus); and by the special discussants Rob van Tulder of Erasmus University, Rotterdam, and Paul de Beer, Jelle Visser, and Anne-Laure Mascle-Allemand of AIAS.

INTRODUCTION

The Dutch Story

Robert Solow

By any reasonable standard definition of "low-wage work," about a quarter of American wage earners are low-wage workers. The corresponding figure is smaller, sometimes much smaller, in other comparable advanced capitalist countries. This fact is not very good for the self-image of Americans. It does not seem to be what is meant by "crown(ing) thy good with brotherhood, from sea to shining sea." The paradox, if that is the right word, is the starting point for the extensive study of which this book is an important part. What are the comparative facts, what do they mean, and why do they turn out that way?

A foundation dedicated from its beginning to "the improvement of social and living conditions in the United States of America" has to be interested in the nature of poverty, its causes, changes, consequences and possible reduction. Low-wage work is not the same thing as poverty, still less lifelong poverty. Some low-wage workers live in families with several earners, and share a common standard of living, so they may not be poor even while working such jobs. Some low-wage workers are on a reasonably secure track that will eventually move them to better paid jobs, so they are not poor in a lifetime sense. But some low-wage workers are stuck with very low income for a meaningful length of time. For them, low-wage work does mean poverty in the midst of plenty.

Of course, the incidence of poverty can be reduced by transfer payments outside the labor market. Nevertheless, in a society that values self-reliance, and in which productive work confers identity and self-respect as well as the respect of others, income redistribution unconnected or wrongly connected with work is not the best solution except in special cases. In that kind of society, ours for instance, the persistence of low-wage work is felt as a social problem on its own. It first has to be understood if we are to find satisfactory ways to diminish its incidence or alleviate its effects.

One obvious basis for low-wage work is low productivity, which

may be primarily a characteristic of the worker, as is often simply assumed, or may be primarily a characteristic of the job. If it inheres in
the job, equity could be achieved by passing the job around, so to
speak, like boring committee assignments or military service, but
that would have no aggregate effect. Wherever low pay originates,
however, raising productivity provides a double benefit: it diminishes
the amount of low-wage work to be done, and it increases the useful
output of the whole economy.

Low productivity, and therefore low-wage work, tends to repro-
duce itself from generation to generation. This is an important additional reason why a high incidence of low-wage work is a "social
condition" that needs to be improved. Growing up in a chronically
low-wage family limits access to good education, good health care,
and to other ladders to social mobility. So a persistent high incidence
of low-wage work, when confined to a relatively small group, contra-
venes the widely accepted social goal of equal opportunity.

These are among the reasons why, in 1994, the Russell Sage Foundation inaugurated a major program of research on the nature,
causes, and consequences of low-wage work and the prospects of low-
wage workers. This initiative replaced a successful but more conventional program of research on poverty. It was called, rather
grandly, *The Future of Work*. One of its key motivations was the need
to understand how poorly educated, unskilled workers could cope
with an economy in which most jobs were becoming technologically
advanced, and therefore more demanding of cognitive power and refined skills.

This formulation was intended to call attention both to workers
and to jobs, the natural subtext being that low-end jobs might be disappearing faster than low-skilled workers. This potential disparity
presented the danger that low-wage workers could be stranded in an
economy that had no use for them. The research mandate was interpreted quite broadly.

The Future of Work program was, as a matter of course, focused on
the United States. It produced a large body of useful and original research, some of which was collected and summarized in the 2003
volume *Low-Wage America: How Employers Are Reshaping Opportunity in the Workplace*, edited by Eileen Appelbaum, Annette Bernhardt, and Richard Murnane. One of the refreshing aspects of these
studies was precisely that the needs and capacities of employers

shared the stage in the low-wage labor market with the abilities and motivations of workers.

One interesting hypothesis that emerged from this work was the notion that employers have significant discretion about the way they organize their use of low-skilled workers and the value they put on the continuity and productivity of their work force. The extreme versions came to be labeled "low-road" and "high-road" modes of organization. At the low-road extreme lie employers such as the typical car-wash, whose workers are regarded as casual labor, interchangeable parts that can be picked up off the street freely under normal labor-market conditions. There is no advantage in doing otherwise. At the other extreme are employers who regard their unskilled workers as an asset whose productive value can be increased by more training and longer attachment to the firm.

The point of this distinction was the belief that in some market situations both styles can be viable. An employer's place on the continuum is not uniquely determined by technology and the intensity of competition in the product market. Satisfactory profits can be earned by somewhat higher- and somewhat lower-road modes of organization; in some industries, examples of both can be found coexisting.

Of course, the nature of the technology and the competitive intensity in the industry are important determinants of labor-market outcomes. That is not in doubt. In some situations, however, there may be scope for several levels of wages and job quality for unskilled workers. It is important here to note that job quality covers much more than the current wage and benefits paid; it includes the length and slope of the internal wage scale, the degree of job security, the training offered and the possibilities of promotion within the firm, small creature comforts, the pace of the work itself, the autonomy and ergonomic character of the work, and so on. Each of these has a cost to the firm and a value to the workers, and the two are not always the same.

It hardly needs arguing that these elements of job quality can be important for the satisfaction and self-respect attached to a job. It then becomes important to the researcher to understand the broad factors that govern the typical choices made by employers. These may include historical precedents, legislation, the working of the educational system, collective bargaining, and other "institutional" biases.

At this stage of the argument, the advantages of a comparative cross-country study stand out. Most of those broadly institutional factors cannot be studied empirically within the United States because they change so slowly in time, and because there is not much locational variation. One cannot actually see them at work in a still snapshot. One can speculate and make thought-experiments, but that is not the same thing. So the idea sprouted within the Russell Sage Foundation in 2003 that it might be very useful to observe systematically how the fate of low-wage labor differs across a sample of European countries. Not any countries will do: one wants countries with somewhat different but not radically different political and institutional histories; but they must be at the same level of economic development as the United States if lessons are to be learned that could be useful in the United States. In the end, the countries chosen included the three indispensable large countries—France, Germany, and the United Kingdom—and two small northern European countries—Denmark and the Netherlands. The choice was consciously limited to Europe in order to avoid the complication of drastically different sociopolitical systems. A competition was held, and a local team selected for each of these five countries.

The planners of the project framed it in such a way that would sharpen the inferences that could be made from cross-country comparisons. Most centrally, five target jobs were chosen as objects of close study, the same five in each country. They were nurses' assistants and cleaners in hospitals, housekeepers in hotels, checkout clerks and related occupations in supermarkets and retail stores specializing in electrical goods, packagers, machine tenders and other unskilled occupations in two branches of food processing, namely confectionary and meat products, and low-skilled operators in call centers. (This last choice took advantage of an already ongoing international study of the call-center industry.) These are all low-wage jobs in the United States. The fact that some of them are not low-wage jobs in some of the five countries is an example of the value of cross-country comparisons. The simple fact invites, or rather compels, the question: Why not?

Each national team was asked to compile a statistical overview of low-wage work in its country, with special but not exclusive attention to the five target jobs. The team was also asked to complement the routine data with a survey of the historical, legislative, educational and other institutional infrastructure that is believed to underlie its own particular ways of dealing with low-end jobs and low-skilled workers. The final part of each country report is a series of case studies of each of the target jobs, including interviews with employers, managers, workers, union representatives and other participants. (When temporary work agencies were used to provide some or all of the relevant workers, they were included in the interviews wherever possible.) The national teams met and coordinated their work in the course of the research. This book is the report of the Netherlands team.

There will be one more stage to complete the project. A six-country group of participants, including Americans, will prepare an explicitly comparative volume, job by job. They will try to fathom what deeper attitudinal, institutional, and circumstantial factors might explain the sometimes dramatic differences in the way these six modern nations engage with the problem of low-wage work.

One big, somewhat unexpected, finding is the one mentioned in the first paragraph of this introduction. The six countries differ substantially in the incidence of low-wage work. ("Incidence" is defined as the fraction of all workers, in the country or in a specific sector, who fall into the low-wage category.)

There is an interesting and important definitional issue that arises immediately. Uniformly in Europe (and elsewhere), a low-wage worker is anyone who earns less than two-thirds of the national median wage (usually the gross hourly wage, if only for data-availability reasons). This obviously makes the incidence of low-wage work an index of the inequality or dispersion of the wage distribution: multiplying or dividing everyone's wage by ten leaves the number of low-wage workers unchanged. The same applies to the measurement of poverty. In the United States, the poverty line is an absolute income. It was initially chosen as an empirical compromise, never entirely appropriate and less so as time passes, but nevertheless an absolute income. The United States has no corresponding definition for low-wage work, but the same approach could be taken. There are arguments to be made on both sides of this issue; for the purposes of this project, the choice of a low-wage threshold makes little practical difference. We use the European definition because that is the way their data are collected.

There is yet another practical reason to use the European definition. As noted, the two-thirds-of-median index simply reflects the degree of wage dispersion: a low incidence of low-wage work means a relatively compressed wage distribution, at least in the lower tail. This measure makes international comparisons more meaningful. Comparing absolute real wages between the United States and other countries is problematic because pensions, health care, payroll taxes, employer contributions and other such benefits and deductions are handled differently in different systems. Relative comparisons are subject to similar distortions, but considerably less so.

Here are the basic facts. In 2005, the incidence of low-wage work was 25 percent in the United States, 22.1 percent in the United Kingdom, 20.8 percent in Germany (2004), 18.2 percent in the Netherlands (2004), 12.7 percent in France (2002) and 8.5 percent in Denmark. The range is obviously very wide.

In a way, that is helpful, because figures like this cannot be interpreted to the last decimal. Here is one interesting example of an unexpected twist. It turns out that the Dutch are the part-time champions among these countries, with a significantly larger fraction of part-time workers than elsewhere. This appears to be a voluntary choice, not something compelled by the unavailability of full-time work. Part-time workers tend to be paid lower hourly wages than full-time workers in the same or similar jobs, even in countries where it is against the law to discriminate against part-timers. The incidence measures given in the preceding paragraph are based on a head-count: 18 percent of all Dutch workers earn less than the low-wage threshold. One could with reason ask instead what fraction of the hours worked in the Netherlands falls into the low-wage category; the answer is about 16 percent. The fact that the hours-based incidence is lower would be common in all countries, but the difference is particularly large in the Netherlands.

A key issue is the degree of mobility out of low-wage work that characterizes each country's system. The seriousness of the "problem" turns almost entirely on the transitory nature of low-wage work. It is impossible to be precise about inter-country differences, because the data are sketchy and definitions vary. It is clear, however, that there are substantial differences among the countries, although mobility is fairly substantial everywhere, if only because younger workers eventually propel themselves into better jobs. The Danes appear to have the shortest residence times in low-wage work. For Americans the take-away lesson is that the self-image of an extremely mobile society is not valid, at least not in this respect.

Of course, there are many uniformities—often just what you

would expect—among these countries in the pattern of low-wage work. The "concentration" of low-wage work in any subgroup of the population is defined as the incidence in that subgroup divided by the incidence among all workers. For instance, any subgroup with a higher incidence than the country at large will have a concentration index bigger than 1. This is the case for workers in the service sector of the economy, for women, for young people, for part-timers, and for those with little education. In most instances, the particular sectors we have picked out for study have a high concentration index; together, retail trade and "hotels and catering" have a concentration ratio of about 3 in the Netherlands. The categories mentioned obviously overlap, but the data do not permit us to zero in statistically on young part-time secondary-school-only women working in supermarkets. Nevertheless, the odds are very high that they fall into the low-wage category.

The cross-country differences are more interesting, however, because they at least offer the possibility that we can find explanations for them in the circumstances, institutions, attitudes and policies of these basically similar economies. It is important that these are basically similar economic systems with broadly similar labor markets. They differ in certain historically established social norms, institutions and policies. One can hope to figure out which of these fairly small differences underlie the observed variation in the conditions of low-wage work. This would be difficult or even meaningless if we were comparing radically different economic systems.

Here is one example of commonality that illustrates the point. In some of the target jobs, in several instances and several countries, there has been a noticeable increase in the intensity of competition in the relevant product market. Low-cost German chains compete with Dutch food retailers. Large food retailers, domestic and foreign, put pressure on meat processing and confectionary prices in every country. The spread of international hotel chains—along with the availability of exhaustive price comparisons on the internet—has made the hotel business more competitive. In all such instances, business firms respond to intensified competition by trying to lower their own unit costs (as well as by product differentiation, quality improvement, and other devices).

The urgent need to reduce costs seems almost invariably—though not exclusively—to involve particular pressure on the wages of low-skilled workers. It is not hard to understand why this should happen in every country, precisely because they are all advanced capitalist market economies. The main reason is that low-wage workers usually have very little "firm-specific human capital." That is to say, since they have few skills of any kind, they have few skills that are difficult to replace for the firm that employs them. If they quit in response to wage reductions, they can be replaced with little cost, especially in a slack labor market. Low-wage workers have few alternatives, so they cannot defend themselves well. For similar reasons, they have little political power and usually little clout with their trade unions, if they have any union protection at all. Firms seeking profit will respond similarly, though not identically in every detail. Country-specific institutions can modify the response, but not entirely.

A closely related common factor has to do with "flexibility." Partly because technology now permits it, and partly because a globalized market now demands it, business firms find that their level of production has to fluctuate seasonally, cyclically and erratically. Sometimes it is not so much the total but the composition of production that has to change, often with short notice. Under those circumstances, it is an advantage if the firm can vary its employment more or less at will; otherwise, underutilized labor constitutes an unproductive cost. The low-end labor force is likely to bear the brunt of this adjustment, for the same reasons already mentioned in connection with wage pressure. Low-wage workers cannot do much to defend themselves against or prepare themselves for these vicissitudes, other than to try for even lower-wage part-time jobs or to resort to public assistance.

There is always a possibility that observed cross-country variation in low-wage employment practices are somehow "natural," in the sense that they can be traced to underlying differences that were not chosen and could not be changed, such as geographical or topographical characteristics, resource availability, or perhaps even some irreversible bit of historical evolution. That does not seem to be what is happening in these six countries. In many instances, cross-country differences are the result of legislation, with minimum wage laws being an obvious example. A more unusual example, at least to Americans, is the fact that many European governments, such as those in France and the Netherlands, can and do extend certain collective bargaining agreements to cover employers and workers in the industry who were not parties to the bargaining itself. In this way, even comparatively small union density can lead to much broader coverage by union agreements.

This need not be an unalloyed benefit to workers. Companies have been known to arrange to bargain with a small, weak union and then press for the resulting favorable agreement to be generalized. But the practice may also reflect a desire by employers to eliminate large wage differentials as a factor in inter-firm competition. It is interesting that when the abolition of this practice of extending collective bargaining agreements was proposed in the Netherlands, the employers' federation opposed the proposal. It is a toss-up which event seems more outlandish to an American: the practice of mandatory extension or that employers should oppose abolishing it.

Explicit legislation is not the only source of institutional differences that affect the low-wage labor market. All sorts of behavioral norms, attitudes, and traditions on both sides of the labor market can have persistent effects. The country narratives describe many such influences. For example, the German report outlines a distinctive system of wage determination and labor relations, based on diversified high-quality, high-value-added industrial production, along with "patient," mostly bank-provided, capital, and participation of employee representatives in company supervisory boards.

This system may be coming to an end, undermined by international competition—especially from the ex-communist countries of eastern Europe, including the reunification of Germany—and shifts in public opinion and political power. It is still a matter of controversy among specialists whether the traditional system had become unsustainable or simply unsustained. The German "mini-job," low wage, frequently incurring lower non-wage employment costs in practice, and limited to very short hours per month, is an example of a device to encourage both demand and supply for certain kinds of low-wage work.

This introduction is not the place for a detailed description of each national system. The individual country narratives will provide that. It is important, however, to underline the fact that the components of each national system often hang together in some way. It may not be possible to single out one component and think: "That looks clever; why don't we try it in our country?" The German mini-job, for example, is occupied mostly by women, and may work the way it does because the social welfare apparatus in Germany is still organized around the notion of the single-breadwinner family. The concept of a labor relations "system" may suggest tighter-fitting than the facts justify; a word like "pattern" might be more accurate. But the basic point remains.

The four continental countries in the study correspond in a general way to the common notion of a "European social model" in contrast with the more individual-responsibility oriented approach of the United States. The post-Thatcher United Kingdom probably falls somewhere in between. It would be a bad mistake, however, to ignore the differences among Denmark, France, Germany, and the Netherlands. To do so would be to miss the variety of conditions for low-wage labor that is possible for advanced capitalist market economies. Only the briefest characterization is possible here, but the individual reports are quite complete.

The Danish "flexicurity" system has achieved the status of a buzzword. The idea is to allow wages and job quality to be determined in an unregulated labor market (except for considerations of health and safety, of course) but to combine this flexibility with a very generous safety net, so that "no Dane should suffer economic hardship." For this system to be workable, the rules of the safety net have to push most recipients into whatever jobs are available. Even so, the system is likely to be expensive. Apparently the *lowest* marginal income tax rate is 44 percent (which is higher than the *highest* rate in the U.S.). One would need to know more about the details of the tax system in order to understand the content of any such comparison, but the details are unlikely to reverse the presumption that Danes are less tax-averse than some others.

To describe the Danish labor market as "unregulated" means only that there is very little intervention by the government. In fact, the labor market is regulated through centralized negotiations between representatives of employers and employees, who have very wide scope. For example, there is no statutory minimum wage, but a minimum labor scale is negotiated by the "social partners." It (almost) goes without saying that there is some evasion of this scale in traditional low-wage sectors, including some covered in the case studies. One reason why this is tolerated is that many of the affected workers are young people, especially students, who are only engaged in low-wage part-time work as a transitory phase. Denmark is a country that is low on university enrollments but high on vocationally-oriented post-secondary, non-university education.

There is a neat contrast here with France, which lives up to its reputation as a rather bureaucratically organized society. As the French report says, "Low hourly wages are fixed in France—perhaps more than in any other country—at the political level, not through collective bargaining agreements, and these wages are set in a centralized, not a decentralized, manner. Thus, the legal minimum wage plays a crucial role in France." Since 1970, the SMIC (minimum inter-branch growth wage) is indexed not only to inflation but also to the growth of overall productivity and wages. The intent was specifically to resist what was felt to be a tendency in the market toward excessive wage inequality.

The SMIC has been set at a fairly high level, and one consequence of this has been the disappearance of some unskilled jobs, to be re-placed by unemployment (especially long-term unemployment), participation in active labor market policies, and withdrawal from the labor force. Other forces have been at work, however—urban land-use regulation in food retailing, for example—so the simple-minded causal connection between the SMIC and high unemploy-ment is not exact. France is also distinguished by having a trade union movement that is rather strong at the national level, but has very little presence on the shop floor. This may account for some eva-sion of labor market regulations at the low end.

The low-wage labor market in the United Kingdom is especially interesting because it is an example of changes in institutions and outcomes brought about in a relatively short time by deliberate acts of policy. The Thatcher government chose as a matter of principle to weaken or eliminate preexisting supports for the occupants of low-quality jobs, and to undermine the ability of the trade union move-ment to compress the wage distribution. As a result, the incidence of low-wage work increased in the late 1970s and after. The Blair gov-ernment, looking for a work-based solution to the problem of poverty, undertook measures to increase the supply of low-wage workers, but it also introduced a (fairly low) National Minimum Wage in 1999. The net outcome appears to have been a steady in-crease in the incidence of low-wage work from the late 1970s until the mid-1990s, and a leveling-off since then.

In effect, the United Kingdom has changed from a system rather like the other continental European countries to something much closer to the United States. The incidence of low-wage work has then followed the same trajectory. Of course, other economic factors, com-mon to many countries, were also at work.

The Netherlands occupies a position somewhere between the

Nordic model and the United States model, but not in a simple average sense. Many of the institutions are peculiarly Dutch; together they are described as the "Polder" model. One of its features is the important extent to which organizations representing employers, the government, and labor act jointly to regulate the labor market and much else, sometimes in a very detailed way. For instance, the minimum wage for young workers is substantially lower than for adults. The proliferation of part-time jobs, many of them occupied by students and young people, may be a consequence of this in part, though it may have other roots as well.

It is striking to an outsider that these tripartite institutions are more than merely regulatory. They are described as "deliberative," and apparently much of the serious public discussion of issues underlying socioeconomic policy takes place within them. This fact may make fairly tight regulation palatable to the Dutch public. The system has had considerable success; for example, the national unemployment rate fell from over 10 percent in 1984 to under 4 percent in 2001, when the widespread recession supervened. As will be seen in the Dutch report, however, it has its problems.

The purpose of these brief vignettes is definitely not to provide a summary of the pattern evolved in each of these countries with respect to low-wage job quality. That information is to be found in each of the separate country studies. The goal of this introduction is to illustrate the important general point that there are several viable systems of labor-market governance, including the mode of management of the low-wage labor market. The issue is not uniquely determined by the needs of a functioning market economy, or by technology, or by the imperatives of efficient organization. The system in place in each country has evolved in response to historical circumstances, cultural preferences, political styles and fashion in economic and social ideas. One cannot avoid noticing that relatively small countries, like Denmark and the Netherlands in our sample, and the other Nordic countries, Austria and perhaps Ireland outside it, seem more able than large countries to create and maintain the amount of trust that is needed for tripartite cooperation. This observation begs the question as to whether successful policy aimed at improving the relative status of low-wage workers may require a degree of social solidarity and trust that may be beyond larger, more diverse populations.

There are certainly many common influences as well: the response to intensified competition; the role of women, immigrants, and minorities; limitations on productivity; and so on. But there is no unique or best pattern. It even seems likely that the same "principles" of organization, applied in different institutional contexts, would eventuate in quite different practices. Some of this may emerge in the detailed comparative volume that is still to come.

The Netherlands has had in many respects a remarkable success story. After a bad patch in the 1980s, aggregate employment has increased strongly, and the unemployment rate has fallen well below the average for the European Union. During the same period, however, the incidence of low-wage employment has increased from 14 to 18 percent, and its composition has shifted slightly toward adult men and women. Part of the mechanism for these changes has been a strong increase in the number of small part-time jobs, which now make up about 70 percent of all low-wage jobs. Taking all wage levels together, 46 percent of all Dutch workers are part-time (15 percent for adult males, 75 percent for adult females), compared with about 17 percent in the United States (6 and 20 percent, respectively). It is obviously important to understand this development: Does it reflect a genuine preference to sacrifice market income in favor of leisure and home production of household services? Is it a defensive reaction against adverse developments in the labor market? Or is it perhaps related to the Dutch educational system, given the importance of part-time jobs for youth?

The report in this volume on low-wage work in the Netherlands looks closely at this history in the context of the "Polder model," which has characterized the specifically Dutch approach to labor market policy since the end of World War II. The essence of the Polder model lies in the important role assigned to bipartite (employers' federation and labor unions) and tripartite (including the government) organizations in regulating the labor market on the basis of consensus. This role extends beyond wage setting to other job quality issues; it can also address the wider economic issues that may be relevant. A key instrument is the collective labor agreement and its mandatory extension beyond the original parties to the negotiation. These organizations were intended to function as more than mere loci for bargaining, and to a remarkable extent they do: they provide a forum for serious discussion of national economic problems. To them should be added the Central Planning Bureau. Established in 1945 in conjunction with the consensual institutions, this is not a planning bureau per se, but a major public center for research and policy analysis.

As already mentioned, the rise in the incidence of low-wage work in the Netherlands has been accompanied by a rise in the number of part-time workers, who today make up 70 percent of all low-wage workers. The largest increase in the incidence of low-wage work occurred among the young (for whom there are especially low minimum wages); in 2002 the incidence of low-wage work among the young was 61 percent, up from 40 percent in 1979. But the incidence among adult men has also risen: from essentially zero in 1979, it increased to 5 percent in 2002 (and from 6 percent to 12 percent among adult women). At the same time, low-paid jobs are increasingly being held by better-skilled workers. The fluidity and changeability of these jobs makes it very difficult for them to be adequately represented by unions, and this is a challenge for the Dutch system.

In other respects, the Dutch experience is fairly typical of continental European countries. The concentration of low-wage work among immigrants (including the second generation) is high and has increased rapidly since the mid-1990s. The service sector has a higher incidence than the goods-producing industries, but we must keep in mind that the service industries differ widely among themselves; not surprisingly, the retailing and hotel subsectors, which are among our case studies, generate a very large quantity of low-wage work, as this report and the others show.

Some American readers may be surprised to discover that a much larger fraction of the Dutch population (37 percent) is classified as having "low" educational attainment than in the United States (20 percent). The Netherlands is one of those countries where many students who in the United States might go to college or university instead move on to senior secondary education that is mainly vocational in character. One consequence of this path is the creation of a large supply of students who are candidates for part-time jobs; another is that completion of the course leads to a credential that is widely accepted by employers.

A small economy like the Netherlands is inevitably more exposed to international competition than a larger one. Dutch firms have always had to compete with foreign rivals, both at home and in export markets. Its proximity to the much larger German economy exposes the Netherlands to competitive pressures emanating from or transmitted by Germany. For example, chronically weak internal demand in Germany leads German firms to seek markets next door, and when German firms find themselves pressed by competition with the lower-wage economies of eastern Europe, they transmit this competitive pressure to the Netherlands. On top of this economic fact, a further strain on peculiarly Dutch institutions comes from the political fact of European integration and the homogenizing effect of directives from the European Union.

The Dutch team is pessimistic about how the system is likely to evolve under the play of these forces, including the sheer flexibility of low-wage employment. If unions learn from their limited success, they may find ways to reduce labor market volatility and improve the quality of low-wage jobs. The team is not certain, however, how far such adjustments can bring them. That only adds to the interest of this volume.

CHAPTER 1

The Debate in the Netherlands on Low Pay

Wiemer Salverda, Maarten van Klaveren, and Marc van der Meer

Employment performance in the Dutch labor market is exceptional in several ways. Today the employment rate in the Netherlands is the highest of the euro zone, and the unemployment rate the lowest. As the country has passed through several deep recessions, the structure of production has shifted from an industrial to a service economy, with the help of a gradual adaptation of the institutional structure. Firms have responded strategically to competitive and institutional pressures by changing their product market strategies, work organization, and human resource policy. In this study, we evaluate the effects for various groups of low-paid workers who are experiencing a growing income differentiation, increasingly diverse patterns of working time, and an overrepresentation of part-time contracts and more unpleasant working conditions than those in jobs higher up the pay ladder. We examine the quality of their jobs and attempt to answer the question of how job quality is affected by the environment of Dutch labor market institutions.

This chapter introduces the national debate on low pay and employment, together with the predominant characteristics of Dutch governance of the labor market and the economy. This debate has long roots that go back all the way to the aftermath of the Second World War, riding three successive "waves" of policymaking regarding wages and social insurance. The waves were all generated or accommodated by the organizational-institutional setup first put in place in 1945 and retained by the country ever since, though its functions have evolved over the course of the intervening sixty years. In addition, the chapter sketches the shape of the discussion on the organization of low-wage jobs—that is, their content and role in firms' division of labor. We conclude with the layout of this volume. But first we summarize the three central features of the research that led to this work: the analysis of institutions, firm strategies, and job quality. These issues are pursued in more detail later, particularly in chapter 4.

THREE CORE ISSUES: INSTITUTIONS, FIRM STRATEGIES, AND JOB QUALITY

This volume combines an institutional analysis of low-wage employment in the Dutch national economy with an in-depth study of forty companies and organizations: eight in each of these five industries: retail trade, health care, food production, call centers, and hotels. Our goal is to show how low-wage jobs have been shaped in a small and open consultation economy that operates in an environment of intensifying and increasingly worldwide competitive pressures, capital mobility, and rapid technological change. The study by Eileen Appelbaum and her colleagues (2003) guided our own study. It charts well these extremely interesting premises and shows that both institutions and firm behavior matter a great deal in determining the quality of low-wage work. This has inspired us to combine three key concepts: institutions, firm strategy, and job quality.

Examining Institutions

Institutions are widely discussed as formal and informal rules that guide human behavior, but their particular effect on low-wage work is seldom well understood. In this work, we raise questions about how institutions fit a wider economic framework and about their effects. We distinguish between two broad categories of institutions affecting, first, the reward of work to the individual employee and the costs to the employer and, second, the content of the job and the organization of work, including the skill level of jobs in interaction with the educational attainment of workers, their flexibility in interaction with employment protection, and their working conditions in interaction with health and safety rules and sickness and disability insurance.

Grasping Firm Strategies

Virtually throughout the twentieth century, the dominant firm strategy was focused on the organizational concentration of enterprise activities. In our case studies, we show how this orientation toward "internalization," aimed at reducing external constraints and uncertainties, has given way to strategies of "externalization" through the outsourcing of staff, jobs, and departments and resulted in an extensive internal and external flexibilization of work processes. This shift makes firm behavior a key element of this research. How do firms design their organization, particularly regarding job quality, given that the institutional environment in which they operate may constrain them but may also stimulate them?

OPERATIONALIZING JOB QUALITY

The decline of industrial employment and the shift to a service economy, combined with a constant pressure to "upgrade" and enlarge the remaining low-skilled jobs, have led to a decline in the number of routine and standardized jobs. Over the past two decades, the fraction of employees performing monotonous, hazardous work has decreased and employees have generally been given more autonomy on the job. At the same time, however, jobs increasingly require workers to be flexible and to accept more responsibility than in the past. In our study, we try to evaluate how particular forms of low-wage work have developed over time, possibly in interaction with the broad industrial environment. This brings us to a key question: under which institutional preconditions can "high-road" approaches be achieved by firms from which low-wage earners can gain?

We elaborate on these questions in chapter 4.

THE DEBATE ON LOW PAY

After the Netherlands, stirred by political unrest and industrial action, introduced universal suffrage after the First World War, more political attention was paid to issues of interest to the newly enfranchised wage-earning population. The legal basis was created for collective labor agreements (CLAs) in 1927, and for the government's right of formal extension to other firms not involved in the negotiating associations in 1937. These laws are still in force today. Before the war social developments basically stopped here. Only limited insurance covering invalidity (1913) and sickness (1930) was made available to certain segments of the dependent working population.

A sea change took place in the wake of the Second World War

when trade unions, employers, and the government established en- tirely new cooperative institutions.[1] In May 1945, the social partners started the Foundation of Labor (STAR) to provide a forum for union-employer talks at the national level. In the same year the gov- ernment established the Central Planning Bureau (CPB), headed by the future Nobel laureate Jan Tinbergen. This organizational-institu- tional setup was completed in 1950 with the creation of the Social and Economic Council (SER), a tripartite body with employer and union representatives and government-appointed experts.

There were strong relationships between union and employer del- egations to SER. In a symbiosis with the STAR and CPB, SER became the most influential adviser for a very broad range of economic and labor market policy issues—for example, wage setting, health care, education, and European unification. It is difficult for policymakers in the Netherlands to ignore agreements on socioeconomic matters reached under this framework. The three institutions, CPB, SER, and STAR, taken together make up a consensus machinery that has tended to depoliticize the socioeconomic debate—until the present day.

When this setup was first established, unions and employers had clear and different power bases: a high membership density on both sides, partly compulsory for employers. The 1945 trade-off granted the unions a position at the national and sectoral bargaining tables. Industry-level collective agreements covered issues of job classifica- tion, wage compensation, training, and employee development. For a large majority of employees under the 1950 Works Councils Act, workers were entitled to representation in joint works councils in the firm, first still chaired by the employer. For decades afterward, the recognized unions turned their backs on issues of work organization and technology, subordinating these issues to national union (wage) policies (Buitelaar and Vreeman 1985). Thus, a dual system of labor relations developed: union presence at aggregate levels, but absence on the work floor.

In the first postwar decades of rebuilding what was at that time both an agricultural and industrial economy, the government was the dominant actor in labor relations, negotiating with business represen- tatives and trade unions about the terms and conditions of employ- ment in the sectors and branches. Within this elitist system, policy- making on low pay was often handled in a rather bureaucratic manner, resulting in a comparatively limited public debate on poverty or the nature of employment and pay—let alone the quality of low-wage work, which is of central concern to us here.

Three issues can be identified in the low-wage debate:

1. The household income of those workers who earn the least

2. The unemployment position of the least-qualified workers

3. The economic nature of the lowest-paid employment

These issues are intricately linked and have been on the agenda of wage formation and social insurance in different formats during three phases of postwar policymaking: a long regulatory phase up until the early 1970s, a short-lived nonregulatory (to avoid using the word "free") phase in the 1970s, followed by a long deregulatory phase that has prevailed ever since. During the first phase, the wage negotiations of unions and employers were strictly controlled for a long time, the statutory minimum wage was introduced, and social insurance expanded slowly at first but then strongly, culminating in the alignment of net minimum benefits with the net minimum wage and the evolution of the latter with negotiated wages. Starting in 1945, this first phase ended for wages in 1964 under the pressure of a tight labor market and concomitant strike activity, and for social insurance in 1974. The phase of strong, unregulated, and diverging wage growth that followed ended in 1979, well before the time of the Wassenaar Accord (1982). Social insurance benefit levels improved in the wake of rapid wage growth. The third phase, which began in 1979 and has extended until the present day, has seen a return to wage restraint in a different format and a long, drawn-out, but cumulatively important dismantling of many of the social insurance provisions (entitlements as well as levels) that had been built up during the first phase; this dismantling continues today. Both trends have a clear and strong negative effect on low wages and minimum benefits. Their employment effects are more disputed, though many consider them the source of the Dutch employment "miracle" (Visser and Hemerijck 1997).

BEFORE 1980: LOW PAY AS PART OF GENERAL WAGE FORMATION

For much of the first phase, low pay was an integrated part of general wage formation. After the war and until the early 1960s, all outcomes of collective wage negotiations had to be officially approved by government-appointed officials first; as a result, there was considerable universal wage moderation in the Netherlands, with minimal differentiation up to 1959. The approval of collective agreements included an explicit checking of the minimum-wage income that would be available to a full-time, unskilled breadwinner and his family (SER 1997, 88). Evidently, the underlying worry concerned the income of the household, not the quantity or nature of low-wage employment. There was broad consensus about the importance of STAR's 1945 recommendation on a "social minimum wage." This mechanism of wage control led the country through the two economic recessions of the 1950s (in 1953 and 1958), but it lapsed in the massive strikes that occurred when the boom of the early 1960s brought unemployment down to very low levels—below 1 percent of the labor force. In the same years employers and the government started bringing in "guest workers" for menial, low-paid jobs in manufacturing—the Spanish, Italians, and Portuguese were brought in first, then later replaced by Moroccans and Turks.

In 1964 the social partners agreed between them on an economy-wide minimum wage, a round figure of 100 guilders a week, which was still meant for the household breadwinner. In 1969 a statutory minimum wage was established by law (NLG 143.50) and was applicable to anyone age twenty-four or older, men as well as women, irrespective of their household position. It should be noted, however, that adult female employment participation was still low at that time. A few years later the threshold was lowered to the age of twenty-three (the "adult [statutory] minimum wage"), and finally in 1974 the famous long tail of Dutch youth minimum wages was introduced after long years of opposition from employers. Note that this occurred some thirty-five years after the United States instituted its federal minimum wage. Thus, low pay, identified as the minimum wage, came to be treated separately from wages in general after 1964. At the same time, however, the government created an up-rating mechanism that linked the evolution of the minimum wage at regular half-yearly intervals to the growth of average negotiated wages, with some time lag. Together with a few special up-ratings in the early 1970s, this mechanism effectively kept low pay part and parcel of wage formation.

The government was forced around 1970 to give up its far-reaching prerogatives vis-à-vis private sector wage formation. The new Incomes Policy Act allowed future government control of wages under exceptional circumstances and for a restricted period only.[2] More than before, wage negotiations were now considered the prime and sole responsibility of unions and employers. The government now had to enter into negotiations with them to target wage growth and/or employment. Unilateral government control of public sector wages remained in force, but wage growth in this sector was effectively linked to private sector developments (the "trend").

During the same period from 1945 to 1974, public social insurance was established. It complemented the wartime health care insurance scheme, which was retained and enacted into law in 1964. Several important schemes with population-wide applications, such as a public old-age pension, were established. More important for our purpose was the creation for employees of unemployment insurance in 1952 and the improved coordination and organization of various schemes, including sickness insurance, and the introduction in 1967 of disability insurance, which replaced the outdated prewar invalidity provisions. The culminating point in the development of social insurance was the linking between 1969 and 1974 of the minimum benefits of all social insurance provisions to the minimum wage on a basis net of tax and contributions. Until the end of the 1970s, wages went up considerably, and given the up-rating and linking mechanisms in place with a focus on welfare, minimum wages and benefits went up equally and there was little discussion of poverty. The purchasing power of the minimum wage/benefit reached its apogee in 1979, as happened at about the same time with the minimum wage in the United States.

SINCE 1980: A DIFFERENT TREATMENT OF LOW PAY

The evolution of both wages and social insurance changed dramatically during and after the deep recession of the second oil crisis of 1980 when a period of prolonged wage restraint and strong and continuing welfare reform started. In the early 1980s, unemployment soared to unprecedented levels, especially for youth, and at the same time international capital movements were liberated in the wake of Margaret Thatcher's policy changes in the United Kingdom. These changes gave employers more room for maneuver vis-à-vis unions and government. Until then, the three parties of the consultation economy had to accommodate each other because none of them had access to an outside option.

From 1981 to 1984, several high-level government advisory groups recommended strengthening industrial policies and improving market conditions for manufacturing. Interestingly, the service sector was hardly discussed. These advisers proposed "a New [Industrial] Elan," but also advocated putting an end to the centrally guided wage policies and stopping the automatic consumer-price indexation in wage setting (Van Dellen 1984). After the 1982 Wassenaar Accord, the newly appointed center-right Lubbers I coalition committed itself to the principles of free wage setting in the market sector without state intervention. That commitment was the outcome of a long political debate that had started with the adoption in 1974 by the CPB of a new view on the effects of wage growth on employment in firms. According to the "vintage model," wage growth would negatively affect the technologically less developed and therefore less productive parts of the production apparatus, together with the corresponding employment.

Negotiated real wage growth was moderated from 1980 on. The statutory minimum wages, which fell under the sway of the government, were lowered even in nominal terms and also in real terms by subsequent "freezes" after 1981—first until 1989, and then again in the period 1993 to 1995 and recently from 2003 to 2005. The perennial argument was that holding down minimum wages was beneficial to employment. It also lowered minimum wages in relative terms, as cumulatively they lagged far behind average wages. As a result, the purchasing power of the adult minimum wage fell between 1979 and 1997 by almost one-quarter, followed by a limited increase of 4 percent up to 2003 and a subsequent decline. Its ratio to adult average wages also declined after 1997 and fell from 62 percent in 1979 to 45 percent in 2004 in spite of the fact that average wages were restrained. We conclude that after 1981 minimum wages and benefits were treated differently from other wages.

Negotiated public sector wages followed a similar course as the minimum wage as the government used its power to cut the link to private sector wage growth. After a unique 3 percent nominal lowering in 1984, public sector wages were also frozen for many years. A steep absolute and relative fall until 1985 resulted, followed by a constant level and then a limited increase after 1996 (figure 1.1). This diverging treatment was a major but little-known provision of the

Figure 1.1   Negotiated Wages, Private and Public and
Youth, and Minimum Wages, Deflated,
1957 to 2005

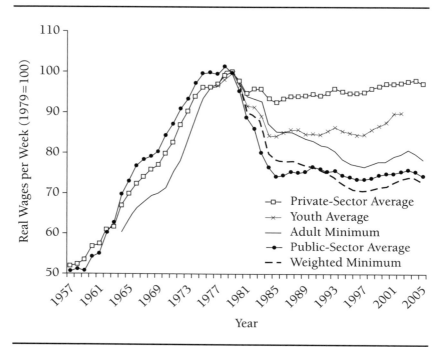

Source: Statistics Netherlands (CBS), Historical Series Statline.

Wassenaar Accord endorsed by the social partners. It helped cut public expenditures—of which wages are the major part—and also
helped keep up net wages while restraining gross wages. Though private sector moderation started in 1980 with some decline in real
wages, its main thrust was not a lagging of wages behind prices but
behind productivity, the primary and enduring element of the Wassenaar Accord. Endorsing this moderation very strongly until 1989—
and again between 1993 and 1995—the Netherlands was a forerun-
ner in Europe. The labor share in GDP fell substantially as a result. In
exchange for this moderation, the second major element of the
Wassenaar Accord was the agreement to shorten the full-time working week and encourage part-time employment.

Since 1980, the entitlements of social insurance have also progres-
sively been diminished or abolished, and the process is still continu-

ing. Cuts in social insurance in the 1980s led to a (strongly opposed) change of direction that significantly affected the purchasing power of social benefits. The revisions of the 1990s went deeper and altered the levels and entitlements more as a matter of principle. In spite of unemployment levels in the early 1980s that had never been seen before, little was done by the government to remedy the employment situation for low-wage workers directly. Only later, when unemployment seemed to be of a structural nature, did the government initiate a variety of active labor market policies. Finally, in 1992, the Youth Guarantee Fund was started, and the government coalition of 1994 to 2002 supported the creation of low-skilled jobs in the public sector and introduced lavish subsidies for employers to reduce the costs of low wages. The cabinet also monitored the utilization of the lowest wage scales of collective agreements. There has been recurrent political debate on the level of the minimum wage and youth minimum wages. The most recent policy change on low pay was to revisit an old policy by freezing the minimum wage—for two and a half years through the end of 2005.

Importantly, the daily organization of social insurance as introduced in 1952 was revised in the 1990s. Step by step the social partners were ousted from the governance of various employee schemes, since their involvement was believed to have encouraged the take-up of social insurance benefits, which were thus misused as a device for solving their problems of reorganizing production. By the early 2000s, most social insurance programs had been renovated according to "work first" principles, and newly integrated social insurance and active labor market programs had been started that attempted to "reintegrate" individuals receiving benefits into the labor market.

Given the steepness of the decline in minimum wages and benefits, that decline has stirred surprisingly little political debate about poverty, in spite of systematic reporting by Godfried Engbersen and others on the subject and on illegal work in the second half of the 1990s. The Netherlands is not familiar with a poverty line such as the United States has. Basically, poverty in the political debate is believed to have been solved by the 1974 equivalence of the net minimum benefits and minimum wage. Recent research on households with a minimum income, however, shows an incidence of poverty of around 10 percent of all households; this figure, the Dutch employment "miracle" notwithstanding, has declined only slightly in recent decades, and then only between 1997 and 2001 (SCP 2005, 20).

THE DEBATE ON WORK ORGANIZATION AND JOB QUALITY

Working conditions and job quality have been promoted primarily by government intervention, under the pressure of employee representatives supported by academics. In the heyday of Dutch Taylorism, the first criticisms of the dominant trend in work organization were heard. In the 1950s, Louis Kuylaars (1952) advocated job enlargement. In the 1960s, field experiments with work structuring were developed at the shop-floor level at, for example, Philips Electronics and the national post and telephone company. The 1970s saw experiments with enhanced employee participation and "industrial democracy," first by the association of Protestant employers and later by the SER. The unions mainly did not participate in these developments (Van Klaveren, van de Camp, and Veersma 1997).

Until the early 1980s, most experiments with new forms of work organization proved to be vulnerable to changes in economic and technological conditions and a lack of managerial commitment. Later on the basis of new forms was strengthened, both scientifically and politically. The theoretical foundation of the Dutch variant of the modern socio-technical (MST) approach developed rapidly, in close interaction with organizational redesign stimulated by the seminal work of Ulbo de Sitter. In 1981 he published an influential plea for organizational renewal that was critical of both the omnipresence of traditional Taylorist work organization in Dutch manufacturing and the aloofness of the unions in this field. A public debate about the "humanization of work" followed, stimulated by studies pointing to the increasing gap between job levels and the educational attainment of the workforce. This "qualitative discrepancy" was widely used as an argument for introducing new forms of work organization and trying to improve job quality. At the same time, the first version of the Working Conditions Act, still concentrated on workplace health and safety, came into force.

Yet over the course of the 1980s, the government and the social partners hesitated to pursue policies to improve job quality in connection with innovations in work organization. For the unions, shop-floor representation continued to be a problem owing to the statutory position of the works councils, the depletion of the ranks of union activists, and the predominance of industry-level collective bargaining. For works councils, a breakthrough came in 1979 when a revision of the law introduced mandatory councils and elections by and from the workers, independent of the employer, and endowed them with powers of information, consultation, and, with respect to personnel policy regulations, co-determination.

Under these conditions, deploying new, innovative union strategies proved to be difficult. Union leaders warned against compromising and dissuaded their members from involving themselves in organizational change.[3] Indeed, union leadership had to take declining membership and the poor state of in-company union representation into consideration, but it did not attempt to shift the shop-floor frontiers of control (Van Klaveren and Sprenger 1994). Over the course of the 1980s, the progress of the "micro-electronic revolution," with its perceived negative consequences for employment and job quality, caused major worries in the union movement. At the same time, the rise of service-sector employment was fully underestimated.

Regarding issues of wage formation and work organization, the agendas of SER and STAR have broadened over the last two decades. In 1992 SER supported the participation of the open Dutch economy in the Economic and Monetary Union but simultaneously advocated further withdrawal of the state from wage setting. In the subsequent STAR agreement, the "New Course Accord" of 1993, unions lifted their veto against a further flexibilization of work processes in exchange for attention to lifelong learning, implying that employers had granted them a position in the workplace. In a subsequent agreement in 1996, the social partners addressed the topics of flexibility and security, and the new law of 1999 included their agreement on flexible employment contracts, in particular those of temp agency workers. Thus, the emerging firm strategies of outsourcing, rationalization, externalization, and internal flexibilization received a regulated response in labor contracting.

As this volume shows, the flexibility of labor is promoted above all in the spread of part-time work, variable working hours of employees, and differentiated company opening hours, all of which result in the internal flexibility of companies and the deployment of optimal staffing strategies (Tijdens 1998). Simultaneously, on the supply side of the labor market, the inflow of new entrants into the labor market—of women in particular—has facilitated the flexibilization of working practices. The normalization of part-time work (Tijdens 2005; Visser 2000) and the "flexicurity" strategy (Wilthagen 1998) with respect to temporary employment and temp agency work have resulted in an extensive diffusion of forms of labor contracting. Large majorities of part-time workers state in survey research that they voluntarily opt for these jobs and do not want to work full-time. We would add that flexible labor contracting, though it has grown over the past decades, still appears to fluctuate with the economic cycle, rising during the upswing and falling during the decline (SCP 2005; Tijdens et al. 2006).

In the 1990s, the firm-oriented strategies of the trade union movement shifted away from influencing technology and toward a variety of issues related to the organization of work. All major unions have tried to incorporate vocational training, career development, the scheduling of work time, equal opportunities, child care, and related labor issues internal to the firm into collective agreements. Yet these efforts have aggravated the problems of workers' representation: monitoring and specifying provisions in collective agreements for these issues are tasks that have been increasingly left to the works councils. The same happened with new legislation on occupational health services, working times, and child care. The fact that many of these new "programs" have been initiated from the top down may at least partially explain the problems that firm and shop-floor representatives of both management and workers have had putting them in practice (Van het Kaar et al. 2007). The consequent distraction of the attention of workers' representatives has tended to harm the interests of the low-paid, particularly with respect to issues of job quality, unless specific support projects have intentionally been put in place to counteract that risk. Indeed, in the 1990s unions launched a number of such projects—aimed, for example, at supermarket checkout operators, call center agents, and workers in physical distribution. Yet within the union movement these projects did not gain sufficient legitimacy and remained outside what leadership overwhelmingly perceives as the unions' core business in the realm of collective bargaining (Van Klaveren and Sprenger 2004).

Lately, the debate on low pay and low-wage employment seems to be giving increased attention to the actual working of the low-wage part of the labor market. Apart from a few studies (see, for example, De Beer 1996), this has remained a much-neglected issue. The political awareness of connections between low-wage employment and other labor market issues—such as the massive growth of part-time employment and of female and youth employment—is rather limited. Perhaps policymakers' increasingly acute perspective on the aging of the population and the potential shrinking of the labor force will reinforce the need for a better understanding of how to integrate people into employment. The title of a recent policy document, "Because Everybody Is Needed" (RWI 2005), illustrates this need. The effects of actual policymaking on low-wage employment, however, remain to be seen.

THE OUTLINE OF THE BOOK

This volume proceeds in two steps. First, in chapter 2, we scrutinize the evolution and structure of the Dutch labor market in general and its low-wage segment in particular. Chapter 3 provides an in-depth examination of the institutions that govern the establishment of and changes in labor market policies and the effects of such changes, in particular on low-wage employment. This provides the context and background to the second step: the focus in chapters 4 to 9 on the five target industries and the case studies. This step starts with a discussion of the research design and the playing field of the industries, which are then discussed individually in the five subsequent chapters. Finally, in chapter 10, we bring the two steps together in our conclusions about institutions, firm strategies, and their effects on job quality in the target occupations.

NOTES

1. The High Council of Labor, created in 1919, was a tripartite predecessor.
2. The act was later adapted to ILO rules and made even less strict in 1987. Limited interventionist measures were taken between 1979 and 1982 (Van der Heijden 2003) and between 1974 and 1976.
3. The chairman of the largest industrial union characterized efforts to achieve a better quality of work as "sticking plasters on a wooden leg."

REFERENCES

Appelbaum, Eileen, Peter Berg, Ann Frost, and Gil Preuss. 2003. "The Effects of Work Restructuring on Low-Wage, Low-Skilled Workers in U.S. Hospitals." In *Low-Wage America: How Employers Are Reshaping Opportunity in the Workplace*, edited by Eileen Appelbaum, Annette Bernhardt, and Richard J. Murnane. New York: Russell Sage Foundation.
Buitelaar, Wout, and Ruud Vreeman. 1985. *Vakbondswerk en kwaliteit van de*

arbeid. Voorbeelden van werknemersonderzoek in de Nederlandse industrie [*Unions Work and Job Quality: Examples of an Employee Survey in Dutch Industry*]. Nijmegen, Netherlands: SUN.

De Beer, Paul. 1996. *Het onderste kwart. Werk en werkloosheid aan de onderkant van de arbeidsmarkt* [*The Bottom Quarter: Employment and Unemployment at the Lower End of the Labor Market*]. Rijswijk and The Hague: SCP / VUGA.

De Sitter, L. Ulbo. 1981. *Op weg naar nieuwe kantoren en fabrieken* [*Towards New Offices and Factories*]. Denventer, Netherlands: Kluwer.

Kuylaars, Louis. 1952. *Werk en leven van de industriële loonarbeider, als object van een sociale ondernemingspolitiek* [*Work and Life of an Industrial Worker as an Object of Company Social Policy*]. Leiden, Netherlands: Stenfert Kroese.

Raad voor Werk en Inkomen (RWI). 2005. *Omdat iedereen nodig is* [*Because Everybody Is Needed*]. The Hague: RWI.

Sociaal en Cultureel Planbureau (SCP). 2005. *Arbeidsmobiliteit in goede banen* [*Mobility of Labor under Control*]. The Hague: SCP.

Social and Economic Council (SER). 1997. *Werken aan Zekerheid I* [*Working on Security 1*]. The Hague: SER.

Tijdens, Kea G. 1998. *Zeggenschap over arbeidstijden. De samenhang tussen bedrijfstijden, arbeidstijden en flexibilisering van de personeelsbezetting* [*Authority over Working Hours: The Interaction Between Office Hours, Working Hours and Flexibilization of Personnel Scheduling*]. Amsterdam: Welboom.

————. 2005. "How Important Are Institutional Settings to Prevent Marginalization of Part-time Employment?" In *Low-Wage Employment in Europe*, edited by Ive Marx and Wiemer Salverda. Leuven and Voorburg, Netherlands: Acco.

Tijdens, Kea, Maarten van Klaveren, Hester Houwing, Marc van der Meer, and Marieke van Essen. 2006. *Temporary Agency Work in the Netherlands*. Working paper. Amsterdam: AIAS/UvA.

Van Dellen, H., editor. 1984. *Een nieuw elan. De marktsector in de jaren tachtig* [*A New Élan: The Market Sector in the Eighties*]. Deventer, Netherlands: Kluwer.

Van der Heijden, Paul. 2003. "Het loonmaatregel-spel" ["The Wage Moderation Game"]. *Nederlands Juristenblad*. Accessed at http://staging.njb.nl/NJB/mem/archief/art10327.html.

Van het Kaar, Robert, Evert Smit, Wout Buitelaar, Robin Collard, Marc van der Meer, Jan Popma, and Frank Tros. 2007. *Vier scenario's voor de toekomst van de medezeggenschap* [*Four Scenarios for the Future of Employee Participation in Management*]. Delft, Netherlands: Eburon.

Van Klaveren, Maarten, and Wim Sprenger. 1994. "Vakbeweging en technologie" ["Unions and Technology"]. *Informatie* 36(3): 174–81.

————. 2004. "Tiptoe Through the Tulips: The Uneasy Development of Strategic Unionism in Polder Country." In *Strategic Unionism and Partnership: Boxing or Dancing?* edited by Tony Huzzard, Denis Gregory, and Regan Scott. Basingstoke, U.K.: Palgrave Macmillan.

Van Klaveren, Maarten, Ankie van de Camp, and Ulke Veersma. 1997. *The Dutch Comment on the Green Paper of the European Commission: Partnership for a New Organization of Work.* Eindhoven and Tilburg, Netherlands: STZ/Tilburg University.

Visser, Jelle. 2000. "The First Part-Time Economy in the World: A Model to Be Followed?" *Journal of Social European Policy* 12(1): 23–42.

Visser, Jelle, and Anton Hemerijck. 1997. *"A Dutch Miracle": Job Growth, Welfare Reform and Corporatism in the Netherlands.* Amsterdam: Amsterdam University Press.

Wilthagen, Ton. 1998. *Flexicurity: A New Paradigm for Labour Market Policy Reform.* Discussion Paper FS I 98-202. Berlin: WZB.

CHAPTER 2

Low-Wage Work and the Economy

Wiemer Salverda

This chapter discusses the level and composition of low-wage employment from a combined cross-sectional and time-series perspective. It also considers how low-wage work fits the national economy and the labor market. We start with a quick overview of the most striking features of the national economy and the labor market before describing the low-wage segment in more detail; then we combine these two topics. The chapter continues with a discussion of the individual dynamics of low pay; it concludes with a summary of the findings.

THE PROMINENT GROWTH OF A PART-TIME ECONOMY

In recent decades, the Netherlands has managed a strong growth of the per-capita employment rate (EPOP). The country became known for its employment "miracle" in the 1990s, and indeed, its labor market has changed almost beyond recognition, together with the pattern of the economy. At the same time, as we will see, the aggregate economic performance was not exceptional but rather average.

In 2005 the Dutch EPOP was at a high level of between 71 and 72 percent, comparable with the United States (see table 2.1). The two countries' unemployment rates, calculated in the standard way over the entire labor force, were also comparable, at a good 5 percent. The present picture differs significantly from that of 1979, when the Dutch EPOP was well below the American figure. Considerable growth has both bridged the gap with the United States and matched U.S. growth, but interestingly, it has hardly altered the levels of unemployment in both countries. The figures include self-employment, which fell significantly in the Netherlands over the period, and therefore the outcomes for employees alone are more favorable than shown here.

Table 2.1 Employment and Unemployment Levels and
          Composition, 1979 to 1983 and 2004 to 2005

	Netherlands		United States	
	1979	2005	1979	2005
Unemployment rate	3.4%	5.2%	5.9%	5. 1%
Employment-population rate				
(age fifteen to sixty-four)	64	71	68	72
For youth (age fifteen to				
twenty-four)	55	62	61	54
For adult women	44	65	55	69
For adult men	90	81	87	83
	1983	2004	1983	2004
Part-time share of employment	33	46	18	17
For youth (age fifteen to				
twenty-four)	34	69	35	42
For adult women	74	75	23	20
For adult men	11	15	5	6

Source: Eurostat, European Labor Force Survey (ELFS), and Organization for Economic Cooperation and Development (OECD), Labour Force Survey (LFS), by sex,
with correction for 1979.
Note: Employment data for the 1970s differ widely. OECD Labour Force Survey data
suffer from important series breaks and underestimate employment levels of the
1970s especially for the Netherlands. Here a correction has been made with the help
of figures of CPB (2UOO6) and the OECD's *Economic Outlook Database.* The year
1979 is chosen as a cyclically neutral year instead of the often-used mid-1980s which
was at the deep bottom of the cycle and naturally shows a much more favorable development since.

Broken down by age and gender, the main international differences in EPOPs today are generally concentrated among youth (defined as age fifteen to twenty-four). Since 1979, the youth EPOP in
the Netherlands has shown a unique growth of almost nine percentage points, though at the same time the youth share in employment
fell because of demographic decline. The EPOP of adult females has
grown even more strongly, up from 44 percent to an internationally
comparable level of almost 66 percent, an increase of no less than
twenty-one percentage points. Women's share in employment also
rose, from 25 to 37 percent. By contrast, there is little change or international variation for adult men. Their EPOP has fallen to a limited extent, though more than in the United States, but still is very

high compared to women and youths, and adult men's share in employment fell from 52 percent to 47 percent. Young workers and adult women evidently did better, but they came from rather low levels by international standards; moreover, the current female EPOP is average, not outstanding.

The rapid evolution of youth and women in the labor force rests on an explosive growth of part-time jobs, up to an aggregate share of 46 percent (see table 2.1), which is unique to the Netherlands.[1] We can add that working part-time is very popular in the sense that very few persons with a part-time job would have preferred a full-time one and that many with a full-time job would prefer to work less. It is outside the scope of this study to explain this phenomenon, which may result from women's increasing preference to participate in paid employment combined with not only a cultural change wrought by increasing educational attainment but also the growing need of households to maintain their income in the face of, for example, wage moderation. Part-time employment has also been strongly stimulated by the government, as we discuss in chapter 3. It has increased particularly among youths—who often work part-time as they pursue their education, as we also see later.

Part-time work is very important for adult women and has grown in line with the strong increase in female employment. The Netherlands traditionally had a low level of female employment—the outcome of a long social struggle against child labor and the pressure that long female working hours exerted on household care at the end of the nineteenth century. Present-day part-time work reflects an attempt to combine paid labor with household responsibilities. Naturally, the limited provision of child care facilities plays a role as well, but it is difficult to say to what extent that also reflects the same underlying views. It is important to add that two kinds of women in particular—women who share a household with a partner and female single parents—have increased their employment participation, up to the level of single women (figure 2.1).[2] As a result, one-earner and two-earner households have traded places as percentages of the population.

One implication of this shift is that most job employment growth has gone to households that were already working; much less of that growth has been seen in reductions of the high level of household worklessness, as also argued by Paul Gregg and Jonathan Wadsworth (2000, 68). Other women, mainly teenage and adult children still liv-

Figure 2.1 Employment-Population Rates of Women Age
Fifteen to Sixty-Four, by Household Type,
1977 to 2006

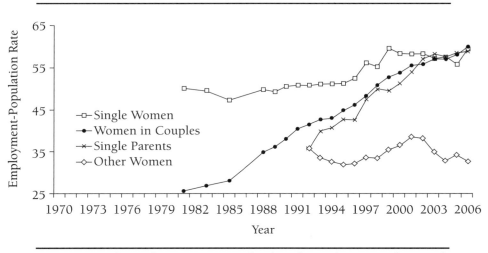

Source: CBS/Statline, Labour Force Survey (LFS), and Sociaal-economische Maand-
statistiek (SEM) 96/11, 29–45.
Note: Employment is defined as working at least twelve hours per week.

ing with their parents, have a much lower and hardly growing employment rate. However, virtually all of the gap between them and
the other groups is bridged by their extensive employment in small
jobs of less than twelve hours per week that are not covered by the
figure. No fewer than 27 percent of women in this demographic category hold such a small job, as against 3 to 8 percent of women in the
three other categories. Apparently, a strong role is played by young
women without a household of their own in small part-time jobs.

Figure 2.2 shows, for employees only, the very divergent developments of the employment rate in terms of persons who are working
(head count) and hours worked (full-time equivalents [FTE], defined as 1,840 working hours per year).[3] The former rate shows an
increase between 1979 and 2005 of 10 percent, while the latter rate
remained, on balance, at the same level of 48 percent.[4] The FTE approach brings the employment rates for young persons and women
down considerably while maintaining the position of adult males at a
steady majority share of 60 percent of total employment hours. The
Dutch evolution contrasts with changes in the labor market in the

Figure 2.2   Head-Count and Hours-Count Employees-
Population Rates, 1970 to 2005

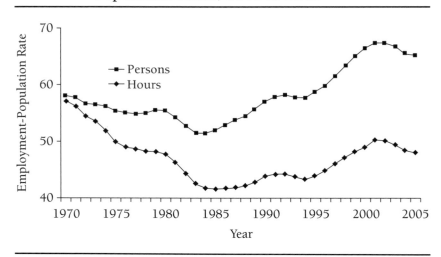

Source: Author's calculations from Central Planning Bureau (CPB) (2005, table
A.7), keeping annual full-time hours at 1,840.

United States, where both head-count and hours-count employment
rates increased, though the latter grew less than the former.

Table 2.2 considers the education of the population in 2002 by
three levels of attainment: low, intermediate, and high. A large segment of the population had little education, and with a stake of 22
percent in the total EPOP, they also played an important role in employment with a relatively high EPOP of 58 percent within their own
educational group. There is an increasing overlap between youth and
low educational attainment, since the cohorts manage more than
ever to reach educational levels beyond the youth level when they get
older. The role of the low-skilled in the American economy is much
more restricted, not only because their share in the population is
smaller but also because their chances of employment are less—and
the fewer talented people there remain in the low-skilled group when
it gets smaller, the more often these two aspects of their situation are
seen together.

The educational accomplishments of the employed make up one
side of the story; the other half is the skill level demanded by the jobs
that people occupy. The two are not identical and should not be con-

Table 2.2 Population and Employment by Level of Educational Attainment, 2002

| Attainment Level | Population by Educational Attainment | | Employment-Population Rate | | | | Concentration Ratio by Educational Attainment (Average = 100) | |
| | | | By Educational Attainment | | For Educational Groups | | | |
	Netherlands	United States	Netherlands	United States	Netherlands	United States	Netherlands	United States
Low	37%	20%	22%	9%	58%	43%	80%	62%
Intermediate	42	48	33	35	79	72	108	103
High	21	32	18	26	87	83	119	119
Total	100	100	73	70	73	70	100	100

Source: OECD, Labour Force Survey (LFS).
Note: Defined by the international classification of education (ISCED) as levels 0 to 2, 4 to 3, and 5 to 7, respectively.

Table 2.3 Lower-Level Jobs (Twelve Hours per Week or More), 1977 to 2004

	1977	1987	1996	1999	2004
Head-count					
Elementary	6.4	6.5	6.7	7.1	7.0
Lower-level	44.0	32.2	25.7	24.6	24.0
Total	48.6	38.7	32.4	31.7	31.0
Hours-count (FTE)					
Elementary		6	6.3	6.5	6.4
Lower-level		31.7	25.0	23.8	23.3
Total		37.7	31.3	30.3	29.7

Source: CBS/Statline Labour Force Survey (LFS) (1977), linearly extrapolated back from 1987 on the basis of Batenburg et al. (2003, 21); hours volume approximated with the help of class means of three categories: twelve to nineteen, twenty to thirty-four, and thirty-five or more hours per week.

fused. Statistics Netherlands operates a classification of job levels that closely resembles the international classification of occupations (ISCO), which builds on a tradition going back to 1960. Table 2.3 summarizes some of its results for the lower end of the range.[5] Amazingly, the lowest-level, elementary jobs have retained their role in employment, but the next-higher-level jobs have witnessed a strong decline. Interestingly, given the strong increase in employment, there has been no decline in the absolute numbers of low-level jobs, but it should be taken into account that they have below-average working hours and a higher percentage of them are part-time.

It is important to realize that lower-level jobs are increasingly occupied by better-educated employees. In the early 1970s, virtually all lower-level jobs were occupied by the low-educated; in 2004, by contrast, 43 percent were taken by the better-educated, including some who were highly educated. Vice versa, the share of low-level jobs among low-educated employees has roughly doubled, from 37 percent in 1971 to 71 percent in 2004. Since there is no obvious lack of low-skilled persons, these figures do not necessarily point to a general overschooling, which in the end could lead to a 100 percent occupancy rate of better-skilled persons. Again, there seems to be an important role here for students, who work small, part-time jobs and who are still pursuing their education beyond the intermediate level already obtained, and also for married women, who may continue to fulfill household obligations while working by accepting lower-level jobs that are nearby or have suitable working hours.

Highly relevant to low-wage labor is the growing role of migrants and minorities, especially those from non-Western countries.[6] Their population share has steadily grown among fifteen- to sixty-four-year-olds, from 1 percent to 2 percent in the early 1970s and 3 percent in 1979 to 11 percent, or 1.2 million, at present, especially in recent years. These figures include the first and second generations and therefore describe a broader group than the foreign-born population of many international statistics. Though the second generation is growing faster, it still is a minority (2.5 percent) in this group.

Migrants and minorities are significantly underrepresented in employment compared to their population share—men by 20 to 25 percent and women by 30 to 35 percent. They contributed only 10 percent to aggregate employment growth between 1996 and 2002. Up to 700,000 are employed today, some 10 percent of them in small, part-time jobs. Compared to the native population, minorities are strongly overrepresented in low-level jobs (by two times) and among those with flexible contracts (by two to three times), and low-educated migrants are even more highly overrepresented. The concentration of all migrant workers in the very lowest-level jobs is almost three times higher than for natives; the concentration for low-skilled migrants is five times as high. Their relative employment position improved somewhat over the second half of the 1990s, and interestingly, their position seemed not to change during the recent post-2001 recession. Nevertheless, their unemployment rate is far higher than the rate for natives.[7]

THE ECONOMY

The level of GDP per capita in the Netherlands is 20 percent below the United States, and consumption (private and public together) out of GDP is 25 percent less. The main reason, as for other European countries, is that the population works fewer hours, not that productivity (per hour) is lower. International trade (imports and exports) as a percentage of GDP is very important—the Netherlands is lonely at the top, though many exports are actually re-exports. The country has had a sizable trade surplus for many years.[8] GDP per capita has increased by 47 percent since 1979 (figure 2.3), which is an average pace internationally but less than the United States (60 percent). GDP growth has registered two significant declines: in the early

Figure 2.3 Macroeconomic Aggregates, 1970 to 2005

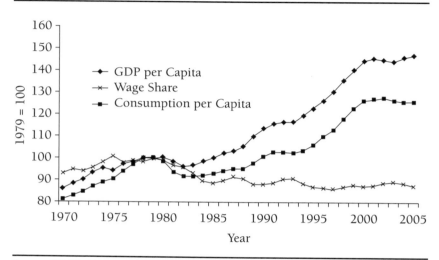

Source: OECD, Economic Outlook.
Note: GDP and consumption: volumes per capita of population age fifteen to sixty-four. Wage share as a percentage of GDP.

1980s (which took ten years to repair), and again in recent years; there was also a standstill in the early 1990s. During the recent recession, total real disposable household income fell by 3.5 percent, in strong contrast to the preceding growth and the rise in incomes in other countries.

An increasing gap has opened up in the growth of consumption per capita, which has lagged in international comparison. Wage moderation hit the share of wages in GDP, which declined substantially, by six percentage points, between 1979 and 1986 and has slowly gone further downward since then. It is currently slightly above 50 percent. The late 1990s showed both a strong growth of GDP and consumption and a recovery, albeit feeble, of the wage share. At the same time, productivity growth declined substantially and was particularly low during the 1990s, as the trend shows. It lagged behind internationally and tucked down below the American trend (figure 2.4). In other words, economic growth became more labor-intensive or employment-generating, which is viewed positively but comes at a potential cost to productivity growth.

The average aggregate economic performance hides important

Figure 2.4 Annual Growth of GDP Volume per Hour Worked, 1970 to 2005

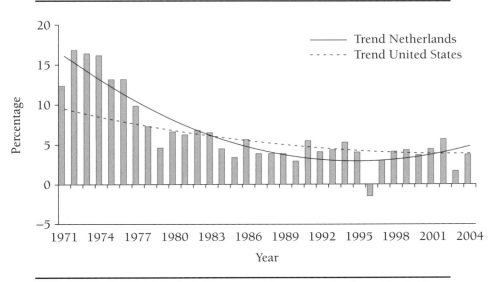

Source: OECD, *Economic Outlook* (Germany without correction for unification).
Note: The polynomial trend is added and is also shown for the United States (dotted line).

shifts in the composition of the economy (figure 2.5). Over the 1979 to 2003 period, manufacturing employment (head-count) declined significantly, by six percentage points, though less than in other countries. By contrast, employment in services grew, by fifteen percentage points, significantly more than elsewhere. As a result, there is no employment gap left compared with the United States. Structural change, measured as the sum of absolute percentage-point changes for the three sectors, was considerable (21 percent) and exceeded the United States (18 percent). Apparently, the Netherlands and some other European countries were flexible enough to manage such enormous change in a short period of time. Within the expanding services, the size of the transportation and communication industries is virtually identical internationally and has undergone very little change. Financial and business services in particular experienced strong growth (up from 6 percent to 14 percent of employees), but so did communal services and trade. The Netherlands closely resembles the United States in each of these industries. In

Figure 2.5   Head-Count Employment-Population Rate, by Industry, 1979 to 2003

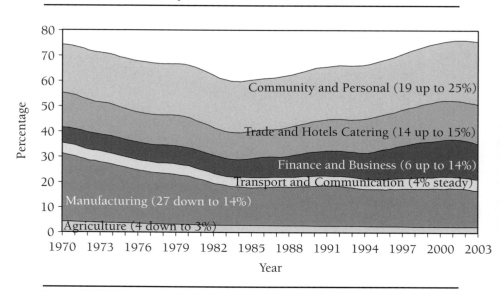

Source: OECD/Structural Analysis Indicators Database (STAN).

terms of full-time equivalents, however, the service sector has a considerably smaller current employment rate (15 percent) than the head-count figures suggest and a slower growth of services comparable to other countries. Naturally, this is because of the high incidence of part-time jobs. This low employment rate directly links the changes in the industrial structure to those in the labor market. In manufacturing, full-time jobs held by men disappeared, a decline that was roughly compensated by the growth of services. The net addition of services to employment was primarily in new part-time jobs for women and youth.

The high rates of part-time employment of youth and adult women also keep their unemployment rates down in the statistics because they inflate the employment denominator, over time as well as compared to other countries. Adult men have remained largely outside these developments. Basically, they have the same employment and unemployment position at present as before. They have also largely maintained their share in the overall volume of employment (FTE).

So several striking characteristics about Dutch employment point to a significant change:

- Strong growth in the employment rate

- Growth in a rate of youth employment that is already higher than in any other OECD country

- The most rapid growth of female employment

- A relatively low rate of unemployment

- An industrial economic structure that closely resembles the United States for head-count employment but not for hours-count employment

- A rate of part-time jobs that is higher than in any other country

Accounting for the hours of part-time work, however, takes away a good deal of the preceding miracles and also helps us to understand how the level of part-time work combines with an average economic performance, which, after all, is a volume effect. We will see that the same phenomenon has been even more extreme in the country's low-wage employment.

CHARACTERISTICS AND EVOLUTION OF LOW-WAGE EMPLOYMENT

Now we turn to the level and composition of low-wage employment. Low pay concerns wage earnings only, and therefore employment data in this section are restricted to employees, in contrast to the discussion in the previous section, where figures included the self-employed.

Figure 2.6 pictures the distribution of hourly wages on both a head-count and hours-count basis to account for the astonishing role of part-time jobs. Hourly pay is the only appropriate concept that enables us to include part-timers and full-timers in the same study of low pay. Naturally, part-timers with a better hourly wage can still earn an annual income that is less than a living wage, but this outcome is clearly the consequence of their working hours, not their level of pay. In 2005, 7.0 million people were engaged in wage employment in the Netherlands, providing 5.9 million FTEs of work

Figure 2.6 Distribution of Hourly Wages and Earnings Thresholds, 2005

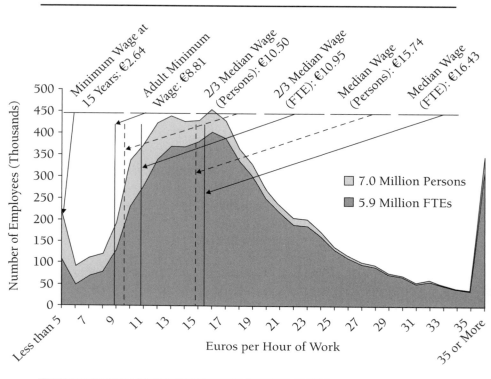

Source: Estimated from CBS, Structure of Earnings Survey (2005), tabulated data.
Note: Truncation of the data explains the flapping wings at the two tails.

(defined as thirty-five hours per week)—a difference of more than 1.0 million, or 15 percent. A comparison between the upper and lower distributions in the figure shows that the difference is concentrated in the lower ranges of the distribution. This indicates where in the distribution most part-time jobs are found.

The consistently defined level of the adult minimum wage is €8.81 per hour. It may be surprising that so many jobs appear to be paid below this level, but that is because of the long tail of specific youth minimum wages, which start at €2.64 for fifteen-year-olds; we come back to this in chapter 3. The low-pay threshold is defined in accordance with what has become the standard in international research: two-thirds of the median wage. Consequently, its level fol-

Table 2.4 Wage Levels Expressed in Euros and U.S. Dollar PPPs, 2005

	1979		2005	
	Euros	U. S.$ PPPs	Euros	U.S.$ PPPs
Low-pay threshold (hourly, FTE-count)	8.93	10.90	10.95	13.37
Threshold in actual practice[a]			9.59	11.70
Decile 1 (hourly, FTE-count)	8.70	10.62	9.70	11.84
Decile 5 (hourly, FTE-count)	13.40	16.35	16.43	20.05
Decile 9 (hourly, FTE-count)	21.92	26.76	29.22	35.67
Adult minimum wage (weekly, head-count, actual practice)	370.00	452.00	292.00	356.00
Average minimum wage (age weights of 1979, weekly)	315.00	384.00	226.00	276.00

Source: Calculated using OECD, National Accounts PPP exchange rates for consumption; see also figure 2.7.
[a] Disregarding holidays, and so on.

lows that of the median. This threshold wage differs between head-count measurement (€10.50) and hours-count measurement (€10.95). In the hours count, the median wage is at a higher level, since low-paid jobs weigh less because of the higher incidence of part-time hours.[9]

What these wage levels, measured at the price level of 2005, amount to in U.S. dollars at the purchasing power parity (PPP) exchange rate of 2005 is shown in table 2.4. The comparative American median wage in 2005 amounted to $14.29, with a low-pay threshold of $9.53 (Mishel, Bernstein, and Allegretto 2007, table 3.4).[10] That seems best compared to the threshold in actual practice of PPP-$11.70 mentioned in the table. The Dutch figure is considerably higher than the American. For a forty-hour working week, the adult minimum wage amounts to $8.90, while the average (weights of 1979) minimum wage of 2005 would be valued at $6.90. The latter is close to the intended increase of the U.S. federal minimum wage of $7.25, but below the minimum wage of several American states.

After the thresholds, we consider their evolution and the incidence of low-wage employment over time. One caveat is that the picture is a rough approximation using tabulated, interpolated data for six bands of weekly hours of work, together with microdata that may not always be fully consistent. Second, the improvement in the data observations between 1994 and 1995, especially at the lower end of the distribution, may lead to an overestimation of the increase in the 1990s. The nature of the coverage improvement makes this more relevant to part-time employment; the increase in full-time low-wage employment (see figure 2.8), however, suggests that part of the increase is certainly real.

Naturally, the evolution of the threshold is identical to that of the median wage. The dashed line in figure 2.7 indicates this evolution, corrected for inflation, and shows how it fits the overall distribution of wages. All three decile levels mentioned (first, fifth, and ninth) declined in the 1980s and started to climb again over the course of the 1990s. The wage distribution has widened as the ninth decile has grown more strongly than the median and first deciles, especially in recent years. The median did better than the bottom, growing by 21 percent, as did the low-pay threshold. The threshold was virtually identical to the first decile for a long time, but in the 1990s a gap opened up when that decile started to lag behind and, on balance, grew by only 1 percent. On an FTE basis, the picture is rather different. The first decile did much better, with 12 percent growth, though it is still only half the growth of the median (23 percent) and one-third that of the ninth decile (33 percent). So inequality also increased with the hours count. The explosive growth of part-time jobs at the bottom explains the difference. The 8 percent hours-heads difference for the first decile peters out quickly to only 3 percent for the median and 2 percent for the ninth decile. Apparently, higher up in the distribution the effect of part-time hours is small and uniform.

In 1979 the incidence of low pay was about 10.9 percent and 10.7 percent of total employment for the head-count and hours-count approaches, respectively (figure 2.8). After a remarkable initial fall, the incidence of low pay among employees went up substantially, reaching a peak in 1998 at 17.9 percent and 16.3 percent, respectively. This was followed by some stabilization and a renewed increase to 18.2 percent and 16.0 percent in 2004. In that year, more than 1.25 million out of 6.9 million employees (950,000 out of 5.9 million FTE) were working for low pay. On balance, the incidence grew by 7.5 percent for persons and 5 percent for FTE. Naturally, it implies that better-paid employment, its complement, fell by the same percentage of employment.

Figure 2.7 Deciles of Hourly Wage Distribution and Low-
Pay Threshold, 1979 to 2005

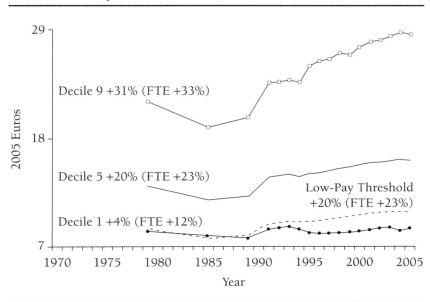

Source: Author's calculations from CBS, Structure of Earnings Survey microdata for
1979, 1985, 1989, 1996, and 2002, and tabulated data for other years.

Figure 2.8 Head-Count and Hours-Count Low-Wage
Employment, 1979 to 2005

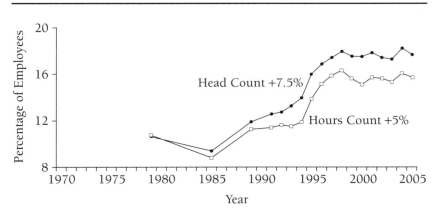

Source: Author's calculations from CBS, Structure of Earnings Survey microdata for
1979, 1985, 1989, 1996, and 2002, and tabulated data for other years.

The Composition of Low-Wage Employment

We check for low-wage employment in the three important categories of employment growth discussed earlier: part-timers, youth, and adult women. Starting with the distinction between part-time and full-time (defined at a threshold of thirty-five weekly working hours), we find that the incidence among part-time workers is always higher than among full-timers and also that the two have grown apart considerably (figure 2.9). Today, low-wage jobs are basically part-time jobs. The initial fall of low-wage employment in the 1980s, pictured in figure 2.7, applies to the full-time low-paid only. After this decline, they stayed at that same level until a slight increase occurred after 1994. The incidence among full-timers in 2005 (10.0 percent) was at virtually the same level as in 1979 (9.7 percent). Part-time employees, by contrast, had a much higher incidence at the start (16.6 percent), showed no fall in the early 1980s, but remained at a stable level, and then, from the mid-1980s on, they underwent a rapid increase, up to 29.3 percent in 1998. This was followed by a significant decrease and a renewed increase to 28.2 percent in 2004. As a result, the share of part-timers in low-wage employment as a whole rose from one-quarter (25 percent) to more than two-thirds (70 percent).

Part-time employment covers a wide range of weekly working hours, from one to thirty-five. This is especially important because, first, shorter hours are quantitatively important, and second, shorter hours link with lower pay. Of the 46 percent overall incidence of part-time employment (figure 2.3), 12 percent concern jobs of less than twelve hours. The incidence is particularly high among the group with the shortest hours, since roughly half of them are low-paid on an hourly basis (figure 2.10). The group that works up to twenty hours also has a high incidence. Those who work more hours deviate little from the overall average, though they are clearly above the 10 percent level of full-time workers. On an hours-count basis (see figure 2.10, right-hand panel), the incidence of low pay in the hours band remains the same, but the shares in total low-wage employment differ radically from those of the head-count approach, as the dark bars indicate. The shortest hours contribute only a tiny volume of no more than 8 percent, contrasting with 32 percent for the head count. Full-time workers provide 54 percent or the majority of all low-paid hours.

The demographics of employment have changed considerably as a

Figure 2.9 Part-Time and Full-Time Low-Wage
           Employment, 1979 to 2005

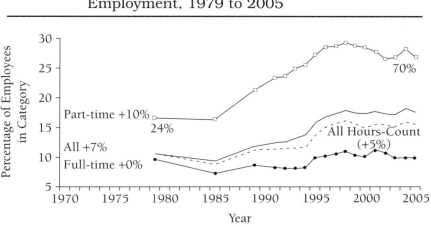

Source: Author's calculations from CBS, Structure of Earnings Survey microdata for
1979, 1985, 1989, 1996, and 2002, and tabulated data for other years.

Figure 2.10 Head-Count and Hours-Count Low-Wage
             Employment by Working Hours, 2005

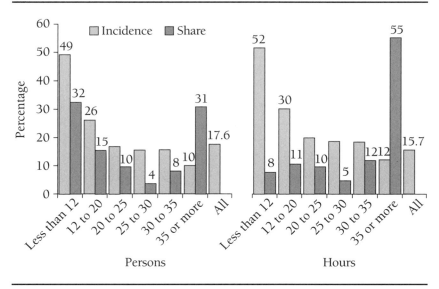

Source: Author's calculations from CBS, Structure of Earnings Survey microdata for
1979, 1985, 1989, 1996, and 2002, and tabulated data for other years.

Table 2.5 Low-Wage Employment for Demographic Groups and the Low-Skilled, 1979 to 2002

	1979	1989	1996	2002
Low-paid among:				
Youth	40%	46%	59%	61%
Adult women	6	6	12	12
Adult men	0	1	4	5
Low-skilled	14	14	22	33
Among low-paid:				
Youth	89	80	60	59
Adult women	8	14	25	26
Adult men	3	6	14	15
Low-skilled	88	62		60

Source: Author's calculations from CBS, Structure of Earnings Survey microdata for 1979, 1985, 1989, 1996, and 2002, and tabulated data.

result of growing adult female and youth employment. This has an important bearing on low-wage employment (table 2.5). Young workers were faced with a growing incidence of low pay until the mid-1990s (between 40 and 60 percent) and most have been low-paid since the end of the 1980s. Young workers are found four times more than average in low-wage jobs. At the same time, the youth share in low-wage employment fell from 89 percent to 59 percent for demographic reasons. The adult female incidence and share grew significantly, the former from 5 to 12 percent and the latter from 8 to 26 percent. Thus, adult women make up one-quarter of all low-paid today. Their concentration in low-paid work has been increasing but is still below average. The incidence of low pay among adult men also increased, from 0 to 5 percent in 2002; nowadays they make up 15 percent of low-wage employment, but their concentration is still far below average. In the same vein, the incidence of low pay among low-skilled employees doubled in the 1990s, to one-third in 2002 after having remained stable over the 1980s. The concentration of low-skilled employees in low-paid work increased at the same time to almost twice the average. Their share in low-wage employment fell, together with their share in total employment, but over the 1990s it increased again, parallel to the incidence. A comparison between head-count and hours-count shows clearly that young workers worked longer hours than adults on average in 1979, while the opposite is true now.

Clearly, adult women and young workers play as important a role for the evolution of low pay as for employment in general, though the role of adult men in low pay has also increased in contrast to aggregate employment. The link between low-wage employment and aggregate employment is considered in more detail in the next section.

THE SIGNIFICANCE OF LOW-WAGE EMPLOYMENT FOR THE NATIONAL ECONOMY

The incidence of low pay among employees tells only half the story if not combined with the evolution of their employment. Here we examine how the two interact (figure 2.11). We find, first, that the head-count low-wage EPOP (ages fifteen to sixty-four) has roughly doubled over the period as aggregate employment and the low-paid share rose in tandem. As a result, 5.9 percent of the population had a low-paid job in 1979, as against 11.5 percent in 2005. The 5.6-percentage-point increase is a very sizable portion of the 10 percent aggregate employment rate increase. Until the mid-1990s, all additional employment was low-paid, and only after 1997 did the employment rate of the better-paid reach a level over and above its position at the start of 1979. During the last few years, it fell again, while the low-wage employment rate remained unchanged.

The figure explores these developments also on an hours-count basis (the lines in contrast to the bars). In spite of some fluctuations, the aggregate employment rate was back in 2005 at 48 percent, almost exactly where it began in 1979. The low-paid employment rate increased by 2.6 percent, but strikingly, the better-paid rate never fully regained its initial level and on balance declined by more than two percentage points—in spite of the increased educational attainment of the population. As a result, people in the Netherlands are spending significantly fewer hours in better-paid jobs today than at the end of the 1970s and more in low-paid jobs.

LOW PAY AND DEMOGRAPHICS

Understandably, this evolution is differently allocated among demographic groups. The rise of the incidence of low pay among young workers from 40 to 60 percent implies that the low-wage employment rate among the young population almost doubled, from 21 per-

Figure 2.11   Head-Count and Hours-Count Employment-
Population Rates for Low-Paid and Better-
Paid, 1979 to 2005

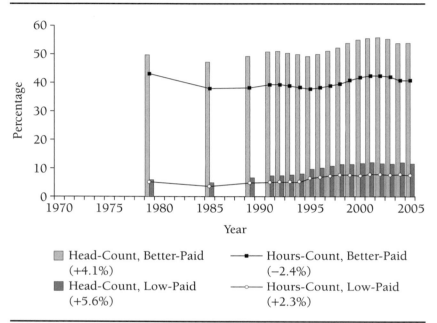

Head-Count, Better-Paid
(+4.1%)

Head-Count, Low-Paid
(+5.6%)

Hours-Count, Better-Paid
(−2.4%)

Hours-Count, Low-Paid
(+2.3%)

Source: CBS, Labour Force Survey, and Author's calculations from CBS, Structure of
Earnings Survey microdata for 1979, 1985, 1989, 1996, and 2002, and tabulated
data for other years.

cent to 39 percent. Thus, much more than the full net seven-percent-
age-point rise in the youth employment rate is located in low-wage
employment, and their better-paid rate fell from 33 percent to 25 percent. We can say that over a period of twenty-five years, youth employment has changed beyond recognition. Jobs are much more frequently part-time, low-paid, and flexible at the same time, as
illustrated by figure 2.12. In 1979, 26 percent of all young workers
were found in at least one of the three employment states depicted in
the figure, but in 2002 this percentage had risen to 57 percent.

Similarly, with the steady incidence of low pay among adult females, 6 percent of their 21 percent net employment rate growth is in
low-wage employment. Finally, the adult male employment rate fell
between 1979 and 2005, from 90 percent to 81 percent. The incidence of low pay among this demographic group grew by four per-

Figure 2.12 Head-Count Youth (Age Fifteen to Twenty-
Four), by Types of Industry, Job, and
Contract, 1979 to 2002

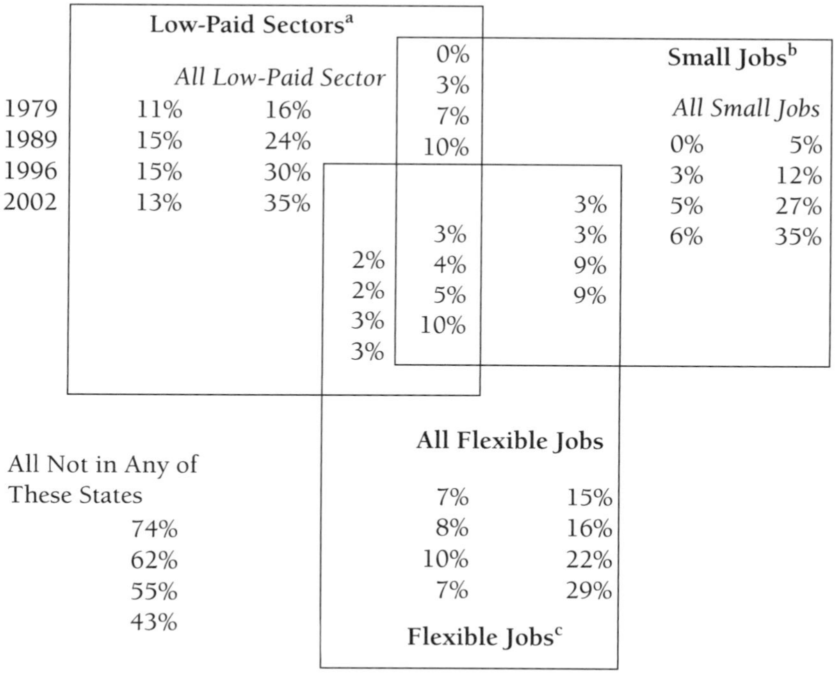

	Low-Paid Sectors[a]				Small Jobs[b]	
			0%			
		All Low-Paid Sector	3%			
1979	11%	16%	7%			All Small Jobs
1989	15%	24%	10%			
1996	15%	30%			0%	5%
2002	13%	35%			3%	12%
				3%	5%	27%
			3%	3%	6%	35%
		2%	4%	9%		
		2%	5%	9%		
		3%	10%			
		3%				

	All Flexible Jobs	
All Not in Any of		
These States	7%	15%
74%	8%	16%
62%	10%	22%
55%	7%	29%
43%	Flexible Jobs[c]	

Source: Author's calculations from CBS, Structure of Earnings Survey microdata for
1979, 1985, 1989, 1996, and 2002, and tabulated data for other years.
[a] Retail and hotels and catering.
[b] Less than twelve hours per week.
[c] Temporary contracts and temp agency work.

centage points, and consequently their better-paid wage employment
rate made an astonishing fall from 90 to 78 percent.

Finally, table 2.6 examines the position of immigrants from non-
Western countries vis-à-vis low-wage employment. In 2002 one-
quarter of the FTE employment of this demographic group was in
low-paid hours. Low pay was almost two-thirds more likely for them
than for employees of native origin, up from 50 percent more in
1996. They had a stronger presence in low pay in all three demographic groups compared to natives, and as a result young immi-

Table 2.6 Immigrants and Natives on Low Pay, 1996 to
2002

	1996		2002	
	Non-Western Origin	Native Origin	Non-Western Origin	Native Origin
In low-paid jobs	4.1%	93.0%	12.5%	83.8%
Among low-paid jobs	23.3	15.8	19.7	12.5
Concentration (overall share = 100)				
All	147	99	164	96
Youth	412	374	403	346
Adult women	124	76	171	65
Adult men	79	26	69	30

Source: Author's calculations from CBS, Structure of Earnings Survey microdata for
1996 and 2002, and tabulated data.
Note: "Immigrants" includes the second generation born of parents who immigrated
from non-Western countries. Immigrants of Western origin are left out.

grants (mainly second-generation) were very substantially overrepresented in low-paid work. Though adult non-Western men were not
overrepresented, the difference between them and native men was
relatively stronger than for women and youth.

The immigrant share in low-wage employment has grown considerably over this short six-year period, from 4 to 12.5 percent, implying that they were responsible for two-thirds of the growth of the
low-paid EPOP between 1996 and 2002. This contrasts sharply with
their 10 percent share in overall employment growth found earlier.
Between these two years, the position of adult non-Western females
has deteriorated. On an hours-count basis, the situation is slightly
worse than for the head-count, indicating that immigrants work
longer hours in low-wage jobs than natives.

LOW PAY AND INDUSTRIAL STRUCTURE

It is also important to understand how low-wage employment links
to different types of economic activity. Table 2.7 provides some insights by detailing the evolution of FTE low-wage employment at the
meso-economic level of sectors and industries. Aggregate low pay
grew by 4.2 percentage points of total employment, or almost 40 per-

Table 2.7 Industry and (Hours-Count) Low-Wage Incidence, 1999 to 2002

	1979	2002
Total low-paid share (national)	10.7%	14.9%
Non-services		
Total	35.1	24.8
Low-paid incidence	9.4	11.1
Low-paid share (national)	3.3	2.7
Services		
Total	64.9	75.2
Low-paid incidence	11.4	16.2
Low-paid share (national)	7.4	12.2
Of which:		
Retail, hotels, and catering		
Total	7.6	9.2
Low-paid incidence	33.3	45.7
Low-paid share (national)	2.5	4.2
Other services		
Total	57.3	66.0
Low-paid incidence	8.5	12.1
Low-paid share (national)	4.9	8.0

Source: Author's calculations from CBS, Structure of Earnings Survey microdata for 1979, 1985, 1989, 1996, and 2002, and tabulated data.

cent of the initial level. This differed between the two main sectors of the economy, services and the rest (agriculture and industry, including utilities and construction). In the former, the incidence grew slightly more than average, but because of its predominant share in employment, it contributes largely to this average. In the latter, the pace was only half as rapid. Without the shifting over time of employment toward services, the increase in the national incidence of low pay would have been somewhat less—3.7 percent as against 4.2 percent. As a result, most of the increase was due to a rising incidence of low pay among employees. The diverging incidence between the two main sectors implies that their shares in total low-wage employment grew even further apart. On a per capita basis, all of the 2.3 percent increase (see figure 2.11) was concentrated in services.

Within the service sector, the growth within the two notoriously low-paying sectors, retail and hotels and catering, showed a huge increase in the incidence of low pay, from one-third to almost one-half of all hours worked.[11] The percentage-point growth was much less for the other services, which include many better-paid services (for example, government, education, health care, and finance and insurance) but also include temporary work agencies and cleaning and personal services, which are often low-paid. However, the speed of the increase was virtually the same, and the intraservices employment shift between these two components hardly mattered for the growth of low-wage employment.

THE PROBABILITY OF BEING LOW-PAID AND EARNINGS MOBILITY

Finally, we turn to the chances of people being low-paid and their mobility over time out of low pay. A look at these issues can help us to see which variables—age, gender, part-time work, or industry—play a more important role and which ones reflect a concentration of the other variables. There is very little systematic information available because of a lack of appropriate panel data. Elsewhere (Blázquez and Salverda 2007), we have used the eight waves (1994 to 2001) of the European Community Household Panel (ECHP) dataset to study these issues. It is the detailed results of that study that underlie this text. Unfortunately, an important limitation is that for jobs of less than fifteen hours per week ECHP lacks the information on hours worked that is needed for determining hourly pay. This is a serious drawback with so many jobs that are in that range and also have a very strong link with low pay.[12] However, the fact that a majority of these small jobs are occupied by young persons mitigates the problem, because it diminishes the risk of erroneously capturing as upward career mobility the transitions of students who take low-paid jobs but after finishing their studies move on to very different job markets corresponding with their expertise. Nevertheless, the inability to determine hourly pay from the ECHP dataset is a serious caveat that should be kept in mind.

The Probability of Low Pay

A probit model analysis of the probability of being low-paid confirms that women run a higher chance of low pay than men, and young persons a much higher chance than older workers. Importantly, the fact of being in a part-time job (but remember the fifteen-hour lower threshold) increases these chances only a little. Most adult women, who for the most part are found in part-time jobs, may therefore be better off than young workers, though they are still penalized compared to adult men. Apparently, it is the concentration of youth and women in these jobs that counts, not their part-time nature. This is consistent with the equal treatment of part-time pay, which we discuss in chapter 3. As to educational attainment, the difference between the lowest level and the next is modest compared to the highly educated. The same holds for low- and middle-range tenure within the same firm compared to longer tenure (five years or more). Interestingly, previous unemployment experience does not really matter either. This seems consistent with the overwhelming effects of young age, gender, and low tenure. People are at risk of low pay at the beginning of their working life.

On the interaction with the economic environment of the worker, the firm where the job is located (captured in three dimensions: public or private; agriculture, industry, or services; firm size within the private sector) has no significant impact on the probability of low pay. Having a service or retail occupation, however, certainly "helps" one's chances of being on low pay. In the same band are skilled workers in agriculture and fishery and craft workers, while elementary jobs enhance the risk of low pay even more. Also, it seems plausible given their elementary nature that in these jobs previous unemployment does not really matter. On-the-job training helps one stay out of low-paid work.[13] It also helps to have a permanent contract, to be male, or to be highly educated.

Estimations using a different (nonpanel) matched employer-employee dataset that includes the smaller jobs but covers only the private sector—the labor conditions survey of the Labor Inspectorate—confirm several of these effects. However, they also show a significant negative effect of increasing firm size on the probability of low pay and diverging effects of more detailed industries, including an upward effect of temp agency work, but this disappears when firm characteristics are taken into account. These estimations also show the importance of certain characteristics of the firm's workforce that could be established from this dataset. Notably, the share of employees not covered by collective labor agreements strongly lowers the probability of low pay and takes away the distinction between CLA coverage and noncoverage for the individual employee. We find that new hirees are significantly more likely than stayers to be in low-wage employment and that this difference is especially pronounced when firm effects are taken into account. Regarding the type of contract, workers holding permanent contracts earn significantly more than those with fixed-term contracts. In contrast, temporary agency workers are found to earn significantly less than the reference—but intriguingly, only when firm effects are not taken into account. When controlling for these effects, we find no significant differences in earnings between temporary agency and fixed-term workers. The individual probability of being low-paid is much higher the higher the percentage of female employees, the lower the average age of employees within the firm, the lower the proportion of workers with higher levels of education, and the lower the proportion of people with longer experience with the current employer. In other words, there is reason to think that firms specializing in a young, high-turnover, female-dominated, and less-educated workforce are using low pay as an instrument for rewarding their personnel.

Mobility Out of Low Pay

If low-wage employment is a temporary experience for individuals, then there is less cause for concern than there would be if individuals who enter low-wage employment are unlikely to leave it. The study of earnings mobility out of low pay over the course of the seven years covered by the ECHP can help to examine this issue. We find that more than 40 percent of low-paid workers experience an upward transition in the earnings distribution, 43 percent remain in low pay, and 16 percent move toward a non-employment situation: unemployment, inactivity, and discouragement. The last group suggests the possibility of a "low pay, no pay" cycle, which, unfortunately, we could not further examine. Males appear not to be more likely than females to escape from low-wage employment and take better-paid jobs. Age, by contrast, significantly influences the likelihood of escaping from low-pay segments of the labor market. This seems to confirm the important role of young workers in low-paid work found earlier. For workers age twenty-five to forty-nine, the probability of moving upward in the earnings distribution is about two times that of younger employees (age sixteen to twenty-four). The effect becomes even more pronounced for workers age fifty to sixty-five.

Their probability of an upward transition is almost five times higher than for the young reference category. However, they also have an equally higher probability of moving toward non-employment. It is an interesting question for further research how these mechanisms work at older ages.

The results also reveal that higher educational levels are related to higher transitions out of low pay as well as lower probabilities of moving to non-employment. Notably, low-paid part-timers are less likely to escape from low-wage employment and to take better-paid jobs than their full-time counterparts, and they are more likely to make a transition toward non-employment.

On-the-job training does not exert a significant effect on the probability of moving upward in the earnings distribution, but we find a negative and significant effect on the probability of moving toward non-employment.

The type of contract is another factor affecting transitions out of low-wage employment. In particular, the results show that holding a permanent contract significantly increases the likelihood of moving from low-wage to high-wage employment and decreases the probability of moving toward non-employment. For low-paid workers with job tenure between two and five years, the probability of moving to a better-paid job is around two and a half times higher than it is for those with less than two years of seniority. From five years' tenure on, however, we do not observe a significant effect of seniority on the probability of escaping from low-wage employment.

For males, being employed part-time significantly reduces the likelihood of getting a better-paid job, while it does not significantly affect the likelihood of making a transition to non-employment. In contrast, the marginal effect of working part-time is not significant for females when estimating their probability of getting a better-paid job, but it clearly increases their likelihood of moving from low pay to non-employment.

SUMMARY

This chapter has shown that in recent decades:

*   Low-wage employment doubled as a percentage of the working-age population and increased by 50 percent as a share of hours worked per capita.

- The hours-volume of *better*-paid jobs suffered a striking decline relative to the working-age population, especially among adult men.

- Particularly youths but also adult women and—especially since the mid-1990s—immigrant minorities played a very important role in the evolution of both employment as a whole and low-wage employment.

- This role was strongly related to the explosive growth of small part-time jobs, which now make up 70 percent of all low-paid jobs.

- Related to this explosive growth in part-time jobs, the Dutch economy has fundamentally altered the time structure of employment, combining a very strong growth of head-count employment with a rather modest evolution of FTE employment, the latter seeming more consistent with the average economic performance in international comparison.

- Interestingly, part-time employment in itself does not show a substantial pay penalty, though small part-time jobs show a very high concentration of low pay.

- Amazingly, the head-count share of the lowest-level jobs was largely unchanged over the period, but it should be taken into account that small part-time jobs are highly concentrated in this category.

- The determinants of the probability of low pay have been the usual suspects (age, sex, low education, and low tenure), they seem to relate to the start of a career, and the personnel policies of certain firms may systematically utilize this information.

- We found substantial mobility of employees out of low pay, which increases with age; however, a significant share of the low-paid remain in low-wage employment, part-time low pay bears an increased risk of leaving employment, and the possibility of a "low pay, no pay" cycle seems nontrivial.

NOTES

1. Unfortunately, owing to lack of earlier data, 1983 was the earliest year we could use in comparing breakdowns by age and gender. Note that the recession in 1983 leads to overestimation of the subsequent performance (compare to figure 2.2).

2. This contrasts strongly with the figure of 39 percent for 1999 given in OECD (2001, table 4.1).

3. Based on a forty-hour working week and forty-six such weeks in a year. This is equivalent to thirty-five hours each week.

4. Both the CPB and OECD/STAN (Structural Analysis Indicators Database) indicate a 3.7 percent increase, but their figures do not control for the decline in annual full-time hours.

5. On the assumption that all jobs of less than twelve hours per week are at the lowest level, the head-count level among all workers in 2004 would rise substantially, to 17 percent; the hours-count level would rise to 8 percent.

6. There are an equal number of immigrants of Western origin, who seem better off in employment.

7. Internationally, the Netherlands has the highest overrepresentation of unemployed foreign-born (OECD 2006, chart I.9).

8. The size of the trade surplus may be related not only to superior export performance but also to lagging imports for consumption.

9. All amounts are gross before taxes and employee contributions to social insurance, but they do not include the employer contribution to compulsory health care insurance, which is part of taxable income but in daily practice not considered part of the gross wage. We mention two caveats. First, the earnings used here do not include annual bonuses such as holiday allowances (statutory minimum of 8 percent), profit sharing, end-of-year bonuses, and overtime earnings. As these increase with earnings, from 3.4 percent at the minimum wage to 9 percent at three times the minimum wage (SZW 2005, 91), the low-pay threshold may be underestimated and therewith the incidence of low-wage employment. Second, following the definition of Statistics Netherlands, the hourly amounts relate to hours of work on an annual basis after the deduction of days off for shortening the working week that people are entitled to when they stick to the full working week. On average, employees had 2.7 such days in 2004. This hourly wage cannot be applied directly to the case studies, where earnings are defined over contractual hours and people continue to earn during holidays. Including holidays but excluding days off, the hourly amounts are lowered by about 15 percent, bringing the FTE low-pay threshold down to €9.46 and the adult minimum wage to €7.69.

10. These are head-count figures, which, given long working hours in the United States, differ little from FTE-count figures.

11. Low-paying industries seem to be universally the same across countries, while high-paying industries are more diverse (Salverda et al. 2001). The former conclusion is also supported by the ranking of interindustry wage differentials (Teulings and Hartog 1998).

12. In the 1994 to 2001 waves of the ECHP, 14 percent of Dutch head-count employment was below fifteen hours per week; the other countries ranked between 1 and 6 percent. Youths and adult women were strongly overrepresented in this category in all countries.
13. This does not necessarily imply that causality runs this way.

REFERENCES

Batenburg, Ronald, Karel Asselberghs, Fred Huijgen, and Peter van der Meer. 2003. *De kwalitatieve structuur van de werkgelegenheid in Nederland, deel V. Trends in beroepsniveau en overscholing in de periode 1987–2000* [*The Qualitative Structure of Employment in the Netherlands, Part V: Trends in Professional Levels and Overtraining in the Period 1987 – 2000*]. Tilburg, Netherlands: OSA.

Blázquez Cuesta, Maite, and Wiemer Salverda. 2007. *Low-Pay Incidence and Mobility in the Netherlands – Exploring the Role of Personal, Job and Employer Characteristics*. Working Paper 06-46. Amsterdam: Amsterdam Institute for Advanced Labour Studies, University of Amsterdam.

Centraal Planbureau (CPB). 2005. *Macro-economische verkenning 2006* [*2006 Macroeconomic Outlook*]. The Hague: CPB.

Gregg, Paul, and Jonathan Wadsworth. 2000. *Two Sides to Every Story. Measuring Worklessness and Polarisation at Household Level*. Working Paper No. 1099. London: Centre for Economic Performance.

Mishel, Lawrence, Jared Bernstein and Sylvia Allegretto. 2007. *The State of Working America 2006/2007*. Washington D.C., and Ithaca, N.Y.: Economic Policy Institute/Cornell University Press.

Organization for Economic Cooperation and Development (OECD). 2001. *Employment Outlook 2001*. Paris: OECD.

———. 2006. *International Migration Outlook 2006*. Paris: OECD.

Salverda, Wiemer. 2007. "The Bite and Effects of Wage Bargaining in the Netherlands, 1995–2005." In *Collective Bargaining in Europe 2006*, edited by Maarten Keune and Bela Galgóczi. Brussels: European Trade Union Institute (ETUI).

Salverda, Wiemer, Brian Nolan, Bertrand Maitre, and Peter Mühlau. 2001. *Benchmarking Low-Wage and High-Wage Employment in Europe and the United States*. Report. Brussels: European Commission Department of Employment and Social Affairs.

Sociale Zaken en Werkgelegenheid (SZW). 2005. *Arbeidsvoorwaardenontwikkeling in 2004* [*Development of Working Conditions in 2004*]. The Hague: SZW.

Teulings, Coen N., and Joop Hartog. 1998. *Corporatism or Competition?* Princeton, N.J.: Princeton University Press.

CHAPTER 3

Labor Market Institutions, Low-Wage Work, and Job Quality

Wiemer Salverda

The ultimate question in this study of low-wage work across countries is this: does low-wage employment differ across countries because of a difference in institutions? That is, do firms shape these jobs differently because of the way their country's institutions are organized and affect the labor market? Chapter 4 elaborates on firm strategies, while chapters 5 through 9 address the double question of whether the target jobs are shaped differently and, if so, how they are affected by the institutional environment. This chapter prepares the ground by taking stock of a selection of institutions that may be at play in low-paid work and job quality. It is important to stress the introductory nature of this discussion, because the role of institutions—a vast and quickly expanding subject—has become all the vogue in recent years and often has strong political implications. The purpose here is to do down-to-earth groundwork, not to try to do justice to the whole debate on institutions and the labor market or determine the actual significance of these institutions for low pay and job quality, though what we know and find will be indicated as much as possible. In the end, not only are the case studies that follow essential, but so is an international comparison with the findings of the other low-wage studies. This chapter aims to provide the building blocks for these two steps.

Nevertheless, this chapter throws up interesting questions about institutions as well as about low pay, and one inference is that the role of institutions should not be overestimated to the disadvantage of the role of the economy. Firm behavior does not simply follow from the institutional environment. The chapter, like the book as a whole, focuses on the Netherlands and, to find sufficient change, uses a long-term approach. In the end, however, international comparison is absolutely vital for establishing the effect of institutions in a national context.

We start with some caveats about the role of institutions and the way this role can be examined. The rest of the chapter tours a range of institutions deemed relevant. It focuses on their properties and their actual impact on firm behavior and low-wage employment, thus going beyond their theoretical characteristics.

ANALYZING AND SELECTING INSTITUTIONS

The research project on low-wage work in the five European countries has not adopted a common approach to institutions and their effects. This is no surprise, since no generally accepted analysis of institutions and their economic effects is available—particularly not for employer behavior in low-wage labor markets and the quality of jobs—and developing it is neither simple nor our aim here. The concepts in the literature seem either too general (Bowles 2004; Hodgson 1988; North 1990) to be useful for our precise subject or too empirical to ensure that their use is not selective "ad hocery" serving a political agenda. The Organization for Economic Cooperation and Development (OECD) has admirably scrutinized various actual rules and legal provisions in many countries but, unfortunately, works its way back from labor market outcomes to an arbitrary selection of (single) institutions.[1]

The risks are several. First, the concept of institutions comes in different flavors, and the taste is not always clear: how to distinguish between large-scale organizational setups—for example, Peter Hall and David Soskice's (2001) deliberative institutions—and specific regulations, between legal and informal rules, between rules and policies or programs, and, ultimately, between institutions and culture. The nature of an institution may depend on policy, as the minimum wage illustrates: though a legal provision in force in the United States since 1938, the real meaning of the minimum wage depends on its level, which is a policy issue.

Second, how do institutions come about? Are they exogenous entities affecting their environment, or are they endogenous—that is, outcomes of the workings of the economy or of factors that also underlie the economy? This may directly bear on the causality of their effects; for example, institutions may codify (economic) behavior that has already developed.

The third issue regards the conceptualizing of the effects of institutions. How do institutions fit a wider economic framework that can define how their workings sort an effect? No convincing framework is available. For example, the supply-and-demand framework misses out on the intermediation between both—such as what is provided by deliberative institutions or contractual relations—and it also is not self-evident for studying job quality.

Fourth, do institutions hang together, or can they be considered in isolation? It is well known by now that individual institutions cannot simply be copied from one country to another, let alone copying complete "models." (The Swedish, Danish, Finnish, Dutch, German, Austrian, American, Australian, and New Zealand models have all been very popular at one point in time or another.) If they hang together, they may all relate to some underlying factor (perhaps a country's culture?), and they may have joint effects that depend on the presence of other institutions, whether the effects of those other institutions are mitigating or reinforcing.

Fifth, looking at institutions theoretically without asking about their actual impact may overstate their effects. Regulations can look more ambitious or dramatic than they are in actual practice, either because their application is more lenient than theoretically envisioned or because institutions mutually compensate for each other. It is also important to realize that their costs and benefits can settle in separate places—sometimes places far away and unexpected.

Last not least, job quality in relation to institutions is virgin territory. First, "better" job quality may have economic content (for example, higher productivity), and it may come at a cost to the individual (for example, time spent training, commuting, or working longer hours) that has to be taken into account. Also, in contrast to quantity, the concept of quality may evade study at the aggregate level to the extent that it depends on the individual.

We conclude, first, that there is no ready-made framework available for organizing the institutional analysis and that economic explanations should be explored to the maximum. Second, international comparison is essential for making progress in this field. Therefore, the approach chosen here is to prepare the ground for comparison with similar studies of low-wage work in Germany, France, the United Kingdom, and Denmark. This approach implies that the treatment of institutions should be modest in conception and selection and conceptually broad with respect to deliberative and regulatory applications, both formal (law) and material (policy), as well as to fields of action. Thus, we divide the broad concept of the quality of (low-wage) jobs into two parts (see figure 3.1):

1. The incomes of workers and the costs paid for labor: institutions with a direct financial effect

2. Job content and work organization: institutions that affect the quality and quantity of labor supply, the division of labor within the firm, and the matching of demand to supply

The distinction is not hierarchical but presentational, aimed at keeping the treatment of the institutions focused. It is also not a one-to-one mapping to aspects of job quality. Institutions may bear on more than one aspect at the same time; they are listed according to their primary field of action.

The issue at stake is whether firm strategies, and particularly their behavior vis-à-vis the quality of low-wage jobs, are fully determined by institutions or whether significant room exists for individual maneuver. The next section examines the deliberative institutions, and the following sections cover the two groups of regulatory institutions. We describe what the institutions stand for and discuss their impact on low-wage employment, with a focus on changes over time. For the concept of firm strategies, we refer to chapters 1 and 4.

THE FOUNDATIONS OF DUTCH LABOR MARKET INSTITUTIONS: THE "POLDER MODEL"

As in any country, the prime actors in the Dutch economy are firms and individuals supplying labor (and demanding commodities), but in many cases they are represented by collective actors who may seek to influence their behavior. This is what the Polder model is about: the specific collective actors that affect the environment in which individual firms and workers operate are an important determinant of social and economic evolution. The model has been in operation since its establishment in 1945 in spite of occasional setbacks. Its workings are much broader than wage formation (discussed in a later section). Here we focus on the tripartite organization of the negotiations responsible for establishing most of the laws and regulations that govern the labor market and many of the consequent policies.

Figure 3.1 Overview of the Institutions Relevant to Job Quality and Low Pay

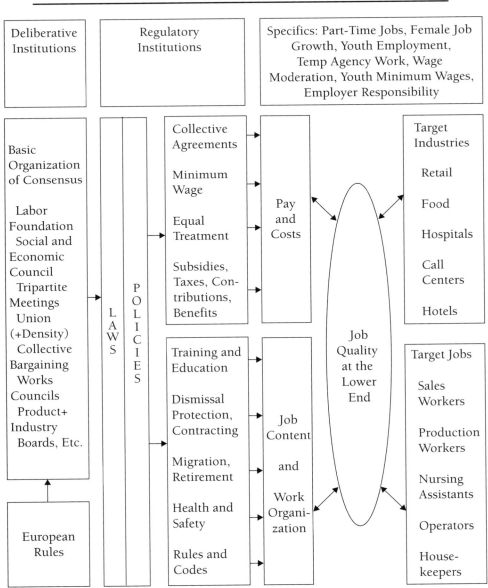

Source: Author's compilation.

Compared to other countries, this organization seems to go further in both its tenure and its resilience in different periods, in the broadness of the areas it covers, and in its impact in those areas.

First of all, employers' associations and trade unions are important actors in the development of socioeconomic policy and in wage determination in particular (figure 3.2). The bipartite Foundation of Labor (STAR), founded in 1945, and the tripartite Social and Economic Council (SER), created in 1950, play the main role, providing platforms for negotiation between employers, employees, and the government. The underlying corporatist arrangements are based on the far-reaching trust and consensus seeking embedded in statutory provisions. In addition, product and industry boards were established in the 1950s that regulate vertically integrated sectors, such as the food industry, and industries with many small firms and self-employed, such as retail. The number of boards has declined over time, and their regulatory power has diminished (SER 2006)—retreating from, for example, wage determination.

Second, the state gives substantial freedom to the social partners for self-regulation, with the aim of achieving optimal interaction between legislation and self-regulation. Many laws open the possibility of adaptation through CLA regulations, with a reinforcing or mitigating effect. Finally, public spending is an important instrument in the government's give-and-take negotiations with unions and employers.

Third, the codetermination at the company level developed by employers' federations and mainstream unions after 1945 led to a dual system of labor relations: general union-employer negotiations outside the firm and the organizational, within-firm involvement of works councils. The councils are not involved in wage bargaining and therefore do not appear in figure 3.2. They are endowed, however, with powers of information, consultation, and codetermination on matters of personnel policy, including working time, working conditions, training and education, and rules for appointing, promoting, and firing personnel. The formation of a council is mandatory for companies with more than fifty employees. A large majority of works councils, however, have problems functioning properly (see, for example, van het Kaar and Looise 1999; Visee and Rosbergen 2004) because of workload, problems of expertise, and the often great distance between councilors and their constituency, especially in industries that have many low-wage workers and are facing rapid change (internationalization, price wars, major reorganizations).

Figure 3.2 The Dutch Model of Socioeconomic Governance and Wage Bargaining

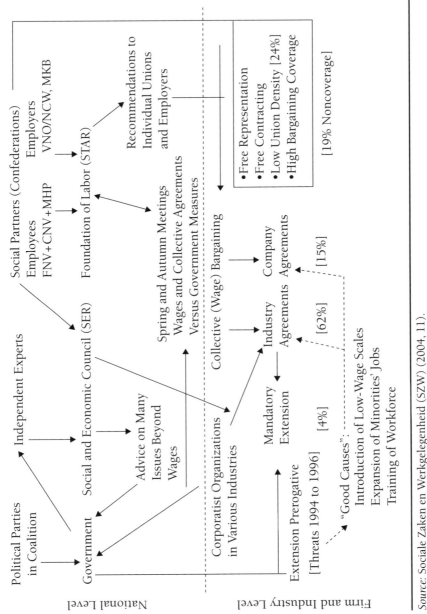

Source: Sociale Zaken en Werkgelegenheid (SZW) (2004, 11).

[a] Noncoverage is 3 percent management, 1 percent in covered enterprise, and 16 percent in noncovered enterprise.

Moreover, many employers still take a lukewarm attitude toward works councils.

Important confederations operate on both sides. The predominant role in representing workers is played by industry-based trade unions that are affiliated with three national confederations. Non-affiliated unions have little influence, and very few unions are based on individual companies. (IKEA's union is one example.) Unionized wage earners have never been a majority in the Netherlands as in, for example, Sweden, and in recent decades union density has steadily declined, decreasing to 26 percent in 2005 (figure 3.3). Workers at the lowest, most elementary job levels are much less unionized, and union density at these levels is falling very rapidly, from 20 percent in 1997 to 12 percent in 2004 (figure 3.4). Density among part-time employees is also low but has not fallen recently. Differences by educational level are small and may reflect higher density among older workers who have less education (and may soon leave employment). Women are also underrepresented, but in recent years they have maintained their membership rate better than men. Unions have shown a growing awareness of gender issues in collective bargaining and have been incorporating these in CLAs since 1983.

Despite the decline in union density, collective bargaining has proven remarkably stable, as we see in the next section. The very important role of collective agreements still makes the trade unions essential actors in the system of industrial relations. The collective agreements address a much broader range of issues nowadays than "simple" wage formation. Unions and employers are expected to contribute to active labor market policies. The importance of this contribution in practice, however, remains to be seen.

THE WORKINGS OF THE MODEL

In the history of the Polder model, wage restraint has always been the first, reflexive response to economic crisis and growing unemployment (Visser and Hemerijck 1997). Here we must take into account that the propensity to strike is low and declining (Akkerman 2000; van der Velden 2000; van Kooten 1998) (figure 3.3). The period 1970 to 1982 was a relatively discordant time marked by substantial industrial unrest and the two oil crises (1973–74). This ended with the first major central agreement: the Wassenaar Accord of 1982. The "Mother of All Accords" offered a single-choice menu: wage modera-

Figure 3.3 Percentage of Union Members and Employees on Strike Among All Employees, 1950 to 2005

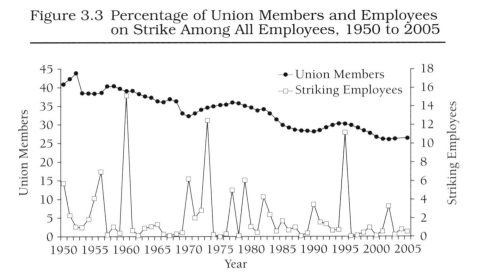

Source: CBS/Statline (union members, strikes) and CBS/Tijdreeksen and Central Planning Bureau (CPB) (2007) (employees).

Figure 3.4 Union Membership by Personal Characteristics, 1997 and 2004

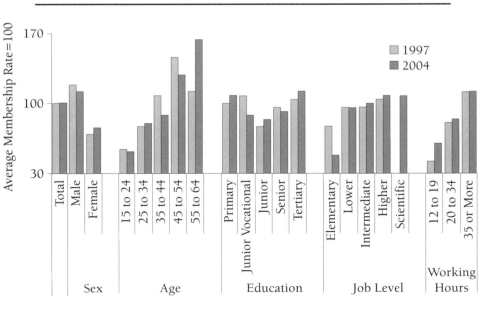

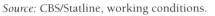

Source: CBS/Statline, working conditions.

tion in exchange for a reduction of working hours. Furthermore, it marked the beginning of a period of "organized decentralization" (Traxler 1995). Government intervention in wage setting was minimized, and the responsibility for wage setting was devolved, first to industries and some major companies and later on to firms within industries. This allowed the confederations to define the policy agenda for decentralized negotiations rather than specific targets or outcomes (Van der Meer, Visser, and Wilthagen 2005).

The subsequent "New Course Accord" of 1993 paved the way for the extension of collective bargaining to areas such as employability, career structuring, training, working-time scheduling, the monitoring of legal provisions for disadvantaged groups, child care, and reinsurance of social benefit entitlements, which were reduced as a result of the government's welfare reforms. The governing coalitions mainly left these issues to the social partners or, as with the reinsurance issue, provoked the social partners to settle them (Van der Meer et al. 2002).

The Wassenaar Accord was also important because it created the opportunity to stimulate all forms of working-time reduction. The government thus encouraged the development of the "first part-time economy in the world" (Visser 2000; Freeman 1998). Part-time work was already progressing over the 1970s but had not yet reached the highest rate in the world. Under pressure from a coalition of unions and women's organizations, part-time work became demarginalized in the second half of the 1980s when the government proposed equal treatment (Salverda and Beukema 1996, 9–11). A large majority of part-time workers are covered by CLAs and thus enjoy legal protection and working conditions equal to those of full-timers (Visser 2000). In a second round of negotiations to shorten working time that followed the 1993 STAR recommendations, a standard thirty-six-hour working week was introduced for the majority of Dutch employees (Tijdens 2002).

Between 1988 and 2000, the Dutch economy grew rapidly, especially after 1994, until in 2001 a recession started.[2] Before that hard landing, "the Dutch disease" had been transformed into "the Dutch jobs machine." U.S. President Bill Clinton, British Prime Minister Tony Blair, and German Chancellor Gerhard Schröder sang the praises of Wim Kok, the leader of the two consecutive "purple" government coalitions (and former FNV chairman) for his guidance on "the Third Way." The revitalized consultation machinery functioned rather effectively. Macroeconomic stability and growing microeconomic dynamism, with private consumption playing a strong role, created near-full employment.

A main critique of the Polder model concerns the slow pace of decisionmaking, the erosion of the primacy of politics, and the limited degree of wage differentiation (Wellink and Cavelaars 2001). Despite this critique, the Polder model infrastructure is still functioning. The national employer and employee confederations meet twice annually with the government, in the spring and in the autumn, to exchange their views on wages, taxes and public spending, social insurance, and the state of the economy. Also, outside the sphere of wages STAR continues to influence the collective bargaining agenda at the industry and company levels by making recommendations on issues such as training and employability (1996, 1998, 2006), reconciling work and family life (1997), and the possibilities for individual choice, or à la carte agreements (1999). However, both union and employers' negotiators seem to use STAR (and SER) recommendations, mainly if those recommendations suit them (Tros 2001). Thus, the parties often take the initiative, especially in areas where the government has long played a passive role—for example, in child care.

Increasingly, European unification is adding to Dutch rules and regulations, as it has done in other countries as well. In line with the consensus model, and because they draw on efforts that the social partners should provide in any event, the adoption of these rules is normally subject to SER and STAR consultation (Salverda and Beukema 1996). Finally, a steadily increasing number of new national regulatory authorities are supervising the behavior of the market parties in private industries (finance, telecommunications, and so on), and also in, for example, collective pension funds. These independent bodies, which are subject to little or no democratic control, could undermine the Polder model institutions, as the recent takeovers of the Anglo-Dutch steel company Corus and the major Dutch bank ABN-AMRO tellingly illustrate. In the interests of shareholders, Corus was auctioned by order of the British takeover regulator. Thus, the Dutch part of the group, a flagship of social entrepreneurship and trade union power on the work floor, was acquired without any say from the personnel or the unions.

In conclusion, the Polder model provides an enduring framework for establishing and changing institutions. Given the low union density in the Netherlands, the role of employer confederations is important. Unions largely stay away from the workplace but have a strong, institutionally reinforced role at the national and industry levels. With the inclusion of the government, the three parties play a game that all try to win at the same time. Increasingly, however, CLAs concluded by two parties are monitored by the third, the government, not only for their general effects but also for the adoption of specific policies (for example, life course arrangements).

In the next two sections, we consider the outcomes of the model in terms of laws, rules, policies, and effects—on costs and incomes, on the one hand, and job content and work organization, on the other.

THE INSTITUTIONS THAT AFFECT COSTS AND INCOMES

We consecutively consider collective labor agreements, which determine the structure of wage scales and annual wage increases; the statutory minimum wage and equal treatment, which put legal constraints on wage formation; and finally, subsidies, taxation, social contributions, and benefits, which contribute to actual revenues and costs of labor.

COLLECTIVE LABOR AGREEMENTS

Collective bargaining is a core institution in the Netherlands, as it is in most continental European countries. The legal foundation of collective bargaining was laid in 1927, and the possibility of mandatory extension was introduced in 1937. This framework remains basically unchanged, so what counts for its effects during the period under scrutiny is the substance actually given to the institution of collective bargaining. Employers and unions negotiate wage increases as well as the grid of relative wages for different tasks, often with scales relating to tenure. In recent decades other issues, such as training and working hours, have been added to the negotiations.

The settings of the Dutch bargaining process are very different from those in the United States, as is well explained by Richard Freeman, Joop Hartog, and Coen Teulings (1996). There is more freedom for employers in the Netherlands, and there is no mechanism of workforce voting; employers are free to conclude a contract or not, and they may do so, for example, by coming to an agreement with only one small union and asking for mandatory extension, leaving other, more important unions out of the process. This makes the role of employers' associations even more important for understanding the high coverage of CLAs, which, in contrast with the much lower union density, cover about 80 percent of all employees. The high density of employer membership in associations and the overrepresentation of larger employers are essential. In the private sector, 46 percent of all firms are negotiating partners to a CLA, covering 74 percent of all employees. This compares to a union density in the private sector of about 19 percent. Only 15 percent of firms, employing no more than 5 percent of all employees, are covered by the mandatory extension. The remaining 40 percent are non-CLA firms employing 21 percent of all private sector employees (SZW 2005a, 78). The CLAs may help firms to solve collective action problems and to realize working conditions that they would be unable to organize individually. CLAs can also improve labor market transparency for both workers and employers.

Mandatory extension is granted by the Minister of Social Affairs, but this is almost a formality and applies to only a small percentage of employees. Nevertheless, the objection was raised that extension might augment the general wage level. Thorough analyses, however, demonstrate that it has no effect, or only a very small upward effect, on wages (Freeman, Hartog, and Teulings 1996; Rojer 2002). Employers gain from the system by the fact that distributional conflicts are resolved outside because unions do not care too much about having a strong presence within the firm. Political threats to do away with the extension mechanism have been perennially opposed by employers, who fear the end of equality and tranquillity in the labor market and in the workplace, as well as an increase in the transaction costs of wage negotiations. The extension legislation has always offered opportunities for dispensation, and increasingly CLAs also allow individual treatment of employees. The extension threat connects bargaining to political decisionmaking, but this does not necessarily work out in favor of low-wage workers, as we will see.

The outcome of the bargaining process is also different from the American situation in that it applies to the entire relevant workforce—there is no individual union wage premium. The CLAs provide a grid that links jobs to wage scales irrespective of the occupant, and most CLAs are closely linked to job evaluation schemes, which may go all the way down to the lowest job levels. Such schemes can be agreed upon by employers and trade unions at the industry or firm level or used by a firm at its own initiative. Larger companies are more likely to use them. Since the early 1990s, all large classification schemes have been checked for gender discrimination, especially in health care. The existence of job evaluation implies that employers have only limited freedom to choose the wage that goes with a job. Once established, a job evaluation scheme will be in place for a long time and thus acts as an institutional constraint on the level of CLA wages. In addition, job evaluation schemes can affect the organizational setup of firms and the career pathways that are open from one job to another.

CLA wage rates provide the starting point for determining actual individual earnings. Figure 3.5 indicates that they are the single most important determinant, though the wage drift and changes in employer contributions to social insurance are certainly not trivial.[3] Negotiated wages have become more sensitive to the economic situation, as indicated by the unemployment rate. Previously, at similar levels of unemployment the aggregate increase was larger. Cumulatively, negotiated wages are lagging increasingly behind actual earnings, but when prices and productivity are taken into account, we see that actual earnings have also behaved quite modestly since the end of the 1970s (figure 3.6). The line showing deflated wages shows the real earnings income for the employee, and the line controlling for producer prices and productivity indicates the costs for the employer. After 1979, in seven out of twenty-six years, real earnings declined, and in no fewer than seventeen years real labor costs fell. Though since the early 1990s unions have taken forecasted increases in producer prices and productivity as a starting point for their wage demands, the actual outcomes have often lagged behind. Unsurprisingly, the labor share in GDP has fallen, from 58 percent in 1979 to 50 percent since the mid-1990s. Such wage-to-productivity moderation is the hallmark of the Dutch model of wage formation. Started in the immediate postwar years, this model, which was very strong in the early 1980s, has been replicated in other European countries but not very much in the United Kingdom and the United States.

The sensitivity of wages to economic change seems to have increased. Pay also differs substantially between agreements for industries, on the one hand, and individual companies, on the other.[4] The latter have 11 percent higher wages, after correction for the composition of the workforce, up from only 4 percent in 1996 (table 3.1). In-

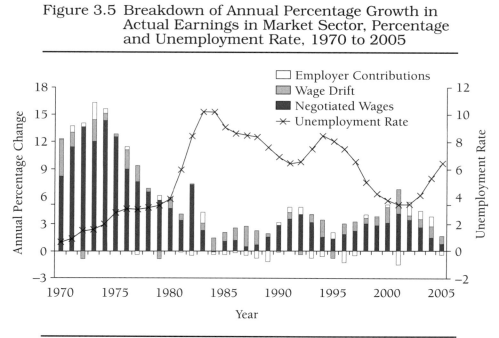

Figure 3.5 Breakdown of Annual Percentage Growth in Actual Earnings in Market Sector, Percentage and Unemployment Rate, 1970 to 2005

Source: Central Planning Bureau (CPB) (2006, table A.6).

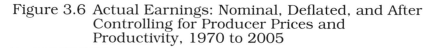

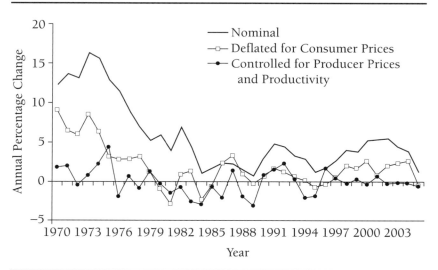

Figure 3.6 Actual Earnings: Nominal, Deflated, and After Controlling for Producer Prices and Productivity, 1970 to 2005

Source: Central Planning Bureau (CPB) (2006, table A.6).

Table 3.1 Differences in Gross Hourly Earnings by Type of CLA Coverage, 2004

Employees Covered By:	Hourly Wage, 2004	Uncorrected Difference, 2004	Corrected Difference[a]		Employment Share, 2004
			1996	2004	
Industry CLA	€12.90	—	—	—	62%
Company CLA	17.10	32%	4.3%	11.0%	15
Mandatory extension of industry CLA	10.14	–19	–0.7*	–1.1*	4
Non-CLA workforce in a CLA firm	20.20	56	7.4	11.5	1
Non-CLA workforce in a non-CLA-firm	14.10	9	–0.6*	–0.4*	16

Source: Sociale Zaken en Werkgelegenheid (SZW) (2005a, VI, 11 and 97).
[a] Individual employee earnings have been corrected for sex, age, working week, tenure, educational attainment, special wage components, job level, type of job, industry, and firm size.
*Nonsignificant at 95 percent

dustry CLAs cover 62 percent of all employees, and company agreements 15 percent. The industry agreements do not neatly follow statistical classifications of industrial activity, and sometimes more than one CLA may apply—offering employers a choice. The pay for workers covered by mandatory extension is not significantly different from that for workers under direct coverage, and this has not changed over the years. However, this applies after correction for composition differences. The uncorrected average wage for firms under mandatory extension is below the low-pay threshold. The 4 percent coverage among employees may therefore concern a substantial proportion of low-paid workers. By contrast, workers in covered firms whose pay is not subject to CLA regulation earn significantly and increasingly more, but this is still a very small group of only 1 percent. Apparently, CLA wage formation has contributed to the moderation of wage growth for those covered directly or indirectly but may have difficulty covering the better-paid. CLA wage growth is also remarkable for its rather uniform outcomes across industries—actual earnings, however, may differ. The uniformity within the private sector seems to have grown in recent decades despite the decentralization of negotiations.

Opening Up the Lower End   It is important to realize that CLAs normally offer a wage grid for low-level jobs. Therefore, low-paid workers' earnings may rise for several years if they stay on the job. The rise may be too modest, however, to bring them above the low pay threshold. A formal instrument for government intervention in wages is the statutory minimum wage. Its effects partly depend on whether the CLAs allow this low level of pay. Figure 1.1 showed that wage rates have to a substantial extent followed the decline of the minimum wage, particularly for young people.[5] Nevertheless, the lowest wage scales laid down in collective agreements are often situated above the minimum wage, for both adults and youth, with a strong variation by industry. In 1993 the government started pressing for bringing the lowest CLA wage scales down to the minimum wage, supposedly to stimulate employment opportunities, especially for disadvantaged groups. STAR and SER repeatedly (1990, 1993, 1995, and 1999) made this recommendation to the social partners, stressing the need to create extra jobs for the low-skilled. The issue continues to be monitored by the government in the spring and autumn meetings to this very day.

The importance of CLAs containing a lowest scale below 105 percent of the minimum wage has grown extensively, from 20 percent (of covered employees) in 1993 to 82 percent in 1997 (Tros 2001). These effects are reflected in figure 3.7. Until 1993, the lowest scales first followed the trend of the average wage rate, diverging from the minimum wage up to 13 percent. Then they were lowered, first quickly and then more slowly; the gap was thus reduced to around 5 percent today. After deflation for consumer prices, the lowest scales have fallen on balance by more than 10 percent compared to the initial level of 1983.

As we have seen in chapter 2, low-wage employment increased after the mid-1990s, and this increase seems suggestive of an employment effect of these measures. However, the policy may have largely been an academic exercise as in CLAs relevant to low pay people low-wage scales already existed while in other CLAs—such as, for example in the building trade—the new, lower scales may not have been used in actual practice. The Labor Inspectorate found in 1998 that the overwhelming majority (86 percent) of companies did not use the new scales and that only 6 percent of their employees were found on them (Ackerman and Klaassen 1998). It is also telling that between 1995 and 2005 the percentage of employees earning up to 105 percent of the minimum wage tended to decline.

By way of conclusion, it seems fair to say that collective agreements are a more passive or—in a more positive vein—more flexible

Figure 3.7 Lowest Scales, Average Agreed Scales, and Adult Minimum Wage, 1983 to 2005

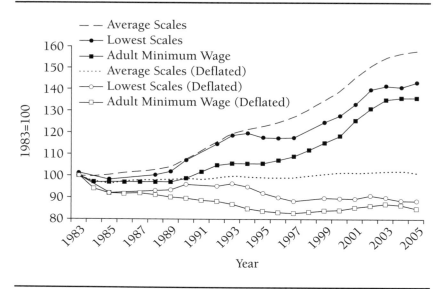

Source: Sociale Zaken en Werkgelegenheid (SZW) (1991); SZW, Spring and Autumn Reports; CBS/Statline, historical series of wage rates 1972 = 100, after 2002 extrapolated with series 2000 = 100; figures 1.1 and 3.8.
Note: Except nominal lowest scales, which are indicated as a percentage of the adult minimum wage.

institution than many may think. Their effects depend on their contents. In spite of the independence of employers and unions as contractual partners, they tend to follow government objectives, especially in bringing the low-wage end of the wage distribution down, albeit under some pressure from the government's threat to bring mandatory extension to an end. However, the effects on actual jobs seem limited.

Constraints on Wage Formation: The Minimum Wage and Equal Treatment

The Minimum Wage: Radical Lowering with Little Effect   As of January 2007, the minimum wage for adults amounted to €300 per week gross, or €257 net after tax.[6] On top of this, employees, like anyone else, are entitled to a minimum annual holiday allowance of 8 percent of gross annual earnings (€14 net per week in 2007). The total gross amount of €332 per week amounts to an estimated $355, and the net amount to $290 (PPPs; see also table 2.4). The minimum wage formally includes all regular payments—such as compensation for shift work, tips, commission bonuses, inconvenience payments, and payments in kind—but not overtime earnings. Employer contributions add to the gross amount. The minimum wage is not defined as an hourly wage— as it is in the United States and the United Kingdom—but relates instead to a "normal working week," which depends on the CLA.

The social partners introduced an adult minimum wage in 1964, and this was put into law in 1969. In 1974 it was complemented with a long tail of youth minimum wages; this internationally distinguishing feature is defined as fractions of the adult minimum for each year of age, starting at 30 percent of the adult wage for fifteen-year-olds. Three arguments are given for this tail by the Ministry of Social Affairs and Employment:[7] young workers are less experienced and trained and have lower productivity; their needs are fewer than those of adults, since they usually live at home and do not maintain a family; and higher earnings would make employment too attractive to young people compared to continued schooling. Unions advocate lowering the age of adult wage to twenty-one or eighteen; in the political debate, by contrast, it is regularly proposed to increase the adult age to twenty-seven.

Until 1993, the minimum wage did not apply to persons working less than one-third of the working week. The restriction was abolished because of its discriminatory effect on women and as a stimulus to part-time employment. The minimum wage is not legally enforced; instead, underpaid employees have to take their employers to court. The Labor Inspectorate found an average of 13 percent underpayment for 0.6 percent of employees in 2004 (SZW 2006). Youths and employees working either under mandatory extension or in smaller firms are more likely to be underpaid.

A legal mechanism exists for biannual up-rating, linked to the evolution of CLA wages (not actual earnings), with some time lag. In principle, this frees the level of the minimum wage from the political process—in contrast to the United States, where the increases are less frequent but considerable. In practice, however, the minimum wage has been very sensitive to political decisionmaking. By special laws, it was nominally lowered in the early 1980s (once for adults, several times for youth) and then "frozen" for many years in the 1980s, part of the 1990s, and again recently between July 2003 and January 2006. The last time the minimum wage was frozen, it was argued that the freeze was a four-year revision, but it occurred in spite of the fact that the inactives-to-actives ratio did not exceed the threshold of 82.6 percent, which was stipulated in a new law in the early 1990s. (Inactives are those who receive benefits, including the public old-age pension; actives are those who are employed, including the self-employed.) This recent experience aptly illustrates the use of the minimum wage as a policy instrument. The government had hoped that trade unions would adopt a similar freeze for all wages. As a consequence, the minimum wage has strongly lagged behind prices (25 to 30 percent) and average wage earnings (28 to 34 percent) (figure 3.8). If we account for the many young workers who earn a (much lower) minimum wage,[8] the decline in the purchasing power of the *average* Dutch minimum wage since its peak in the second half of the 1970s actually matches that of the American minimum wage, which has a single value for all ages. The decline of the ratio to the average wage for all ages exceeds that of the United States, and both ratios are rather similar now.

The pivotal importance of the net minimum wage for all net social benefits and ensuing public expenditure is the key argument for a policy of budget restraint. In principle, there is a poverty concept behind this argument, but it is given no systematic scrutiny, and little has been heard from the government about the poverty implications since it started decreasing minimum benefits and the minimum wage in the early 1980s.

Who are the people actually earning the minimum wage (or less), and how many of them are there? Based on estimations from tabulated data, the incidence of age-related minimum wages has fallen considerably (figure 3.9). This is in line with the literature on the American minimum wage.[9] Changing the minimum wage primarily affects the wage distribution—and therewith inequality—more than employment. The figure also indicates the share paid at or below the single adult minimum wage (including youths earning between the youth and the adult minimum wage). This share has also fallen, but clearly less, and it has remained roughly stable over the 1990s at 10 percent of all employees.

In principle, the decline of the minimum wage has increased the room for maneuver for hiring people at low pay. Figure 3.10 shows the decline, together with minimum-wage employment and low-wage employment. In 1979 the minimum wage was well above the low pay threshold of 66 percent of the median. This changed in the

Figure 3.8 Real Minimum Wages (Prices of 2005) and Relative Minimum Wages, 1970 to 2005

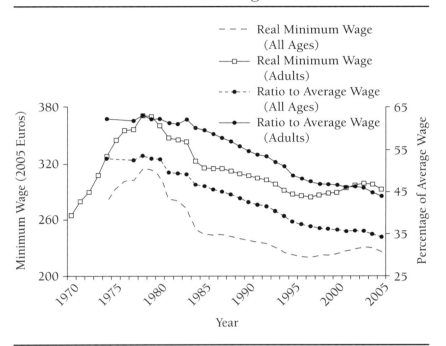

Source: Statistics Netherlands (CBS), Historical Series Statline.

second half of the 1980s, when it came in under that threshold. From that moment on, low-wage employment was positively larger than minimum-wage employment. However, it did not increase but basically stayed at the same level until the mid-1990s, while minimum-wage employment fell strongly together with the minimum wage, from an estimated 14.5 percent in 1979 down to 6.2 percent in 1993. Since then, it has increased slightly, to 7.7 percent in 2004 and 6.9 percent in 2005. The relative level of the minimum wage tended to decline further. Apparently, most of the decline of the minimum wage hardly affected low-wage employment, which quickly increased between 1994 and 1998 and has subsequently been fluctuating around a level that finally exceeds the initial incidence of minimum-wage employment, albeit by only 1 to 1.5 percentage points (but remember the caveat in chapter 2 about a possible series break).

Figure 3.9 Incidence of Age-Specific Minimum Wages, 1974 to 2005

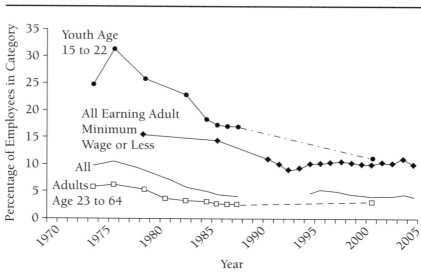

Source: Author's calculations from CBS, Structure of Earnings Survey microdata for 1979, 1985, 1989, 1996, and 2002, and tabulated data for other years; Rienstra and Copinga (2003).

The first, stylized conclusion is that the adult minimum wage fell from 70 to 55 percent of the median, while low-wage employment fully replaced minimum-wage employment and grew somewhat above it. However, though the increase on balance is modest, it hides a considerable demographic composition shift toward adults (see table 2.5). Second, a lower minimum wage may increase opportunities for low pay, but apparently their use depends on economic and labor market conditions more than the other way around. It is clear, nevertheless, that the content given to the minimum wage as an institution has allowed the growth of low-wage employment. However, had the minimum wage remained unchanged, most of the same circumstances would have been labeled "minimum-wage employment," though adults might have had less of a role in it.

Equal Treatment: Help for Women on Low Pay and Part-Time Employees
Policies that aim to diminish the gender wage differentials have been of major importance for low-wage female workers. After 1945, CLAs

Figure 3.10 Relative Minimum Wage, Adult Minimum-
Wage Employment, and Low-Wage
Employment (FTE), 1979 to 2005

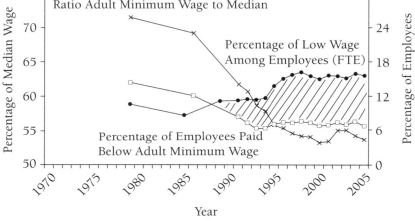

Source: Author's calculations from CBS, Structure of Earnings Survey microdata for 1979, 1985, 1989, 1996, and 2002, and tabulated data for other years; compare also figure 2.8.

put female wages proportionally lower than men's. Later on, international pressure to award equal pay for equal work began to grow, and slowly the formal wage differences and the special female wage scales were abolished—the last for laundries in 1971 (Tegelaar 1972). In 1975 the Equal Pay for Men and Women Act came into force; the act was later integrated into the Equal Treatment of Men and Women Act, both based on European Union (EU) directives. The latter act also covered equal access to jobs, training, and pension facilities. The Equal Treatment Commission received hardly any complaints that touched on wages, from which the Labor Inspectorate concluded that that men and women were seldom found in the same occupations. That conclusion put job segregation on the agenda and led to a fierce debate in the 1990s on the gender neutrality of job evaluation systems (Pott-Buter and Tijdens 1998). Unions criticized the poor weights attached to heavy workloads and to aspects of "care," especially in health care, but with more refined criteria and adequate weights, most of that criticism has now disappeared.

We already mentioned the impressive growth of part-time employment and its importance for female employment. Two complementary laws on equal treatment have strengthened the legal position of part-time workers. One law, passed in 1996, prohibits distinguishing on the basis of working hours between employees with regard to employment contracts. It covers working hours, their effect on pay and bonuses, and so on. The Equal Treatment Commission advised in 2003 that the rules for overtime hours and earnings should also not discriminate between part-timers and full-timers. Another law, passed in 2000, entitles employees to request an adaptation (increasing or decreasing) of working hours, not to exceed the standard working week. The request has to be granted by the employer unless it conflicts with the interest of the business. The law also prohibits discrimination in employment conditions between permanent and temporary jobs, unless objectively justified. Together with the Flexicurity Act of 1999, this law has improved the position of temporary workers. Just over half (53 percent) of all large firms had adjusted their working hours policies prior to the introduction of this law, mostly through the CLA (Muconsult 2003). Though the percentage of firms covered by CLAs that entitle employees to a reduction of individual working hours had increased to 70 percent, in 1998 still less than one-quarter of CLAs explicitly stated that all functions could be performed on a part-time basis (Tijdens 2005). Thus, both new laws stimulated a development already under way by adding individual to collective rights.

The gender wage gap is diminishing, but slowly; in December 2004 women's uncorrected average gross hourly wage was still 19.3 percent below the male average, as against 24.0 percent in 1995. The remaining gap can be explained mainly by the fact that women are overrepresented in low-wage subsectors (sectoral sorting) and in low-wage occupations (occupational sorting). In a number of subsectors, a lack of advancement opportunities in firms (the "glass ceiling") plays a role; in other industries, the gap is due to job segregation or a penalty incurred by women reentering the labor market. Table 3.2 illustrates this. The gender differential seems to be smaller at the lower end of the pay distribution than higher up; witness the fact that the uncorrected female pay gap is even positive below 130 percent of the minimum wage for the lowest job level and for small part-time jobs of less than twelve hours. Low-skilled women do get paid less than men, but the gap is smaller than higher up the educational ladder (SZW 2005a, 64–75).

Table 3.2 Determinants of the Gender Wage Gap, by Industry, 2004

	Uncorrected Wage Gap	Determinants[a]					
		1	2	3	4	5	6
Food and beverage manufacturing	24.8%	+++	+	0	++	0	0
Retail trade	21.8	+++	+	+	++	0	+
Finance	30.3	+++	+	+	+++	0	++
Utilities	18.8	++	+	0	?	0	+
Hotels and catering	11.8	++	0	0	+	++	0
Temp agency workers	2.3	0	0	0	?	+	0
Cleaning	21.0	++	+	+	0	0	0
Hospitals	25.2	+++	+	+	+	0	+
Homes for the elderly	19.1	++	0	+	+	0	+

Source: Calculations based on CBS/Statline (research for the EQUAL and CLOSE projects carried out by Maarten van Klaveren, Kea Tijdens, and Wim Sprenger).
[a] Determinants:
  1. Employment structure/job segregation
  2. Recent changes in employment structure (crowding)
  3. Recently many women re-entrants
  4. Women re-entrants with considerable wage penalty
  5. Negative effects of recent legislation/CLAs
  6. Glass ceiling
Effects on the wage gap:
  + slight
  ++ moderate
  +++ strong

TAXATION, SUBSIDIES, AND BENEFITS

Income taxation, contributions made to social insurance by both employees and employers, subsidies given to firms or individuals, and social benefits that individuals receive under certain conditions affect the take-home pay of workers and the labor costs of employers.

Taxes and Social Contributions   Income tax and social contributions are formally different and evolve in materially different ways over the wage distribution—increasing for tax, decreasing for contributions—but the two have become increasingly intertwined. Since 1990, the contributions to national social insurance (old-age pension, orphans and widows scheme, large health care costs) have been fully integrated into the structure of income taxation, while employee social security contributions (unemployment, disability) have remained separate.[10] Taxation of low incomes is now only 2.5 percent, but contributions amount to 31.15 percent. The progressive nature of income taxation partly explains the popularity of part-time employment with proportionally lower annual earnings. The system of income taxation was drastically changed in 2001 when exemptions of income, depending on personal and household characteristics, were replaced with tax credits deducted from taxes due over all income. The value of an exemption depends on the individual's marginal tax rate, but a tax credit is an equal amount for everyone. The General Tax Credit (€2,000 [US$2,930])[11] is given as a deduction on tax obligations to each taxpayer and is actually paid (up to €2,000 or the taxes paid by the earning partner if these are less) to partners in a household with no income or very low income of their own (up to €5,800 [US$8,496]). The Labor Tax Credit phases in to a maximum of €1,400 (US$2,051), which is reached at about the level of the adult minimum wage (€18,000[US$26,364]). For incomes of less than half the minimum wage, the credit is a very low 2 percent, while over the second half of the minimum wage it is 12 percent of earnings until the maximum credit is reached. The phasing-in was introduced to augment the benefit of paid work over social benefit.

The change of system in 2001 significantly affected take-home pay and marginal tax rates for the low-paid because of the phasing-in of the labor credit, the payment of the general credit to non-earning partners, and the typical effect of tax progression. The three factors work together, especially over the range of earnings between the minimum wage and the low pay threshold. Figure 3.11 indicates present and previous outcomes for earnings up to €25,000 (US$36,611) for two different household types that were—and still are—treated differently: the individual earner who does not share a household or, as a two-earner, shares it with a partner receiving his or her own earnings that are taxed independently (panel A); and the traditional single breadwinner with a nonworking partner (panel B). Out of the minimum wage, the former pays 16 percent in taxes and contributions (26 percent before the change), the latter 4 percent (12 percent before the change). At the low pay threshold, the current figures are 20 and 10 percent, as against 28 and 15 percent before. Teenage minimum wages are so low that young earners effectively pay no taxes.

As a result of the system change and the subsequent increase in the labor credit, the purchasing power of the *net* minimum wage has con-

Figure 3.11 Net-to-Gross Annual Earnings and Marginal Tax Rate, 1998 and 2007

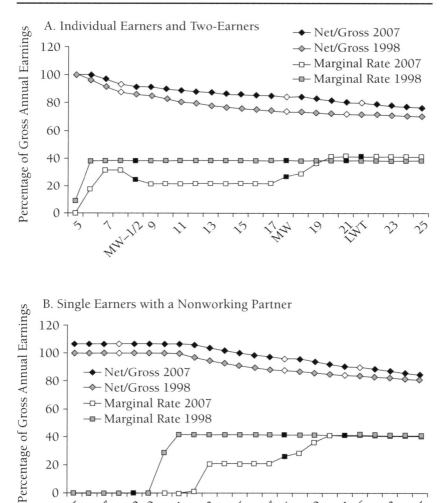

Source: Author's calculations.

Note: Calculated after income tax and contributions to the public pension and the orphans and widow(er)s scheme, which are integrated into the tax system, and including compulsory health insurance, but before employee contributions to social insurance, occupational pensions and early retirement. The presence of children is disregarded.

tinued to increase in recent years in spite of the gross freeze. This was part of the government policy, which was aimed at preventing an increase in the gross labor cost of the minimum wage. Taxation was lowered for all income levels, but the effects were relatively more substantial for lower earnings. This led to a lower marginal tax rate than before below the minimum wage, but also a strongly and further increasing marginal rate over exactly the earnings range from the minimum wage to the low-pay threshold.[12] This seems to create or reinforce a "part-time trap" that can be felt at higher job levels than one might expect as long as total annual earnings remain below the threshold—which they do for more than 40 percent of all adult female year-round workers.

Finally, to understand the gender effect of income taxation, it is important to know that since 1973 the labor incomes of partners sharing a household have been taxed separately.

Subsidies   On the subsidy side, we consider active labor market policies aimed at directly stimulating employers to hire additional workers and other subsidies affecting labor supply.

It should be stressed that in the Netherlands there is no subsidy scheme such as the U.S. Earned Income Tax Credit. The labor credit as it is given between 50 and 100 percent of the minimum wage comes closer to it than anything else, but it does not relate in any way to the income of the household.

The Netherlands shares with many other countries a history of attempts to stimulate employment creation by employers, with at best a limited success (see Salverda 1998a). At present there is no subsidy for such a policy. Special mention should be made, however, of the specific tax rebate (SPAK) scheme, which directly subsidized companies for their workers earning up to 115 percent of the applicable minimum wage between 1996 and 2005—an important period for the evolution of low-wage employment. SPAK take-up was very successful because of its administrative ease and because it did not require additional hiring but the simple presence of the employee. Peter Mühlau and Wiemer Salverda (2000a) found no positive employment effect, but other research was more positive (SZW 2001, 79–80). Nevertheless, the deadweight loss was considered so enormous—92 percent or more—that the subsidy was eventually abolished. Though SPAK did not generate additional employment, it may still have increased the number of workers on low pay, since it was in the employers' interest to keep wages down so as to receive the subsidy. Mühlau and Salverda (2000b) found some indications for such

Figure 3.12 Government Job Creation as a Percentage
of Low-Wage Employment (Persons), 1991
to 2004

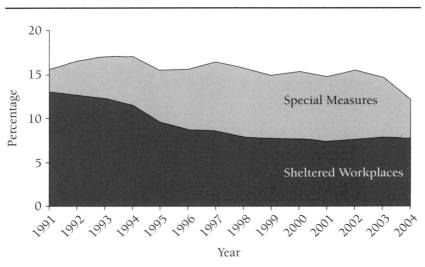

Source: Author's calculations from Sociale Zaken en Werkgelegenheid (SZW),
Social Nota, (various issues), and figure 2.8.

a result. Thus, SPAK may have contributed to an artificially higher
level of low-wage employment for some time.

Another type of subsidy is aimed at direct job creation in the public sector, including hospitals, for low-skilled, long-term unemployed
persons. New measures were introduced in the 1990s for youths and
others, of which the best known were jobs named after Ad Melkert,
then the minister of social affairs (the term was later changed to "ID
jobs"). Indeed, the number of jobs created rose quickly, from 17,000
in the early 1990s to 95,000 in 2002, or from less than 3 percent of all
low-paid persons to almost 8 percent (figure 3.12). However, traditional measures of job creation for the same group should be taken
into account, especially sheltered workplaces (WSW), when determining the net effect. Their role declined because the government
fixed the absolute number, and the combined effect of both of old
and new measures was roughly constant at around 15 percent of low-
wage employment, implying a pro rata contribution to the growth of
low-wage employment but not a special impetus. They may have

contributed, however, to the composition shift of low-wage employment toward adults.

Finally, an unduly neglected subsidy that affects the labor supply and that has also developed swiftly in recent decades is the grant system for students, age eighteen to thirty, in official education. Adopting this view are Rudi Wielers and Peter van der Meer (2001), who show the rapid increase in student labor market involvement. Indeed, there is a very high overlap between education and paid labor in international comparison. Since a universal system of direct grants to all students was put in place in 1986, students have been allowed to combine grants with substantial income from paid work. That income is taxed as usual, but not deducted from the grant as long as it remains below a certain threshold. This income level was increased considerably over the 1990s, and today it amounts to about 70 percent of the statutory adult minimum wage (figure 3.13). Thus, the grant acts as a subsidy that enables students to compete for lower-level, lower-income jobs on a part-time basis, putting pressure on the employment opportunities and pay of persons (mainly young, low-educated people) who depend on full-time jobs for a living. In 2004 and 2005 some €3 billion (US$4.4 billion) was spent on student grants, which compares to total youth wage earnings of €11 billion (US$16.1 billion).

Social Benefits   Employee social insurance covers the risks of unemployment, sickness, and disability. Unemployment insurance (UI) is complemented by means-tested social assistance for the unemployed who do not qualify for the employee insurance. UI can affect the firm directly (financially through its financial contributions and organizationally through employment obligations vis-à-vis its employees) and indirectly (through the labor supply encountered in the market). UI has been in place since 1949 but was drastically changed in 1987, when the replacement ratio fell from 80 to 70 percent; later on, entitlement criteria were tightened several times—most entitlements of young persons were eliminated—and more changes were made very recently, in October 2006. The entitlement depends on the loss of paid work of at least five hours or 50 percent for less than ten working hours. Employees need to have worked for at least twenty-six weeks out of the preceding thirty-six, and to receive more than three months' worth of benefits, an employee must have worked four out of the preceding five years. Benefit duration (up to sixty months un-

Figure 3.13 Student Grants and Allowable Net Earnings Per Annum, 1986 to 2006

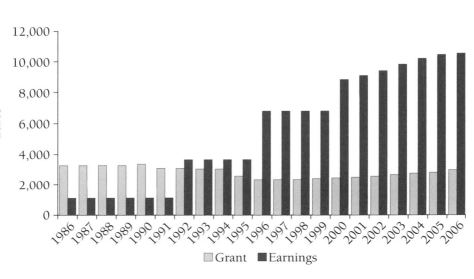

Source: Ministry of Education and Informatie Beheer Groep (IBG).
Note: The basic student grant (independent of parents' income) is for students not living with their parents—about half is needed for fees today.

til October 2006, when benefit duration was reduced to thirty-eight months) and benefit level both increase with the individual's work history and may also be lifted to the minimum to prevent household poverty. The recent change was the result of a long debate, after which the government finally adopted the agreement reached by SER while unions and employers agreed to put more effort into preventing dismissals by using their own industrial training funds.

Those who make up the major part of the labor supply in the low-wage labor market, youths and adult women sharing a household, have virtually no UI entitlements. This will not prevent them from entering the labor market, but it may be one reason they refrain from leaving. No data are available that allow us to link unemployment benefits to persons previously on low pay, nor to their level of educational attainment, but it is clear that unemployment is much higher among the low-skilled (SZW 2005b, 3). However, because youths make up a very significant part of this category, the evolution of their

Figure 3.14 Benefit-Wage Ratios (1979 = 100) and Market-Sector Replacement Rate, 1970 to 2005

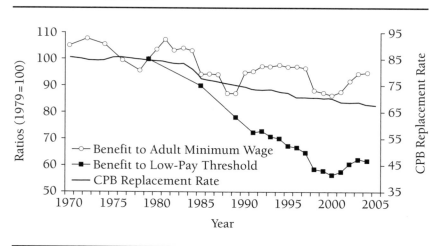

Source: See figures 2.7 and 2.8 for low-pay threshold and minimum wage; Uitvoering instituut Werknemersverze-keringen (UWV) (2005) for average unemployment insurance benefits; and Central Planning Bureau (CPB) (2006, table A.6) for replacement rate.

benefits can give us some indication of this link, particularly because their entitlements have been changed the most over time. Their official UI inflows relative to their employment (more than twelve hours per week) fell from 13 percent in 1987 to 8 percent in 2004, while at the same time those of persons age twenty-five to sixty-four hardly changed (7 percent in both years). It seems plausible that the changes in UI have affected the lower end of the labor market more strongly and diminished the options for receiving unemployment benefits as an alternative to paid work.

Another significant aspect of the evolution of UI policy concerns replacement income. In recent decades, the average replacement rate of social insurance has declined significantly, from 86 percent to 68 percent (figure 3.14). It is important to realize that this lower rate also applies to low-paid workers, because since the change of 1987 benefits are topped up only for households at risk of poverty—which make up no more than a steady 8 percent of all recipients (UWV 2005, 165). The benefit has also fallen considerably compared to the low pay threshold and the adult minimum wage.[13] So even if UI entitlements still offered an alternative income, the level of replacement income has become much less attractive.

INSTITUTIONS THAT INFLUENCE JOB CONTENT AND WORK ORGANIZATION

We now turn to the second group of institutions that more directly affect firm behavior regarding job quality. We focus, consecutively, on education and training, which influence the nature of the labor supply and thus job content; on hiring and firing rules as well as immigration and retirement rules, which all constrain the firm's labor supply; and on health and safety legislation and the corresponding parts of social insurance (disability and sickness), which directly intervene in the firm's working conditions and division of labor. In principle, occupational rules and hygiene codes do the same, but they have applications to specific occupations and industries and seem important for hospitals only and will be considered in chapter 7.

EDUCATION AND TRAINING

The education of job occupants depends on initial education and later on-the-job and firm-provided training. The share of the low-skilled (ISCED 0–2) in the working-age population in the Netherlands—37 percent in 2002—is relatively high compared to various other countries, including the United States, where it is 20 percent.[14] However, the employment rate of the low-skilled, at 80 percent of the national average, is also high in international comparison.[15] Strikingly, the share of the low-educated in the present outflow from the educational system is virtually identical to that of the working-age population up to sixty-four years. The implication is that little progress has been made in educational output recently. Among low-educated school-leavers, three groups can be distinguished: those without a certificate beyond primary level; those with a certificate of junior secondary education; and those who obtained a certificate of junior secondary education but subsequently dropped out of senior secondary education without obtaining a diploma. Up to the mid-1980s, the shares of the first two groups fell considerably, while that of the third group gradually increased. Since then, the first group has roughly stabilized at about 14 percent, while the second group has continued to decline, to 6 percent, and the third to grow, to 19 percent. The second group developed slightly faster than the third group, with a very slow overall decline of the low-skilled as a result. Nowadays half of all low-educated school-leavers are dropouts from senior secondary education. This bad performance occurs within vocational education in particular. Apparently, this segment of the educational system fails to bring students higher up the ladder of educational attainment. It is an important social and political problem that is aggravated by the fact that much of it coincides with ethnic differences among the (youth) population.

The Persistent Problems of Vocational Education   Secondary-level vocational education (VET) has a long history of making policy about the respective roles of the state and business in providing training, and it is also much discussed internationally. Both junior and senior secondary vocational education in the Netherlands were overhauled between 1983 and 1994, on the advice of three committees, each chaired by a former captain of industry. At the junior secondary level, vocational and general education were merged into a single school type in 1999. In 1995 large regional schools were established at the senior secondary level; these are also responsible for practical training for teenage as well as adult students. Eighteen special expert centers have liaisons with particular industries, with two aims: shaping the nature of the training in the schools and certifying the training posts in the firms.

With this change, the two legs of senior secondary vocational education—theory and practice—were brought together. In practice, however, the difference between the options is diminishing as time spent on the work floor in the theory-based leg is increasing. One of the government's two main think tanks, the Social and Cultural Planning Office (SCP), observes that the growing dominance of practice-based education impairs the general knowledge that individuals need for lifelong employability (SCP 2006). Also, many observers think nowadays that the merging of vocational and general education at the junior secondary level is harming general education and encouraging pupils not to choose vocational education after primary school. This pressure, together with the high dropout rate in senior secondary vocational education—up to an extreme 70 percent in the practice-based leg—seems to imply that the recent organizational changes have not solved the problem.

The declining inflows from education into firm training posts il-

Figure 3.15 Inflows into Firm-Based Vocational Training from Initial Education, 1970 to 2005

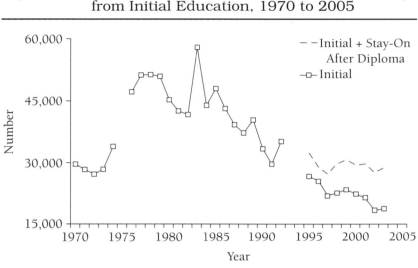

Source: CBS, Matrix of Educational Transitions.

lustrate this (figure 3.15).[16] The problems are caused by the different positions of the stakeholders responsible for the practical training of students and by an in-built weakness: during economic expansion firms and students alike will try to skip education, while during a contraction firms will not want to spend on training positions and people who have already entered may want to stay on. The social partners have been called upon to increase the number of training positions, and recently employers, unions, and the government have agreed to create special informal training positions that qualify more generally for the labor market and target (potential) dropouts. However, substantial numbers of people do not participate in any education or work, and SER (2002) has observed that stimulating education via the social partners will not reach low-educated groups with low employment rates. SER's conclusion is that the government must retain active responsibility for adequate initial education.

Finally, youth from ethnic minorities seem to have much greater difficulty getting accepted for a training post in a firm, which they need to successfully complete practice-based vocational education. In 2005 they made up some 25 percent of all students and 21 percent

Table 3.3 Collective Agreements with Training and Education Arrangements, 2005

Type of Training Facility	Number of Collective Agreements	Workers Covered by These Agreements
Job-oriented training	120	99%
Vocational education and training	56	56
General training	24	19
Recognition of acquired competencies	10	14
Dutch language for migrants	7	3
Total[a]	124	99

Source: Sociale Zaken en Werkgelegenheid (SZW) (2005).
[a] Some agreements offer more than one option.

of all outflows of junior secondary education, but going on from there, they made up 29 percent of all flows into the theory-based leg but only a tiny 8 percent of the flows into the practice-based part. This seems to aggravate the traditional problems of providing vocational training in firms.

Firm Training   Trade unions and employer organizations are developing new initiatives to keep workers employable and protect them from employment loss, including the recognition of acquired competencies (see table 3.3). No information is available, however, about the extent to which these provisions are actually put into practice.

Since the mid-1990s, the social partners have put aside money through the collective agreements for industry-based training funds, which aim to promote the employability of workers and now number more than one hundred. The financing is part of the wage bill. With mandatory extension, all companies within an industry have to contribute. In 2003, 79 percent of CLAs covering 85 percent of all workers had such funds (SZW 2003). Industries that do not have them tend to be less unionized and located in the service sector—the independent call center industry being one example.

The use of the funds is an important problem. Their accumulated savings were estimated at €1 billion (US$1.41 billion) in 2002 (Waterreus 2002, 30). The fact that they are organized through CLAs complicates efficient spending because their large number does not match the structure of vocational education (especially the eighteen

Figure 3.16 Participation in Post-Initial Education, by Educational Level, 2000 to 2004

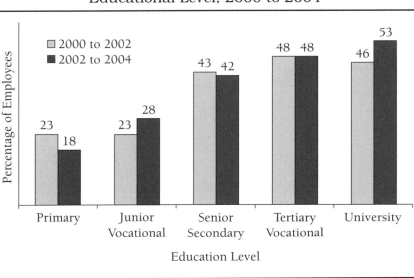

Source: Fouarge et al. (2006, 86).

expert centers). The industry-based financing of the funds also discourages spending on training that would enable employees to leave an industry.

A central issue in our research is the connection between wages, job quality, and education or training. Because unions are better organized among semiskilled and skilled workers, they are not always able—or alert to the need—to deal with training and education for low-wage workers, who are less often found in employment anyway. Most industry-level arrangements are primarily directed at the core workers. This is certainly the case for the efforts of job evaluation schemes to define qualification degrees for various jobs. Such efforts have helped to connect the worlds of formal education and labor market institutions more intensely than two decades ago. Yet in these operations low-skilled and low-paid work tends to be neglected or even forgotten. Approximately one million people in the Netherlands have difficulty reading and writing in the Dutch language. To improve the employment chances of these low-educated workers after their initial education is of utmost importance. Over the past decades the participation of workers in post-initial education has increased, but a dichotomy between high-educated and low-educated workers is visible and seems to be widening (figure 3.16).

A tentative conclusion of this section is that, in the light of the persistently bad performance of vocational training, the Polder model is not well suited to solve the problems of education and the labor market. The low-educated risk being left out. At the same time, it should be noted that students and married women provide strong competition, not only because they prefer to work part-time but also because of their better educational attainment. For example, the least-educated quartile of women workers is better educated than their male counterparts, while at the same time their average job level is lower, implying a greater overeducated competition of female talents. Unsurprisingly, the share of the better-skilled among the occupants of low-skilled jobs increased to 43 percent in 2004, as we saw in chapter 2.

Hiring and Firing

The ease with which employers can hire or fire employees naturally affects job security for workers, but it may also influence the way jobs are organized by the firm.[17] Between 1979 and 2005, the number of people with an employment contract grew by 2 million, or more than 40 percent. This enormous growth does not exactly provide prima facie evidence that employment protection legislation (EPL) is a relevant constraint. Naturally, it may be more important for certain groups in the labor market—such as youths, the low-skilled and the low-paid—than for others. The issue plays an important role in international debates and comparisons, particularly those of the OECD. EPL concerns the options that are available to the employer to terminate a permanent employment contract, conclude a nonpermanent, temporary, or fixed-term contract that will end without the need for a legal dismissal procedure (though the economic cost of unemployment benefits may still have to be borne), or hire through an intermediary such as a temp agency. Unsurprisingly, EPL goes back again to 1945, when a wartime regulation, the Buitengewoon Besluit Arbeidsverhoudingen (BBA), was reaffirmed. Meant as emergency legislation for hiring and firing in the private sector, it superseded other rules and laws governing the employment relationship, including the Civil Code.

For employees with a permanent position, dismissal is forbidden for a range of specified reasons but allowed for a "compelling reason." The employer needs to observe a notice period of one to four months, depending on seniority, though the CLA may reduce the period. The employee can appeal to a court in the case of an "obviously unreasonable" dismissal and claim financial compensation. There is a "dual system" offering two options for dismissal of individual employees: through an administrative body or in court. First, the employer can ask permission from the public employment service—since 2002 the Center for Work and Income, an independent administrative body. This organization checks the legal rules, ranging from the firm's economic circumstances to the individual employee's behavior or disability and the activities undertaken by the firm to prevent the dismissal. The procedure entails certain administrative obligations, and it can take some time before a decision is reached; there is also a risk that the permission will not be granted (as happened in 7 percent of cases in 2005).[18] The important advantage, however, for the employer—particularly small and medium-sized enterprises—is that no severance pay is awarded to the worker. The second option is to request a court to dissolve the employment contract, a procedure that is thought to be less time-consuming.[19] In stark contrast to the administrative option, however, the court normally awards compensation to the employee, depending on earnings, tenure, and age, with a possible "correction" for the culpability of the employer or the employee. The compensation makes this option much more costly to the employer (estimated at five to six times more by van Zevenbergen and Oelen 2000). No further statistical detail about reasons is available for court cases, but the refusal rate was estimated at 3.5 percent for 1997 to 1999 (Van Zevenbergen and Oelen 2000, xiii).

In case of collective dismissals of at least twenty employees, the employer has been required by law since 1976 to follow the administrative procedure. Since January 1, 2006, the administrative body no longer evaluates the economic arguments of the firm if the unions agree with the arguments when the request is submitted. Evidently, the selection of employees for dismissal is an important issue. After 1995, a choice was offered between two guiding principles—"last in, first out" (LIFO) and mirroring the composition of the relevant workforce—but in March 2006 the former was forbidden because of a new law implementing the European directive against age discrimination in the labor market. The purpose of abolishing LIFO was to improve the labor market position of marginalized groups, but at the same time the position of incumbent workers was strengthened by a more rigorous check on the employer's efforts to prevent dismissal, a procedure that now incorporated the possible shift to another job or the adaptation of the current job within twenty-six weeks, including the possibility of training.

The dual system remains a hot and recurrent issue in a long, drawn-out political debate that also relates to UI. A new round of discussion was provoked in 2000 when a government committee advised abolishing the administrative option and adapting the legal framework of the court option. In 2003 STAR opposed the proposal—in line with its earlier view. Unions reject proposals to abolish protection, and some employers fear an increase of financial compensation costs.[20] All parties share the fear of an unnecessary juridification of dismissals. Recent discussions between unions and employers have not led to a joint view, though all parties wish to diminish unnecessary court cases in situations where the parties agree on substance and need only a formal endorsement of the ending of the contract and a severance payment.[21]

Following the Flexibility and Security Act of 1999, direct fixed-term contracts can be renewed only twice—a third renewal automatically transforms it into a permanent contract—and they can last no more than three years in total. However, CLAs can increase both the number and cumulative duration of contracts, and in 2004 57 percent of agreements did so for the former and 20 percent for the latter.[22] The law was the result of the 1996 agreement on job flexibility and security concluded by the social partners in STAR whereby they exchanged an improvement of the protection offered to temporary workers—especially those working through temp agencies—for a slightly diminished employment protection for permanent jobs. The partners agreed on precise legal phrasing that was adopted in the law of 1999. Legal rules also provide some protection for temporary contracts that do not fully specify the number of work hours and the times of work (call contract, zero-hour contract, or min-max contract), such as a minimum level of pay or a steady contract after a certain number of consecutive contracts. Again, CLAs may change these rules (see, for example, chapter 6).

Strongly Increased Flexibility   Before the 1970s, labor market intermediation was a state monopoly, temporary agency work (TAW) was practically illegal, and only a minor group of mala-fide labor brokers was active. Then both the number of licensed agencies and the acceptance of agency work started to grow, but the general idea remained that intermediation should be left to the state. In the 1990s, the government, SER, and the social partners discussed the regulation of TAW and the public employment service, resulting in major changes for both. Also, the European Union issued the Posted Workers Directive and, in 2004, the Services Directive, which defined a level playing field for the international mobility of employees, both permanent and temporary. In 1998 the temp work agency license system was abolished and more than nine thousand new agencies sprang up; however, about half of them went broke after some time. Today a new CLA is being discussed that aims to equalize the hiring conditions of foreign temp workers, especially Poles, by paying them at least the Dutch minimum wage and providing proper housing. The temp agency industry has developed into a mature, self-regulating industry that prevents illegal practices, and TAW has become an accepted form of flexibility.

The legislation on temp work agencies is strongly intertwined with that on temporary contracts and employment protection. The agencies were directly involved in the conclusion of the 1996 flexicurity agreement, and a CLA for temp work was concluded as part of the deal. Because the limitation on the number of temporary contracts and their total duration also applies to TAW, permanent contracts between temp workers and temp work agencies are made in due course. The share of permanent contracts has thus grown quickly—to one-third of all temp workers in 2002.

Although the OECD unequivocally advocated the relaxation of EPL in its 1994 Jobs Study, now it finds that the theoretical effect of EPL and empirical studies are both ambiguous (OECD 2004, 63). To improve on the empirical work, the organization took stock of EPL and developed an overall indicator based on dismissal protection for permanent contracts, additional rules for collective dismissal, and contract options for temporary work (OECD 2004, ch. 2). Methodologically, however, OECD's fixed weighting scheme denies variation across countries or over time. For example, TAW rules weigh as much or as little in the Netherlands as elsewhere in spite of the diverging incidence. The indicator attributes to the Netherlands relatively strict rules for individual protection (way above the American level), average rules for collective dismissal, and rules for temporary work that are lenient in international comparison but still well above

Table 3.4 OECD Summary Index of EPL Strictness and Its Three Components, 2003

	Total	Protection of Regular Workers Against (Individual) Dismissal	Specific Requirements for Collective Dismissal	Regulation on Temporary Forms of Employment
United States	0.69	0.08 (0.08)	0.48	0.13 (0.13)
Netherlands	2.29	1.29 (1.28)	0.50	0.49 (0.99)

Source: OECD (2006b, figure 3.9), OECD (2004b, ch. 2), and OECD (2004a).
Note: The three components are grouping eighteen basic measures and are weighted $5/12$, $2/12$ and $5/12$ respectively for the total. Figures for the late 1980s are in parentheses (not available for collective dismissal).

the United States (table 3.4). Since the late 1980s, regular protection has not changed, but temporary protection has been halved. To get a better handle on the impact of dismissal regulation, we consider the dismissals of the dual system and the evolution of flexible contracts in more detail.

In 2005 slightly more than half of all dismissal cases followed the administrative option. Figure 3.17 shows the striking change behind this development. The increase in court cases is a recent phenomenon. In 1989 they made up no more than 12 percent of dismissal cases. In terms of individual dismissals, they are a majority now because 16 percent of all administrative cases concern collective dismissal and another 20 percent regard dismissals because of disability, the settlement of which through court is discouraged. The present 60 percent is double the share for 1993. Second, compared to the two previous dismissal peaks, the total number of the present peak has not changed much. Because employment has grown substantially, dismissals as a percentage of employees have fallen. However, compared to the rate of unemployment, which indicates the economic situation, the rate of dismissals has become more sensitive. This is due entirely to the evolution of court cases. Thus, dismissal flexibility has increased considerably in spite of an unchanged institutional setting.

As to the low-skilled, the OECD (2004, 86) concludes that EPL may positively affect employment by limiting layoffs when the economy slackens, but that it may also boost the use of temporary contracts, leading to unstable labor market careers. Unfortunately, no direct data about the importance of EPL for low-wage employment are

Figure 3.17 Dismissal Requests at the Center for Work
and Income and in Court, 1970 to 2005

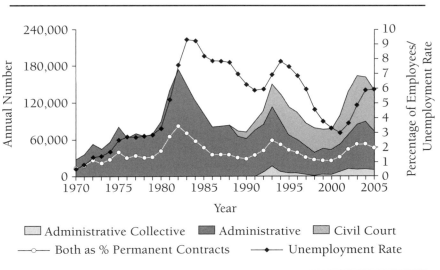

Source: Sociale Zaken en Werkgelegenheid (SZW), Dismissal Statistics (several years); and Central Planning Bureau (CPB), (2006, table A.12).
Note: Missing figures for 1983 and 1987 were interpolated for ease of presentation.

available, neither for the administrative route nor for the court cases. Roelof van Zevenbergen and Udo Oelen (2000, xiv) find that the least-skilled are not overrepresented among formal dismissals, though employers more often think that a person is low-skilled than the employees themselves do.

The complement of dismissal regulation—the other "half" of EPL—is the use of flexible employment contracts. Van Zevenbergen and Oelen (2000, iv) estimate that 1 million employment contracts were terminated between October 1997 and October 1999. Almost half of this number (48 percent) were automatic endings of temporary contracts. Another 14 percent did not make it through probation, and 17 percent ended with the consent of both the employer and the employee. As a result, less than 20 percent of all separations were channeled through the dual system of dismissals. Apparently the role of temporary contracts is extremely important.

Flexible employment as a percentage of all employees has doubled, with some cyclical fluctuation, from 7 percent in 1970 to 15

Figure 3.18 Concentration of Flexible Jobs, (Average Incidence = 100), 2004

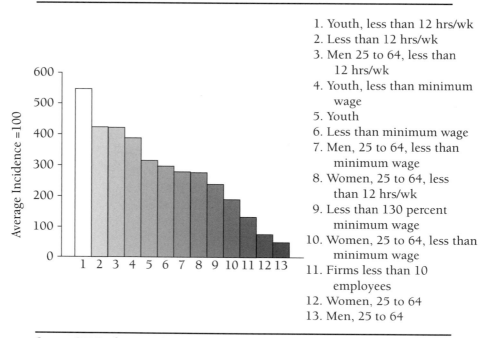

1. Youth, less than 12 hrs/wk
2. Less than 12 hrs/wk
3. Men 25 to 64, less than 12 hrs/wk
4. Youth, less than minimum wage
5. Youth
6. Less than minimum wage
7. Men, 25 to 64, less than minimum wage
8. Women, 25 to 64, less than 12 hrs/wk
9. Less than 130 percent minimum wage
10. Women, 25 to 64, less than minimum wage
11. Firms less than 10 employees
12. Women, 25 to 64
13. Men, 25 to 64

Source: CBS/Statline Employment and Earnings Statistics.

percent today. In contrast to dismissals, flexible work has clearly increased over time. Much of the rise over time—and particularly the sharp rise most recently—is concentrated among young workers. The low-paid more often have temporary contracts. However, simple cross-tabulation suggests that first and foremost small jobs of less than twelve hours per week are vulnerable; next most vulnerable are young workers, and then coming in third are the low-paid as represented by those earning up to 130 percent of the (age-dependent) minimum wage (figure 3.18). Naturally, these characteristics often overlap: young workers on small jobs are up to almost six times more likely than average to experience flexible contracting. Surprisingly, small firms have only a modestly higher incidence. This situation was pretty stable over the last decade.

The Netherlands is well known also for its high rate of temp agency work, which is part of the flexible contracts just discussed.

Figure 3.19 Employment Share of Temp Agency Work,
            1986 to 2005

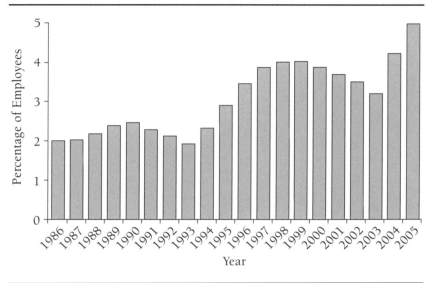

Sources: CBS/Statline Employment and Earnings Statistics, and Quarterly Statistics
of Temp Agency Sales, 1986 to 2002.

Donald Storrie (2002, 28) calls the Netherlands "the most TAW-in-
tensive country." The current share in employee hours worked can be
estimated at 5 percent, after a significant increase over the second
half of the 1990s and a decline during the previous and present economic recessions (figure 3.19). Again, young workers are largely
overrepresented. Temp agency work is basically low-paid. The mean
temp agency workers' wage stood at 94 percent of the low-wage
threshold in 2003–2004, and over 40 percent of male temp agency
workers and over 50 percent of female temp agency workers earned
130 percent or less of the age-dependent minimum wage in 2004. In
this respect, the temp agency industry resembles the notorious low-
wage sectors of retailing, hotels, and catering.

    The external numerical flexibility of firms also includes second-
ment and the hiring of (so-called) self-employed and freelancers.
These practices, which are more widespread today, are badly captured
by official statistics. The same applies to outsourcing, which shifts activities that no longer belong to the firm's core business to the outside

world. This practice has grown rapidly in recent years, especially in value chains in the manufacturing industry, giving rise to, on the one hand, "hollow companies" and, on the other hand, mature supply structures, including large suppliers of cleaning, IT, human resource management activities, and other (shared) services (Van Halem, van Klaveren, and Wetzel 2002).[23] In statistical terms, however, insourcing and outsourcing are fluid, and the numbers of workers involved are hard to trace. Moreover, these forms of internal and external flexibility may not be affected by any clear legislation, because they remain at the discretion of the employer.

Dismissals, temporary contracts, and flexible contracts are certainly not the full story of firm flexibility: firms can also attempt to vary the hours of incumbent employees (overtime compensated in money or time, extension of part-time contracts, or flexible working hours) or use functional flexibility of staff across job categories, overcoming job demarcation lines. Firm strategies vary greatly across industries, depending on CLAs and the job levels for which flexibility is needed. TAW and work on-call are more often applied at low skill levels. Also, the gender composition of the industry plays a role: on-call work is applied more often in the case of predominantly female staff and temp agency work in the case of male staff. Overtime hours amount to 3 percent extra hours, which is not much less than current TAW. The low-educated perform the least overtime hours but are much more likely to be paid if they do.[24] Annualization of working hours applies to fewer than 1 percent of all wage earners. Other forms of internal mobility are difficult to measure. Internal functional flexibility occurs when, within a firm, persons in one job category take over work from another category. In 2004 more than 40 per cent of employees indicated that they took over tasks from workers in other job categories within the firm more often than just coincidentally (Fouarge et al. 2006). This is a very substantial level compared to other types of flexibility.

We conclude, first, that the OECD methodology disregards the actual patterns of flexibility and that its measurement overestimates the impact of EPL in the Netherlands. Second, formal dismissals, in spite of their increased importance because of the increasing use of the court option, are dwarfed by the use of flexible contracts and the flexibility of incumbent staff. Third, we see a strongly increased contractual flexibility and no clear restraining effect of EPL on employment, neither for employers nor for employees. However, the low-paid and low-skilled may bear the brunt of temporary contracting and temp agency work.

LABOR SUPPLY CONSTRAINTS: MIGRATION AND EARLY RETIREMENT

Naturally, increases in the participation of women in the labor market or of youth in education affect the labor supply. We have already discussed both issues. Here we are interested in two supplementary institutional effects that can either constrain or augment firms' choice of employees and thus the size or composition of their workforce, in particular the low-paid workforce: immigration and early retirement.

The labor supply of immigrants has been strongly connected to low-wage employment from the start. In the early 1960s, the first "guest workers" were recruited for menial jobs. Most of them returned to Italy, Spain, or Portugal when job prospects there improved. Recruitment then turned to Morocco and Turkey, closely supervised, if not actually organized, by the government. Again the idea was that people would return to their home countries in due course, but instead family reunification added new immigrants, followed by a growth of the minority population. Migrants from Suriname just before its independence in 1975 and political and economic asylum seekers in the 1990s added to the inflows.

Already in 1979 the Scientific Council for Government Policy drew attention to the unemployment of these groups, but its efforts remained unsuccessful. Later, in spite of a government note in 1983, an advisory statement by the SER in 1987, and STAR's 1990 recommendations aimed at realizing equal representation in employment within five years, the conclusion was drawn in 1996 that neither the social partners nor the government had succeeded. In the meantime, a new law had been introduced in 1994—at the initiative of the Parliament, not the government—obliging companies with at least thirty-five employees to draft plans to remedy underrepresentation. The law met with massive civil disobedience from firms and was replaced in 1998 with a softer, temporary law aimed at "stimulating" minority employment (Salverda 1998a). On the strength of the argument that most companies were taking or considering measures, this law was finally abolished in 2004 as part of deregulation measures, though it was also clear that underrepresentation persisted. Part of the explanation is that equal representation became a moving target as non-Western numbers doubled in the Netherlands during the 1990s from 600,000 to the present 1.2 million.

In 1998 the first measures were taken to control immigration, and ever since increasing demands have been put on immigrants by new and sharper laws, culminating in the Integration Act of 2006. All immigrants are now obliged to undergo an "integration examination," which includes knowledge of the Dutch language. As a result, net immigration steeply declined in recent years: from a peak of 50,000 in 2000–2001, immigration turned negative in 2003 and decreased to a net outflow of 30,000 in 2006. Though individuals from Western countries made up 90 percent of the net outflow, most of the decline was attributable to individuals of non-Western origin, whose numbers went down from inflows of 45,000 to outflows of 3,000. This change contributed to slowing down the annual growth of the minority population, from 6 percent in 2000 to less than 2 percent today. It is still growing, however, mainly because of the second generation, whose growth rate, though substantially diminished since the mid-1990s, is still 9 percent. As the growth rate is still positive and also because there is room for expanding the immigrant employment rate, which currently is twenty percentage points below that of the native population, the potential minority labor supply is not constrained.

Older workers (age fifty and older) pose another possible constraint on the labor supply (see OECD 2005). The general age of retirement has been sixty-five since the introduction of the public old-age pension in 1957. During the employment crisis of the early 1980s, however, extensive early retirement schemes were set up in many industries, with government support. The employment rate of older workers—traditionally low because of very low female participation in that age group—declined from 49 percent to 35 percent between 1973 and 1985. The new schemes mitigated the consequences of mass redundancies from manufacturing, which over that period shrank from employing 22 percent of the total working-age population to 16 percent; the decline was probably much greater among older workers. In addition, older entrants into UI (age fifty-seven and a half and older) were relieved from the duty to apply for jobs and received benefits until the pension age of sixty-five. As part of aging policies, this provision was abolished in 2003, but with little effect on the older unemployed. In 2006 the system of early retirement was virtually abolished. This caused an uproar in the Polder model that was solved only after the unions had organized a mass demonstration in the autumn of 2004. The system was still abolished, but some options remained open. Workers age fifty-five and older retained most of their entitlements, since they would have no feasible alternative way of building up private savings. In addition, the new "life course scheme" of tax-deductible individual savings for use as income during periods of leave for maternity, schooling, and so on, was opened also for early retirement. Its pickup depends on individual decisions, however, and thus turns out to be very small, in contrast to the collectively organized retirement schemes.[25] Finally, increased savings for occupational pensions were allowed that still enable retirement before the age of sixty-five.

The strong opposition was partly motivated by the fact that the social partners had already taken measures to change the retirement system, in agreement with the pension covenant concluded between STAR and the government in 1997. Older workers' employment behavior had already been rising secularly since the mid-1980s, reaching a level of 46 percent in 1997 and 56 percent today—well above the level of the 1970s and hardly affected by the recent recession. This change in performance was the most rapid of all OECD countries. Again, it seems that the measures chiefly codified a behavioral change already under way. Because of their growing participation and swelling population size, the contribution of older workers to low-wage employment has tended to increase, up from 6 percent to 9 percent between 1996 and 2002. The incidence of low pay among older workers increased at the same time, but slightly less than average.

Health and Safety and Working Hours

Health and safety are essential components of job quality, and also a field of intense policymaking with direct links to European rule-making. A broad legal framework lays down the responsibilities of employers and employees. The regulation of working conditions and working hours has become increasingly tied up over the last fifteen years with the reform of social insurance for sickness. Much of its take-up was attributed to the behavior of employers and employees, and the conditions of entry imposed on employers and employees were made more stringent, though, as a compensation, CLAs often agreed to additional benefit entitlements. Finally, at the initiative of the government, in recent years industry-level tripartite agreements of the government, employers, and unions (working conditions covenants) have been added as an instrument for change.

The Working Conditions Act (1998)—the second revision of the original law of 1980—contains a code of conduct for health and safety policy. The revisions watered down the initial goals concerning "well-being at work": and the role of works councils but introduced risk analysis and evaluation and the certification of private working conditions service providers to firms. One revision was aimed at developing tailor-made rules and strengthening the responsibilities of employers and employees, but also reinforcing official workplace inspection. The formal obligation of employers to inform unions and works councils was weakened, especially with regard to accidents, and rules for firms with fewer than twenty-five employees were diminished. But the social partners are now also expected to spell out their practices in so-called labor conditions catalogs. Within the unions, this provision caused some worry about the position of the less-skilled in particular, who are exposed to serious health and safety risks, and the major confederation FNV (Dutch Trade Union Federation) opposed the proposal, unsuccessfully. The new law took effect in January 2007.

Employers are obliged to create the most favorable working conditions for their employees in cooperation with the works council. This includes the rhythm of work, the workload, and measures to stem aggression, violence, and sexual harassment. It should be emphasized that nowadays 90 percent of the executive decrees on working conditions are based on European Union rules and International Labor Organization (ILO) treaties. Employers tend to interpret these as a maximum (Popma 2003, 86). EU regulation, however, is limited to the "classical" elements of health and safety at work and occupational risks, while the organizational and psychological dimensions of job quality, particularly individual autonomy at work, remain peripheral. The working conditions covenants are based on voluntary cooperation and are growing in importance and number. (There were fifty-seven in 2006.) They aim to improve working conditions, curb sick leave, and reduce the numbers of the occupationally disabled. Characteristically, the covenant approach means that measures are not imposed top-down but instead stimulated from the bottom up. Until 2002, their primary goal was the prevention of sick leave and occupational disability. The second-phase covenants are increasingly being used, however, as tools to reintegrate disabled people into work and advise the social partners to stimulate task enrichment at low job levels.

Second, the Working Hours Act of 1996 replaced its predecessor of 1919, which had introduced the famous eight-hour working day. The increasing demands for working time flexibility from both employers and employees led to a total revision of the law. The present law aims to protect the "safety, health and well-being of employees in relation to their work" and to promote the "reconciliation of work and family life, as well as other responsibilities outside the workplace." It provides standards for working times, breaks, shift work, and so on, but CLAs may impose norms that fit better. An evaluation of the effects of the law in 2002 motivated a government proposal for change in 2003, followed by an agreement of the social partners in 2005 and the introduction of the new rules in April 2007. The change implies a softening of the constraints on hours of work, bringing the legal level down to the minimum of European regulations. The law may have a direct effect on wages by changing the definitions of overtime and night shifts.

The third important legal institution is the Gatekeeper Improvement Act of April 2002. Inspired by social security reform, it has considerable implications for firm behavior. The main goal is to check entry into social benefits. This is done by obliging the employer and the sick employee to maintain the employment relationship, possibly by adapting the workplace or the job, and to prevent the sickness from becoming long-term and turning into disability, with the help of an obligatory individual plan for reintegration.

The Sickness Benefits Act, dating back to 1930, was fully privatized in 1996. The employer is obliged to continue paying a sick employee's wage, first for one full year and, since 2004, for two full years, and the employer can purchase private insurance to cover the risk. The obligatory level is 70 percent of earnings, but many CLAs impose 100 percent. When the two-year period expires, those still unable to work should qualify for disability insurance.

Comprehensive disability insurance, introduced in the mid-1960s, was changed rather drastically very recently.[26] In the 1980s, benefits were lowered from 80 percent to 70 percent; later on, entitlements were restricted, with the aim of ultimately providing a minimum benefit only. A parliamentary inquiry held in the early 1990s concluded that the social partners were abusing the scheme as a superior unemployment benefit to solve problems in the work organization.[27] This brought about a paradigm shift in social insurance and ousted the social partners from its governance. Employers and employees were obliged to take responsibility for finding an appropriate solution in case of sickness and disability. Experience rating was introduced to increase the contributions of firms generating levels of disability. In 2001 a drastic change was proposed—abolishing partial disability. This was opposed by the social partners, whose detailed alternative was rejected by the government. Vehement opposition merged with the uproar over early retirement and forced the government to virtually adopt the alternative. The new law, which started in January 2006, stipulates that people with less than 35 percent disability will remain employed in their firm and that firms are obligated to enable such employees to continue to work and are also allowed to buy private insurance for this purpose. Unions promised to support the process. In exchange, the experience rating for firms was abolished and the benefit increased to 75 percent of previous earnings. A first evaluation (Van Horssen and van Doorn 2007) shows that many of those with less than 35 percent disability do lose their jobs in spite of the obligations and promises.

On paper, disability insurance coverage and benefit levels are generous in international comparison. Nevertheless, the average benefit has shown exactly the same downward trend as UI (figure 3.14), and spending as a percentage of GDP (2.3 percent in 2004) has not been so low since 1975. Collective agreements, however, may stipulate a top-up, paid from corresponding contributions.

The Impact of Regulations. The Labor Inspectorate monitors compliance with the health and safety regulations and has several means of (drastic) enforcement. In the early 1990s, it embarked upon an ambitious program of design-oriented inspection and monitoring aimed at identifying and advertising "good practices" of technology and organizational design and consequently of job quality. In recent years, however, it has focused heavily on abuses, such as illegal labor, illegal temp work agencies, and so on. Under the new Working Hours Act, inspectors can impose direct fines on firms—as an analogue to the Working Conditions Act of 1999—to enable more effective control.

Table 3.5 Employees Experiencing Working Conditions, by Level of Education, 1997 to 2002

	Use of Force	Time Pressure	Use of Vehicles	Vibration 1[a]	Vibration 2[b]	Noise	Use of Screen
1997							
Total	36%	61%	13%	14%	21%	21%	55%
Low	52	52	23	21	35	29	30
Intermediate	39	61	13	15	23	22	57
High	12	72	2	3	4	12	79
2002							
Total	37	59	13	14	21	22	62
Low	56	48	24	22	36	30	33
Intermediate	41	60	13	16	23	24	63
High	13	68	2	4	5	14	86

Source: CBS/Statline, working conditions by personal characteristics.
[a] Vibration 1 = vibration of tools/machinery.
[b] Vibration 2 = vibration of tools/machinery and vehicles.

Increasingly, regulation draws on the cooperation of the social partners, as the working conditions covenants illustrate. The attention paid in the CLAs to various working conditions varies widely and remains at a rather low level. It is doubtful whether this can replace the effectiveness of strong regulation, especially for the lower end of the labor market.

Table 3.5 pictures the incidence of various working conditions. It shows high levels of time pressure and little change for all variables between 1997 and 2002. Apart from computer use, the pressure of working conditions is higher among the low-skilled, often substantially so. A classic assumption is that variations in working conditions are reflected in variations in sick leave rates. Unfortunately, the privatization of sickness insurance has hampered statistical observation of recent trends and therefore also the effects of the privatization. The least-educated show the highest sick leave rates, and so do workers in jobs at elementary and lower levels. The lowest wage categories show the highest rates, for both frequency and duration.

Finally, we take a look at the impact and effectiveness of disability insurance. Benefit receipt is widespread—11 percent of all employees, 75 percent of them age forty-five to sixty-four—and seen as a tenacious political problem, though levels in other countries, includ-

Figure 3.20 Inflows and Outflows on Disability Insurance

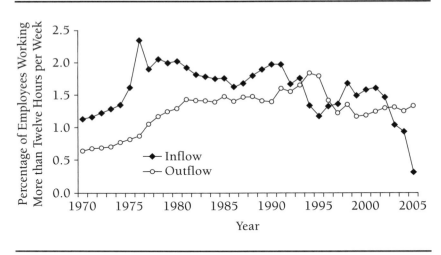

Source: CBS/Statline.

ing the United States for the low-educated, are not much different (OECD 2003, 25). The incidence is high primarily because of the long duration of stay—once on the scheme, people have great difficulty obtaining a job and exiting. The inflows, however, are modest and relatively important at younger ages, not older ages; the older-age stock figures are high because of cumulative duration (OECD 2005, table 3.4). Ill health is still an important determinant of disability, and among the low-skilled the incidence of health problems (32 percent for the Netherlands) is high in international comparison. Figure 3.20 shows clearly how outflows lag behind inflows, implying the role of durations. In addition, table 3.6 suggests that the shift in employment from youth to adult women, because of the latter's higher incidence, has contributed to maintaining the disability stock at high levels. No direct data are available for the incidence among the low-skilled and low-paid. However, the low average level of the benefits actually paid suggests that disability is largely a matter of concern for the low-paid. In recent years, the percentage of the potential labor force with a labor handicap has tended to increase and their employment participation to decrease. The former percentage is twice as high among the low-skilled compared with the high-skilled.[28]

Table 3.6 Stock of Disabled by Demographic Characteristics, 1998 and 2005

	Total	Fully	Partial	Youth	Adult Women	Adult Men
1997						
Number	728,700	214,020	514,130	5,380	285,080	438,240
Share	100%	29%	71%	1%	39%	60%
Percentage of employees	12	4	9	1	15	14
2005						
Number	699,990	234,810	464,740	2,190	321,500	376,230
Share	100%	34%	66%	0%	46%	54%
Percentage of employees	11	4	8	0	14	12

Source: CBS/Statline.

We conclude that although rules may become more lenient when EU rules are adopted, the general and specific organizational demands on firms tend to increase. The introduction of covenants and rules in CLAs must be negotiated and put into practice, and the workplace itself may have to be adapted to enable prolonged employment of employees who would otherwise receive disability benefits. The position of incumbent workers is reinforced by the employer's obligation to continue the employment relationship for two years during the employee's sickness—and indefinitely for the partially disabled—although that protection is not statutory. Such protection should be based on the social partners' activity, but it may not work that way in practice.[29] The risk is a negative effect on the selection of new employees, though discrimination by health is forbidden. For employees, the outside option of a disability benefit has become much less attractive. It is difficult to say whether the privatization of sickness insurance has had a favorable effect on the sickness rate.

CONCLUSIONS

After this tour of labor market institutions, we underline again that it serves to prepare for the case studies and not to analyze the role of institutions for low-wage employment as such. At the start of the chapter, we mentioned six caveats; here we can conclude that it is essential to go beyond the theoretical significance of institutions and consider their impact. In several cases, the same formal institution was associated with significant changes in both firm and employee behavior in the labor market (for example, dismissal), on the one hand, or, on the other, changes in an institution did not matter much for outcomes (for example, education). It would be foolish, however, to think that the effects of institutions can be settled here, and conclusions certainly cannot be drawn in isolation from an economic analysis of employment. Nevertheless, we quickly consider here the relationships between these institutions and the major findings on low-wage employment reported in chapter 2, and also what new stylized facts we can add from the overview in this chapter. We also list the institutions that remain for further scrutiny in the case studies. Before proceeding, however, we would ask: where have changes occurred, and what mutual relations exist between the individual institutions, if any?

To answer these questions, we begin by looking at three categories of institutional change. First, the minimum wage, equal treatment, social benefits and social security organization, and employment contracts and temp agency work have all changed considerably. Changes in these institutions are emblematic of the third postwar period, during which time low pay began to be treated differently (see chapter 1). Second, by contrast, the deliberative institutions, collective agreement law, and dismissal law were not altered during any of the three periods. Third, and finally, changes were made to the works councils, working conditions law, the vocational education and training system, public job creation, immigration, and income taxation. Some of these changes were modest and occurred gradually over the course of time, and others were more radical, but the radical changes have taken place so recently that very little can be said yet about the effects.

Collective labor agreements provide a clear case of mutual institutional linkages. With social-partner negotiations at the industry level, CLAs seem to have become the workhorse of Dutch industrial relations, going over and above their role in setting wages for 80 percent of all employees. Virtually all other institutions have gradually been put in its cart: the minimum wage, with the lowest scales; hiring, with the modifications of flexicurity law provisions; firing, with the union contribution to speeding up the workings of administrative-route dismissals; education and training, with the establishment of industrial training funds; health and safety, with the working condi-

tions covenants; social insurance, with the topping up of legal entitlements, especially where they had shrunk, as had happened with
sickness and disability. The whole collection is loosely termed the
"good" or "virtuous" aims of CLAs. This development seems to reflect a decentralization of policymaking and has incited an increased
monitoring of CLAs by the government. That monitoring, however,
primarily regards the formal adoption of rules in CLAs, not the actual
effects on firm or employee behavior. The consequences of CLA rules
for the effectiveness of these institutions may be reinforcing or weakening or neutral. This role of CLAs makes it increasingly difficult to
determine the effectiveness of certain institutions. (For example,
Trudie Schils (2007) shows that through CLA's EPL deviates significantly from the national rules.) Adoption of rules in CLAs can either
strengthen the policy impact on firms or have the opposite effect of
adding a layer of defense around firms. The case studies shed more
light on this effect.

That brings us to the first new stylized fact that can be added: the
amazingly strong role of the deliberative institutions—particularly, in
certain areas, the social partners vis-à-vis the government. The
agenda is not actually set by these institutions—to the contrary, that
role often falls to the government, as disability insurance and many
other issues illustrate. However, in pursuing its agenda, the government depends on the cooperation of the partners, who try to impose
their views. In several cases, the social partners quite literally formu-
lated new laws for adoption by the government and the Parliament—
for instance, laws on contractual flexibility, disability, and unemployment insurance. The role of employers deserves special mention,
since without their high associational density the coverage of collective labor agreements would certainly be much less extensive. At the
same time, however, that role may limit the significance of CLAs, all
the more because they are actually concluded at the firm or industry
level, not at the national level, where nowadays only recommendations are agreed on. Wage formation is an obvious outcome, but for
the virtuous aims, which may be more exacting of firm behavior, the
effects seem less convincing, and sometimes no more than lip service
may be paid. Inclusion in CLAs may actually obscure responsibilities,
lock in policymaking, or lead it down dead ends. The longtime un-
fortunate state of vocational education and training—which cannot
find a way to reduce the number of low-educated school-leavers—
seems to illustrate this. This lack of success also casts doubt on the

new policy approach to social insurance, which banks on changes in firm behavior concerning job structure and working conditions vis-à-vis individual employees. Finally, it should be stressed that no change has occurred in these deliberative institutions since their postwar establishment and also that the behavior of the collective actors has shown no fundamental change in spite of fluctuations.

Wage moderation is the second new stylized fact, the hallmark of Dutch industrial relations. It was standard practice until the mid-1960s; after an interlude, wage moderation returned with a vengeance in the early 1980s, and it seems to have become even more marked in recent years. Because wage moderation is concerned with the negotiated wages laid down in CLAs, it affects actual wage earnings. However, negotiated wages and actual wage earnings are increasingly diverging, and the CLAs risk losing significance for the higher end of the earnings distribution. At the lower end, they are constrained by the statutory minimum wage and its pivotal role for the level of social security benefits and thereby social expenditures. Thus, CLAs also risk losing significance for low pay when they neglect the interests of the low-paid workforce, who are at risk of marginalization in industrial relations—witness their rapidly falling union density. Potential marginalization is reinforced by vanishing UI entitlements and declining benefit levels. Risks of in-work poverty may be increasing with the growing adult share in low-wage employment. Wage negotiations in general are also affected because the uprating of the minimum wage is based on the average outcome. Unions are regularly pressed by the government to demand zero wage growth, with the threat of either stopping the up-rating or cutting the linkage to benefits. Prolonged and almost automatic wage moderation seems another lock-in of policymaking that focuses exclusively on "jobs, jobs, jobs." Because it neglects potential negative and self-reinforcing effects on the labor market and the economy, moderation may beget moderation. There are three obvious negative effects of moderation: slower productivity growth in firms because of a cheaper supply of labor; the disincentive to schooling for workers because of compressed earnings perspectives; and the curbing of consumer demand out of wages. That demand is particularly important for low-wage labor, which is strongly concentrated in consumer-oriented services as underlined by Andrew Glyn and others (2007). Interestingly, wage growth was less restrained during the employment boom of the late 1990s, and consumption was buoyant, also driven by soaring house prices and rapidly growing household debt to one of the highest levels internationally. As long as all wages are moderated, there is also no room for improving low wages—unless by net income transfers through the tax system.

In chapter 2, we found two stylized facts: the explosive growth of part-time employment with strong links to low pay and the significant role of young workers in low-wage employment.

For the first issue, figure 3.21 brings together the evolution of part-time employment with the many relevant measures that have been taken. The evolution is almost linear, and each time its pace does not seem to have been accelerated by the changes—sometimes the pace even slows down—though clearly potential institutional hindrances have been taken away. Naturally, such visual inspection does not show the absence of an institutional effect but can only underline the lack of prima facie evidence of such an effect. The steady growth may depend on a cultural effect of increasing female educational participation or the economics of households that try to escape from moderation, or it may depend on the job offers of firms. The growth might have occurred in spite of institutional hindrances, as the growth prior to the later changes seems to imply. Institutional change may thus serve to codify behavior that has already changed for most actors, with the causality running to instead of from the institutions. Such codification will discipline only a few remaining actors. The two institutional changes that occurred at the moment when flexible employment had already reached its highest point (figure 3.21) are consistent with this view, but the actual growth of temp agency licenses within unchanged institutional rules may have contributed somewhat. However, several observations can be made. The many measures are sequential and do not by themselves imply a coherence of institutions. They may again illustrate a lock-in of policymaking, as potential negative effects seem to be disregarded. For example, we found that, for women, working part-time on low pay increases the probability of exiting employment. Other research has uncovered wage penalties that endure after moving to a full-time job (Taner and Hendrix 2007, 35). Last but not least, the part-timing of low-level jobs may hamper the career prospects of the low-skilled, who depend on full-time employment for a living wage. Especially important in this regard is the tax change of 2001, which came at a time when any new stimulus to the growth of part-time employment was redundant.

Because flexible contracts are particularly important for young

Figure 3.21 Part-Time and Flexible Employment and
Institutional Change, 1970 to 2004

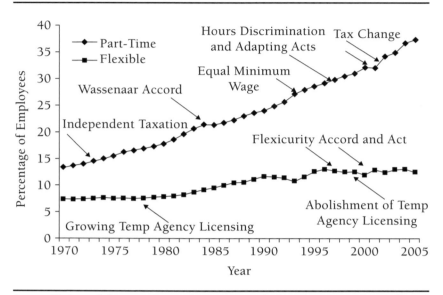

Source: Estimated from total according to Central Planning Bureau (CPB) (2006) and full-time and part-time employed according to CBS, Labor Account Statistics. *Note:* Part-time employment is on a normal contract, while flexible employment is contractually defined and can be either part-time or full-time. Full-time employment at normal conditions makes up the difference to 100 percent.

workers, the above applies mutatis mutandis to the second stylized fact of youth and low pay. The other institutions most significantly related to youth are the long tail of youth minimum wages and student grants (figure 3.22). The government lowered youth wages compared to the adult minimum in 1981 and 1983 and followed with further freezes. The decline of youth minimum wages more than matched that of the U.S. federal minimum wage and opened up a wide gap with the low-pay threshold. The employment incidence of youth minimum wages fell simultaneously, giving support to the literature that stresses the effects of the minimum wage on equity instead of employment. However, low pay did show a considerable increase among youth. The part-timing of low-paid jobs and the grant system may be better candidates to associate with that growth. Finally, the steady high rate of school-leavers with low skills produced by the educational system has maintained a high level of low-wage

Figure 3.22 Young Workers' Low-Wage and Minimum-
          Wage Employment and Institutional Change,
          1970 to 2004

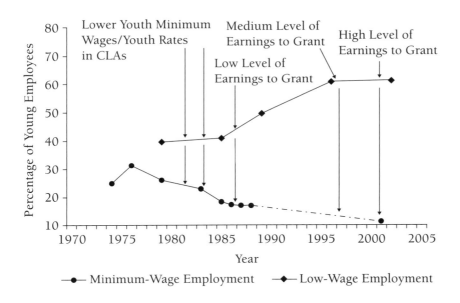

Source: Author's calculations from CBS, Structure of Earnings Survey microdata for 1979, 1985, 1989, 1996, and 2002, and tabulated data for other years.

young workers who have difficulty finding full-time occupations to settle themselves in the labor market.

The case studies that follow cannot possibly deal with all these institutions. Methodologically, the effects of some are better explored at the aggregate level than in individual interviews. Practically, the workload of a comprehensive study would not have been feasible for the cases and would have been too demanding of the respondents. Therefore, we leave behind here the issues of taxation and social contributions, subsidies and student grants, unemployment insurance, equal treatment, and dismissal regulations. However, the deliberative institutions of unions and employers at the industry or firm level and of employees and employers within the firm—the works councils— are central to the case studies. They were already important for securing research access in some industries. Collective labor agreements are of prime importance because of their lower wage scales and job classifications and also for the significance of their supplementary role to legislation, such as for temporary contracting. The minimum wage, vocational education and training, and working conditions and working time regulations are other evident candidates.

Before proceeding with the case studies in chapters 5 through 9, chapter 4 introduces the five target industries and discusses the basics of the research concepts and methodology.

NOTES

1. Compare Richard Freeman's (2005, abstract) criticism of "the current 'lawyer's case' empiricism in which priors dominate evidence."
2. From 1994 to 2001, the employment rate of the working-age population grew by ten percentage points, to 76.1 percent; it fell back to 73.3 percent in 2005—the largest fall among the five EU countries under study. For a discussion, see Salverda (2007).
3. Elsewhere (Salverda 2007), I consider wage drift in detail and argue that over the last ten years collective bargaining affected directly only 40 percent of the earnings increase. The figures presuppose full compliance with CLAs and may also include some composition effects.
4. These are not necessarily large companies. The company-size effect is limited and more constant.
5. The age earnings differential seems particularly large in the Netherlands and has grown considerably since 1979 (Salverda 1998b).
6. Until recently, health care insurance was also included, but as of 2006 this depends on the composition of the household.
7. For the full text of this argument, see the Ministerie van Sociale Zaken en Werkgelegenheid (SZW) web page at http://home.szw.nl/navigatie/dossier/dsp_dossier.cfm?set_id=77&doctype_id=9.
8. Weighted with the age distribution of 1979: (1) fifteen to twenty-two years and (2) twenty-three years and older.
9. See William Even and David MacPherson (2004). EC/Eurostat (2006) puts the employment incidence of the U.S. minimum wage at 1.4 percent in 2004.
10. Note that the Dutch qualify for national social security regardless of contributions made or not. After a life of low incomes because of part-time work, these employees still receive the full public old-age pension. We leave out employee social security contributions here because they are more complicated to describe. In contrast to taxation, they are basically levied on the hourly wage and may differ somewhat

between parts of the economy. Over time not only the percentage levied but the party obliged to pay—employee or employer—has changed. As of July 1, 2006, an employee pays 5.2 percent for unemployment insurance (UI), and the employer 8.13 percent for disability insurance below the minimum wage and 11.58 percent above that level—disregarding obligatory health care insurance contributions (6.5 percent).

11. Unless otherwise noted, all currency conversions based on prevailing rate in December 2007.

12. Employee social security contributions with an exemption up to about the minimum wage, such as for UI, reinforce the increase. So do pension contributions with a franchise up to the minimum wage, but they may be considered individual savings instead of social contributions.

13. The direct benefit–low pay ratio fell from an estimated 110 percent in 1979 to 68 percent in 2004. The upward movements of the early 1990s and 2000s may reflect mass unemployment, which also hurts the better-paid.

14. France is at a level similar to the Dutch level. ISCED reflects the diploma structure of the educational system. In terms of literacy, the low-skilled in continental countries, including the Netherlands, seem to do relatively well, especially compared to the United States (see, for example, Freeman and Schettkat 2000; Mühlau and Horgan 2001).

15. A higher share may include more talented people and therefore show a higher rate of employment. See Glyn and Salverda (2000), who use a quartile approach to educational attainment to correct for such sorting.

16. Almost two-thirds of the inflows into the practice-based leg of vocational education are from outside the educational system. The 70 percent failure rate includes them.

17. I am grateful to Robert Knegt of the University of Amsterdam for putting his data at our disposal and providing comments. For more information on temp agencies, see the special working paper by Kea Tijdens, Maarten van Klaveren, Hester Houwing, Marc van der Meer, and Marieke van Essen (2006).

18. In 2005, 8 percent of requests were withdrawn by the employer. These primarily concerned the (perceived) behavior of employees, and apparently the Center for Work and Income plays a role as a mediator here.

19. Surveyed employers expected a similar duration for both (Van Zevenbergen and Oelen 2000, 33).

20. Of surveyed employers, 41 percent had no opinion, 25 percent supported the dual system, 12 percent preferred the administrative system alone, and another 12 percent preferred the court system (Van Zevenbergen and Oelen 2000, 84).

21. No less than two-thirds of all court cases are formal, according to van Zevenbergen and Oelen (2000, 16).
22. CLAs can also modify, within limits, other elements of EPL. See Trudie Schils (2007) for further detail.
23. The maturity of labor relations often lags behind in new configurations of economic activity (see chapter 8).
24. See the article at Statistics Netherlands (CBS), *Webmagazine*, "Ruim eenderde werknemers werkt regelmatig over" ["More than One-Third of Employees Regularly Works Overtime"], August 15, 2005.
25. Fewer than 6 percent of employees working at least twelve hours in 2006 participated in the life course scheme. Participation was twice as high among the high-skilled as among the low-skilled (CBS/Statline).
26. For a discussion of the problems of Dutch disability and the policy changes, see OECD (2005, 71–79).
27. However, the fact that inflows into disability insurance develop procyclically seems to contradict this argument (see figure 3.20).
28. See CBS/Statline, Profiel arbeidsgehandicapten [Profile of Handicapped Experiencing Problems in the Labor Market].
29. Cora van Horssen and Esmerelda van Doorn (2007) show high rates of dismissal of the partially disabled after the legal two-year term.

REFERENCES

Ackerman, C. H. and C. Klaassen. 1998. *De onderkant van de arbeidsmarkt in 1998 [The Lower End of the Labor Market]*. The Hague: Ministry of Social Affairs and Employment.

Akkerman, Agnes. 2000. *Verdeelde vakbeweging en stakingen: concurrentie om leden [Divided Unions and Strikes: Competing for Members]*. Amsterdam: Uitgeverij Thela Thesis.

Bowles, Samuel. 2004. *Microeconomics: Behavior, Institutions, and Evolution*. New York and Princeton, N.J.: Russell Sage Foundation and Princeton University Press.

Centraal PlanBureau (CPB). 2006. *Macro economische verkenning 2007 [2007 Macroeconomic Outlook]*. The Hague: CPB.

———. 2007. *Centraal Economisch Plan 2007 [Central Economic Plan 2007]*. The Hague: CPB.

EC/Eurostat. 2006. Minimum Wages 2006. *Statistics in Focus, Population and Social Conditions, 9/2006*. Luxembourg: Eurostat.

Even, William, and David MacPherson. 2004. *Wage Growth among Minimum Wage Workers*. Washington: Employment Policies Institute.

Fouarge, Didier, Anne Gielen, Rob Grim, Marcel Kerkhofs, Amelia Román, Joop Schippers, and Ton Wilthagen. 2006. *Trendrapport Aanbod van Arbeid 2005. [Labor Supply Panel 2005]*. Tilburg, Netherlands: OSA.

Freeman, Richard. 1998. "War of the Models: Which Labour Market Institutions for the 21st Century?" *Labour Economics* 5(1): 1-24.

———. 2005. *Labor Market Institutions Without Blinders: The Debate over Flexibility and Labor Market Performance.* Working paper 11286. Cambridge, Mass.: National Bureau of Economic Research.

Freeman, Richard, and Ronald Schettkat. 2000. *Skill Compression, Wage Differentials and Employment: Germany vs. the US.* Working Paper 7610. Cambridge, Mass.: National Bureau of Economic Research.

Freeman, Richard, Joop Hartog, and Coen Teulings. 1996. *Pulling the Plug: An Analysis of the Role of Mandatory Extension in the Dutch System of Labor Relations.* The Hague: OSA.

Glyn, Andrew, and Wiemer Salverda. 2000. "Does Wage Flexibility Really Create Jobs?" *Challenge, Magazine of Economic Affairs,* 43(1): 32-43.

Glyn, Andrew, Wiemer Salverda, John Schmitt, Michel Sollogoub, and Joachim Moeller. 2007. "Employment Differences in Distribution: Wages, Productivity, and Demand." In *Services and Employment: Explaining the U.S.-European Gap.*, edited by Mary Gregory, Wiemer Salverda, and Ronald Schettkat. Princeton, N.J.: Princeton University Press.

Hall, Peter A., and David Soskice, editors. 2001. *Varieties of Capitalism: The Institutional Foundations of Comparative Advantage.* New York: Oxford University Press.

Hodgson, Geoffrey M. 1988. *Economics and Institutions.* London: Polity Press.

Muconsult. 2003. *Onderzoek ten behoeve van evaluatie Waa en Woa. Eindrapport* [*Research to Evaluate the Working Hours Adjustment Act and the Working Hours Differentiation Act: Final Report*]. Amersfoort: Muconsult.

Mühlau, Peter, and Justine Horgan. 2001. *Labour Market Status and the Wage Position of the Low Skilled.* Working Paper 05. European Low-wage Employment Research network LoWER. Accessed at http://www.uva-aias.net/files/lower/05MuehlauHorgan.pdf.

Mühlau, Peter, and Wiemer Salverda. 2000a. "Effects of Low-Wage Subsidies: The Example of 'SPAK' in the Netherlands." In *Policy Measures for Low-Wage Employment in Europe,* edited by Wiemer Salverda, Brian Nolan, and Claudio Lucifora. Cheltenham, U.K.: Edward Elgar.

———. 2000b. *Low–Wage Subsidies, Employment and Wages The case of SPAK in the Netherlands.* Paper to EALE-SOLE world conference of September 2000, Milan.

North, Douglas. 1990. *Institutions, Institutional Change, and Economic Performance.* Cambridge: Cambridge University Press.

Organization for Economic Cooperation and Development (OECD). 2003. *Transforming Disability into Ability.* Paris: OECD.

———. 2004. *Employment Outlook 2004.* Paris: OECD.

———. 2005. *Aging and Employment Policies: Netherlands.* Paris: OECD.

————. 2006a. *OECD Economic Surveys: Netherlands*, vol. 2006/2. Paris: OECD.

————. 2006b. *Employment Outlook 2006*. Paris: OECD.

Popma, Jan. 2003. *Het arbo-effect van medezeggenschap* [*The Working Conditions Effect of Co-determination*]. Alphen aan de Rijn, Netherlands: Kluwer.

Pott-Buter, Hettie, and Kea Tijdens, editors. 1998. *Vrouwen—leven en werk in de twintigste eeuw* [*Women - Life and Work in the Twentieth Century*]. Amsterdam: Amsterdam University Press.

Rienstra, M., and M. Copinga. 2003. *Banen van Jongeren* [*Jobs of Young Workers*]. The Hague: Dutch Statistics (CBS).

Rojer, Maurice F. P. 2002. *De betekenis van de CAO en het algemeen verbindend verklaren van CAOs* [*The Significance of Collective Labor Agreements and Declaring of Collective Labor Agreements to be Universally Binding*]. The Hague: Ministry of Social Affairs and Employment.

Salverda, Wiemer. 1998a. "Vergroting van de onderkant van de arbeidsmarkt? Een overzicht en eerste beoordeling van beleidsmaatregelen" ["Expanding the Bottom of the Labor Market? An Overview and Preliminary Evaluation of Policy Measures"]. *Tijdschrift voor Politieke Ekonomie* 21(1): 24–57.

————. 1998b. "Incidence and Evolution of Low-Wage Employment in the Netherlands and the United States, 1979–1989." In *Job Quality and Employer Behavior*, edited by S. Bazen, C. Lucifora, and Wiemer Salverda. Basingstoke, U.K.: Palgrave.

————. 2007. "The Bite and Effects of Wage Bargaining in the Netherlands, 1995–2005." In *Collective Bargaining in Europe 2006*, edited by Maarten Keune and Bela Galgóczi. Brussels: European Trade Union Institute (ETUI).

Salverda, Wiemer, and Nico Beukema. 1996. *Four Reports on the Role of the Social Partners in Implementing the Conclusions of the Essen and Madrid European Councils in the Netherlands* as a Member of the Group of Experts for the European Commission, Directorate-General for Employment. April 1996 to February 1997.

Schils, Trudie. 2007. *Employment Protection in Dutch Collective Labour Agreements*. Working Paper 07-56. Amsterdam: Amsterdam Institute for Advanced Labour Studies, University of Amsterdam.

Sociaal-economische Raad (SER). 2002. *Het Nieuwe Leren* [*The New Learning*]. Advisory report on lifelong learning in the knowledge-based economy. Advice 2002/10. The Hague: Social and Economic Council.

————. 2006. Option PBO (product and industry boards). Accessed at http:// www.ser.nl. The Hague: Social and Economic Council.

Sociale Zaken en Werkgelegenheid (SZW). 1991. *De laagste CAO-lonen in de periode 1983–1990, een voorlopige analyse* [*The Lowest Collectively Negoti-*

ated Wages in the Period 1983 - 1990, A Preliminary Analysis]. The Hague: SZW.

———. 2001. *Aan de Slag, Eindrapport van de werkgroep Toekomst van het Arbeidsmarktbeleid*. [*Final Report of Working Party Future of Labor Market Policies*]. The Hague: Ministry of Social Affairs and Employment.

———. 2003. *Voorjaarsrapportage CAO-afspraken 2003* [*Spring Report on 2003 Collective Labor Agreements*]. The Hague: Ministry of Social Affairs and Employment.

———. 2005a. *Arbeidsvoorwaardenontwikkeling in 2004* [*Development of Working Conditions in 2004*]. The Hague: Ministry of Social Affairs and Employment.

———. 2005b. *Najaarsrapportage CAO-afspraken 2005* [*Fall Report on 2003 Collective Labor Agreements*]. The Hague: Ministry of Social Affairs and Employment.

———. 2006. *Werknemers met een bruto-loon op en onder het wettelijk minimumloon in 2004* [*Employees Earning a Gross Wage at or Below the Statutory Minimum Wage in 2004*]. The Hague: Ministry of Social Affairs and Employment, Labour Inspectorate.

Storrie, Donald. 2002. *Temporary Agency Work in the European Union.* Dublin and Luxembourg: European Foundation for the Improvement of Living and Working Conditions / Office for Official Publications of the European Communities.

Taner, Bilal, and Peter Hendrix. 2007. *De armoedeval. Een nieuwe kijk op een oud probleem* [*The Poverty Trap: A New View of an Old Problem*]. The Hague: Ministry of Social Affairs and Employment.

Tegelaar, Petronella J. C. 1972. "Gelijke beloning voor mannen en vrouwen" ["Equal Pay for Men and Women"]. *M&O* 26(3): 150–66.

Tijdens, Kea G. 2002. "Arbeidsduurverkorting en het Akkoord van Wassenaar" ["Shortening Working Hours and the Accord of Wassenaar"]. *Tijdschrift voor Arbeidsvraagstukken* 18: 309–18.

———. 2005. "How Important Are Institutional Settings to Prevent Marginalization of Part-time Employment?" In *Low-Wage Employment in Europe*, edited by Ive Marx and Wiemer Salverda. Leuven and Voorburg: Acco.

Tijdens, Kea, Maarten van Klaveren, Hester Houwing, Marc van der Meer, and Marieke van Essen. 2006. *Temporary Agency Work in the Netherlands.* Amsterdam: AIAS/UvA.

Traxler, Franz. 1995. "Farewell to Labour Market Associations? Organized versus Disorganized Decentralization as a Map for Industrial Relations." In *Organized Industrial Relations in Europe: What Future?* edited by Colin Crouch and Franz Traxler. Aldershot, U.K.: Avebury.

Tros, Frank. 2001. "Arbeidsverhoudingen: decentralisatie, deconcentratie en empowerment" ["Employee-Employer Relations: Decentralisation,

Deconcentration and Empowerment"]. *Tijdschrift voor Arbeidsvraagstukken* 17: 304–18.

Uitvoeringsinstituut Werknemersverzekeringen (UWV). 2005. *Kroniek van de Sociale Verzekeringen 2005 [Chronicle of Social Insurances, 2005]*. Amsterdam: UWV.

Van der Meer, Marc, Jelle Visser and Ton Wilthagen. 2005. "Adaptive and Reflexive Governance - The Limits of Organised Decentralisation." European Journal for Industrial Relations 11: 347–65.

Van der Meer, Marc, Adriaan van Liempt, Kea Tijdens, Martijn van Velzen, and Jelle Visser. 2002. *The Trade-off Between Competitiveness and Employment in Collective Bargaining: The National Consultation Process and Four Cases of Company Bargaining in the Netherlands*. Geneva: ILO.

Van der Velden, Sjaak. 2000. *Stakingen in Nederland. Arbeidersstrijd 1830–1995 [Strikes in the Netherlands: The Labor Struggle, 1830-1995]*. Amsterdam: Stichting Beheer IISG/NIWI.

Van Halem, Arjen, Maarten van Klaveren, and Ed Wetzel. 2002. Eindrapport sociale aspecten van uitbestedingsrelaties binnen netwerken *[Final Report Social Aspects of Outsourcing Relations in Networks]*. Utrecht: FNV Bondgenoten.

Van het Kaar, Robert H., and Jan C. Looise. 1999. *De volwassen OR. Groei en grenzen van de Nederlandse ondernemingsraad [The Mature Works Council: Growth and Limits of the Dutch Works Council]*. Alphen aan den Rijn, Netherlands: Samsom.

Van Horssen, Cora, and Esmerelda van Doorn. 2007. *Onderzoek naar de reïntregratie van werknemers die minder dan 35% arbeidsongeschikt zijn [Study of Reintegration of Employees who are less than 35% Disabled]*. Final report to STAR. Amsterdam: Regioplan.

Van Klaveren, Maarten, Wim Sprenger, and Kea Tijdens. 2007. Dicht de loonkloof! Verslag van het CLOSE-onderzoek [Close the Gender Pay Gap! Report of the CLOSE Research Project]. Eindhoven and Amsterdam: STZ Consultancy & Research / AIAS

Van Kooten, Gerrit. 1998. *Stakingen en Stakers: een theoretische en empirische verkenning van fluctuaties in stakingsactiviteit in Nederland, 1951-1981 [Strikes and Strikers: A Theoretical and Empirical Inquiry of Strike Activity in the Netherlands, 1951-1981]*. Delft: Eburon.

Van Zevenbergen, Roelof, and Udo Oelen. 2000. *Het duaal ontslagstelsel – beëindiging van arbeidrelaties in de praktijk [The Dual Termination System - Termination Employment in Practice]*. Leiden, Netherlands: Research voor Beleid

Visee, Hetty, and Edward Rosbergen. 2004. *Achterban over de OR. Onderzoek door MuConsult BV [Supporters of OR. Research by MuConsult BV]*. The Hague: Department of Social Affairs and Employment.

Visser, Jelle. 2000. "The First Part-time Economy in the World: A Model to Be Followed?" *Journal of Social European Policy* 12(1): 23–42.

Visser, Jelle, and Anton Hemerijck. 1997. *"A Dutch Miracle": Job Growth, Welfare Reform, and Corporatism in the Netherlands.* Amsterdam: Amsterdam University Press.

Waterreus, Ib. 2002. *O&O-fondsen op herhaling* [*Training Funds Inventory*]. Amsterdam: Max Goote Kenniscentrum

Wellink, Nout and Paul Cavelaars. 2001. "De ontwikkeling van de Nederlandse economie: zijn de polderinstituties klaar voor de toekomst?" ["The Development of the Dutch Economy: Are the Polder Institutions Ready for the Future?"]. In *Nederland Kennisland?* [*Netherlands: Knowledge-based Country?*], edited by Jeroen Kremers, Jarig van Sinderen, and Raymond Gradus. Groningen, Netherlands: Stenfert Kroese.

Wielers, Rudi, and Peter van der Meer. 2001. "The Increased Labour Market Participation of Dutch Students." *Work Employment and Society* 15: 55-71.

CHAPTER 4

The Position, Design, and Methodology of the Industry Studies

Maarten van Klaveren

This chapter aims to provide the bridge between the first three chapters, which were focused on the national level, and the next five chapters, which concentrate on the target industries and subsectors at the meso level and the case study establishments at the micro level. The research targets five industries and specific target occupations within each one:

- The retail trade, divided into the subsectors of supermarkets and consumer electronics retail, with the target occupations of checkout operators and sales clerks, respectively

- Hotels, with the target occupation of room attendants

- Hospitals, with the target occupations of nursing assistants, nutrition assistants, and cleaners

- Call centers with a focus on the finance sector and utilities, distinguishing between independent and in-house centers, with the target occupation of call center agents or operators

- Food processing, divided into the subsectors of meat processing and confectionary, with the target occupation of production workers

I begin by situating the target industries and subsectors in the economy and in employment. Then I consider the incidence of low pay in the industries and subsectors and relate this to a number of potentially influencing factors. In the next section, I discuss the levels and yardsticks that will serve to make firm strategies operational, focusing on the distinction between high-road and low-road strategies. Finally, the chapter provides an overview of the research design and methodology used in the industry studies and the case studies.

THE DEVELOPMENT OF EMPLOYMENT IN THE TARGET INDUSTRIES

Industrialization started rather late in the Netherlands, and from an international perspective the share of manufacturing in employment remained rather low, reaching its peak between 1947 and 1960. By 1975 employment in commercial services exceeded that in manufacturing, excluding construction (table 4.1). Deindustrialization took off after 1975. Between 1975 and 1990, male employment in manufacturing fell by ten percentage points, and at the same time female employment increased by twenty-five percentage points, mainly in services and part-time employment. In 2004 the employment share of manufacturing among employees had fallen to 12 percent, commercial services stabilized at about 47 percent, and other services (government and other noncommercial), which had oscillated around 30 percent over the last three decades, accounted for 34 percent. Seven percent was left for agriculture, fishing, mining, and construction. The table shows the employment figures of our target industries and subsectors, at the NACE four-digit level (but five-digit for the food-processing subsectors). In fact, the food-processing subsector is even smaller (10,000) than the table suggests (27,400), since meat processing is analyzed here without slaughtering and poultry processing and confectionary in our study does not include cocoa processing. The figures concerning call centers typically cannot be based on official statistics. We were able to use recent Statistics Netherlands microdata that specified call center employment. These data applied to independent call centers, however, not to in-house call centers, which cover about 80 percent of call center employment. For the size of that employment we have to rely mainly on market research sources. The last row of the table indicates that the combined share of the target industries increased more than fourfold over the half-century, from 2.4 percent in 1947 to 10.7 percent of all employees in 2004. Yet it remains of limited importance.

Only one of the target industries is a classic manufacturing industry: food processing. Although a stronghold of Dutch manufacturing, its significance is diminishing, as is true of manufacturing production occupations in general. After having grown until 1975, employment in slaughtering and meat processing decreased both in absolute numbers and relative to total employment. The same happened after 1960 with cocoa, chocolate, and confectionary manufacturing. By

Table 4.1 Employees in Selected Industries (Head-Count × 1,000) 1947 to 2004

	1947	1960	1975	1990	2000	2004
Total	3,612.0	4,169.0	4,683.0	5,626.0	6,998.6	6,947.3
Manufacturing industry	1,105.0	1,279.0	1,213.0	1,150.0	960.6	835.3
Food and beverages	186.7	199.2	179.2	159.0	145.0	128.2
Slaughtering & meat-processing	8.3	20.0	23.5	19.8	26.6	20.4
Cocoa, chocolate, confectionary	11.2	14.3	9.8	7.1	8.9	7.0
Commercial services	807.2	961.3	1,283.1	2,036.1	3,279.8	3,234.3
Retail industry	167.9	174.2	320.0	469.1	625.2	612.9
Supermarkets	—	(6.6)	(58.0)	(124.0)	201.7	198.7
Consumer electronics	0.8	2.1	(6.0)	(16.0)	22.7	20.9
Hospitality industry	37.2	44.3	66.0	127.0	254.4	257.6
Hotels	11.2	18.1	(24.0)	(38.0)	58.0	73.0
Call centers	—	—	—	7.5	110.0	180.0
Other services, including government hospitals	642.0	780.4	1,062.6	1,974.0	2,082.4	2,348.2
	55.4	86.2	(125.0)	(165.0)	214.1	241.3
Total target subsectors	86.9	147.3	(246.3)	(377.4)	642.0	741.3
Target subsectors as percentage of employees	2.4	3.5	(5.3)	(6.7)	9.2	10.7

Sources: CBS, censuses 1947, 1960; Labour Force Survey (LFS), 1975; Enquête Beroepsbevolking (EBB), 1990; Enquête Werkgelegenheid en Lonen (EWL), 2000, 2004 (Statline); Groningen Growth and Development Centre, 60-Industry Database, September 2006, accessed at http://www.ggdc.net; for call centers, see chapter 8.
Note: Author's estimates are in parentheses.

contrast, the share of employees in retail has doubled since 1947, but this mainly reflects the decline of self-employed and cooperating family members. Changes in retail have been substantial. In 1947 supermarkets were still unknown, but by 2004 they employed nearly 3 percent of all employees. Wage employment in consumer electronics retail grew noticeably in the 1980s and 1990s. In these years the hospitality industry also expanded rapidly, although this growth was again marked by the declining numbers of self-employed and cooperating family members. The hotel subsector came along in this expansion. The first Dutch call centers emerged in the early 1990s, and recently the employment share of this industry seems to be approaching that of the supermarkets. Finally, over the nearly six-decade period, the hospital subsector has been the single largest industry under study, although in the 1980s and 1990s the growth of its share lagged behind that of the retail and hospitality industries.

THE INCIDENCE OF LOW PAY BY INDUSTRY

For the target industries and occupations, we established the incidence of low pay and other details using Statistics Netherlands (CBS) microdata. Unfortunately, we had to leave out meat processing and confectionary because the sample size made the results unreliable. The industries that could be selected employ 7 percent of all employees. Table 4.2 shows that the average low-pay incidence in the target industries was 32 percent, compared to 16 percent in all other industries and an overall average of 17 percent. Low-pay incidence varied significantly within the targeted segment, from 7 percent in hospitals to 57 percent in supermarkets. The female share in the target industries' employment was 64 percent. The incidence of low pay among them in the target industries deviated little from the total incidence, but their concentration in low-paying industries gives them a higher incidence overall—21 percent as against 17 percent.

Table 4.2 Shares of All Employees and Female Employees Under the Low-Wage Threshold, 2002

	Total	Female
Supermarkets	57%	53%
Consumer electronics retail	19	19
Hotels	26	31
Hospitals	7	6
Independent call centers	32	54
Subtotal target industries	32	31
Other industries	16	20
Total	17	21

Source: Author's calculations from CBS microdata Enquête Werkgelegenheid en Lonen/ Enquête Beroepsbevolking (EWL/EBB) (2002).

Table 4.3 brings together information on the average wage levels in the target industries from two sources, comparing these with the basic wages in the relevant CLAs (the first step in the lowest grades for adults) and the statutory minimum wage (SMW) for adults. The WageIndicator data add value because they are more recent than the CBS microdata and allow a closer look at adult wage levels, leaving out the influence of youth wages. Except for hospitals, more recent official hourly wages data are available only at the two-digit level. However, the WageIndicator is a voluntary survey, and for some industries and occupations its results can be less reliable. In any event, in the next chapters WageIndicator data will be used to indicate recent wage levels. Taking into account the average CLA hourly wage increase of 6.3 percent from 2002 to 2006, the differences between the 2002 CBS microdata and the 2006 WageIndicator outcomes are limited. The largest differences are those for food and call centers. For meat processing, the WageIndicator produces an average 2006 adult wage that is 19 percent below the average microdata wage, 12 percent below for confectionary, and 14 percent below for the independent call centers.

The gap between the levels of the lowest adult wages laid down in the CLA scales and the average adult 2006 wages based on WageIndicator information varies widely. Accounting for the average 1.2 percent hourly CLA increase in 2005–2006, this gap was 22 percent for the supermarkets, 29 percent for confectionary, and 42 percent for hotels, growing to 50 percent for call centers, 52 percent for consumer electronics retail, 74 percent for meat processing, and 104 percent for hospitals. The more substantial gaps are caused by factors such as extensive layers of higher-skilled and -paid (hospitals), the spread of performance-based pay (consumer electronics), and empty lower wage scales (food).

Concerning the shares of the target occupations in the target industries, the microdata categories are not insufficiently detailed. Thus, we have to rely on the indications that the industry chapters provide (in FTEs):

• Checkout operators in supermarkets: 42 to 45 percent

• Salespersons in consumer electronics retail: 50 to 60 percent

• Room attendants in hotels: 25 to 30 percent

Table 4.3 Average Wages in Subsectors, 2002 and 2005–2006

	CBS Microdata Average Hourly Wage, 2002 (Euros)	WageIndicator Average Adult Hourly Wage, 2006 (Euros)	Collective Labor Agreement Basic Wage, 2005/Lowest-Grade Adults, 2005 (Euros)	Statutory Adult Minimum Wage (Depending on Collective Labor Agreement Hours per Week) 2005 (Euros)
Supermarkets	9.84	11.22	9.09	8.07
Consumer electronics retail	12.51	13.61	8.07	8.07
Hotels (cleaning)	11.46	11.95	8.33	7.69
Hospitals	18.02	17.39	8.49	8.07
Independent call centers	12.72	11.56	8.40	7.30
Meat processing	16.42	14.05	8.07	8.07
Confectionary	14.56	13.65	10.46	8.07
Subtotal target industries	13.52	13.35		
Other industries	13.91			
Total	13.74			

Source: Author's calculations from CBS, Structure of Earnings Survey microdata (2002); WageIndicator data, January 2004 to September 2006 (level 2006); relevant collective labor agreements.

- Cleaners, department assistants, and nutrition assistants in hospitals: 5 percent

- Agents in call centers: 85 percent

- Production workers in meat and confectionary processing: 50 to 60 percent

The incidence of low pay may be influenced by a number of factors. Workers may receive low wages because they are poorly educated or because their jobs require low levels of skill. Collective bargaining coverage may be important, assuming that a CLA will prevent covered workers from being paid a low wage. Union membership may cause a similar effect. We may assume that being employed on a permanent employment contract ensures higher pay levels. Being female, having short tenure, working in a small company, working in a small part-time job, or receiving little on-the-job training increases the likelihood of being a low-wage earner. Labor economists might add that high labor intensity also increases this likelihood.

We do not have microdata available to strictly test these assumptions, mainly because union membership and collective bargaining coverage are hardly registered in Dutch surveys of individual workers. However, table 4.4 offers a glimpse of the causal relationships. We present aggregate data on the incidence of eleven factors in the eight subsectors, together with the average for these subsectors, combining WageIndicator data with data gathered for the industry chapters. Most indicators speak for themselves; training length has been defined as the average scores on a scale ranging from 0 (no training required) to 7 (training more than one year required). For each factor (row), the four factors least important for the likelihood of being in low pay are shaded. For example, the first row shows union density and shades the four subsectors where union density has the highest likelihood of resulting in high pay: meat, confectionary, in-house call centers, and hospitals. These are also the four subsectors above the 24 percent average in the last column. The four shaded figures in a row are almost always those above or below the average, with the notable exception of working less than twelve hours per week. Here the large share of small jobs in supermarkets, 35 percent of the sample, raises the average.

Most effects work out in the expected direction, except (partially)

Table 4.4 Factors That May Influence Wages in Subsectors, 2004 to 2006

	Food		Retail		Cleaning[a]	Call Centers		Hospitals[b]	Average
	Meat	Confectionary	Supermarkets	Electronics		In-house	Independent		
1. Union density	22–40%	20–35%	10–17%	12–19%	16–20%	28%	12–18%	36%	24%
2. Covered by collective labor agreement	78	84	85	76	72	73	59	96	83
3. Low-educated	27	28	23	11	32	8	7	2	18
4. Permanent employment contract	75	80	69	70	60	81	60–61	91	75
5. Female	25–29	30–38	54–56	29–38	62	64–70	61–75	69	58
6. Tenure (single employer) less than 10 years	69	58	83	84	90	73	91	58	76
7. Working hours less than 12	12	4	33	4	14	15	13	3	19
8. Training length	4.17	4.02	2.71	4.27	3.25	3.05	3.21	4.50	3.42
9. Firm size less than 100	67%	78%	75%	77%	30%	63%	46%	16%	55%
10. Labor intensity[c]	12	20	47	45	33	74	72	?	?
11, Hourly gross wage (2006 euros)	14.05	13.65	11.22	13.61	11.95	14.20	11.56	17.39	13.35

Sources: 1–9 and 11, unless indicated **bold**: WageIndicator web survey, January 1, 2004 to June 15, 2006, N: unweighted 11,216; weighted by age, gender, and working hours. 10, and indicated **bold**: other sources; see chs. 5–9.

[a] No distinction could be made between hotels and other cleaning firms, except for labor intensity.

[b] Academic hospitals and nursing homes are excluded.

[c] Labor costs: total operating costs, including purchasing (2004).

those of education, gender, and firm size. Most striking is the position of the two food-processing subsectors, where low levels of (initial) education do not exclude comparatively high average wages. Here, industry CLAs aiming to include the low-skilled, a traditional strong union position, substantial on-the-job training, long tenures, and low labor intensity jointly outdo the eventual negative influences of low education and small firm size.

FIRM STRATEGIES: HIGH ROAD AND LOW ROAD

Firm strategies provide a crucial link between the factors discussed here and the outcomes for low-wage workers in terms of job quality, including wages. Recently the discussion has grown about the possible existence of different firm strategies within comparable environments and product and service markets, and about the opportunities that high-road market strategies may offer for enhancing work organizations and improving job quality. This debate concentrates on the benefits of new, non-Taylorist forms of work organization. In this respect, the international influence of the Scandinavian experiences cannot be overestimated (Deutsch 2005). When drafting the European Commission Green Paper "Partnership for a New Organization of Work" (1997), the main author drew considerably on these experiences. The green paper advocated a combination of flexibility, security, and social dialogue in order to develop a high-road strategy for European firms. Even though there was no real policy follow-up to this EC initiative, research continued, and that allowed us to clarify the relations to be considered.

In the strand of literature dealing with organizational change, high-road market strategies are strongly associated with innovation, either in the field of R&D or in work organization. The outcomes of a U.K. research project, claiming evidence from innovation-based models of change grounded in workplace partnership, may typify this: "The high road . . . demonstrated clear benefits in terms of competitiveness, employment and quality of working life" (UKWON 2001). High-road forms of organization are supposed to be competitive in global markets, delivering better products faster, unleashing creativity, generating new knowledge, and promoting the convergence between improved competitiveness and improvements in job quality (Totterdill, Dhondt, and Milsome 2002). The argument is that management practices labeled high-performance work systems (HPWS) generate superior market performance because employees are spurred to greater efforts when they are offered conditions of relative autonomy, participation in work decisions, and different material and intrinsic rewards. These practices include functional flexibility, working in self-directed teams, and investment in workers' skills. The development of high-trust relations between managers, workers, and their representatives eventually leads to the "mutual gains enterprise" (Kochan and Osterman 1994; see also Appelbaum and Batt 1994; Appelbaum et al. 2000). Job security is thought to be one such mutual gain, since opportunities are created for long-term worker participation and employers have incentives to invest in training and in new forms of work organization.

The empirical evidence on the association of HPWS and related high-road approaches with superior firm performance, however, is not unambiguous. Some U.S. and U.K. studies show rather positive outcomes, but others show more negative outcomes (Danford et al. 2005, 5). Notably, researchers from these two countries suggest that the actual economic, social, and institutional conditions may work to favor the dominance of the low-road path in most industries. In particular, they point to the weakening of organized labor and the weakness of shop-floor worker representation. We would add the growing importance of short-term shareholder value considerations and related constraints connected with the exposure to global market forces. These conditions may also have a considerable impact on the effects of HPWS in terms of job quality, although here the picture is not unequivocally black. Based on extensive surveys, Richard Freeman and his colleagues (2000) concluded that in the United States "employee involvement" had a strong and positive impact on employee well-being. Thomas Bauer (2004) shows for fifteen EU member states that higher workers' involvement in HPWS is associated with higher job satisfaction, indicating that workers value higher autonomy and increased shop-floor communication. Case studies (Milkman 1998; Danford et al. 2005) confirm that workers who have experienced authoritarian management regimes broadly prefer high-road approaches. Yet at the same time, surveys suggest, for both the United States and European countries, that several features of HPWS, especially the intensification of work and job rotation, are causally related to increased occupational hazards (Askenazy 2001; Askenazy and Caroli 2002; Savage 2001). And though the evidence is more scattered, workers in high-performance workplaces are reported to be exposed to higher work-related stress levels and to encounter a growing sense of job insecurity. Based on our own research (Van Klaveren and Tom 1995), we assume that these negative effects follow segmented patterns. Their incidence among low-skilled workers may be higher than among the high-skilled. The development of HPWS has diverted attention—including that of researchers—from the tendency to externalize employment, which is often related. By externalizing production, employers can avoid the trade-off between high performance and employment protection (Altmann 1994; Sprenger 1995). Indeed, as Arne Kalleberg (2001, 482) has pointed out, "Studies of HPWS have tended to neglect flexible staffing strategies involving non-standard forms of employment." The claim that a high-performance work system embodies a high-road firm strategy that offers long-term job security seems hard to substantiate. At least, differentiation between outcomes for various groups of workers seems justified.

The high-road versus low-road distinction seems a key element of the present research. However, fields of application, variables, and criteria differ substantially between researchers and practitioners, partly depending on varying national backgrounds. In *Low-Wage America*, the distinction is particularly used in the last chapter, where differences between smaller manufacturing establishments in central New York are analyzed (Appelbaum, Bernhardt, and Murnane 2003). Derek Jones and his co-authors characterize the observed firm strategies as high-road if basic wages and employment policies place the establishment in the top tier of plants in the relevant labor market, with a no-layoff strategy and generally low turnover rates; moreover, the incidence of HPWS should be above average, implying high levels of training, job rotation, multiskilling, employee involvement, teamwork, employee stock ownership, and profit sharing. Low-road strategies are sought in the opposite direction where "systems of performance evaluation and compensation (pay grades) are traditional and quite bureaucratic, and job ladders have few rungs" (Appelbaum, Bernhardt, and Murnane 2003, 494). Most if not all such high-road criteria are accepted in Dutch research, but this seems more doubtful for some of the low-road yardsticks. Systems of job evaluation and grading in the CLAs, which may be bureaucratic, are regarded as elements of "high roads" by researchers and practitioners in the Netherlands, as they supposedly contribute to income security and shield the low-paid against arbitrary decisions. Job ladders with few rungs are also valued differently: researchers and unionists tend to recommend such ladders as a means to attain a more equitable organization and a smaller gender wage gap. These examples show that, apart from universally acknowledged criteria, some yardsticks ask for a specific national (and maybe even industry-based) operationalization. Moreover, it seems to us that the concept of a firm strategy as an independent variable needs a definition and criteria of its own, independent from job quality.

Therefore, we differentiate between four aspects of firm strategies with respect to high and low roads, with job quality as the dependent variable:

1. Product-market strategies: high-road strategies characterized by comparatively high value-added production and servicing, aimed at distinctive and high-quality products and services, versus low-cost, low-quality production and servicing

2. Work organization: high-road, enhanced forms of work organization versus low-road organization based on traditional, strict divisions of labor, with outsourcing and offshoring of tasks and processes as a third distinction

3. Human resource policies on recruitment, selection, staffing levels, training, contracts, outsourcing, use of temp work agencies, labor turnover, sick leave, maternity and other leave arrangements, job quality, and firing: high-road if contributing to sustainable, enhanced forms of work organization as well as to job quality by, among other things, challenging workers' skills and competences, limiting work pressure and health and safety risks, and offering ample training, career, and "voice" opportunities

4. The job quality of the target groups of workers, by which we refer to skill use, autonomy at work, work pressure, risks of work stress, health and safety, working time, wages and compensation, training and career prospects, job security, and "voice" (interest representation)

In this setup, product-market and human resource strategies are the more dynamic aspects, while work organization is the restricted one. It is our conviction that mutual relations between these four elements, as well as those with job quality, are often complex and rarely unambiguous. We are inclined to believe that the idea that firm strategies share robust common elements that lead to either a high road or a low road is often too simple to capture firm behavior. In the next chapters, we try to give indications of (dominant) firm strategies and to make aspects of high-road and low-road elements visible.

RESEARCH DESIGN, METHODOLOGY, AND CONTRASTS

The following chapters are based partly on desk research, partly on expert interviews, and partly on establishment case studies. These are basically grounded in the international templates for the industry reports and the guidelines for interviews with management, employees (individual interviews and focus groups), and employee representatives that were developed cooperatively by the five national teams for Denmark, France, Germany, the United Kingdom, and the Netherlands and that underlie all the country studies. These templates and guidelines were somewhat adapted to specific national and industry conditions. Starting from there, the research developed in three phases.

In the first phase, exploratory desk research was combined with expert interviews to build up the story of the industry: the aim was to draw a comprehensive picture of the most significant characteristics and trends in that industry and to relate them to the national economy and the national institutions. Information was gathered from topical research reports; from industry, subsector, and firm reports; from statistics of Statistics Netherlands; from product and industry boards; from the WageIndicator and management consultancies; and from trade journals, union magazines, and related websites. Experts included representatives of employers' and professional associations, unions and, if existing, product and industry boards, as well as independent analysts. Our observation of trends focused on changes in competitive conditions, in institutions, in firm strategies, and in low-wage employment and job quality. First drafts of reports were written for all five industries.

In three industries, research focused on two subsectors in order to contrast production processes, employment structures, products and services, and institutional settings. The retail study focused on supermarkets and consumer electronics retail, the food-processing study on meat processing and confectionary production, and the call center industry study on centers servicing companies in two industries: finance and utilities. One or two additional contrasts were chosen in international agreement. The role of the contrasts was to enable us to relate variations in job quality and wages to differences in economic and institutional contexts as well as to differences in firm strategies. In addition to these international contrasts, some national contrasts were incorporated into the case study selection—notably, the contrast between tight and soft labor markets. During the two-year research, interesting differences developed between the rapidly tightening labor markets of the densely populated western part of the Netherlands, the so-called Randstad conurbation, and the rest of the country.

In the second phase, in accordance with the original research framework, eight case studies were completed in each of the five industries. Desk research and expert interviews provided two out of three points of departure for the selection of case establishments; the criteria decided in the international industry groups of the five countries formed the third. The ease of access to case establishments varied widely, and particularly in retail and the call center industry we met considerable problems. These problems were partly the result of conflicts in labor relations at the time of the research, although developments in product markets (price wars in retail, customer complaints about call centers) also played a role. This diminished the enthusiasm for welcoming outsiders scrutinizing the industry. The generally more cooperative labor relations in food manufacturing contributed to rather smooth access there. Access to the hotel and hospital industries was somewhere in between, although access to hotels was more difficult than easy.

Usually, before proceeding with the interviews, the researchers attempted to visit the establishment and gather essential facts and figures about it and, if relevant, about the parent firm. Researchers' interviews with managers (general, human resource, line) focused on economic context and firm strategy, work organization and job design, hiring and firing, skills and training, and wages and labor costs, including outsourcing and use of temp agency work. Researchers' interviews with individual employees and focus groups concentrated on personal characteristics, work organization and job design, job quality, wages, skills, training and career prospects, job satisfaction, and collective action. Similar topics were discussed with works counselors and union officials; in these interviews, researchers paid special attention to employee representation, collective bargaining, and the perspectives of the firm, the establishment, and the employees. In most case studies, the researchers made specific arrangements concerning reporting on results to interviewees and providing them with other forms of feedback.

In the third phase, the results of the case studies were integrated into the draft industry reports that resulted from the first phase. Since over a year had passed, information on the primary changes in economic and institutional contexts and firm strategies was incorporated into the reports, together with more recent industry statistics. Agreements on feedback to unions, employers' associations, and other experts consulted were fulfilled, and wherever relevant their comments were integrated.

REFERENCES

Altmann, Norbert. 1994. "Production Networks and New Forms of Work Organization." Paper presented to the 100th anniversary Irish Congress of Trade Unions. May 1994, Dublin.

Appelbaum, Eileen, and Rosemary Batt. 1994. *The New American Workplace: Transforming Work Systems in the United States*. Ithaca, N.Y.: Cornell University Press/IRL Press.

Appelbaum, Eileen, Annette Bernhardt , and Richard J. Murnane, eds. 2003. *Low-Wage America: How Employers Are Reshaping Opportunity in the Workplace*. New York: Russell Sage Foundation.

Appelbaum, Eileen, Thomas Bailey, Peter Berg, and Arne L. Kalleberg. 2000. *Manufacturing Advantage: Why High Performance Work Systems Pay Off*. Ithaca, N.Y.: Cornell University Press.

Askenazy, Philippe. 2001. "Innovative Workplace Practices and Occupational Injuries and Illnesses in the United States." *Economic and Industrial Democracy* 22(4): 485–516.

Askenazy, Philippe, and Eve Caroli. 2002. "New Organizational Practices and Working Conditions: Evidence for France in the 1990s." *Louvain Economics Review* 68(1): 91–110.

Bauer, Thomas K. 2004. "High-Performance Workplace Practices and Job Satisfaction: Evidence from Europe." Discussion paper 1265. Bonn: IZA.

Danford, Andy, Martin Richardson, Paul Stewart, Stephanie Tailby, and Martin Upchurch. 2005. *Partnership and the High Performance Workplace: Work and Employment Relations in the Aerospace Industry*. Basingstoke, U.K.: Palgrave Macmillan.

Deutsch, Steven. 2005. "A Researcher's Guide to Worker Participation, Labor, and Economic and Industrial Democracy." *Economic and Social Democracy* 26(4): 645–56.

European Commission (EC). 1997. "Partnership for a New Organization of Work." Green paper. Communication COM (1997) 128. Luxembourg: Official Publication Office of the European Commission.

Freeman, Richard B., Morris Kleiner, and Cheri Ostroff. 2000. *The Anatomy of Employee Involvement and Its Effects on Firms and Workers.* Working paper 8050. Cambridge, Mass.: National Bureau of Economic Research.

Groningen Growth and Development Center. 2006. 60-Industry Database. Accessed at http://www.ggdc.net/index-dseries.html.

Kalleberg, Arne L. 2001. "Organizing Flexibility: The Flexible Firm in a New Century." *British Journal of Industrial Relations* 39(4): 479–504.

Kochan, Thomas A., and Peter Osterman. 1994. *The Mutual Gains Enterprise: Forging a Winning Partnership Among Labor, Management, and Government.* Boston: Harvard Business School.

Milkman, Ruth. 1998. "The New American Workplace: High Road or Low Road?" In *Workplaces of the Future,* edited by Paul Thompson and Chris Warhurst. Basingstoke, U.K.: Palgrave Macmillan.

Savage, Pat, editor. 2001. *New Forms of Work Organization: The Benefits and Impact on Performance.* EWON theme paper. Brussels: European Commission.

Sprenger, Wim. 1995. *In de kern. Bedrijven en de slanke lijn* [*At the Core: Companies and Trimming the Fat*]. Amsterdam: FNV.

Totterdill, Peter, Steven Dhondt, and Sue Milsome. 2002. *Partners at Work? A Report to Europe's Policy Makers and Social Partners.* Unpublished report of the HI-RES (Defining the High Road of Work Organization as a Resource for Policy Makers and Social Partners) project.

UKWON. 2001. Newsletter, February 6, 2001.

Van Klaveren, Maarten, and Toke Tom. 1995. "All-round groepswerk: doen of doen alsof?" ["All-Round Group Work: Do or Pretend?"]. *Tijdschrift voor Arbeidsvraagstukken* 11(1): 21–33.

CHAPTER 5

The Retail Industry: The Contrast of Supermarkets and Consumer Electronics

Maarten van Klaveren

The regular customer in a Dutch supermarket usually encounters a rather segmented work organization in the store: a lineup of checkout operators, most of them female; at various spots in the store, shelf-stackers, mostly boys, who are busy with physical distribution; and in a glass room or customer greeting area near the entry, a gentleman in a suit, the store manager. The visitor to a Dutch electronics store gets a picture of a completely different organization: sales clerks who are nearly all well-dressed gents, and all carrying out more or less the same tasks; and sometimes a few ladies of a similar kind.

A closer look at the reality of the shop floor reveals a slightly different picture. Both WageIndicator data and case study evidence reveal that in the supermarkets those in the target occupation, the checkout operators, make up about half of the head-count supermarket workforce. Yet they are not the only ones carrying out checkout tasks. About one-third of the shelf-stackers occasionally also perform checkout duties, while a slightly smaller share of the checkout operators also fulfill shelf-stacking duties.[1] This overlap in duties often happens informally, however, and is sometimes hardly perceived by the store management. This kind of functional flexibility is flourishing under pressure: it is almost inevitable if the shop-floor organization is pressed and tight financial and personnel standards do not allow idle hours.

Such flexibility was never really promoted by the human resource policies of the supermarket chains. In the late 1990s, the market leader, Albert Heijn (AH), took some steps toward promoting teamwork and functional flexibility in its supermarkets (Horbeek 2003), but this attempt did not survive the recent supermarket price war.

Now that the price war seems to have come to an end and the super-market chains are rediscovering good customer service as a major competitive edge, high roads in human resource strategy and work organization will get a new chance. However, human resource management in retail generally seems weak and not very responsive to changes in the economic context.

From the employees' point of view, the situation in consumer electronics outlets seems much more comfortable. In their daily functioning, sales clerks, accounting for 50 to 60 percent of the head-count workforce, have built-in functional flexibility. Their professional attitudes often inspire them to stand in for colleagues, a practice strengthened by the importance of (higher) sales not only for the store but for their personal incomes. As in many professional organizations, however, the boundaries of such flexibility are unclear; for the sales clerks in our case studies, flexibility repeatedly led to high workload and work-related stress. Moreover, the wages of electronics retail clerks are strongly dependent on bonuses and compensations, and the wage floor offered by the CLA is low. As far as we could trace, the human resource policies of the main consumer electronics retailers hardly play a role in protecting their employees against excessive flexibility. These policies remain weak and mainly concentrate on training aspects.

THE METHODOLOGY

The contrasts between firms within the industry were chosen with respect to the production process, the employment structure, and products or services. First, four cases were selected in supermarkets and consumer electronics, respectively. The second contrast was low-end versus high-end market position, with the following as indicative yardsticks: product quality, service quality, price levels, and assortment offered. In addition to these internationally uniform contrasts, the national contrasts chosen were: international/national ownership, high/low levels of process innovation, and tight/soft local labor markets.

Getting access to establishments was a serious problem, for different reasons. First, our research in the field was just starting when the two supermarket CLAs expired on April 1, 2004; negotiations between the social partners for new CLAs were cumbersome and did not result in a new agreement until June 2005. Second, the supermarket price war seriously hampered access for a long time. Third, some consumer electronics chains withdrew earlier promises of access. Nevertheless, eight cases were completed, although, unfortunately, not always with the official cooperation of firm headquarters. In total, forty-seven people were interviewed. In three cases, we interviewed individual workers in the target jobs, in four cases we worked with focus groups of shop-floor workers, and in one case we did both. Table 5.1 gives an overview of the most important "hard" characteristics of the retail cases.

The chains owning or franchising the stores in which the supermarket cases have been carried out had a combined market share in 2005 of about 16 percent, while the consumer electronics chains had about 23 percent. We should acknowledge that the sample is very small: 8 stores out of 767 in the eight chains covered here, and out of 10,000 supermarkets and consumer electronics outlets in the country as a whole. With so small a sample, we must be very careful in generalizing our case results.

With the opportunities available to the supermarket and consumer electronics chains to develop high-road human resource strategies as the leading theme, we unfold the landscape of retail as follows. The next section treats the economic and institutional context, presenting an overview of retail employment. That is followed by a section on how the results from the eight cases relate to this context. Finally, we consider the potential for a high-road strategy to have a positive effect on employment prospects, job quality, and wages in the target jobs.

THE ECONOMIC AND INSTITUTIONAL CONTEXT

EMPLOYMENT

The retail trade is a major part of the service sector. At the end of 2005, the retail industry as a whole employed 714,400 persons (head count): 610,000 (85 percent) being employees and 104,400 (15 percent) being employers and cooperating family members. These employees represented 8.7 percent of wage and salary employment in the Netherlands (CBS/Statline).

From the early 1990s until 2002, retail experienced a decade of prosperity, with continuous growth in employment and substantial

Table 5.1 The Case Study Retail Establishments

	Supermarkets				Consumer Electronics Retail			
	SUP A	SUP B	SUP C	SUP D	CER A	CER B	CER C	CER D
Market share	5.5%	1.2%	1.8%	7%	11%	7%	2%	3%
Number of Dutch stores	89	49	45	380	22	41	29	112
Ownership	Dutch	Dutch	Dutch	Dutch/French	German	British	Dutch	Dutch
Product/service strategy[a]	Low, soft discount	Middle, fresh food	Low	High	Middle	Middle	High	Low
Total workforce[a] (international/Dutch)	13,500	4,100	5,200	15,000	37,000/1,500	28,000/1,000	600	1,100
Store workforce[a]	84	87	95	31	93	22	16	10
Store surface (square meters)	880	1,200	1,400	500	4,500	1,000	900	300
Share part-time[a]	86%	89%	85%	84%	20%	36%	38%	40%
Share female[a]	74[b]	88[b]	83[b]	81[b]	14	4	13	0
Share target jobs	45–51	48–57	59	52	51	55	63	70

Source: Author's compilation from case studies by the researchers.
[a] Head count
[b] Share of regular full-time/part-time workforce.

profit margins. The Industry Board for Retail (HBD, Hoofdbedrijf-schap Detailhandel) even characterized the 1990s as the "golden years" (HBD 2005a, 5). From 1990 on, wage and salary employment grew by 32 percent, a stronger growth than in the United States, Denmark, and France (Groningen Growth and Development Center 2006). In 2001 and 2002, employment growth had already slowed down, yet the decline in 2003 of 2.1 percent (head-count) came as a shock. That year total retail sales fell by 2 percent, followed by a similar decline in 2004. Consequently, 2004 witnessed a further decline in wage and salary employment (1.0 percent, head-count; 2.0 percent, full-time equivalents [FTEs]). In 2005 retail sales began to recover, and sales decreased by only 0.3 percent and the (head-count) employee workforce by 0.9 percent for the year as a whole. FTE retail employment, however, fell by no less than 2.4 percent (CBS/Statline). Interestingly, the head-count male workforce grew by 0.3 percent, but female numbers continued to diminish, by 1.7 percent.

Part-Time Employment   The figures presented earlier also indicate the dominance of part-time work in retail: the FTE/head-count ratio was 58 percent in 2005; compared to 65 percent in 1995 and 61 percent in 2000, this points to a continuous growth of the share of part-time jobs. In 2005 no fewer than 80 percent of female retail workers and half of all males worked less than thirty-six hours per week. The growth of retail employment from 1995 to 2005 can be attributed fully to the growth of part-time work for both sexes. By contrast, for both men and women the absolute numbers of full-timers were lower in 2005 than a decade earlier.

The supermarket subsector is by far the largest of the retail branches: in December 2005, it employed 200,700 workers (head-count), nearly one-third of the retail total. In the supermarkets, part-time employment is even more widespread than in retail as a whole: in 2005 its FTE/head-count ratio was 47 percent. Therefore, individual supermarkets have a comparatively large workforce: the average head-count number of workers in the stores of the national chains varies between 50 and 115. This implies that managing the cooperation and working hours of such a workforce is a major challenge for management. The supermarket subsector is less feminized than retail at large. With 55 percent female workers in 2005, it ranked only tenth out of fifteen branches.

Consumer electronics retail is much smaller. In 2005 it employed

20,800 workers (head-count), or 3.4 percent of the retail workforce (CBS/Statline; HBD 2005c). Here the FTE/head-count ratio was 67 percent. Moreover, with 63 percent male workers, consumer electronics had the second-largest male share in retailing. The figures for the two subsectors underline their different employment structures and staffing strategies. This was the main reason we chose these two subsectors as a contrast for retailing.

Gender   The retail workforce was feminized in the 1990s, though less strongly than in the economy as a whole. In 2000, 64 percent of the workforce was female, against 56 percent in 1992. Recently the share of women stabilized at 63 percent, but in the supermarkets the female share fell between 2000 and 2005, by two and a half percentage points, and even in consumer electronics retail, by three and a half percentage points. As we will see later, in the supermarkets deliberate policies to save on labor costs played a major role in this respect; the causes for the diminishing female share in consumer electronics are less clear.

   In a cross-country perspective, the share of women in Dutch retail is not particularly high. It is lower than in Germany and France and equal to the United Kingdom, but higher than in Denmark. The same picture holds true for the supermarkets. At first sight, this is astonishing: in the supermarkets 85 to 88 percent of the checkout operators turn out to be female (based on WageIndicator data and the case studies), about ten percentage points higher than in the United Kingdom, France, and Germany. The inevitable conclusion seems to be that Dutch supermarket chains allow themselves a comparatively large male staff in management and logistics.

Age   Dutch retail relies heavily on young workers, but this reliance appears to diminish over time according to the retail benchmark set for European countries in this low-wage project, the share of workers under age thirty. In 1995, 60 percent of the retail workforce were workers age fifteen to twenty-nine, while in 2005 the share was 53 percent.[2] However, the share of the youngest category, fifteen- to nineteen-year-olds, is growing. In 2005 they made up over one-quarter of the retail workforce, against one-fifth in 1995 (CBS/Statline). Already in 2004 the Industrial Board for Retail (HBD) pointed to the smaller cohorts of juveniles entering the labor market and expressed its concern about the future of the retailing labor supply. Yet in

2004–2005 retail employers concentrated even more on recruiting young people under age twenty, who filled two-thirds of all vacancies. Obviously the human resource management of the main chains has not been very responsive to warnings about the changing labor market.

The fact that students account for just one-quarter of all newcomers in retail suggests that three-fifths of the young newcomers are rather low-skilled teenagers who may not regard a retail job as a temporary occupation (HBD 2005a, 23; 2005d; Dribbusch 2003, 23). The nonstudent category seems to contain predominantly those with no aspirations or opportunities for postsecondary education and training. In the large cities, second-generation migrant workers are the majority in this group. Nevertheless, scattered evidence suggests that about 10 percent of the retail workforce age fifteen to twenty-four fosters aspirations for a career in retail. This group includes a substantial number of minority workers who are active in family enterprises. It should be noted that "ethnic supermarkets" are on average successful and expanding quickly (Van den Tillaart and Doesborgh 2004).

Combining the available sources, we estimate that in 2005 the supermarket workforce contained 74,000 fifteen- to nineteen-year-olds (37 percent of the total), 44,000 twenty- to twenty-two-year-olds (22 percent), and 12,000 twenty-three- to twenty-four-year-olds (6 percent). Thus, approximately 118,000 individuals, or nearly three-fifths of the workforce, were under twenty-three years of age. Their pay is found in the youth wage scales of the CLAs. About 110,000 formally had a job as auxiliary workers employed on a fixed-term contract (based on CBS/Statline; CGB 2006; HBD 2005a; WageIndicator data).

At first sight, the supermarkets seem to offer interesting workplaces to juvenile workers, especially students. There are opportunities to work outside the traditional opening hours but not at unappealing hours such as at night or on Sunday, and supermarkets also present young people with more opportunities to work closer to home, perhaps even in their own neighborhood. Three-quarters of the young people employed in supermarkets who answered the WageIndicator survey lived less than one-quarter of an hour from their workplace, compared to fewer than 50 percent of those working in other branches. Against these advantages, many young people obviously take the low supermarket wages for granted. Their gross hourly wages are on average 20 percent less than they could earn elsewhere while working much shorter working weeks. As a result, a nineteen-year-old on average earned €130 (US$191) per week in the supermarket, against €183 (US$269) elsewhere (Van Klaveren and Tijdens 2005). However, young people pay virtually no taxes on such low incomes.

Consumer electronics retail also has a rather young workforce, but this is due to the large share (nearly 40 percent) of those who are age twenty-three to thirty-five. This subsector illustrates the increase in average tenure that has occurred since 2000. Male retail employees age twenty to twenty-four in particular have tended to stay with their employer. The share of those with tenure of five years or more grew from 4 percent in 2000 to 23 percent in 2005 (author's calculations from CBS/Statline).

COMPETITIVE PRESSURES AND INDUSTRY PERFORMANCE

Production and employment structures in Dutch retail have been moving toward a low-wage model. The management strategies of the large chains have been focused on lowering prices, saving on labor costs, and augmenting the numerical flexibility of labor; countervailing human resource policies have been lacking. Elsewhere (Salverda, Moeller, and Sollogoub 2005), we concluded that between 1979 and 1996 retailing moved toward low pay in the Netherlands and the United Kingdom and away from it in the United States and Germany. We may assume that, in the aftermath of the "golden years," competitive pressures in the Netherlands led to a continuation of this pattern. From 1996 to 2005, hourly retail wages lagged behind the national wage trend by two percentage points for male employees and by five percentage points for females (author's calculations from CBS/Statline).

We have identified four main competitive pressures, which are treated in the next sections:

1. The slowdown or even decline of disposable income growth and the changes in consumer spending patterns

2. Price wars and the spread of discounting

3. The liberalization of zoning regulations and opening hours

4. The development of supply-chain management systems, linked
    with front- and back-end innovations

Changing Consumer Spending Abundant retail growth declined in
2002, initially because of the slowdown in disposable income growth
and hesitant consumer spending. It took until the second half of
2005 before consumer spending started to grow again, and this recovery initially concentrated on durable consumer goods, not food.
In May 2006, food sales finally expanded: compared to May 2005, supermarket sales grew by 7 percent, of which volume effects accounted for six percent points (CBS, press release, July 14, 2006).

The position in their respective areas of the supermarkets and the
consumer electronics outlets has developed contradictions. The
number of supermarket establishments is falling (9 percent from
2000 to 2005, ending up with 5,664 stores as of January 1, 2006), but
the share of supermarkets in consumers' food expenditure continues
to grow, from 61 percent in 1991 to 75 percent in 2005. Yet the supermarkets are predominantly *grocery* sellers: the 2005 share of nonfood in supermarket sales was only 14 percent (author's calculations
from CBS/Statline).

Since the early 1980s, the number of electronics goods stores,
about 4,100 at present, has also been diminishing. Notably, 2004 and
2005 were bad years for these stores: they lost to other sales channels
in all categories. Their market share in large household appliances
(white goods) sales even fell by seventeen percentage points, to 55
percent, and their shares in audio and video equipment (brown
goods), small household appliances, and computers (grey goods) declined too. Household articles stores, do-it-yourself (DIY) stores, supermarkets, and Internet sellers were their main competitors (HBD
2004a).

Price Wars and Discounting   The worldwide expansion plans of the
largest Netherlands-based retailer, Ahold, ignited the recent supermarket price war. This war fit the pattern of low-road market strategies that already prevailed in grocery retail, with, in cross-country
perspective, low consumer price levels and small assortments. AH,
the large Dutch supermarket chain of Ahold, had to generate the
huge amounts of money needed for the megalomaniac ambitions of
its CEO. In the winter of 2002, shrinking food spending turned
against AH in particular because consumers regarded its stores as too

expensive. Many switched to cheaper alternatives, like the German hard-discounters Aldi and Lidl. In February 2003, it turned out that Ahold's expansion had been partly built on fraud and sales-boosting practices in the United States, Latin America, and Scandinavia. Banks and stock markets reacted strongly. Finally, AH was freed from its role as cash generator because the CEO was forced to quit. In October 2003, the firm lowered the prices of 1,200 top-brand articles to a maximum of 35 percent. It was the start of a price war that went far beyond the usual price skirmishes in retail. AH went on until October 2006 with thirteen consecutive discount rounds.

From January 2004 until December 2005, the supermarket price levels went down each consecutive month. Already during the period 2002 to 2004 the average net margin of the supermarkets fell from 3 to around 1 percent. First, the leading supermarket chains reacted with cost-cutting strategies, concentrating on labor costs. In particular, they replaced "expensive" elderly frontline staff, mostly women, with "cheaper" young people. In the spring of 2004, many elderly checkout operators in an FNV (Dutch Trade Union Confederation) survey complained that they were "bullied away." Women with family responsibilities reported that employers often made unilateral decisions about days off and holidays, frustrating them and sometimes forcing them to give up their jobs. Over the course of 2004–2005, store managers admitted these practices, stating that they "had to do this in order to survive" (De Volkskrant, March 24, 2005; Bondgenoten Magazine, July 2004). We did not find any counterefforts from human resource managers at company headquarters. Moreover, the supermarkets continued to concentrate their hiring policies on the youngest youths, supported by the practice of not renewing the fixed-term contracts of eighteen- to twenty-two-year-olds. These rather ruthless hiring and firing policies generated bad press and accusations of age discrimination (CGB 2006).

Second, the supermarket chains shifted the burden of their lower prices to food suppliers and farmers. After having made massive replacements of top brands with private labels, they pushed down the margins of the private-label manufacturers—since 2003, on average from 2.5 to 0.5 percent (Koen de Jong, IPLC consultant, NRC-Handelsblad, October 21, 2006). The Dutch dairy and meat-processing industries in particular have been severely hit as they were squeezed between raw material suppliers and large retailers (see chapter 9). The employment effects were substantial. Over a period of only one and a half years—up to April 2005—the staff cuts in supermarkets and in distribution centers and food manufacturing establishments related to the supermarket price war were estimated at 34,000 (FTEs) by two leading retail consultants (Laurens Sloot and Jan-Willem Grievink, quoted in *NRC-Handelsblad*, April 30, 2005).

In October 2006, AH announced the end of the price war after having reached its main goals: midmarket positioning; a market share of 28 percent, which exceeded its 2002 level; and a record profit margin of 6.3 percent in the first half of 2006 (*NRC-Handelsblad*, October 21, 2006). The major loser has been the composite Laurus supermarket chain, in which the French Groupe Casino took a majority share in 2004. Laurus lost one-third of its market share before it was dismantled by the selling of two of its three supermarket chains—to AH and medium-sized competitors. In the end, a number of these competitors, organized in the Superunie buyers' group, also did quite well. Initially in the price war the traditional distinctions between "servicers" and "soft" and "hard" discounters became blurred, especially when restrictions on assortments became part of the sales strategies of all major supermarket chains. Yet this reached its limits rather soon. Over the course of 2005, growing numbers of customers were said to be annoyed that supermarkets were reducing their range of products (HBD 2005b, 5–6). Reactions to this customer displeasure may suggest a break away from the prevailing low road in grocery market strategies. Various competitors—AH, C1000, Jumbo, and Super De Boer—are trying to develop strategies that combine comparatively low prices with good (fresh) quality and a broad assortment. A crucial prerequisite for the success of this strategy will be heavy investment in up-grading the sales and product expertise of staff. If such strategies gain ground, they may—under the pressure of the unions, training institutes, and so on—generate positive effects on the quality of supermarket jobs, including improved career opportunities for checkout operators. From this perspective, it is an interesting sign that AH announced in 2006 that the customer service skills of its frontline staff needed improving and that it was launching training programs for fifty thousand workers for that purpose (*NRC-Handelsblad*, February 21, 2006). Notably, C1000 and Jumbo have followed this training path as well. Yet it is still far from clear whether the companies' headquarters will incorporate high-road human resource policies into their reorientation.

The main worry of consumer electronics retailers is not to be squeezed by the speeding up of new product cycles. Increasing volumes should allow their sales to stay ahead of the continuous decline of price. This effort failed in 2004–2005, and sales collapsed by 16 percent (CBS/Statline). Knockout pricing led to the reduction of net margins to, on average, 0 percent in 2005. Yet half of all consumer electronics outlets are independent firms and are not included in chains or buyer groups (author's calculations, based on HBD 2005c, and company websites). The latter are regarded as countervailing powers against the large electronics manufacturers. Competition is fought on sales, especially regionally, with many baits and "cheapest buy" guarantees, but also on advertising service quality, knowledgeable staff, and reliable technical backing. The most ambitious contenders are MediaMarkt, owned by the German Metro Group, which, with an aggressive marketing profile, opened the largest stores of this kind (4,500 to 8,000 square meters), and BCC, a subsidiary of the U.K.-based KESA Group, which plans to double the number of its stores in the Netherlands (*NRC-Handelsblad*, May 27, 2005, May 10–11, 2006).

Liberalization and Economies of Scale   The size of retail outlets recently got a boost. Over the long run the increase in scale has been clear, in grocery and nonfood retailing alike. In grocery retail, the average store surface grew from 35 square meters in 1968 to 91 square meters in 1987 to 172 square meters in 2004; the comparable figures for nonfood retailing are 85 square meters in 1968, 154 square meters in 1987, and 253 square meters in 2004. Nevertheless, Dutch stores remain comparatively small (Evers, van Hoorn, and van Oort 2005, 31). Apart from the small national market, the detailed rules that the national authorities maintain for the establishment of large shopping centers on the edges of towns are crucial. Recently this policy has been abolished; decisionmaking on the location of large retail outlets has been decentralized to provinces and municipalities. The governmental Spatial Planning Bureau (RPB) suggests that the coming of "mega malls" and "big box boulevards" is inevitable. However, consumer preferences may play a role here. Dutch consumers' propensity to accept a massive development toward hypermarkets seems low. In a 2006 survey among five hundred consumers, over 60 percent said they did not expect to do their shopping in hypermarkets (NRC-Handelsblad, May 29, 2006).

Recently it was emphasized that the value-added per retail worker in the Netherlands was by far the lowest of the five countries under study (Creusen et al. 2006, 13).[3] The OECD blames remaining product-market regulations. Although with the 1996 Shop Closing Act maximum shop opening hours were increased from fifty-five to ninety-six per week, the OECD argues that the Netherlands maintains less liberalized opening hours than other member states (OECD 2006, 92). However, after the 1997–98 boom, most supermarkets retreated and reduced their opening hours. Labor supply problems and feelings of being unsafe in the streets after dark contributed to a decline in supermarket sales in the evening hours, to a low point of 9 percent of total sales in 2004 (HBD 2005b, 6). It seems doubtful whether OECD policy advice has captured this reality.

Supply-Chain Management and Innovation   For large retailers, large-scale supply or purchasing ("merchandising" in the United States) provides a larger competitive edge than cost savings on the selling side. Global supply chains, increasingly buyer-driven and under the command of retailers, are fully profitable if supported by supply-chain management systems with low inventory and just-in-time delivery as ultimate goals. American researchers have linked the giant U.S. retailer Wal-Mart with this "lean" retailing. They stress that advances in IT largely drive this supply revolution: scheduling software, data warehousing, use of hand-held scanning computers for stock keeping, and so on (Abernathy et al. 2000; Bernhardt 1999). In the 1990s, U.K.-based Tesco, French Carrefour, the German Metro Group, and AH brought their exploitation of these back-end innovations up to par with Wal-Mart (Kirsch et al. 1999, 23). Linking with front-end innovation is essential. Electronic consumer response (ECR) systems have been implemented in order to develop demand-led logistic chains, using information from cash scanning terminals. In the coming years, supply-chain management could be technically perfected by the introduction of radio frequency identification (RFID) technology instead of bar coding, although the real breakthrough of RFID will most likely take another three to five years.[4]

    A decade ago, American researchers observed that merchandising reforms, highly productive and profitable as they were, hardly affect, much less enhance, retail *sales* jobs, with their low wages and low promotion chances (Bailey and Bernhardt 1997, 195). Even this may be too optimistic for the near future, as the large retailers are integrating supply-chain management software with programs supporting optimal-staffing strategies and personnel benchmarking. Optimal staffing has become vitally important for both headquarters and store managers in order to manage the gap between opening hours and individual working times at the establishment level. For headquarters, internal benchmarking based on strict staffing targets is a major instrument to control the amount of labor (Kirsch et al. 1999; Tijdens 1998; Voss-Dahm and Lehndorff 2003). Our cases confirm the pivotal importance of such benchmarking in managerial decisionmaking. Under the pressure of these managerial strategies and tools, high roads in human resource strategies seem even less open than before.

Frontline operations will constitute the next major rationalization area. In mid-2005, after pilots of medium-sized chains with self-scan cash registers, AH announced the large-scale introduction of these devices. The firm suggested that the social outcomes would not be very negative because redundant checkout operators could stay on as "advisers" (*Distrifood Nieuwsblad*, cited on http://www.zibb.nl/food, June 6, 2005). The FNV Bondgenoten union, on the other hand, expects the introduction of self-scanning to lead to the short-term loss of one-fifth of all checkout operator jobs. An additional reason for the perseverance with which AH has fought the price war may well be the firm's expectation that the frontline in its supermarkets hides a large rationalization potential—to be unleashed by the adoption of self-scanning and RFID technology.

INSTITUTIONS AND LABOR RELATIONS

Collective Labor Agreements and Employers' Associations   Retailing as a whole is covered by thirty-five subsectoral CLAs. In January 2005, these agreements covered all but twelve thousand retail workers, who were concentrated in some small branches (HBD 2005e), implying 98 percent coverage. The central employers' organization in retail is RND, the Council for Netherlands Retail. Retailers are RND members through their branch associations. A main goal of RND in recent negotiations was the trimming down of CLAs that supposedly contained too many rules. The unions emphasized that the vulnerability and low wages of most retail workers left no room for "lean" CLAs (author's interviews with FNV Bondgenoten union officials, July 2006).

Eighteen large supermarket chains maintain their own employers' organization, VGL (Association of Grocery Multiple Stores). VGL negotiates the "VGL-CLA" with two unions, FNV Bondgenoten and CNV Dienstenbond. Smaller, independent grocery retailers have started an organization of their own, Vakcentrum, which negotiates the CLA for grocery companies with the same unions. Actually, the two CLAs are virtually identical. The VGL-CLA has a few extras for early retirement and child care and contains an additional protocol on changes in employment and a (small) training fund. After eleven rounds of negotiation, in June 2005 new supermarket CLAs were agreed upon for the period April 1, 2004 to April 1, 2007. The fifteen months in between were without a CLA, that is, without wage increases. Since the national statutory minimum wage was frozen at the same time, the gap between CLA wages and the SMW remained the same.

Contrary to the more "political" behavior of the supermarkets' association, UNETO-VNI, the employers' organization in consumer electronics, acts mainly as a professional association and concentrates on vocational training.

Vocational Training   In the autumn of 2004, about thirty-five thousand students followed the two dual-learning schemes for retail, the one practice-oriented and the other more theory-based. In the preceding years, the number of practice-oriented students had grown, especially at levels 3 and 4, while those following the theory-oriented curriculum had fallen, notably at levels 1 and 2. The vocational training institutions attribute this falloff to the lack of available internship posts. Yet, the different match between the supplied education and pupils' capacities and motivations obviously played a role as well. Dropout rates are low in the more practice-based scheme and higher among theory-based pupils (Kenniscentrum Handel 2004; HBD 2005a, 27).

We estimate that in 2005 about 85,000 retail workers, or 15 percent of the workforce, had a "dual retail learning" background with at least two completed years of training. The coverage of the Dutch vocational training system remains low, certainly compared to Germany, where 81 percent of the retail workforce had completed vocational training at this level (Voss-Dahm 2005). While the prevailing German production model in retail may develop into a *skill-oriented* low-wage model, we definitely have to leave out "skill-oriented" for the Netherlands.

The Industrial Board   In retail, as in two of the other subsectors under study, hotels and meat processing, a classic institution of Dutch corporatism plays a role: the Industry Board for Retail Trades, or HBD. In HBD, employers' associations and the two main trade unions, FNV Bondgenoten and CNV Dienstenbond, cooperate. HBD has the authority to lay down basic pay and conditions for retail workers not covered by a CLA in a regulation, and in the past it did so in the VAD (Verordening Arbeidsvoorwaarden Detailhandel). By mid-2004, however, this mechanism had been abolished. Already before the price wars, a political debate had started about the usefulness of the product and industry boards (see chapter 3). The price wars confirmed the limited significance of HBD as a labor relations institution, although notably FNV officers did not go along with the suggestion that the wars as such eroded HBD. It is quite understandable that unionists would not give up the opportunities an institution such as HBD offers to act as a center of expertise, monitoring the labor market and other social aspects and exerting some pressure on employers to behave not too shortsightedly.

Employees' Representation   Unionism is a difficult issue in retail, not only in the Netherlands but also, for example, in Germany and the United Kingdom. Based on a comparison of these three countries, it has been argued that there is no specifically anti-union resentment among retail workers, but rather a lack of opportunity to join the unions (Dribbusch 2003). The Dutch practice supports the thesis that union organizing meets structural constraints, especially the predominance of small workplaces and part-time and contingent employment. Union density in retail remains about 12 percent, of which two-thirds are organized in FNV Bondgenoten. In large firms the well-organized distribution centers—strategic points in the logistical chain—add considerably to union membership and the deployment of union power. Yet in the majority of supermarkets and electronics outlets, union consciousness is low, as the eight cases we investigated confirm. In a focus group, one supermarket checkout operator said:

> We don't have any contacts with union officials, and nobody here is a union member—if anybody is a member, she better keep it secret. About a year ago, a union guy visited our store. He only spoke with the manager and was not allowed to contact us. Yet we would like to

discuss some pressing problems with unionists, if necessary outside the store, especially the short-notice messages on our working hours.

Works councils also have a difficult task in retail. Compliance with the Works Councils Act is one of the lowest of all industries: about 180 councils cover only one-third of all retail workers. Most of the approximately 1,200 lay representatives of the FNV Bondgenoten union who are active in retail are works councilors, which means that 40 to 50 percent of all councilors are Bondgenoten members (Dribbusch 2003, 96; information also from FNV Bondgenoten). Nevertheless, union officers feel that many works councils in retail are largely under management control.

Labor Relations   Although he characterized the supermarket chains as tough opponents, one union officer pointed out that more than other retail employers they are inclined to maintain a minimum level of regulated labor relations. Their backgrounds and interests work in this direction. First, they have reached higher levels of professionalism than other retail businesses. Second, all grocery chains worry about their public image. It is not inconceivable that a bad image results in lower sales. In 2004 several clashes occurred between Aldi and the unions, for example, over dismissals of "talkative" workers, and a leading industry analyst saw the related negative publicity reflected in a lower Aldi market share (Joop Holla, quoted in *De Volkskrant*, February 19, 2005). Since then, Aldi's Dutch headquarters has avoided conflicts with the unions. A third factor contributing to regulated labor relations at the supermarket chains is the outside threat of the potential penetration of the Dutch food market by foreign competitors.

During the price war, developments in labor relations mirrored the positions taken in product markets, and old distinctions were blurred. Since 2003, Albert Heijn, once the "social face of Dutch retail," has lost this aura. Headquarters' demands for strict cost control often clash with practices that AH store managers want to pursue. On the other side of the spectrum, union-management relations at Aldi and Lidl seem to have left the low point behind. Obviously, Lidl has learned from the Aldi experience: the second German discounter is adapting to the prevailing labor relations in its host country (FNV Bondgenoten officer, interview with the author, July 2006).

CASES IN CONTEXT

EMPLOYMENT, WORK ORGANIZATION, AND FLEXIBILITY

As we indicated earlier, in many supermarkets store management is burdened with considerable organizational problems. The extremely high share of young part-timers plays a major role here. Working less than twelve hours per week is the dominant pattern for the many young workers age fifteen to nineteen. In the boom years of 1995 to 2000, the Shop Closing Act of 1996 allowed longer opening hours, and thus the share of jobs of less than twelve hours per week among the youngest category went down in favor of jobs lasting twelve to nineteen hours. The decisive element was the integration of order reception and shelf-stacking—which until then had been carried out outside opening hours—into regular work schedules. Since 2000, a return to the small-jobs pattern can be observed, and in 2005 the official statistics showed that two-thirds of the youngest age group worked less than twelve hours.

At the same time, employers' strategies toward numerical flexibility became manifest. While in the 1990s less than one-fifty of retail employees had half-year or shorter contracts, this figure went up steeply in the early 2000s, and then to 74 percent in 2004–2005. HBD explicitly relates this to the larger risks for employers in case of sickness and occupational disability of permanent staff (Dribbusch 2003; HBD 2005a, 23–24). In the case studies, such comments were made in all management interviews. The practice of leaving logistics and shelf-stacking to auxiliary workers, mostly employed on flexible contracts, provides a functional equivalent to outsourcing, that is, the use of temp agency workers. In our cases, we found only a very small number of temp workers in the target jobs.

From the viewpoint of work organization, numerical flexibility seems to have reached its limits. Notably in the large cities in the Randstad conurbation, the size of the core supermarket staff is only about 8 to 10 percent (head-count). Guiding the young workforce and making a substantial recruitment effort is a tough job, as all (assistant) store managers interviewed explained—even more because, first, they have to operate in centrally structured organizations that maintain strict personnel and financial benchmarks, and second, the supermarkets they run are—at least formally—hierarchically structured. Only in two case supermarkets had the store management been left some discretion concerning assortment and discounts, allowing managers to adapt to local preferences. In all four cases, store managers, within the discretion left by the financial and personnel benchmarks, were allowed to make recruitment, promotion, and dismissal decisions concerning frontline staff.

Managers who apply optimal staffing strategies in hierarchical organizations may encounter a fair number of practical problems, as overtime in retailing for women illustrates. In October 2005, the frequency of overtime among females in retail was more than twice the national average: 6.5 percent against 3.1 percent (CBS/Statline). The unpredictability of consumer behavior may play a role, but our field experience convinced us that full reliance on numerical flexibility often does not work. Allowing some functional flexibility is definitely needed if supermarket chains commit themselves to minimizing lines for the checkout. Recent demands for improved service may add commercial arguments and put pressure on chains to allow local management more discretion and to stimulate *and* reward the functional flexibility of frontline staff.

Among the case supermarkets—that is, among their parent chains—different strategies could be observed. Supermarket A had no clear policies on customer fluctuation and lines for the checkout. Frontline staff were slow to adapt to the number of customers lining up at checkouts as they opened. If this was inevitable, it was informally settled within cultural peer groups, often without informing store management. Contrary to this case, the store management of supermarket B had clear policies to keep lines short through the flexible opening of new checkouts. If necessary, staff was added from counters and from the ranks of experienced shelf-stackers. Management encouraged functional flexibility practices, although they were neither formalized nor rewarded.

This contrasts with consumer electronics retail, where functional flexibility is well developed, openly practiced, and not an object of much debate. The rewards of flexibility practices for both management and sales clerks are usually clear. These practices offer opportunities to learn in adjoining technical fields. Even in the large stores, A and B, where sales clerks had to function for some time as checkout operators (which could be interpreted as a demotion), they tended to accept such tasks as a simple matter of mutual support. Such attitudes and codes are characteristic of a professional environment. Indeed, next to the fact that electronics retailers are sales-based firms that leave considerable leeway to store managers and salespersons in making decisions about sales, they function to a large degree as professional organizations.

JOB QUALITY

Skill Use, Task Variety, and Autonomy   Breakdowns of job levels in retail reveal that in 2005 a majority of employees worked at the two lowest levels: 54 percent of the men and even 72 percent of the women. Moreover, from 1996 until 2005, the average job level in retail fell. The official statistics that enable a comparison of job level and educational level suggest a growing underutilization of workers with completed secondary and higher education—in 2005, 62 percent of the sample. In that year, 57 percent of those with secondary education worked at levels 1 and 2 (national average: 27 percent), and 33 percent of those with completed higher education (national average: 5 percent) (author's calculations from CBS/Statline). We assume that most of the latter are young people recruited by the supermarkets who kept their jobs because of lack of labor market prospects.

The typical supermarket checkout job has a narrow job profile and scores mainly on the executing tasks of the job description. Except for the small supermarket in our sample, these operators had no preparing tasks, limited supporting tasks (cash control, simple maintenance of cash register), and very limited organizing tasks (contacts with first cashier, participation in workers' consultation). This target job scores low on autonomy, especially in those supermarkets where management has no policies to limit the lines before the checkout stand.

On the other hand, the typical salesperson in consumer electronics retail has a broad job profile, or a "full" job, besides executing tasks (demonstrating, selling, advising) including preparing, supporting, and organizing tasks. The employees interviewed especially valued the direct contacts with suppliers. Although these contacts were sometimes risky and possible sources of tension between colleagues, they allowed sales clerks considerable discretion in pricing and promoting articles and could be the basis for bonuses. Thus, under normal conditions workers in this target job enjoyed considerable autonomy.

Work Pressure, Health, and Safety   In supermarkets, limited task variety and autonomy do have consequences for employees' workload and work stress levels. This was already convincingly demonstrated in the early 1990s when union-initiated research compared the workload and work stress of supermarket checkout operators and department store cashiers. The latter were in jobs with a broader function, usually including showing merchandise. The outcomes were in line with expectations. Workloads and stress were consistently worse for the first group, who experienced significantly higher levels of headaches, tiredness, and other symptoms of work-related stress. The researchers advocated organizational development, job enrichment, and changes in the checkout equipment formation (Meerman and Huppes 1993). Since then, in nearly all supermarkets standard checkout equipment has been improved ergonomically, although modern equipment does not prevent ergonomic problems and RSI (repetitive strain injury) risks per se. Modern equipment divides the weight of heavy loads more evenly, but the loads that a checkout operator has to manipulate remain high, most likely up to three to five hundred kilograms per hour. Thus, task variety, job rotation, and regular pauses continue to be important for the job quality of checkout operators.

In supermarkets A and C, checkout operators pointed to customer harassment as contributing considerably to work pressure. In case A, harassment was explicitly linked with long lines, but not in case C; there complaints included customers reacting with irritation on the self-scanning equipment. In this store the orientation of this chain toward a high level of process innovation was not supported by policies of training and supporting staff in adopting new technology.

In the 2003 Dutch Survey on Working Conditions, workers in supermarkets and department stores, asked whether they *always* felt work pressure, scored just below the national average (Smulders and van den Bossche 2004, 5). Our case experiences suggest that work pressure for checkout operators is more a matter of "often" or "sometimes," that is, that pressure is greatest during peak hours and when there are long lines. Our cases also indicate an interesting positive relationship between higher service levels and improved job quality: shorter lines tend to diminish work pressure and work-related stress. Our focus groups emphasized that checkout operators are motivated by direct customer contacts, which are eased by short lines.

We gathered from our consumer electronics cases that the work pressure felt by salespersons is normally "sound" and challenging. In some situations, work pressure can become more structural and lead to work stress. Our interviewees suggested that this was the case when suppliers launched new products and product knowledge in sales initially proved to be insufficient. In that event, the high autonomy of salespersons may turn into a disadvantage. Other complaints were related to customer harassment (notably in cases A and D) and frequent shop theft (case D). In case D (the smallest store), the employees interviewed regarded the total of the various constraints a serious threat to their well-being.

Working Time

In retail the working time issue is nearly always closely related to work organization and staffing strategies. A recurrent worker complaint in the supermarkets is that of unilateral employer decisions concerning working times and days off, low staffing levels, and employers who do not pay according to hours worked. Union officers and laypeople get a lot of complaints about violations of the strict terms of notice for changes in working hours laid down in the CLAs. In all four supermarket cases, we heard complaints about working times and hours worked, about the inflexibility of the store management with respect to personal wishes concerning working hours (case A), about late notice concerning requested changes of working hours (cases C and D), and, most common, about not being paid according to hours worked (cases B, C, and D). Obviously, curtailing the payment of all worked hours is a widespread practice among store managers that helps them to live up to the benchmarks set by headquarters.

In the consumer electronics cases, the complaints most frequently registered were about working at unsocial hours (cases B, C, and D). In two cases, such practices seemed to be perceived merely as a disadvantage linked to being employed as sales clerk, but in case D complaints had a more serious undertone and were obviously connected with understaffing.

WAGES AND COMPENSATIONS

The typical larger supermarkets show five job levels and four hierarchical levels—if a formal hierarchy is absent between shelf-stackers and checkout operators:

- Shelf-stacker/prospective checkout operator/sales assistant (A)

- Checkout operator/sales assistant (B)

- Assistant department manager/first checkout operator (C)

- Assistant store manager/department manager (D, E, F)

- Store manager (F, G, H, I)

The actual wage scales in the supermarket CLAs can be characterized as follows:

- In the A to D range, large overlaps and rather minor differences between the wage levels

- Short scales and thus low seniority rights: scales contain a maximum of five yearly steps

- The youth scale A wage at age fifteen starts 22 percent above the youth SMW level

- The adult scale A wage starts 16 percent above the SMW level, but 13 percent under our low-wage threshold; these wages will reach the threshold after four annual steps, and those in B (checkout operators, sales assistants) after the first yearly step

The WageIndicator data deliver mean adult wages in the three occupations of €11.28 (US$16.59) for checkout operators, €11.11 (US$16.34) for sales assistants, and €11.21 (US$16.49) for shop assistants and shelf-stackers. These wages are 6 percent above the average of the CLA scales A and B. The gap between these scales and the wages reported through the WageIndicator is much larger for fifteen- to twenty-two-year-olds: 15 to 20 percent above the age levels of scale A. Yet the reported hourly wages of twenty-one- to twenty-four-year-olds is only 2 to 8 percent above the respective scale A levels. These outcomes confirm that the supermarket chains are mainly interested in employing the youngest youths in the target jobs. In particular, the labor market position of twenty-one- to twenty-four-year-olds is weak.

The scales in the CLA for the electro-technical retail trade are astonishingly low; only the end wages in steps 7 and 8 of scale E and those in steps 6 through 9 of scale F exceed the low-wage threshold. Yet, based on WageIndicator data for 2004 to 2006, the mean adult hourly wage in consumer electronics retail was €13.61 (US$20.02) (level 2006)—37 percent above the CLA scales. In this respect, the 20 to 35 percent gap between actual and CLA wages that we found in the four case stores is even rather modest. Moreover, we must take into account that on top of this last figure salespersons in larger electronics stores often receive a combination of individual and group-based performance pay and compensations for working overtime and unusual hours. In the two cases in which we received indications of the amount of bonuses and compensations, these varied from 10 to 35 percent of basic wages. This may mean that a substantial group of salespersons earn, including all compensations, €15 to €19 (US$22 to US$28) hourly. We estimate that less than 20 percent of the consumer electronics retail workforce is actually paid below the low-pay threshold. Of course, the existence of such low CLA scales is intriguing, also because they remain the basis for unemployment benefits. Most likely they stem from some decades ago, when small, rather ailing local stores dominated the electronics retail subsector. Obviously, unions have not yet been able to translate the arrival of large firms into higher guaranteed wages. For FNV Bondgenoten, the lack of "critical mass" seems to play a role. The position of what is a small subsector in a large, amalgamated union may have led to a certain neglect.

RECRUITMENT, TRAINING, AND CAREERING

In the case supermarkets, labor turnover in the target job varied between 20 and 35 percent annually. This is rather low, considering that since the mid-1990s the national figure has been about 40 percent (Dribbusch 2003, 64; HBD 2004a). Although recruitment and training were very demanding activities for store managers, they seemed to regard high churning rates as merely "a fact of supermarket life," the exception being case A. Here, in a supermarket in the low-cost, no-frills segment, an interesting link had been developed between recruitment and training which particularly seemed to benefit migrant workers.

The only labor supply sources for supermarket A were young people and older women, both of migrant origin. The store manager had doubts about the qualifications of most applicants and added that there were problems with labor morale. In the past, traditional recruitment procedures had led to high rejection rates. For a few years, however, in-company training had been part of the recruitment procedure, and this had worked as a rather efficient screening device. Moreover, the newcomers felt that they were given special attention and were tied to the firm.

After the extremely tight labor market for retail jobs of 2001–2002, supermarkets in the Randstad conurbation continued to be confronted with persistent labor shortages, especially if their geographical location vis-à-vis their labor supply was unfavorable. Employees with small part-time jobs clearly favor short commuting times and may judge a one-way trip of thirty minutes to be too long. Against this backdrop, local unemployment rates do not give good indications of the labor market position of supermarket checkout operator jobs. Our case studies suggest that in the Randstad cities the reservoir of young people is near exhaustion, certainly for evening work. Characteristically, headquarters' human resource departments—maybe with the exception of chain A—did not show much interest in these labor supply problems. Again, their responsiveness to external changes was low.

We could not trace career ladders for the target job in the case supermarkets. Promotion opportunities were few, and recent efforts to eliminate the assistant store manager or department manager level had diminished these opportunities even more. We did not find any women at the level of assistant store manager or higher in the case stores. This fits the general picture: experienced women, acting as first checkout operators, hardly get any chances to be promoted to (assistant) store manager—certainly not if they are working part-time. Generally, the lack of policies toward upgrading incumbent staff skills is striking. All four supermarkets had apprenticeship posts, covering 3 to 6 percent of the workforce, but except in case A, supervising the apprentices was done rather haphazardly.

Training facilities in consumer electronics retail are substantial and are often linked with suppliers' training offers to keep product knowledge up-to-date. The employers' association already in 2004 worried about a lack of supply of higher-qualified specialists. Yet a survey on staffing needs did not reveal many worries among their constituency (HBD 2004b). Our case findings confirm this rather careless attitude; only case A managers envisaged serious labor shortages in the near future, notably for senior salespersons.

CONCLUSIONS

The supermarket price war in particular has been a catalyst for developments already under way, developments that may worry retail employees and their representatives. Under the pressure of the prevailing low-road market strategies, human resource managers have predominantly chosen low-road policy options, and efforts to take "high roads" in human resource management and work organization have been close to invisible. Retailers' development of management tools based on supply-chain management puts the brakes on efforts to address the low-road job quality for checkout operators in particular—even though some of them are revising the low-road market orientation. Without suggesting too rosy a picture, we can say that consumer electronics retailing nevertheless functions as a convincing contrast, not least because that retail branch is sales-based and knowledgeable salespersons are regarded as valuable assets. Yet especially in smaller outlets, various factors sometimes lead to high levels of work-related stress among the staff, and human resource management of the chains does not always seem to be aware of such dangers.

Working time and scheduling issues stood out prominently in workplace relations in the supermarkets. Store managers tried to live up to headquarters' benchmarks by curtailing paid working hours. Recurrent complaints among staff were about employer decisions concerning working times and days off, low staffing levels, and being paid for fewer hours than were actually worked. In consumer electronics retail, the working time issue was much less prominent, partly because of the lower share of part-timers in this retail branch, partly because of the higher wage levels, and partly because of the compensations paid for working overtime and unusual hours.

In the short run, the local labor market situation is marked by more than contrasting high-road/low-road strategies; the tight versus soft labor market contrast is also relevant for variations in job quality, at least with regard to training opportunities but also with respect to (informal) shop-floor cooperation patterns. Here causal relationships may well be contrary to those assumed. Because of their labor market position, supermarkets in the low-cost segment may feel forced to offer jobs linked to training. Human resource management of the former high-end supermarket chains may well be reacting rather lazily here. They seem to opt for firm strategies that bet on the dissemination of labor-saving technology.

The most striking aspect of the retail story is the relative absence of Dutch labor relations institutions. In the supermarket subsector, these institutions, including the Industry Board, have hardly made a move to counteract the low-road trend, although the board does signal labor market problems. It will be highly interesting to follow the subsectors under investigation when the economy keeps on recovering and labor markets are tightening further. Will the reservoir of checkout operators and shelf-stackers, for hire at the present terms of employment, be exhausted? Are employers right in gambling on technological solutions? If these solutions do not result in much lower employment levels, then growing and more quality-oriented consumer spending and labor shortages may offer employees, unions, works councils, and industry training institutions opportunities to break through the dominant low-road human resource orientation and the poor job quality related to it. Naturally, in the supermarket subsector such opportunities are likely to be accompanied by a struggle with major firms over their strategies based on supply-chain management.

NOTES

1. Author's calculations, based on interviews with union officials, case study evidence, and WageIndicator textboxes, September 2004 to September 2006.
2. This was about the same as in Danish retail, slightly higher than in the United Kingdom, but substantially higher than in France and Germany.
3. Yet, because of the very high part-time share in the Netherlands the value-added per hour worked is a better indicator. In 2004, the value-added per hour in Dutch retail, recalculated in U.S. dollars, was 8 to 10 percent below that in Germany, the United Kingdom, and the United States, and 25 percent below that of France (EU KLEMS 2007).
4. Conclusions drawn from the trade press as well as from study visits of the author, Anja van de Westelaken (STZ), and Dorothea Voss-Dahm (IAT) in the summer of 2005 to the Metro Group Future Store in Rheinberg and Metro's Innovation Center in Neuss (both in Germany).

REFERENCES

Abernathy, Frederick H., John T. Dunlop, Janice H. Hammond, and David Weil. 2000. "Retailing and Supply Chains in the Information Age." *Technology in Society* 22(1): 5.

Bailey, Thomas R., and Annette D. Bernhardt. 1997. "In Search of the High Road in a Low-Wage Industry." *Politics and Society* 25(2): 179–201.

Bernhardt, Annette. 1999. "The Future of Low-Wage Jobs: Case Studies in the Retail Industry." Working paper 10. New York: IEE (March).

Commissie Gelijke Behandeling (CGB). 2006. *Advies Commissie Gelijke Behandeling inzake Leeftijdsonderscheid in de supermarktbranche "Te Jong Te Oud" op verzoek van de CNV-Jongerenorganisatie* [Recommendation of the Equal Treatment Committee Regarding Age Discrimination in the Supermarket Branch: "Too Old, Too Young," at the Request of the CNV Youth Organization]. The Hague: CGB.

Creusen, Harold, Björn Vroomen, Henry van der Wiel, and Fred Kuypers. 2006. *Dutch Retail Trade on the Rise? Relation Between Competition, Innovation, and Productivity.* The Hague: CPB.

Dribbusch, Heiner. 2003. *Gewerkschaftliche Mitgliedergewinnung im Dienstleistungssektor. Ein Drei-Laender-Vergleich im Einzelhandel* [Union Recruitment in the Service Sector: A Three-Country Comparison in Retail]. Berlin: Editions Sigma.

Evers, David, Anton van Hoorn, and Frank van Oort. 2005. *Winkelen in Megaland* [Shopping in Megaland]. Rotterdam/The Hague: NAi Uitgevers/Ruimtelijk Planbureau.

EU KLEMS. 2007. *EU KLEMS Growth and Productivity Accounts.* March 2007. Accessed at http://www.euklems.net.

Groningen Growth and Development Center. 2006. *60-Industry Database.* Accessed at http://www.ggdc.net/index-dseries.html.

Hoofdbedrijfschap Detailhandel (HBD, Industry Board for Retail). 2004a. *Branches in detail 2004. Supermarkten* [Branches in Detail 2004. Supermarket]. Accessed at http://www.hbd.nl.

———. 2004b. *Brancherapportage detailhandel* [Retail Branch Report]. Accessed at http://www.hbd.nl.

———. 2005a. *Arbeidsmarkt in de detailhandel 2005* [Retail Labor Market]. Accessed at http://www.hbd.nl.

———. 2005b. *Branches in detail 2005. Supermarkten* [Branches in Detail 2005. Supermarket]. Accessed at http://www.hbd.nl.

———. 2005c. *Branches in detail 2005. Wit-, Bruin- en Grijsgoedzaken* [Branches in Detail 2005. Consumer Electronics Stores]. Accessed at http://www.hbd.nl.

———. 2005d. *Bestedingen en marktaandelen 2004* [Spending and Market Shares 2004]. Accessed at http://www.hbd.nl.

————. 2005e. *Verantwoordingsverslag 2004* [*Accountability Report 2004*]. Accessed at http://www.hbd.nl.

Horbeek, Henricus J. 2003. *De buigzame werkvloer. De implementatie van interne flexibiliseringsmaatregelen nader beschouwd* [*The Flexible Shop-Floor: Implementation of Internal Flexibility Measures Reconsidered*]. Rotterdam: Tinbergen Institute.

Kenniscentrum Handel. 2004. *Arbeidsmarkt en beroepsopleidingen in de sector handel 2004* [*Labor Market and Vocational Education in the Commercial Sector in 2004*]. Ede, Netherlands: Kenniscentrum Handel.

Kirsch, Johannes, Martina Klein, Steffen Lehndorff, and Dorothea Voss-Dahm. 1999. *"Darf's etwas weniger sein?" Arbeitszeiten und Beschaeftigungsbedingungen im Lebensmitteleinzelhandel. Ein europaeischer Vergleich* [*"Can I Have a Little Bit Less, Please?": Working Hours and Employment Conditions in the Food Retail Sector: A European Comparison*]. Berlin: Editions Sigma.

Meerman, Martha, and Gjalt Huppes. 1993. *Werk aan de winkel* [*Shop Work to Be Done*]. Leyden, Netherlands: Wetenschapswinkel Leiden.

Organization for Economic Cooperation and Development (OECD). 2006. *OECD Economic Surveys: Netherlands*, vol. 2006/2. Paris: OECD.

Salverda, Wiemer, Joachim Moeller, and Michel Sollogoub. 2005. "Retail Employment and Wage Rigidities." In *Low-Wage Employment in Europe*, edited by Ive Marx and Wiemer Salverda. Leuven and Voorburg, Netherlands: Acco.

Smulders, Peter, and Seth van den Bossche. 2004. *Nationale enquete Arbeidsomstandigheden 2003* [*2003 National Working Conditions Survey*]. Hoofddorp, Netherlands: TNO.

Tijdens, Kea G. 1998. *Zeggenschap over arbeidstijden. De samenhang tussen bedrijfstijden, arbeidstijden en flexibilisering van de personeelsbezetting* [*Authority over Working Hours: The Interaction Between Office Hours, Working Hours, and Flexibilization of Personnel Scheduling*]. Amsterdam: Welboom.

Van den Tillaart, Harry, and Jan Doesborgh. 2004. *Demografie etnisch ondernemerschap in de detailhandel* [*Demography of Ethnic Entrepreneurship in Retail*]. The Hague: HBD.

Van Klaveren, Maarten, and Kea Tijdens. 2005. *Youngsters in the Supermarket*. Amsterdam: AIAS/UvA.

Voss-Dahm, Dorothea. 2005. "Institutions, Firms' Strategies, and Job Quality in the German Retail Sector." Unpublished paper. Gelsenkirchen, Germany: IAT.

Voss-Dahm, Dorothea, and Steffen Lehndorff. 2003. *Lust und Frust im moderner Verkaufsarbeit: Beschaeftigungs- und Arbeitszeittrends im Einzelhandel* [*Lust and Frustration in Modern Sale: Employment and Working Hours Trends in Retail*]. Gelsenkirchen, Germany: IAT.

CHAPTER 6

Hotels: Industry Restructuring and Room Attendants' Jobs

Ria Hermanussen

In the last decade, the character and structure of the Dutch hotel industry have been quickly transformed. The small-scale, independent family hotel with one or two stars is gradually disappearing, and three- and four-star hotels are taking its place.[1] New forms of cooperation and ownership have evolved, and the influence of foreign corporate chains has increased. These changes deeply affect work organization and job quality in hotels.

The hotel industry is part of the hospitality industry (hotels, restaurants, cafés) and employs approximately 73,000 persons. Hospitality is a labor-intensive industry—one-quarter of each euro in sales goes into wages—with a high share of low-skilled and unskilled jobs. The mean female wages are the lowest of all industries, and male wages are second lowest after retail. Moreover, hospitality jobs offer the least job and income security and are likely to expose workers to health risks. In the hospitality industry, those in our target group, hotel room attendants, belong to the group of low-paid and flexible workers. According to our case studies, room attendants, who are responsible for making beds and cleaning rooms, make up 25 to 30 percent of total hotel staff, depending on the type of hotel (for example, with or without a restaurant). Flexibilization and cost-saving firm strategies recently have had a great impact on their jobs, including the increasingly common strategy of outsourcing cleaning work to external cleaning companies. Nearly all room attendants, regardless of whether they are employed by a hotel or by a cleaning company, earn hourly wages below our low-wage threshold; only the wages of some of those workers with long tenure cross the threshold.

THE METHODOLOGY

Our research design featured eight hotel case studies and interviews and focus groups with room attendants, general managers and executive housekeepers, and, in some cases, human resource managers and works councilors. Interviews were held with a total of forty-nine persons.

Two main factors influenced the selection of case studies. First, we selected hotels that allowed comparisons between hotels in the capital, Amsterdam, and provincial hotels in medium-sized cities in the south of the Netherlands. The Amsterdam hotel industry differs from that in the rest of the country in several ways. First, Amsterdam's much higher hotel density leads to a higher demand for hotel staff. Second, in Amsterdam the labor supply for hotel cleaning jobs mainly consists of migrant women, whereas in other parts of the country it is mostly native women who apply for these jobs. Third, organizational demands between Amsterdam and southern hotels vary as well. Amsterdam is connected to different types of tourist and visitor markets: 87 percent of tourists in Amsterdam come from abroad, against 47 percent in hotels outside the capital. Amsterdam visitors travel more often in groups, and because their arrival and departure times are randomly scattered over day and night, Amsterdam hotels need around-the-clock room cleaning services. Room cleaning in hotels in the south, with more predictable check-in and check-out times, needs to be done before new guests arrive early in the afternoon. The latter hotels offer part-time jobs for a few hours a day, while many Amsterdam hotels want their room attendants to be available for at least six hours a day.

The second selection criterion concerned the outsourcing of room cleaning, a rapidly growing strategy that has a great impact on job quality for room attendants. According to an internal study of the Dutch Executive Housekeepers Association in 2004, 48 percent of hotels had outsourced room cleaning, and an inventory of twenty-four four- and five-star hotels revealed that they outsourced more than half of all cleaning work totally or partly (Executive Housekeepers Association 2004). Five out of the eight selected hotels had also outsourced room cleaning totally or partly. Because of the relevance of outsourcing for the job quality of room attendants, we also interviewed the management of two specialized hotel cleaning companies.

In selecting the hotel cases, we contrasted the middle- and high-level four- and five-star hotels with budget hotels in the two- and three-star classes. Also, we selected a mix of chain and independent hotels, assuming differences in business and management strategies between the two groups. We did not include unqualified hotels or one-star hotels, since doing so would not have added much information. Although still large in numbers, this segment mainly consists of small-scale family hotels with no employees or only very few employees.

Table 6.1 provides an overview of the selected hotels and their characteristics.

THE ECONOMIC AND INSTITUTIONAL CONTEXT

RESTRUCTURING, INTERNATIONALIZATION, AND STANDARDIZATION

For quite some years, the total number of hotels in the Netherlands has been stable, fluctuating around 2,900. Approximately 2,300 have been classified as a star hotel.[2] Dutch hotels vary widely, from modest budget hotels aimed at budget tourists to luxurious hotels aimed at business travelers and conference or training course participants. The international business market is concentrated in Amsterdam and around Schiphol Airport.

In the past decade, the industry has faced major structural changes, as can be seen in table 6.2. First, a major scaling up took place: from 1994 to 2004, beds and rooms were upgraded and their numbers increased, by 22 and 23 percent, respectively. The average number of beds per hotel grew from fifty-five in 1994 to sixty-nine in 2004, while the number of three- and four-star hotels increased and those of their one- and two-star competitors decreased. Hotel capacity largely expanded in Amsterdam and its surroundings, whereas capacity in the south hardly grew.

Chain formation and internationalization deeply affected the industry as well. In early 2004, one out of five Dutch hotels was part of a corporate chain (see table 6.3). The five largest hotel chains, three with a foreign owner, now own about 30 percent of all rooms. These changes in hotel ownership gave rise to new organizational and management concepts, such as franchising, management contracts, and sale and lease-back constructions.

Chain formation encouraged the standardization of hotel products. Branding—developing a recognizable brand for client groups— is increasingly essential in hotels' communication and marketing

Table 6.1 The Case Study Hotels

	Hotel A	Hotel B	Hotel C	Hotel D	Hotel E	Hotel F	Hotel G	Hotel H
Ownership	International chain	International chain	Inde-pendent	International chain	Inde-pendent	Inde-pendent	International chain	International chain
Stars	4	2–3	3–4	5	4	3	5	3
Region	Province	Province	Province	Capital	Province	Capital	Capital	Capital
Hotel workforce	36.5	17[a]	33[a]	ca. 89[b]		25	ca. 150[c]	32[a]
Number of rooms	92	150	192	270	72	79	270	180
Occupancy rate (2004)	72,0	53,6	57	85	90?	74	90?	78,5
Outsourcing?	No	Yes, RAs and supervisors	Yes, only RAs	Yes, RAs and supervisors	No	No	Yes, 60% of RAs outsourced	Yes, RAs and 90% of supervisors

Source: Author's compilation of case study interviews by researchers.
[a] Head count.
[b] Excluding housekeeping.
[c] Partly excluding housekeeping.

Table 6.2 Key Indicators of the Dutch Hotel Industry,
            1994 to 2004

	1994	2000	2004	Percent Change 1994 to 2004
Number of hotels in the Netherlands	2,895	2,835	2,831	−2.2
Number of hotels in Amsterdam	354	363	373	+5.4
Number of rooms (× 1,000)	77.5	87.6	94.3	+23.3
Number of beds (× 1,000)	159.0	182.1	196.1	+21.7
Hotels by number of stars				
One	511	449	379[a]	−26
Two	661	685	622	−6
Three	654	770	851	+30
Four	229	315	337	+47
Five	29	31	31	+7

Source: Bedrijfschap Horeca en Catering (BH&C) (2004a, 2006a).
[a] Figures for 2003.

strategies. Hotel chains are presenting their own concepts with the goal of distinguishing their chain from others with regard to sphere, service, style, and price.

Internationalization and chain-bound standardization have caused reactions. More and more hotels are creating a distinct profile by offering services related to specific themes or specific client groups (Ernst & Young 2004). The aging of the population and cutbacks in health care are expected to support the growing number of care and wellness hotels, leading to the further diversification of the industry. This group of unique, so-called boutique hotels also feels a strong

Table 6.3 The Top Five Hotel Chains, the Netherlands,
            2003

	Number of Rooms	Number of Hotels	Average Number of Rooms per Hotel
Accor (French)	7,124	51	140
Golden Tulip (Dutch)	5,423	65	83
NH-Hoteles (Spanish)	5,349	28	191
Van der Valk (Dutch)	5,327	49	109
Best Western (U.S.)	3,547	50	71

Source: Bedrijfschap Horeca en Catering (BH&C) (2004a).

push to cooperate, owing to high risks, the need to invest in new technologies (such as wifi), the shortening life cycle of products and concepts, and the growing government regulation of environmental and hygiene issues as well as working conditions. Today the hotel industry ranges from hotels that are part of large (international) hotel chains, with access to financial and customer markets, knowledge, and professional management, to a group of small and medium-sized hotels with less knowledge and fewer resources at their disposal. The latter group may be more vulnerable but also more innovative in adapting to changing consumer preferences (Reintjes 2005).

Industry Performance

The hotel industry, which generated sales of about €3.1 billion (including VAT) (US$4.5 billion) in 2005, is relatively small, with a share of less than 1 percent of GNP. More than half of its sales stem from room selling; the remainder stems from selling food and beverages (F&B) as well as renting conference rooms and meeting halls (BH&C 2005b). The sales patterns of hotels are very unstable: demand for hotel services can fluctuate yearly and even weekly. For example, in the third quarter of the year room occupancies almost double compared to the first (BH&C 2005b). Moreover, both prices and occupancy rates are vulnerable to the business cycle. Finally, recent disasters have underlined the industry's vulnerability. Hotels in the higher segment faced rapidly decreasing occupancy rates after the terrorist attacks in New York, Washington, Madrid, and London. Changes in lifestyle, the increased transparency of hotel prices due to the Internet, and the growing supply of cheap flights all play a role in the decisions of business travelers and tourists about where to go, how long to stay, how much to pay, and so on.

The net margins of hotels fluctuate even more than sales. A substantial part of costs are fixed and not easily adaptable to changes in demand for hotel rooms. In 1993 and 2003, years that were particularly difficult for the hotel industry, both occupancy rates and average room prices fell substantially. In both years the decline was intensified by an oversupply of beds and rooms, and the result was dumping, sharpened competition, and lower profits. In 1993 the average occupancy rate of the three-, four-, and five-star hotels dropped to an all-time low of 58 percent, and in 2003 to 65 percent, with a slight recovery to 67 percent in 2004. Yet in that last year the average room

Table 6.4 Three-, Four-, and Five-Star Hotels in the
Netherlands, 2000 to 2004

	2000	2001	2002	2003	2004
Occupancy rate	76.4%	71.7%	70.9%	65.3%	66.7%
Average room price	€104	€106	€114	€102	€98
RevPar (yield per available room)	48.3	49.0	42.2	38.9	38.4

Source: Hoogendoorn and van Bruggen (2005).

price and the RevPar (yield per available room) continued to fall
(Hoogendoorn and van Bruggen 2005). Moreover, the hotel industry
recently experienced an increase in exploitation costs. Especially in
Amsterdam, with its tight labor market, the average payroll expenses
per room employee grew in 2004 by over 10 percent. Energy prices
and the costs of maintenance, publicity, insurances, taxes, and food
safety increased too (BH&C 2004a) (see table 6.4). A large part of
these costs are independent of sales, causing a nearly fatal combination of higher costs, falling occupancy rates and falling room prices,
certainly for the small, independent hotels (Hoogendoorn and van
Bruggen 2005).

INNOVATION

Hotels' need to protect themselves against the effects of decreasing
room prices, rising costs, and sales fluctuations has been an important stimulus for innovation. Hotel firms have followed the combined
strategy of increasing sales and cutting costs. They have joined forces
through international cooperation to invest in scaling up and standardization or specialization. In fact, the hotel industry is generally
seen as the most innovative part of the hospitality sector (BH&C
2005c). Also innovative is hotels' investments in IT applications,
which have led to online booking and yield management. A manager
in an Amsterdam hotel chain said:

The strategy of the chain strongly targets cost saving. Due to scaling
up and cooperation—for example, concerning joint purchase and distribution—cost advantages can be gained. The same is true for joint
innovation. At the chain level, a special task group now is developing

a new restaurant and breakfast concept, covering all aspects, from food to styling and organization. Once this new concept is accepted, all hotels belonging to the same brand are obliged to implement the new concept.

COST-SAVING METHODS

The tight labor market conditions of 2001–2002 gave rise to substantial wage increases in 2003. At the same time, the industry faced high labor turnover and sick leave rates that put the profitability of the industry under pressure, especially when occupancy rates fell after 2002 (BH&C 2005a; Hoogendoorn and van Bruggen 2005; Vos 2005). At the beginning of the 2003 recession, hotels aimed to retain staff, fearing that labor shortages would return if the economy started booming again. As the recession continued, however, hotels considered it impossible to maintain staff levels; dismissals followed, vacancies were not filled, and fixed-term contracts were not renewed. When in 2004 the industry recovered, newcomers were engaged at lower wage levels. The hotel workforce increasingly became composed of flexible staff, including a shift from full-timers to part-timers (BH&C 2004b). Recently, staff optimization in relation to the number of guests became a major employer strategy to improve labor productivity. The advance of software programs enables hotels to improve the predictability of guest volumes and thus they are able to refine capacity planning and staff scheduling. The availability of refined-for-capacity planning techniques was an important impetus for hotel management to consider outsourcing room cleaning to professional cleaning companies.

EMPLOYMENT AND CAREER DEVELOPMENT

In 2005, 255,500 persons (140,400 FTEs) were employed in the hospitality industry (CBS/Statline), of which 73,000 (28.5 percent) worked in hotels (BH&C 2005b, based on Uitvoering Werknemers Verzekeringen [UWV] insurance figures). Between now and 2010, hotel employment is expected to increase by 7,000 to 10,000, growth that, together with replacement of staff, may lead to 17,300 to 24,700 vacancies (BH&C 2006b).

In an average hotel, the internal labor market is strongly segmented, and staff can be divided into three categories. First, 30 per-

cent make up a primary segment with a hospitality-oriented education at the medium or high level; this segment includes managers and
skilled employees in line occupations (reception, kitchen, housekeeping) and overhead occupations (control, marketing, human resource management). Second, those in a low or uneducated group
hold the hotel job as their primary job, including some who have
completed low-level vocational training for kitchen or service jobs.
Others, working in room cleaning or linen rooms, have no specific
education. This second group of so-called primary job-holders
amounts to about 40 percent of total staff. The third group (30 percent), is predominantly made up of young people and women, consists of second-job-holders, and is mainly used to enlarge numerical
flexibility. This third group mostly works part-time on fixed-term
contracts (BH&C 2006c; Bispo 2005).

Opportunities for internal training and career development mostly
apply to the primary segment. Those with a first job do have, compared to second-job-holders, more job security and (owing to long
tenures) higher hourly wages. Yet as far as job content and career perspectives are concerned, their position is close to that of the second-
job-holders. Mobility between the low and high segments is quite limited. Horizontal mobility is also limited, and advancement from the
F&B department to reception or housekeeping, or vice versa, hardly
ever occurs. Educational requirements play a role, but lack of the required personality traits and skills appear to hamper mobility too.

THE ROLE OF INSTITUTIONS

Collective Bargaining   Employers in the hospitality industry are better organized than their employees. More than half of the employers
are members of the main employers' association, Koninklijke Horeca
Nederland (KHN), while union density is only 16 percent (CBS/Stat-
line). The limited union influence came to the surface in 2005, when
unions and KHN negotiated the new CLA. The employers were determined to use the negotiations to enlarge their opportunities for
flexible contracts and working hours. The two largest unions, affili-
ates of the FNV and CNV confederations, resisted the employers'
proposals because of what they perceived as a negative impact on job
quality and income security, and they refused to sign the CLA. Yet the
CLA could be approved when the Unie (workers' trade union), representing only five hundred members in hospitality, was prepared to

sign. The negotiation of this CLA has put labor relations in the industry under pressure. As it is now, the CLA is mandatory for KHN members and covers 65 percent of all workers in hospitality, while nonmembers are not obliged to apply the CLA.

The Working Conditions Covenant and the Gatekeeper Improvement Act
In a recent survey, a majority of hospitality workers perceived their job as physically exhausting (68 percent), and many reported high levels of work stress (45 percent) (Bispo 2005; confirmed by van Klaveren and Tijdens 2008). The high workload is considered to be a main reason for high labor turnover. Depending on the business cycle, annual turnover may be over 50 percent, the result either of workers leaving the industry or of job mobility within (BH&C 2004c). Sick leave rates in the hotel industry are comparatively high: 5.1 percent in 2002 against 2.5 percent in hospitality at large (CBS/Statline). Hotel employers were confronted with the effects of these high rates when the Gatekeeper Improvement Act was introduced in 2002 (see chapter 3).

From 2000 to 2004, the employers' associations and the unions in the hospitality industry agreed on a Working Conditions Covenant, which obliged employers to take measures to reduce health and safety risks. Although evaluations have shown that the covenant contributed to some workload reduction (Vaas 2004), national overviews show that the industry's health risks are still among the highest found among Dutch industries (Houtman, Smulders, and van den Bossche 2006; van Klaveren and Tijdens 2008). This corresponds with our finding that the covenant's impact on work organization and job quality for room attendants' jobs remains quite limited. Obviously, the Gatekeeper Improvement Act has had more impact: all hotels questioned were developing active policies to reduce sick leave—in some cases by paying bonuses to workers for not being sick. Besides having a strong impact on hotel staffing policies, the Gatekeeper Improvement Act gave employers another reason to outsource room cleaning.

Future Pressures on Low-Cost Strategies   With high labor turnover and many small flexible jobs, the hospitality industry relies heavily on local labor markets, particularly in a booming economy with increasing numbers of vacancies. It will soon need to redouble its efforts in local labor markets since aging has considerably shrunk the stock of suitable staff since the late 1990s. In addition, as the educational levels of young people keep going up, school-leavers acquire higher ambitions than the hospitality industry, with the limited career possibilities it is able to offer (BH&C 2006a). Strategies aimed at lowering labor costs and achieving numerical flexibility run the risk of alienating young people from the hotel industry, which would then face serious labor shortages again. Whether this happens depends on the availability of low-skilled workers, and there are already indications that in the Amsterdam labor market such availability largely depends on the labor supply from migrant groups. In this respect, regulations that liberalize the labor market and immigration may be crucial.

One Amsterdam hotel chain manager had this to say:

> I am not happy with the current poor CLA. It is presented as a minimum agreement, permitting hotels to improve the terms of employment according to their own wishes and possibilities. Yet the reality is different. The chain has made some improvements in the newest CLA, but these terms of employment still do not meet those in the former CLA.

ROOM ATTENDANTS AND THEIR JOBS

THE BACKGROUNDS OF ROOM ATTENDANTS

The following list indicates the substantial differences by ethnic background, gender, and personal conditions between room attendants who work in the Amsterdam hotels and those in the hotels in the southern part of the country.

Room Attendants in Amsterdam Hotels	Room Attendants in Provincial Hotels
Mainly migrants	Mainly natives
Women, increasingly also men	Only women
Low- or unskilled, sometimes high-skilled	Low-skilled
Mostly breadwinners	(Mostly) no breadwinners, often women re-entrants
High frequency of working weeks of thirty-two hours or more	High frequency of working weeks between sixteen andtwenty-four hours

Working alone	Mostly working in couples or teams
If employed by cleaning companies, piece-rate wages	No evidence of piece-rate wages in cleaning companies

In the Amsterdam hotels, room attendants are primarily migrant workers. Hotels and cleaning companies suggest that few native women in Amsterdam apply to clean rooms because they cannot perform the job, whether because they cannot cope with the heavy workload, they are not flexible enough, or they have problems with drug or alcohol addiction. In contrast, in the south the hotels and cleaning companies prefer native women, whom they judge to be more reliable and neat. Obviously, the Amsterdam labor market is vastly different from that in the south, in part because of different conditions. The lower end of the Amsterdam market includes more migrant women who may or may not have children but who are almost all breadwinners. In the south, the lower end mainly consists of native low-skilled female re-entrants who prefer to hold a job while their children are at school. One of the employers interviewed in the south hired only female room attendants who had no breadwinner responsibilities. Here working weeks of twenty to twenty-five hours fit not only the hotel's organizational needs but the preferences of these women: working more hours would have been too exhausting. Yet a part-time cleaning wage is not sufficient for an independent living.

In Amsterdam more than elsewhere men are prepared to clean rooms. Recently the share of male migrants in the cleaning firms has increased substantially. The director of one of the cleaning companies argued that men are stronger and have lower sickness rates. Particularly in small hotels that lack elevators and have corridors that are too narrow for carts, the cleaning work is quite heavy and men are thought be better suited to it.

Outsourcing

We already pointed to the growth of outsourcing of room cleaning. Job categories that require little or no contact with guests are considered particularly suited for outsourcing (Wagemakers 2003). A 2003 survey showed that only 18 out of 291 hotels (6 percent) did not outsource cleaning tasks. The others outsourced one or more such tasks, such as personnel administration, laundry, automation, security, and cleaning.

Until the late 1990s, hotel cleaning consisted of the small-scale, regional activities of entrepreneurs, usually spin-offs of the hotel industry who were familiar with the industry's quality standards. In the early 2000s, with hotels confronting increasingly tight labor markets, cleaning companies appeared to be suitable partners, and since then outsourcing of room cleaning has boomed. In 2003, when the hotel industry collapsed, employers' main motives for outsourcing changed from filling labor shortages to achieving flexible staffing practices and reducing their risk of sick leave and occupational disability.

The exact number of suppliers of room cleaning services is not known. Apart from two large nationally operating companies that each employ more than 2,000 room attendants, we know of at least three regionally operating, medium-sized firms, each employing 150 to 200 workers. Our interviews suggest that many small-scale companies offer their services at very competitive prices. It is assumed that they often use illegal workers and pay under CLA levels. We were not able to confirm these rumors, although we expect that the market for these companies is not that large and limited to small, low-end hotels. Hotels run a risk of being fined €8,000 (US$11,679) for every illegal worker they employ, and the provisions of the act on chain liability make them responsible for the financial misconduct of subcontracting firms.

It is also not exactly clear how widespread the outsourcing of room cleaning may be: estimates are anywhere from 30 to 50 percent. Outsourcing is more common in business-oriented hotels, since there are greater fluctuations in their occupancy rates than in those of tourist-oriented hotels. Yet hardly any hotel outsources all cleaning activities. Distinguishing room cleaning from the cleaning of corridors, meeting rooms, and the like, most case study hotels preferred to keep the latter in-house. The same held true for supervising and inspection tasks, which were more often kept under direct management control. Hotels wanted to be able to keep control of cleaning quality and realize functional flexibility.

In all the case studies, including the hotel chains, it was local management who was responsible for the decision to outsource or not to outsource room cleaning. The following pros and cons were taken into account:

The costs of outsourcing: Purchasing one cleaning-hour from a cleaning company is more expensive than one hour of in-house cleaning. Some hotels decided therefore to have the fixed part of the cleaning performed by their own staff and the variable part by the cleaning company.

The quality of outsourced cleaning: Hotels assumed that their own staff was more committed, more motivated, and more prepared to be functionally flexible. For some hotels, this quality argument was another reason to keep room cleaning in-house, at least partly, or to re-source room cleaning—as we found in one case.

The estimated efforts of recruiting and retaining cleaning staff: The staffing problems that hotels expected depended partly on the situation with the local labor market and partly on internal staffing policies or previous experiences with hiring room attendants.

"The role of the forewoman is critical," said one hotel chain manager in the south whose analysis embodied all three factors. "She is the team leader. If she is doing a good job and knows how to organize the team, than turnover rates are fine, and in-house cleaning will be a lot cheaper. Yet if the forewoman leaves, there may be the risk of high turnover, high sick leave, and poor job quality. Then you would like to outsource cleaning immediately."

The hotels paid the cleaning companies a fixed tariff per room. Based on the limited information we got, we calculated that cleaning an average room in a three- or four-star hotel took twenty minutes. The hotel was paying the cleaning company €8 to €9 (US$12 to $13) per room. The tariff for cleaning public spaces and extra cleaning work was €16 to €18 (US$23 to $26), although tariffs were not quite comparable: tenders were tailor-made, and tariffs were set by average room size, number of supplies, the hotel's quality standards, the duration of the contract, and so on. According to a manager of a cleaning company, the tariffs that hotels paid per cleaned room had decreased in the past five years by 10 to 20 percent. The large hotel chains in particular had succeeded in putting tariffs under pressure, and fierce competition had forced cleaning companies to accept lower prices.

THE JOB OF THE ROOM ATTENDANT

Over the years, the content of the room attendant job has not changed much. The main tasks are spotlessly cleaning bathrooms

Table 6.5 Organization and Job Structure of the Housekeeping
           Department

	General Director/ Executive Housekeeper	Supervisor/ Forewoman	Room Attendant	Linen Boy
Supervision and control	X		X (self-checking)	
Division of work and control		X	X	
Executive tasks		X (if needed)	X	
Preparation tasks			X (in small hotels in the lower-quality segment)	X

Source: Author's compilation from case study interviews by researchers.

and making beds quickly and neatly (KHN 2005). The size of
the cleaning department workforce, mostly called "housekeeping,"
makes it one of the larger hotel departments—definitely in hotels
with limited restaurant provisions. In our study, hotel managers
stressed the importance of a well-organized and efficient cleaning department. Table 6.5 shows the organization and job structure in the
case study hotels.

All case study hotels used production standards to evaluate the
work of the room attendants, distinguishing productivity from quality standards. Productivity standards referred to the number of rooms
to be cleaned per hour—between 2.3 and 3 rooms per hour, up to
even 4 rooms per hour in one case.[3] Comparison of standards between hotels remains difficult owing to differences in room size,
number of guest supplies, and materials of wall and floor covering.
On average, however, cleaning companies seem to apply higher standards than the hotels. We derived one example of tougher targets
from a five-star hotel that had recently outsourced room cleaning, including the contracts with the room attendants already working for
the hotel. The union had negotiated that the room attendants would
maintain their initial terms of employment for five years. Their target
remained seventeen rooms per day, whereas their new colleagues
were expected to clean nineteen to twenty rooms for a lower hourly
wage; moreover, none of the latter received a permanent contract.

Hotels were aware that higher productivity standards might easily compromise quality standards. Six out of the eight case hotels used clear quality standards for checking the cleanliness and room appearance of the cleaned guest rooms. Chain hotels in particular applied strict standards, using standardized forms that sometimes included up to 120 aspects of a room to inspect. Besides the level of cleanliness, the order and accuracy of the guest supplies was inspected. For example, soap had to be placed in the right corner of the washing basin so as to show the hotel logo. The general rule was that all rooms were inspected before being handed over to the front desk for renting again. Apart from daily inspections, the hotels made random inspections as well, carried out by the hotel manager or by so-called mystery guests.

Health and Safety   With all the bending and lifting involved, making beds and cleaning bathrooms are highly demanding tasks that can especially strain back and neck muscles. In comparison to other industries with a high physical workload, the awareness of health risks in the hotel industry seems rather limited. The cleaning companies in our study gave some attention to the physical workload in introducing newcomers, but they hardly checked compliance with work instructions. Time pressure played a major role. Room attendants reported that the ergonomic instructions they received could hardly be applied in reality: the extra time required was not available.

Most case study hotels reported that they paid attention to the working conditions of room attendants. They increasingly selected lightweight cleaning equipment and environment-friendly cleaning materials. Some hotels also took ergonomic aspects into account when buying new room furnishings, such as higher beds, beds on wheels, or wardrobes fitted to the ceiling. Other hotels removed the heavy spreads and extra cushions on the beds and adapted bathroom supplies in order to diminish the amount of bending and lifting required. One of the international chain hotels even invested in beds with adaptable heights, but other managers we interviewed did not expect this example to be widely imitated, not only because of the extra costs involved but also because these beds did not fit the concept and style of other hotels. The hotel manager of a four-star design hotel stated: "Only commercial reasons justify high bed investments. Ergonomic reasons don't count." Obviously health and safety at work was not an issue to be discussed in contract negotiations between the hotels and cleaning companies. According to a cleaning company director: "Everyone must take one's own responsibility, and the occurrence of dangerous situations in hotels is limited, so we take the risk."

Besides the physical burdens of cleaning hotel rooms, room attendants and housekeeping management both point to the increasing mental workload. Many room attendants perceive their job as stressful, primarily because of the high cleaning standards. Very dirty rooms disturb their work rhythms and hamper their ability to reach the standards. At this point we found hotel (service) quality and job quality to be negatively correlated. Quality levels are higher in five-star hotels, making cleaning on average more stressful than in a three-star hotel. Moreover, five-star hotels have equipped their rooms with the highest number of guest supplies, a practice that also contributes to the high mental workload that room attendants' experience.

Job Latitude and Autonomy   The Amsterdam hotels differed significantly from the southern hotels with respect to the organization of room cleaning. In the four Amsterdam hotels, the room attendants worked alone and their performance was individually monitored. In the four southern hotels, in contrast, room cleaning was done two by two or even in teams of three. Only hotel characteristics, such as size, whether the hotel is a chain or independent, and star category, could not sufficiently explain these differences. Personnel characteristics, such as the different ethnic backgrounds of room attendants and communication and cooperation difficulties because of different languages, were likely to play a role as well. A housekeeping executive of an Amsterdam hotel argued that working alone was best suited to the hotel culture, which stressed individual performance. If a room attendant did not meet the quality and productivity standards, this was discussed immediately and later on again in the job evaluation interviews. Managers in the southern hotels explained that teamwork was a way to relieve room attendants' workloads. Teamwork allowed more opportunities for mutual help in making beds and for rotating tasks. In fact, these managers suggested, working two by two led to the best division of labor and the most efficient work order.

Job latitude and the task variety of room attendants remain very limited. Even if functional flexibility is applied, it mostly just broadens room cleaning to include other cleaning tasks, such as cleaning corridors and meeting rooms. The influence of room attendants on their work sequence depends on the instructions of the hotel management. Some hotels leave the room attendant free to organize the work herself, but others demand that work be done in a certain order, legitimizing this demand with hygienic and efficiency arguments. One of the case hotels was developing a detailed prescription of the cleaning sequence; the aim of consistently performing all the steps in the required order was to guarantee high cleaning quality and, in the long run, make it possible for the supervisor to spend fewer hours overseeing the work. The high production standards left no room for slowing down the work pace or for taking short breaks, except those scheduled for coffee and lunch.

Working Hours and Contracts   As explained before, we found much variety between hotels with regard to the duration of the working day. Three out of the four hotels in Amsterdam offered room attendants long shifts of seven or eight hours per day. In the remaining hotels, certainly those in the southern provinces, where guests' arrivals and departures were more predictable, room cleaning could best be done in morning shifts of four to five hours.

Room attendants are increasingly given flexible mini-contracts of zero, two, or four hours a week. They may still work as many average hours per week, however, as a room attendant with a permanent contract for twenty-eight or thirty-two hours. Yet if occupancy rates fall, the flexible workers will be the first to be pressed to work fewer hours. Nevertheless, employers do not need flexible working arrangements per se to make more flexible adjustments to shifting occupancy rates. Hotel management's need for more numerical flexibility can be fulfilled with (large) part-time jobs as well, as two hotels in the study showed. The head of housekeeping in a five-star hotel said:

> Our need for flexibility is fulfilled, as we offer contracts for four days per week, between 8 o'clock in the morning and 3 o'clock in the afternoon. In case of extra guests, room attendants are expected to be flexibly available. At the start, they get a temporary contract for one year. Then they get a permanent contract, provided that the productivity and quality of the work is sufficient. Due to the fact that we offer permanent contracts for thirty to thirty-four hours a week, we actually have a waiting list of room attendants that like to come and work with us.

Wages and Benefits   In all the case studies, room attendants were covered by a CLA. Hotels apply the CLA for the hospitality industry; cleaning companies apply the cleaning CLA. Table 6.6 compares the two kinds of CLA. The average hourly wages of room attendants, whether their contract is with a hotel or a cleaning firm, are below the low-wage threshold. The table makes clear that the implementation of the new hospitality CLA in 2005 seriously worsened wages and job security for room attendants. Only after a minimum period of four years is a worker entitled to a basic wage at grade 3; until then, payment is based on the SMW. Under the old CLA, this waiting period was two years, suggesting that many newcomers experienced a wage decrease. The deterioration of job security is also evident: employers are now entitled to offer fixed-term contracts for a five-year period, whereas under the former CLA the period was three years.

From the perspective of room attendants, the differences between the two CLAs are not that large. When the new CLA for the hospitality industry came into force in 2005, the CLA for the cleaning industry even seemed to offer better terms of employment, since allowances for irregular working times could lead to a higher hourly wage. The prospects for getting a permanent job were better too. Yet this picture is too rosy compared to daily practice: cleaning companies seem to comply with the CLA less than hotels do. In Amsterdam we found examples of cleaning companies paying for the number of rooms cleaned. Neither breaks nor idle hours were paid, and the same held true for the extra time needed to clean extra-dirty rooms. This practice may well lead to average hourly wages below the SMW level, and thus to a violation of the Minimum Wage Act. Indeed, the Labor Inspectorate fined one of the cleaning companies involved.

Recruitment, Selection, and Career Opportunities   Hotels and cleaning companies recruit new staff more often through room attendants already employed, or they use ads in local newspapers. They set out no special requirements, and selection primarily aims at finding out whether the applicant fits in with the team and the hotel. Mastering the Dutch language is preferred in the south, while in Amsterdam English will do.

As discussed before, career development is mainly limited to hotel workers who already have an occupation-oriented education at the medium or high level. We found some examples of career development for room attendants who were too highly educated for cleaning

Table 6.6 Wages, Bonuses, and Grades of Room Attendants:
Two Hospitality Collective Labor Agreements (CLAs)
and the Cleaning CLA

	Old Hospitality CLA	New Hospitality CLA	Cleaning Company CLA[a]
CLA year	2003–2004[a]	July 14, 2005 to March 31, 2008	January 1, 2005 to January 1, 2008
Grade	3	3	2
Adult wage applicable from age	22	22	22
Basic wage	€1,436.37	€1,436.84	€1,371.67
Waiting period (before receiving basic wage)	Two calendar years (starting wage = SMW = €1,264,60)	Four calendar years	First half-year in grade = learning period
Maximum monthly wage	€1,706.88	€1,706.88	€1,421.07
Maximum hourly wage	€10.37	€10.37	€9.44
Basic hourly wage	€8.72	€8.72	€8.33
Holiday allowance	8%	8%	8%
Bonus for weekend shift	Saturday: none Sunday: 150%	None	Saturday: 150% Sunday: 215%
Clauses on wage development in 2006 and 2007 contracts		2006: €8.92 2007: €9.00	2006: €8.62 2007: €8.90
	Probation period: two months; three fixed-term; after contracts in three years, a permanent contract follows	Probation period: two months; after six fixed-term contracts in five years, a permanent contract follows; waiting period of one month breaks up the chain	Probation period: two months; after three fixed-term contracts in one and a half years, a permanent contract follows
Minimum working hours	Four hours per week	No minimum	Two hours per week

Source: Collective labor agreements for hospitality industry and cleaning sector; both made a contract in 2005.

[a] Wages based on an average working week of 38 hours and an annual working time of 1,979 hours.

work. A viable career path goes from room attendant to supervisor to head housekeeping, but in practice only a very few take these steps. "Careering is limited," said the head of housekeeping of a three-star hotel. "Hotels don't have a broad range of jobs. Moreover, the knowledge and capacities of the room attendants often don't reach. That is a pity, because older room attendants run a higher risk of labor turnover, and for them the solution could be service work."

"First I had a job in a five-star hotel," said a room attendant in Amsterdam, "with a target of seventeen rooms per day. The cart was very heavy, and so was the bedspread. Yet the most important reason for quitting this job was that the hotel would not offer me a permanent contract. Then I started to work for a cleaning company. Because I always worked more hours than I was being paid for, and because that company wouldn't offer me a full-time contract, I also left that job."

Labor Turnover and Sick Leave   Room attendants working for a hotel as a rule show low turnover rates, particularly those with long tenures and permanent contracts. Turnover of their fellow workers working for cleaning companies is substantially higher—60 to 90 percent against less than 15 percent. High turnover rates in the first year of tenure are indications of the high job demands of cleaning companies, which goal is to retain only the most motivated, precise, and healthy room attendants.

DETERIORATING JOB QUALITY

In the focus groups, the room attendants expressed the high value they put on the following job elements:

Reasonable room targets: "Reasonable" targets take into account the specific characteristics of the rooms. Because room cleaning in five-star hotels is considered more intensive and demanding than in three-star hotels, and targets often were not balanced with these higher demands, nor are wages, the room attendants preferred more standardized work in three-star hotels over work in five-star hotels. When hotels showed a keen eye for the interests and needs of room attendants and did not require extreme productivity levels, attendants were willing to carry out extra tasks when needed.

Job and income security: Having a permanent contract was a major reason for not changing jobs, while a fixed-term contract was a reason to search for a job with more security.

Good work atmosphere and good relationship with the supervisor: For room attendants, a good supervisor is one who defends them in case of guests' complaints and has an open attitude toward problems at work or at home.

We observed, based on our hotel cases, that in recent years hotel management had succeeded in raising room cleaning productivity but that at the same time job quality had generally deteriorated. Room attendants' jobs became more demanding, and wages for the same amount of work decreased. Higher productivity levels had resulted only to a very limited extent from investments in new equipment and materials; more often they resulted from managers finding new ways to organize cleaning. For the room attendants, this had led to two connected trends: working harder in less (paid) time, and getting paid for productive tasks only. "When I started this job in 2000," said the forewoman in a three-star hotel, "I had three minutes per room more at my disposal. We do the same now—or even more—in less time, but the limit is reached and I will not accept any further time reductions. We still have to deal with human beings and not with robots."

Doing More Work in Less (Paid) Time   With regard to job quality, both room attendants and hotel managers agreed that in recent years the workload of room attendants had increased, both physically and mentally. Here a direct connection with increased competition could be traced: renovations and interior adaptations contributed to higher workloads because these materials were more difficult to clean. The more frequent use of marble and dark floors had also clearly contributed to the increased workload, in much the same way as the increase in guest supplies: the extra cleaning these surfaces required added to the number of tasks room attendants had to complete.

Besides being more physically demanding, this development had also increased the mental workload. The risk of making mistakes had been heightened, especially in the five-star hotels. Yet the general manager of a three-star hotel mentioned the same tendency to upgrade rooms. Upgrading and more transparency via the Internet had also lifted quality demands: "One hair in the bathroom can bring much damage to a carefully and expensively constructed hotel reputation." Meeting higher quality demands and coping with the strict quality control systems also contributed to a higher workload. All of these developments had occurred against the backdrop of decreasing available cleaning time per room.

Getting Paid for Productive Tasks Only We found a clear tendency for hotels to reduce the costs of room cleaning by paying only for directly productive cleaning tasks. Outsourcing is the most far-reaching example: this practice allows hotels to adjust cleaning costs precisely to fluctuations in occupancy rates. Both hotel employers and cleaning company managers had found ways to enlarge numerical flexibility, which had led to an increase in flexible contracts and temp jobs. Room attendants as well as hotel managers mentioned hotels going a step further: paying piece rates per cleaned room and not paying for the pauses attendants took between rooms. A housekeeping manager at a four-star hotel explained: "I experienced that between eight and nine-thirty room attendants spent much time waiting for guests to check out or to leave. Therefore, I changed the starting time. Now the room attendants can finish their work without a pause, and they carry out the same amount of work in three hours as they formerly did in four hours."

Altogether, the overall flexible use of manpower contributes significantly to raised productivity levels, but it contributes as well to the strong deterioration of the work and income security of room attendants.

IN SEARCH OF A HIGH ROAD

A number of hotel managers turned out to be worried about the increasingly demanding nature of cleaning work. They talked about "exhausting room attendants," a tendency that was aggravated, in their view, by the outsourcing of housekeeping. These managers questioned the financial motives for outsourcing, which they considered to be rather weak: it seemed to them that outsourcing entailed higher training and learning costs, because the turnover rates of external cleaning companies were much higher. High turnover at cleaning companies also led to the use of room attendants who were less experienced and had a lower commitment to the goals and needs of the hotel, leading to higher control and supervisory costs.

We found two hotels in Amsterdam, a five-star chain hotel and an independent three-star hotel, that preferred in-house room cleaning over outsourcing. Both of these hotels had invested in sustainable relationships with their room attendants. After a probation period, these hotels offered room attendants permanent contracts, mostly for four days per week. Compared to other hotels, they invested more in human resource policies and good social relations, especially with regard to the social climate, health and safety issues, and work intensity. They practiced a human-oriented management style: the needs and problems of the workers were handled respectfully. Because of the weak societal position of this group (for example, many room attendants were single parents or migrant workers), they brought a great variety of problems to the workplace. The housekeeping management of these hotels invested much time and effort in helping their cleaning staff solve these problems. In return, the room attendants who worked for these hotels were more motivated, committed to their job, and prepared to adapt their working times to the needs of the hotel. Other payoffs of this human resource strategy were low turnover and sick leave rates, as well as a good reputation on the local labor market for room cleaners.

The management of both hotels was convinced that the benefits of this organizational strategy outweighed the benefits of outsourcing. They stated that they had reached acceptable productivity levels and achieved enough organizational flexibility to adjust to shifts in market demands, while their labor costs were much lower compared to hotels that outsourced housekeeping. We did not get comparative data on the financial results of the eight case hotels to verify these statements and to draw conclusions about the effectiveness of the various strategies.[4] More managers in the case studies, however, showed an awareness of the advantages of creating win-win situations between the needs of the hotel and the needs of room attendants.

A prerequisite for this strategy is a human-oriented management style, which is usually not a well-developed feature of hotels' human resource policies. We found that most hotel managers were not able or committed enough to deal with the needs of the low-skilled room attendants. Moreover, when hotel managers decide to outsource cleaning work, their decision is at least partly based on the desire to "outsource" a social group with which they feel no affiliation—a group, moreover, that is associated with problems of high turnover and much sick leave. Some managers pointed to a lack of the required management competencies and skills, a result of the poorly developed human resource policies in the hotel industry. More professional human resource policies or the development of decentralized human resource practices might stimulate more hotel managers to develop win-win solutions. "There is so much checking around, and all that checking by supervisors, housekeepers, and mystery guests is very stressing and expensive," noted the executive housekeeper in an Amsterdam three-star hotel.

> Why not invest in motivating and stimulating room attendants? Let them think along with you, do not lift the workload above a reasonable level. Let them check their own work. In doing so, one can save a lot of money. By creating a mixed staff of full-timers and part-timers, you can meet both the hotel's need for more flexibility and the workers' need for more job and income security. One should understand what it means for unskilled workers to be condemned to temp jobs. They will not be able to build a future; they will not get any security.

We expect that the tightening of the labor market and the growing scarcity of room cleaners could have an impact on hotel employers' strategies about organizing room cleaning and inspire them to rethink their wasteful way of dealing with their workforce. Whether this rethinking will take place, however, and if so, how, will be highly affected by the government's revision of immigration policy. Revisions of immigration laws are foreseen in the very near future, and they could lead to an increase in the low-skilled labor supply from Eastern Europe.

It is hard to conclude, based on the experiences of the two Amsterdam hotels, that taking the high road with respect to low-wage room cleaning work, as discussed in chapter 4, is always possible. Their target requirements differed only slightly from those of the other hotels we investigated, and these two hotels did not pay higher hourly wages or offer superior career opportunities. At the same time, we may wonder how much room to maneuver hotels have to pay higher wages, develop enhanced work practices, or provide financial room for education and mobility. Consumers' opportunities to compare hotels on price and quality, together with the otherwise highly competitive environment, pose limits here. Moreover, the educational background of the large majority of female attendants restricts their career opportunities in segmented hotel organizations. The room attendants with whom we spoke, however, highly appreciated the social policies of these two hotels, as was expressed in the long tenures of existing employees and a waiting list of room attendants looking for jobs in these hotels. We may conclude that this firm strategy is at least a good example of decent employership, signaling the possibility of a high road.

CONCLUSIONS

We now return to the initial research question: what impact have the rapid changes in the hotel industry had on the job quality of room attendants in the housekeeping departments of hotels? Our research provides us with many indications that in the past few years room attendants' job quality has deteriorated substantially, expressed by both a decline in job and income security and an increased workload, physical as well as mental. These changes can be attributed, first, to the greater volatility of the worldwide hotel industry: the increased unpredictability of yearly revenues has given hotels a strong impetus to pursue two dominant firm strategies: flexibilization and cost saving. This has led to a strong increase in fixed-term and other flexible contracts. Flexibilization has the greatest impact at the lower job levels, and this is particularly true for cleaning staffs, owing to the increased practice of outsourcing their work.

Second, we found that the internationalization and upscaling that have characterized the restructuring of the industry strongly affect room attendants' jobs. The traditional industry structure of small family hotels is quickly changing, boosted by the development of new product market (branding, standardizing) and cost-saving strategies (economies of scale). For room attendants, these developments come with higher performance standards (with regard to productivity as well as service quality) and stricter and more formalized quality control procedures.

Third, we want to point to the growing effects of IT on room attendants' jobs. Quality demands are pushed up as a result of greater market transparency—consumers can exchange information on the Internet about, for example, the cleanness of hotel rooms—and increased flexibilization, which are facilitated by the electronic booking and more refined capacity planning and staff scheduling software.

The negative effects of changes in room attendants' jobs described in this chapter can be traced most sharply in the Amsterdam hotels, which, more often than the southern hotels, combined low wages, job insecurity, and heavy workloads. The Amsterdam cleaning workforce is increasingly composed of migrant men, recruited because they are thought to be better able to cope with the notable physical workload. Female room attendants in the Amsterdam hotel labor market look more and more like labor nomads, hopping from job to job, looking for permanent work with better terms of employment and better working conditions. Where room cleaning is outsourced, room attendants' jobs have deteriorated even more, as evidenced by still higher production standards or the application of piece rates. The quality level of a hotel, expressed by the number of stars, also seems to have some impact on the quality of room attendants' jobs: working in a five-star hotel is perceived as more demanding than working in a three-star hotel, wages being equal.

The institutional context of laws, rules, CLA negotiations, and union influence has offered only limited protection to room attendants' jobs. We saw some institutions stimulating or supporting an increase in flexible relations (with the subsequent negative impact on income and job security), such as the Gatekeeper Improvement Act, and pushing hotel employers to outsource cleaning activities, such as the agreements on lower wages and more flexible labor relations in the latest CLA. Several factors might explain this deterioration—the weak position of low-skilled (female) workers, the segmented employment structure of hotel organizations, the limited influence of unions in the hotel industry, and the present political climate with regard to liberalizing and flexibilizing labor markets.

NOTES

1. In Europe 20 to 25 percent of hotels belong to a corporate chain—in contrast to 75 percent in the United States (Ernst & Young 2004).
2. Includes both hotels and pensions. About 2,300 hotels are classified according to the Dutch Hotel Classification: the label "hotel" is protected and allowed only if the hotel has at least one star.
3. These figures refer to the targets for check-outs. In most hotels the targets for stay-overs are slightly higher.

4. We do not have the RevPar development of all eight hotels at our disposal. Most of the hotel managers we interviewed were rather reluctant to hand over these figures.

REFERENCES

Bedrijfschap Horeca en Catering (BH&C). 2004a. *Slapen in de Nederlandse horeca* [*Sleeping in the Dutch Hotel, Restaurant and Catering Industry*]. Zoetermeer, Netherlands: BH&C.

———. 2004b. *Horeca-arbeidsmarkt steeds flexibeler* [*Hotel, Restaurant and Catering Industry Labor Market Increasingly Flexible*]. Zoetermeer, Netherlands: BH&C.

———. 2004c. *In-, door-en uitstroom van werknemers in de horeca* [*Inflow, Outflow and Careering of Employees in the Hotel, Restaurant and Catering Industry*]. Zoetermeer, Netherlands: BH&C.

———. 2005a. *Slapen in de Nederlandse horeca* [*Sleeping in the Dutch Hotel, Restaurant and Catering Industry*]. Zoetermeer, Netherlands: BH&C.

———. 2005b. *Barometer 4* (October). Zoetermeer, Netherlands: BH&C.

———. 2005c. *Barometer special Innovatie* [*Barometer Special: Innovation*]. Zoetermeer, Netherlands: BH&C.

———. 2005d. *Horeca in cyfers* [*The Hotel, Restaurant and Catering Industry in Figures*]. Zoetermeer, Netherlands: BH&C.

———. 2006a. *Arbeidsmarktanalyse 2006* [*2006 Labor Market Analysis*]. Zoetermeer, Netherlands: BH&C.

———. 2006b. *Barometer Arbeid* [*Labor Barometer*]. Zoetermeer, Netherlands: BH&C.

———. 2006c. *In-, door-en uitstroom van werknemers in de horeca* [*Inflow, Outflow and Careering of Employees in the Hotel, Restaurant and Catering Industry*]. Zoetermeer, Netherlands: BH&C.

Bispo, Armenio. 2005. *Deelmarkten in de Nederlandse Horeca; over beroepsopgeleiden, bijbaners en hoofdbaners* [*Sub-Markets in the Dutch Hotel, Restaurant and Catering Industry: On Professionally-Educated, Part-Timers and Full-Timers*]. Zoetermeer, Netherlands: BH&C.

Ernst and Young. 2004. *Eyeopener 6.1. Investeren in hotels loont* [*Investing in Hotels is Rewarding*]. Utrecht: Ernst & Young Real Estate, Hospitality, and Construction.

Executive Housekeepers Association. 2004. Internal study about outsourcing housekeeping activities. Not available to non-members. See http://www.executivehousekeepers.nl.

Hoogendoorn, Ewout, and Marco van Bruggen. 2005. *HOSTA 2005: The Benelux Hotel Industry*. Hilversum, Netherlands: Horwath.

Houtman, Irene, Peter Smulders, and Seth van den Bossche. 2006. *Arbobalans 2005: arbeidsrisico's, effecten en maatregelen in Nederland* [*Working*

Conditions Balance 2005: Health Risks, Effects and Measures in the Nether-lands]. Hoofddoorp, Netherlands: TNO.

Koninklijke Horeca Nederland (KHN). 2005. *Handboek functies Horeca, 2005 [2005 Hotel, Restaurant, and Catering Industry Functions Handbook]*. Apeldoorn, Netherlands: KHN.

Reintjes, Martijn. 2005. *Toppertjes in innovatie [Leading in Innovation]*. Dutch hotel award 2005. Doetinchem, Netherlands: Misset Horeca.

Vaas, Fietje. 2004. *Eindrapportage over het arboconvenant werkdruk horeca [Final Report about Safety Covenants in the Hospitality Sector]*. Zoetermeer, Netherlands: TNO

Van Klaveren, Maarten, and Kea Tijdens, editors. 2008. *Bargaining Issues in Europe: Comparing Countries and Industries*. Brussels: European Trade Union Institute for Research, Education and Health and Safety (ETUI-REHS).

Vos, Antwan. 2005. "Incidentele loonontwikkeling in 2003 hoger dan in 2002" ["Incidental Wage Development in 2003 Higher than in 2002"]. *Sociaal Economische Trends* (Heerlen: CBS), 2005-3, 49-52.

Wagemakers, Evelien. 2003. *To Outsource or Not to Outsource? That's the Question*. Rotterdam: Erasmus Universiteit/Hogere Hotelschool Den Haag.

CHAPTER 7

Health Care: Integrated Quality Care Sheltered from Cost Control?

Marc van der Meer

The organization of work processes in hospitals is robustly institutionalized in Dutch regulations, and work processes are strictly planned and scheduled in order to finely calibrate the needs of the organization with the availability of employees. The overall ambition of the system is to provide integrated, high-quality care. For this reason, the integration and upgrading of function levels have been standard practices in all hospitals.

The demand for health care is growing each year, owing to the increase in and aging of the population. The cost implications of increasing demand have resulted in a political debate regarding the governance system for the health sector and the role of institutional intermediary assurance organizations and individual taxpayers in that system. After almost three decades of political controversy, the financial regime for health care was changed in 2006. As a result, budget allocation within hospitals has been decentralized.

The argument in this chapter is that, in this sector where low-wage employment is already a relatively marginal issue, the negotiation of pay is relatively sheltered from the emerging debate on cost control. In our study, we found hardly any nursing assistants or department assistants helping skilled nurses; we did, however, come across a variety of practices for nutrition assistants and cleaners. For all of the occupations under study, the wages were hardly below the national threshold of two-thirds of the median wage. Only the entry-level wages of a few occupations were set below the low-wage definition, but seniority payments easily enabled staff members to cross the threshold. Such jobs were located primarily in facilitating and ancillary services, such as infrastructure, transport, and cleaning.

Where low-wage employment occurs, it is generally true that part-time jobs—and small part-time jobs in particular—are widespread, though wages per hour do not differ for full-timers and part-timers.

Table 7.1 Research Design for the Case Study Hospitals

	Top Clinical Hospital	General Hospital	Nursing Homes
Inside Randstad	Cases 3, 5	Cases 4, 6	Cases 7, 8
Outside Randstad	Case 1	Case 2	

Source: Author's compilation.

Most nurses are female, and many of them are part-timers. The employment flexibility in hospitals derives from the shift system, which enables employees to accumulate bonuses in wages. Furthermore, hospitals make use of internal labor pools, which enable managers to match supply with demand.

The analytical question in this chapter is this: to what extent do hospitals make use of low-wage employment in traditional or enhanced forms of work organization, and how is the conflict between cost control and integral quality maintenance solved?

The empirical research on which this chapter is built concentrates on two subsectors in health care: general hospitals and nursing homes. In each of these types of organizations, professional education and training are provided. Within the hospital sector, we compare general hospitals with hospitals that are among the self-proclaimed "top clinical hospitals," which generally offer specialized training, are larger in size, and are more modern working organizations. All hospitals in the sample are located inside and outside the Randstad conurbation. In addition, we provide information on two nursing homes, which have about the same size and degree of institutionalization as the hospitals. The people being treated in nursing homes have left the hospital but are too ill to go home.

In each of the organizations, we studied the labor market position of three occupational groups: nursing assistants, nutrition assistants, and housekeepers. In addition to the case studies, we conducted interviews with representatives of interest associations, temp agencies, private investors, and the director of a consultancy who set up a proposal for a new job classification system; these interviews let us evaluate the pluses and minuses of the current practice.

This chapter is organized as follows. In the first section, we provide an overview of the main institutional characteristics of the industry and current trends in the labor market. That is followed by a discussion of wages and job quality in the hospital sector in comparison with the case studies under scrutiny. Then we provide an overview of the target occupations. Our conclusions appear in the final section.

THE HEALTH CARE SECTOR

NATIONAL REGULATION

Hospitals are institutions that originated as charitable organizations that were often based on religion or ideology. The functioning and planning of hospital activities is strictly regulated by law, and health care is a universal social right of all citizens laid down in the Dutch Constitution. The Health Care Quality for Health Care Institutions Act (1996) stipulates four general criteria rather than detailed norms about the quality of care expected of those serving the public interest: quality, accessibility, efficiency, and accountability. Government intervention is deemed necessary to overcome market imperfections in the asymmetric relationship between the supply of and the demand for health care, which is unpredictable and cannot be influenced by individual citizens alone.

The Inspectorate for Health Care monitors compliance with the act, as well as with European regulations and tendering procedures, whereas the Minister of Health Care, Welfare, and Sports holds the final responsibility. Individual professionals working in health care are covered not by the Quality Law but by the Individual Health Care Provisions Act. In principle, this law gives full scope to medical actions, though it describes some "reserved medical actions" as procedures that can be conducted only by qualified professionals. The law also includes a penalty clause: harming a person's health is punishable.

SPECIALIZATION AND BUDGET ALLOCATION

Hospitals can be characterized according to their functions and specializations. With better prevention and medications, advanced treatments, and extended life expectancy, the formally separate areas of health care, health cure, and health prevention have increasingly become coordinated, whereas specialization occurs in each of the branches. More and more hospitals organize their departments to provide both long-term treatment and out-patient treatment in clinics. Overall, the average duration of stay in hospitals has decreased, owing to technological advances and cost control. For example, in hospital 1, the average stay of patients declined from 8.8 nursing days per patient in 1999 to 7.1 days in 2003. Those patients who no longer need direct treatment or close supervision are placed in other institutions, such as specialized mental health care institutions, organizations for mentally handicapped persons, nursing homes, or caring homes for the elderly. In addition, the number of home care organizations is growing, and the medical care system has become a preventive one. Given their increased well-being, citizens are also becoming more critical consumers with respect to the nature and quality of the care provided. Consequently, hospitals are applying a strategy of product differentiation and increasingly provide specialized, tailor-made care (Ministry of Health, Welfare, and Sports 2002).

Mergers and scale enlargement have led to a decline in the number of hospitals, from two hundred two decades ago to ninety-eight in 2004, of which ninety are general hospitals and eight are academic hospitals.[1] Both university-affiliated academic hospitals and the nineteen top clinical hospitals are larger in size and in number of beds than the other general hospitals. The largest hospitals have a structure through which they direct several divisions or business units at various geographical locations.

The New Financial Incentives Model   In contrast with the other industries investigated in this book, the health care sector depends on state budgets—except for a small (but growing) number of private clinics located particularly in some larger cities. The fast-rising cost of health care—it was 9.8 percent of GDP in 2003 (WHO 2005)—has made the government aware of the need to control public budgets, and efficient budget allocation is currently at the center of decision-making in every hospital. This tension has resulted in a broad public debate about the quality, accessibility, solidarity, and cost control of health care services (Den Exter et al. 2004; van der Grinten and Vos 2004).

After enduring political immobility and the postponement of political decisionmaking, a new social insurance system was introduced in 2006. Under this system, health insurance organizations that offer standard and supplementary insurance packages of medical and dental treatment compete with each other. All citizens are covered, and the insurance associations are not allowed to refuse to accept any customers.

After 2006, the cost pricing system in hospitals was also scheduled to be gradually changed. In the past, the annual budget of hospitals did not depend on the number of patients it treated; instead, a guaranteed lump-sum payment for fixed and variable costs was provided by the health insurance associations, without a direct correlation between performance, effectiveness, and budget. Now the standard for health care prices is expressed in the so-called diagnosis-treatment-combinations (DTC).[2] The unity of the DTC concept is at the center of a financial system in which one integral cost price per unit of production is calculated. The prices linked to the DTCs are established in separate negotiations between health insurance associations and hospitals. The Exceptional Medical Expenses Act will need to be integrated into this new general insurance system. To get more control of (unfair) market concentration and to stimulate market allocation, a supervisory "Care Authority" was introduced in 2006 to monitor the diversity and spread of the supply of health care.

The two nursing homes we visited were also revising their financial model of budget allocation to acquire a competitive position in the care market. Both organizations were preparing to analyze as precisely as possible the costs of care by calculating the exact time (in labor minutes) spent by each staff member on providing different aspects of care. In contrast to the past lump-sum model of budget allocation, the new time-framed model of individual care is based on the clients' needs.

The overall idea in the health care sector is thus to introduce one common market in which health insurance associations compete and hospitals contend with each other on the basis of price and quality. Within such a "quasi-market" (le Grand and Barlett 1993), cost-consciousness in the organization of hospital care services should be encouraged.

Budget Allocation in Individual Hospitals   Hospitals are labor-intensive organizations: about 60 percent of the costs are related to staff. Reductions in the length of hospital stays have increased duration efficiency, but this is not necessarily cost efficiency. Some hospital board directors in our sample supported the introduction of the DTC system and were putting on political pressure to get it accepted in its entirety (as at hospital 2), whereas others called the introduction of the DTCs a "disaster" and "an unworkable, complex administrative system taking disproportionate amounts of nonproductive time" (hospital 1). Moreover, direct cost control is difficult within hospitals since medical specialists determine the production process and related costs for medicine, lab research, and nursing. Yet only 20 percent of doctors are wage earners, and 80 percent of medical specialists are not directly employed by the hospital but are united in partnerships (maatschap). The partnership establishes, for example, recruitment procedures for supporting staff and salary levels.

In their struggle to control costs, hospital administrators are increasingly using benchmarking techniques to compare different hospitals. The hospital sector owns a sectorwide research center that evaluates organizational costs, costs of production, manpower, and so on. The data are quite complete at the level of hospitals but do not provide much practical information to use in comparing efficiency at the department level in hospitals. One hospital we visited reportedly had a higher cost-per-employee ratio than elsewhere. This hospital had hired a consultancy company to carry out a truly Taylorist time and motion study for nurses to look for ways to increase their efficiency and reduce labor costs.

LABOR MARKET INSTITUTIONS

Health care is a growing sector. The demand for health care is increasing, first, because of the growth of the population, from 16.1 million in 2005 to a projected 17.7 million people in 2040. In addition, there are more individuals living with chronic disorders as the population has aged and life expectancy has increased. Furthermore, it is expected that the growing share of ethnic minorities in the population will lead to higher demand for health care. Finally, the increasing share of single households will also lead to demands for more health care (Van der Windt et al. 2004).

In 2004, the 90 general hospitals had 181,000 employees. According to Dutch statistics, three other sub-sectors dominate the health care sector, notably nursing homes, elderly homes or residential homes and home care services. In the same year, there were 338 nursing homes with 119,000 employees and 588 elderly organizations with 112,000 staff members. The 243 organizations for home care services had 204,500 workers on their payroll. In general hospitals, the majority of health care workers are employed in the nursing profession (58 percent); 17 percent are in general and administrative functions, 13 percent work in hotel and catering, 4 percent work as independent medical specialists, and 5 percent are students.

The employment levels in health care are growing at a higher speed than the economy at large. This is due partly to the growing demand for health care services and partly to the working time reduction from thirty-eight to thirty-six hours, implemented in 1997 and 1998. There are many part-timers in the health care sector and above all women have part-time jobs. Industry statistics show that fifty percent of larger part-time jobs in health care (working more than thirty hours per week) are occupied by men: the share of women in this category is around 30 percent.

In tables 7.2 and 7.3, we compare labor market characteristics of nursing and caring staff in general hospitals with those in nursing homes. In general hospitals alone, in 2005 the number of nurses and caretakers is at 63,000 persons, which is equivalent to 43,000 FTE, making the part-time ratio at 69 percent. The average duration of employment with the current hospital has risen from 9.0 years in 2001 to 10.6 in 2005 (table 7.2.). More elaborated industry statistics point out that the tenure patterns generally are elevated. In 2003, 48 percent of hospital employees had tenure of more than ten years with their current employer, and only 21 percent had worked for their employer for two years or less. The average total work experience of employees in the health care sector as a whole is 17 years (Bekker et al, 2004). The rise in tenure goes hand in hand with the ageing of the work force. As table 4.2 also shows, the average age of the nursing and caring staff in hospitals is 39.1 in 2005, two years higher than in 2001.

In nursing homes, the absolute numbers of nursing and caring staff are quite comparable with those in general hospitals; in contrast, however the share in female jobs is more elevated in the nursing homes. In hospitals 87 percent of nursing and caring employees are women, in nursing homes this percentage is even 95 percent in 2005. In nursing homes, the age figures are somewhat lower than in general hospitals and not indicating a rising pattern.

Sickness levels in the sector are generally considered as substantial, though over the last number of years absence due to illness has declined to 5.9 percent in hospitals and 7.3 percent in nursing homes in 2005, which is in line with the observations of our interviews that personnel managers take this issue seriously and aim to re-integrate ill employees as soon as possible. The gross turnover rates are de-

Table 7.2 Labor Market Characteristics of Nursing and Caring Personnel in General Hospitals, 2001 to 2005

	2001	2002	2003	2004	2005
Number of nurses and caretakers	58,684	61,988	61,708	62,398	62,898
Number FTE's	40,898	41,895	42,484	43,025	43,195
Average working hours per week (fulltime = 100%)	0.70	0.68	0.69	0.69	0.69
Percentage female jobs	87.2	87.3	87.6	87.8	87.9
Gross turnover in percent (persons who leave the work place)	11.7	9.6	8.0	6.7	6.4
Net turnover in percent (persons who leave the sector)	3.5	2.6	2.1	2.1	1.8
Sickness rate in percent	7.1	6.5	6.1	5.8	5.9
Average age (in years)	37.1	37.5	37.7	38.5	39.1
Average duration of employment with current employer (in years)	9.0	9.1	9.3	9.7	10.6

Source: Author's compilation from Prismant and Website Labor Market Information Care and Welfare (accessed at http://www.AZWinfo.nl).

clining as well. They are relatively small in hospitals (6.4 percent) and substantially larger in nursing homes (10.5 percent), though in both sub-sectors many persons leave their work places and find jobs elsewhere in the sector, minimizing the net turnover rate (table 7.2).

Education   The vocational and training system historically focuses on upgrading and improving skill levels. In 1996–1997, a new national vocational education system was introduced to reduce the complex variety of training systems in hospitals as well as the need to update the tasks, competencies, and required skills of staff. The old system was changed into a more transparent system that delivers qualified workers according to a five-level education structure, level 5 representing a new element of medical training: training for nurses at a higher vocational level. Only level 4 and 5 nurses have to be registered to be able to practice their profession. Finally, in 1997 so-called in-service education, through which apprentices are trained inside care institutions, was transferred to external regular educational institutions at medium and higher professional levels (Den Boer, Hövels, and

Table 7.3 Labor Market Characteristics of Nursing and Caring Personnel in Nursing Homes, 2001 to 2005

	2001	2002	2003	2004	2005
Number of nurses and caretakers	64,780	64,412	60,462	60,620	64,151
Number of full time jobs	41,507	40,995	40,968	41,749	43,364
Average working hours per week (full time = 100%)	0.64	0.64	0.68	0.69	0.68
Percentage female jobs	95.4	95.3	95.0	95.2	94.8
Gross turnover in percent (persons who leave the work place)	18.7	15.9	12.8	10.4	10.5
Net turnover in percent (persons who leave the sector)	4.3	3.7	3.3	3.1	4.2
Sickness rate in percent	10.2	8.9	8.2	7.5	7.3
Average age	37.1	38.4	38.8	39.7	37.4
Average duration of employment with current employer (in years)	6.8	6.9	7.0	7.4	7.7

Source: Author's compilation from Prismant and Website Labor Market Information Care and Welfare (accessed at http://www.AZWinfo.nl).

Klaeijsen 2004). Qualification levels in hospitals are substantially higher than in the nursing homes and the elderly homes. In home care services, qualification levels are the lowest on average.

The following outlines the various vocational levels:

- Level 1: One-year training to become a "helper" who provides assistance in the daily care of patients. The work is classified as very low-skilled, and preparatory training is not required.

- Level 2: One-year training at the primary vocational level to become a "qualified helper" who assists with tasks like washing and feeding patients. No preparatory training is required for this low-skilled work.

- Level 3: Three-year training at the secondary vocational level to become an "assistant nurse" who administers daily care, takes simple medical actions, and reports on patients. Preparatory training is necessary. Staff at this level are very likely to work in care institutions and nursing homes, but seldom in hospitals.

• Level 4: Four-year training at the secondary vocational level to become a general nurse who takes medical actions and reports on and monitors patients. Training at this level builds on earlier vocational training requirements.

• Level 5: Four-year training at the tertiary vocational level to become a "nurse" who takes medical actions, coordinates total patient care, and manages the lower nursing staff. The courses at this level also start from earlier qualifications.

The vocational training and education system is organized in various work-school combinations and as apprenticeship training schemes. Students must apply for the job at a training hospital. They start with a job preparation period, which lasts no more than six months and usually exposes the student to a mix of theory and practice. The student signs a job preparation contract. Each month the student receives pocket money equivalent to the net minimum (youth) wage. The employer pays the tuition fees.

After the job preparation period, the student becomes an apprentice and receives practical instruction, laid down in a working contract for no more than thirty-six hours a week. On average, four hours per week of instruction is foreseen in this contract. The salary of such pupils rises on an annual basis.

Employed nurses have many training options, though they seldom climb the occupational job ladder from level 1 to 2 to 3 to 4 to 5. New entering nurses have a level 4 qualification and find jobs at that level (inflow into the occupational ladder thus occurs via a side-entry post). There are few vertical career opportunities in the occupational labor market for nurses, and only a few make it to managerial positions. Many nurses, however, work on their specializations and change from one department to another after several years of experience and thus have a horizontal career path.

The health care sector had a sectorwide social fund for training and reintegration until 2004; it was abolished for reasons of retrenchment. Since that time, individual health care organizations determine their training budgets, which subsequently have declined from about 5 percent to 1 to 3 percent of the wage sum. For low-skilled staff, skills and training policies are now part and parcel of the financial position of hospitals. When hospitals face a precarious financial situation, training opportunities for incumbent employees in the hospital become even more retrenched. In our interviews, we were informed that resources for nurse training had been frozen in a period of financial hardship and that hospitals were sometimes cutting back the number of places they offered for vocational training.

We conclude that for employees in the lower ranks—such as those under investigation in this study—a structural training policy hardly exists. That these staff members are not at all guaranteed additional training negatively affects their career opportunities. In the long run, it also harms the health care sector itself, which already faced substantial vacancies in the period of high conjuncture that occurred around 2001. Also, after 2007 a large increase in vacancies at all levels is expected.

Reward and Compensation   Collective bargaining is the core institution for establishing wage levels, at both the industry level and the individual level. Collective bargaining determines the annual wage increase, number of working hours, social benefits, and pension entitlements for the workforce covered by the terms of the agreement. The collective labor agreement (CLA) stipulates the procedures for the establishment of wage levels for individual employees. In an appendix to the collective agreement, a job classification system is developed (Functiewaardering Gezondheidszorg, FWG). Jobs are graded according to function levels that are connected to one of seventeen wage scales (FWG 5, 10, 15, 20, 25, 30, 35, 40, 45, 50, 55, 60, 65, 70, 75, and 80) for low to high pay levels. Each wage scale consists of nine or ten years of tenure on average. In addition, there are special wage scales for young persons, for new entrants into the labor market, and for participants in the vocational and training system.

Until 1998, one overall CLA covered all 450,000 employees in the entire health sector. Since then, the structure of collective bargaining has been differentiated. Currently, all 185,000 employees of hospitals and rehabilitation centers are covered by this collective agreement, which is negotiated in the name of five (national and sector) trade unions on the employees' side and the hospitals and rehabilitation centers on the employers' side, which are all members of the Netherlands Association for Hospitals. In April 2004, the social partners negotiated an agreement for fifteen months lasting until March 31, 2005. After regular negotiations, a new CLA was reached, valid from January 2006 to February 2008, which maintains its central character while ensuring small wage increases and a revision of the early re-

Figure 7.1 Wage Scales 1 to 50 in the Collective Labor
Agreement for Hospitals

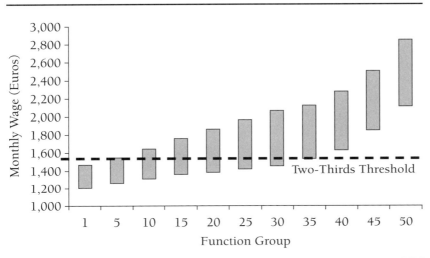

Source: Author's calculations from the text of the collective labor agreement.

tirement conditions. In addition, the unions in the industry are participating in negotiations about reorganizations when employment conditions are at stake.

Yet this job classification system should not be seen as a fixed system but as a guideline for the implementation of individual negotiations between management and employees. Reference points for determining the wages of individual employees are knowledge, social skills, risks, responsibilities and influence, expressive ability, physical mobility, attention, other function demands, and abilities under hard work conditions, whether physical or psychological. The system specifies the characteristics of an individual job. For example, one can find a department assistant in food delivery in three different groups: one job includes only easy fixed tasks (linked to FWG 10); one has fixed tasks but is also rewarded for initiative (linked to FWG 15); and one food delivery job includes responsibility for making up diets (linked to FWG 20).

In figure 7.1, we present the wage structure within the wage scales 1 to 50. It appears that substantial overlap exists between several wage scales and that the wage distribution is relatively compressed. At the same time, each of the wage scales holds substantial tenure compensation, which as a general rule is stepwise paid on an annual basis. The lowest scale counts seven salary grades, and the highest scale (FWG 50) counts eleven.

In table 7.4, we have translated the wage scales into gross monthly wages and gross hourly wages. It appears that the entry wages at the bottom of the wage scales—1 through 35—are under the threshold of two-thirds of median income—which in 2002 was €9.90 (US$14.48) per hour, or two-thirds of €14.85 (US$21.72). However, the seniority compensation in all wage scales is responsible for the fact that many employees, even some in the lower wage scales, are receiving an hourly wage that is above the threshold. For example, a housekeeper with five years of experience who is paid according to (low) wage scale 15 receives a tenured wage that per hour is above the two-thirds threshold.

In addition, the CLA stipulates that employees are entitled to an end-of-year payment (5 percent of annual salary) and holiday pay (8 percent of annual salary).

In table 7.5 we provide the division of employees over the various function wage categories for general hospitals and nursing homes. In general hospitals, most employees are ranked in function group 35 or above. In comparison with 1993, an overall upgrading of wage levels has taken place. After the introduction of the new job classification system in January 2000, most level 4 and level 5 nurses are ranked in wage scale 45 in 2001. Vested employment rights are being respected, and staff members have not been placed in lower employment conditions than they occupied before. In interviews, HRM-managers attributed the overall wage increase of 5 percent connected to the new job classification model to the powerful position of nurses in a tight labor market. In the nursing homes, in contrast, a larger share of employees is ranked in the low wage function groups. Twenty percent is ranked in wage scale 25 or lower, whereas most of the nursing staff is in wage scale 35, exhibiting that many of the nursing staff in the nursing homes are trained at level 3 and not at level 4 or 5 of the professional education structure.

Because of potential problems related to the introduction of the FWG system, trade unions and employers' organizations were allowed to commission an independent consultancy firm to examine a new salary structure. The consultancy concluded that the current system is too complex and the wage levels of the lowest categories of employees are too elevated, owing to the system's focus on attending

Table 7.4 Function Groups and Corresponding Gross Monthly and Hourly Wage Levels

Function Group	1	5	10	15	20	25	30	35	40	45	50
Monthly entry wage	€1,212	€1,265	€1,315	€1,363	€1,390	€1,426	€1,462	€1,542	€1,639	€1,859	€2,121
Monthly maximum wage	1,462	1,542	1,639	1,750	1,859	1,962	2,068	2,121	2,282	2,507	2,848
Minimum hourly wage	7.74	8.08	8.40	8.71	8.88	9.11	9.34	9.85	10.47	11.88	13.55
Maximum hourly wage	9.34	9.85	10.47	11.18	11.88	12.54	13.21	13.55	14.58	16.02	18.20

Source: Author's calculations from the text of the collective labor agreement.

Table 7.5 Employees by Function Wage Group in General Hospitals and Nursing Homes

Function Group	General Hospitals			Nursing Homes	
	1993	2000	2001	1993	2000
25 or lower	1%	2%	2%	15%	20%
30	1	1	1	8	9
35	5	5	4	58	53
40	46	41	25	6	7
45	29	25	35	6	5
50 or higher	18	25	32	6	5
Total	100	100	100	100	100

Source: Van der Windt et al. (2004, 75).

to patients, even if such a duty is performed only once a year. The consultancy has proposed a blueprint for a new classification system with fewer wage scales, room for individual development and reward, and separate functional descriptions that can be implemented in a cost-neutral fashion. Although both the trade unions and the employers' associations were positive about this new system, until now the fear of higher costs has led to non-implementation.

A trade union concern is the average remaining wage gap of 12.3 percent putting employees in the hospital sector at a disadvantage in comparison with the market sector. The top of the occupational hierarchy in hospitals is especially worse off compared to the market sector, whereas the wage difference at the bottom of the occupational hierarchy is relatively small in comparison with the market sector (Vandermeulen, Hoogendoorn, and van Lomwel 2003). The unions proved to be less concerned, however, about the payment level of the low-skilled workforce. "Low-wage workers are a relatively small group that has hardly any union members and who we do not want to compete out of the market," as one union representative put it.

Working Hours   The employment duration on a full-time standard level is 1,878 hours in a year (an average of 36 working hours in a week), though individual agreements make it possible to work forty hours. Annual working hours are based on the gross employment duration minus holiday hours, days off, and public holidays. Ordinary working hours are between 7:00 A.M. and 8:00 P.M. on weekdays and between 8:00 A.M. and 12:00 P.M. on Saturdays. With the agreement of the works council, deviations are possible.

Shift work is well paid, with a 22, 38, 47, 52, or 60 percent hourly bonus, depending on the day of the week and year (Sundays and holidays pay more). Shifts of no more than five successive nights are allowed. When agreed, seven night shifts are possible, and at the most thirty-five night shifts in thirteen weeks. To work on night shifts (that is, between 11:00 P.M. and 7:00 A.M.), employees have to be older than eighteen. There are three other forms of irregular shifts: availability, attainability, and consignment shifts. For these shifts the employee is on stand-by and can be called up for work.

The CLA contains a detailed regulation concerning overtime and irregular shifts. Overtime is unlawful for employees who are more than three months pregnant or those older than fifty-five, unless they agree. The maximum number of overtime hours is an average of 3.6 hours per week, measured quarterly (below FWG 48), or 4.2 hours per week (FWG 48–74). If this number is exceeded, the employee will be assisted or a job vacancy will be announced. Compensation for working overtime consists of the same number of hours in free time and monetary compensation of 25, 50, 75, or 100 percent of the hourly salary, depending on the day and time. The works council is obliged to know the employer's policy on this matter.

According to a general employee survey in the health care sector in 2003, 67 percent of hospital employees were satisfied with their current working hours, 22 percent wanted to work fewer hours, and 11 percent wanted to work more hours. Sixty-seven percent of the respondents stated that they had influence over their work schedule, and 72 percent indicated that they could adequately combine working hours with their responsibilities at home (Bekker et al. 2004).

In several of our case studies, managers considered the working time regulations too rigid. According to them, there is no room for practical solutions and the regulations oppress the labor process. The CLA should be adjusted to give more room to flexible working times. According to a hospital director, employees wouldn't be bothered but trade unions would be an obstacle.

The Netherlands Association of Hospitals (NVZ) holds the opinion that primary labor conditions should be spelled out in the CLA and that secondary labor conditions should be decentralized and implemented on the work floor to give hospitals the freedom to introduce tailor-made employment conditions. On the contrary, trade unions want to settle as many things as possible in the collective labor agreement. Although some hospitals perform less well on working conditions, the NVZ believes that forcing rules on organizations will lead to resistance. Therefore, the NVZ suggests getting works councils involved to monitor implementation of labor conditions.

Corporate Governance and Supervision Boards   At the hospital level, several stakeholders have institutionalized positions. First, works councils (Ondernemingsraad) formally meet with the hospital board every two months, though there are often many close informal contacts to discuss the organization and infrastructure of the hospital, the social policy for employees, employee performances, and the resolution of emerging conflicts of interests. The works councils have information, consultation, and advisory rights in order to represent the interests of employees and safeguard the well-being of the entire organization.

Since 2004, the CLA for the hospital sector has prescribed the establishment of a Nurses Advisory Council, with obligatory membership for all nurses. This body advises hospital management on issues relating to the status and content of the work process. Several respondents were of the opinion that this council was more effective than the works council. In three cases, however, there was lack of interest in such a council. Besides the works council for all employees and the Nurses Advisory Council for nurses, there is a council for doctors, as well as a board of supervisors (Raad van Toezicht) and a client council (Cliëntenraad). The varying composition of these different boards results in a complex auditing and accountability system. One current subject of debate is how to make the corporate governance structure in hospitals more transparent in the years to come.

CHANGING WORK ORGANIZATION AND LOW-WAGE EMPLOYMENT

JOB DESIGN AND WORK ORGANIZATION

In their discussion of low-wage employment in American hospitals, Eileen Appelbaum and her colleagues distinguish between three types of work organization: traditional and enhanced work organizations and outsourcing. They conclude that the labor conditions of nursing assistants and housekeepers are rather poor and lead to a substantial turnover of staff. In some cases, work restructuring resulted in enhanced work organizations, which can be effective in reducing turnover; enhanced job levels, however, hardly influence job satisfaction (Appelbaum, Bernhardt, and Murnane 2003, 110).

Dutch hospitals are organized into separate organizational departments where work organization and job design increasingly are central to the attention of both management and employees. As a general rule, the job territory is defined broadly, and the tasks and responsibilities of certain groups of employees partly overlap. Jobs are organized around the concept of "integrated quality care," meaning that staff members' tasks need to be integrated and upskilled. Given the relatively high work pace and substantial responsibilities of qualified nurses, managers are of the opinion that "their tasks should strike a balance between effort and rest, and less complex tasks are needed to keep this balance straight."

In some hospitals, experimental, self-steering quality circles have been implemented, but as a general rule the internal organization of the hospital can still be characterized as a vertical, top-down management system in which each staff member is responsible for a certain number of patients for whom he or she works intensively, especially since many patients are seriously ill and hospital stay durations are getting shorter and shorter.

In all six hospitals in our sample, the struggle to achieve cost-efficiency according to the new budget model had led to changes in the hospital's organizational structure. Most hospitals had gone from a department structure to a cluster structure, with care in each cluster being centered on certain categories of patients or illnesses. In hospital 5, a business unit structure had been introduced, resulting in new working methods and deliberations about flexible use of staff (table 7.6).

CONFIGURATION OF LOW-WAGE JOBS

When we define low-wage jobs as those jobs that are compensated below two-thirds of the median income (€9.90), it appears that starting wages in the FWG scales 1, 5, 10, 20, 25, 30, and also 35 are just below the threshold. Employees with working experience and seniority, however, easily pass the low-wage threshold. In the following list, we outline the job title and wage compensation for several low-paid jobs in hospital 1.

Table 7.6 Main Characteristics of the Case Study Hospitals

	Case 1	Case 2	Case 3	Case 4	Case 5	Case 6
Number of beds	529	341	881	852	530	250
FTE	1,538	891	1,928	1,819	2,170	520
Top clinical/ non-top clinical hospital	Top clinical	Non-top clinical	Top clinical	Non-top clinical	Top clinical	Non-top clinical
In-/outside Randstad	Outside	Outside	Inside	Inside	Inside	Inside
Financial situation	Declining, still positive	Healthy	Healthy	Unstable	Healthy	Financial crisis
Structure	Cluster	Department	Cluster	Cluster	Business unit	Cluster, integral management
Internal flexibility	Own flexpool with fixed contracts	Own flexpool with 0-hour contracts	Per department 0-hour contracts	Own flexpool with 0-hour or fixed-hour contracts	Own flexpool with fixed contracts	Pool with 0-hour contracts, plus temp workers
Volunteers "paid = work"	No	No	Yes	Yes	No	Yes
Seniority indicator	Average job tenure: 9.4 years	0–4 years: 46%; 5–10: 20%; 11–15: 17%; 16–20: 8.5%; 21–25: 4%; 26–30: 3%				Average job tenure: 5 years
Sickness leave	4.6%	4.5%	4.8% (7% in cleaning)	5.3%	5.9%	5.3%

Source: Author's compilation.

Job Classification of Low-Wage to Average-Paid Jobs in Hospital 1

FWG 10: Position for belt help in washing-up kitchen

FWG 15: Positions as assistant food supply, coworker in washing-up kitchen, bed-supply room, copy corner, household work, kitchen, linen service, traffic warden

FWG 20: Positions as coworker in household work, washing-up kitchen, intern transport, linen service, post

FWG 25: Positions as department assistant, administrative coworker, all-around service work, registration, kitchen, linen service, supply room, patient transport, staff restaurant, reception, cleaning service, telephone exchange, transport, nutrition administration, mechanical engineering, typist, nutrition assistant

FWG 30: Positions as coworker in outpatients' lab, administrative department assistant, lab assistant, administrative coworker, coworker in archives, security, blood samples, architecture, till to operating table, patient transport, reception, telephone exchange, medical secretary, secretary, administration, nutrition assistant, technical service

FWG 35: Positions as coworker in foreman technical service, coworker in foreman garden service, medical receptionist, purchase assistant, cook, diet cook, health visitor, lab assistant, lab assistant heart, X-ray technician, coworker in administration, company office, architecture, electrical engineering, admission, outpatients' lab, service desk, mechanical engineering, medical secretary, secretary, administration, lab supply room, caretaker.

FWG 40 to 45: Nurses

FWG 50 and higher: Specialized nurses

PROFILES OF THE NURSE AND NURSING ASSISTANT POSITIONS IN EMPIRICAL RESEARCH

The most important position in the internal care department of a general hospital is that of qualified nurses. All six hospitals under study explicitly employed only level 4 and 5 nurses, whereas the nursing homes also hired level 3 nurses to work next to level 4 and 5 nurses. In actual practice, the difference between level 4 and 5 nurses is not always visible. Managers have argued that nurses with a practical training background (level 4) often better understand the idiosyncrasies of the workplace and are more directly employable than nurses from a theoretical education track (level 5).

Now we give an overview of the various target occupations and their main tasks, responsibilities, and job territory.

Cleaners and Housekeepers   In all hospitals cleaning is an important function, given the hygiene requirements. Two organizational principles compete in this area. All of the case study hospitals but one had unskilled cleaners or housekeepers on their payroll (wage scales 15, 20, or 25). In hospital 2, we came across a very professional approach to the cleaning occupation; the aim was to give the cleaners themselves responsibility for achieving efficiency gains. Next to in-house cleaning, all of the hospitals also outsourced to specialized cleaning companies to a substantial degree. Such professional cleaning companies were responsible for the entrance halls, corridors, and public spaces within the hospital. Cleaners on the hospital payroll were responsible for cleaning a separate department with sixteen to twenty beds in half a day (that is, in four hours). They cleaned rooms, bathrooms, toilets, windowsills, tables, corridors, and sometimes operating theaters, but not the department kitchen: that work was done by the nutrition assistant.

Cleaners do not clean the direct environment of a bedridden patient; that is the responsibility of the nurse, who must observe the medical condition of the patient. For the same reason, a head nurse will even empty the bedpan, since there is no separate occupation responsible for that task. Nevertheless, there is occasional conflict between nurses and cleaners about cleaning extremely dirty floors, the edges of beds, or toilets soiled from the patient's illness. Though most of the cleaners we interviewed were satisfied with their working environment and the small conversations they could have with many different persons in that environment, some cleaners explicitly complained about being treated badly by nurses who ignored them, did not know their names, and left them work to do that was the nurses' responsibility. In addition, in hospital 5 and in the nursing homes we were explicitly informed about racial harassment and stereotyping between ethnic groups.

The Nutrition Assistant   Nutrition assistant is a low-skilled job that is mostly performed on an individual basis. These assistants distribute beverages and food, under the close supervision of nurses and dietitians. Working hours are flexible, and the working environment allows some communication with patients, which is an attractive employment condition. Like cleaners, many nutrition assistants have been recruited in informal circuits through friends or family. Some nutrition assistants progress to a secretary occupation. Reward is mostly categorized in FWG 25 and sometimes in FWG 30, though not all nutrition assistants were satisfied with their rewards given their responsibility for patients' diets. In some hospitals, nutrition assistants were experimentally given more responsibility for developing ways of treating patients more as a guest lady there to help them eat and drink, sometimes outside of the bed as well.

Nursing Assistants, Caretakers, and Department Assistants   In all but one hospital, a single nursing assistant was employed to assist nurses by generally lending a helping hand, holding up patients, standing by with equipment, fetching materials from the stockroom, preparing coffee and drinks, and so on. In all of the hospitals, such positions were scarce, and the hiring of these employees had often not been done on a structural basis. Many of these nursing assistants were left over from earlier applied job creation schemes. In one case, however, hospital management was discussing the reintroduction of level 3 nurses to fulfill easy tasks and relieve general nurses—also in order to save costs. Given the variety of responsibilities for nursing assistants, payment varied from FWG 10 to FWG 30. There was no formal training for these positions, apart from instruction on the job.

The Joint "Assist" Occupation   Hospital 3 explicitly attempted to integrate the assisting, cleaning, and nutrition functions into one function, called the "assist" function. The three aims of this experiment in enhanced work organization were to raise both employee satisfaction and patient satisfaction, to get insight into costs, and to gain financial benefits (or at least anticipate financial losses).

According to hospital 3, the following results have been achieved:

1. After nine months, the majority of employees were satisfied, and nurses saw working with an assist as innovative and an improvement. Nurses were performing considerably fewer of the tasks that had been assigned to assists, from 26.4 percent in 2003 to 7.6 percent in 2005, and they had more time directly spent with the patient (35.2 percent in 2005 against 30.0 percent in 2003).

Figure 7.2 The Assist Project: Three-in-One

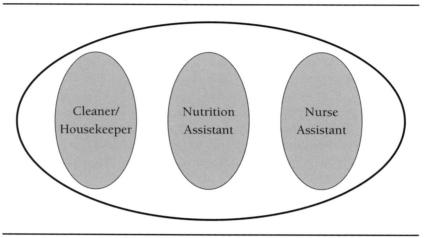

Cleaner/ Housekeeper

Nutrition Assistant

Nurse Assistant

Source: Author's compilation.

Nutrition assistants, however, were unhappy about having had to exchange their care and nourishment tasks for general hospitality and cleaning tasks they did not like.

2. The patients appeared to be rather pleased with the innovation. In department 1, patient satisfaction increased from 7.9 (on a 10-point scale) in 2004 to 8.4 in 2005. In department 2, patient satisfaction increased from 7.7 to 7.9.

3. It was difficult to measure the costs of introducing the assist, but the innovation seemed to have very positive results: with the same costs, production increased by 12 percent.

Volunteers in Related Areas   In all six hospitals and in the two nursing homes, a high number of volunteers were active in function domains that were closely related to but did not overlap with those of nursing assistants. Volunteers fulfilled tasks such as giving patients directions, taking care of flowers, bringing mail and newspapers to patients, riding the mobile library, and organizing the Sunday church service, as well as more work-related tasks, such as helping at the information desk, serving coffee and tea, distributing food trays, and transporting patients.

Officially, volunteers couldn't do paid work. Hospitals dealt with this limit in different ways. Some hospitals did not take the rule too strictly. In one hospital, volunteers took care of a substantial part of the patient's transport, an issue that was being considered for further professionalization. Another hospital filled gaps in the work schedules of nutrition assistants by bringing in volunteers. The border between paid and nonpaid work was thus blurred and gave hospitals some room for maneuver to let volunteers take over tasks that were usually done by employed personnel.

Nevertheless, both line and personnel management usually lacked a clear overview of the tasks and responsibilities executed by volunteers and were unaware of the tasks volunteers were carrying out in the hospital. Hence, volunteers worked not for economic motives but for traditional reasons. Their compensation varied by hospital: in one hospital, volunteers received €3 (US$4.39) per half-day of service and some compensation for transport, and in other cases volunteers were invited for the annual Christmas dinner.

Students   In actual practice, students from the vocational training system filled the most important helping position. They provided additional labor and could help nurses wherever it was deemed necessary. We conclude that to some extent they were the functional equivalent of nursing assistants, especially when they had some work experience and took less supervision.

WORKING CONDITIONS AND JOB QUALITY

INTERNAL AND EXTERNAL FLEXIBILIZATION

To solve staffing problems, hospitals apply both external and internal flexibilization strategies. Internal flexibilization occurs in varying degrees. On the wards, staff members are generally cooperative and help each other when needed, as is understood in the broad functional flexibility of the nursing job. Staff members also are willing to work with each other to change their prefixed work schedules to match their personal preferences and needs. In the interviews it also came out, however, that hospitals (as well as nursing homes) have established work cultures. Notwithstanding collegiality and cooperative work effort, sometimes there is a misbalance of work on the teams: some staff members suffer from work pressure as the demands from doctors and patients are increasing. Moreover, internal reorganization is sometimes met with resistance because employees are attached to their colleagues and nurses are unwilling to leave their vested rights within their local department.

External flexibility is sought primarily in the form of outsourcing and temp agency work. In all but one hospital, temp agency work was not used on a regular basis because the overhead costs were thought to be too high. In this context, temp agencies in this market offer a highly specialized contingent of workers—for example, nutrition assistants and specialized nurses.

In hospital 1, where no temp workers were used except for exceptional cases, outsourcing was practiced for a part of the cleaning staff, for kitchen personnel, and for several auxiliary jobs. The most important form of internal flexibilization of nurses was applied through an internal labor pool called Mobiflex. The eighty Mobiflex nurses (5 percent of overall staff) were employed by the hospital itself. The use of an internal labor pool was considered to be cheaper because, among other reasons, it was possible to avoid value-added taxation in comparison with hiring regular temp workers. Other advantages included the maintenance of quality levels and the attachment of flexible workers to the hospital. The hospitals argued that, to maintain quality, nurses in permanent jobs had to work at least twenty hours per week.

Hospitals 2, 4, and 6 had established a labor pool of people with a so-called zero-hours contract. The nursing homes had also adopted this strategy. "Zero-hours" employees have a written employment contract with the hospital and can be called on to work when needed. The employee has no obligations and can refuse to accept the task, and the employer has no obligation to offer a minimum number of working hours. As a general rule, both permanent and temporary contracts are applied, whereas the number of hours per week is differentiated. The expectation is that the use of internal labor pools will rise in the near future.

ETHNICITY

The number of workers in health care from ethnic minority backgrounds is relatively low in comparison with the national average. According to sector data, the share of ethnic minority workers is significantly higher in the nursing homes and homes for the elderly (5.5 percent) than it is in hospitals (3.3 percent) and in home care services (2.7 percent) (Van Til et al. 2001, 46). Surinamese and Antillean employees perform better than Turkish and Moroccan employ-ees, in part perhaps because among the latter health care has a very low status. Non-Western ethnic minorities are employed in assisting or auxiliary health care jobs more often than indigenous workers; they also are less likely to have a permanent contract and more often hold their job through a subsidized job creation scheme. Few ethnic minorities pass the threshold of level 3 in the education system, so many remain in care jobs and hardly progress to the fully responsible nursing occupation (Van der Meer and Roosblad 2004).

Although the working environment in general is classified as rather pleasant—among ethnic groups as well—we found that ethnic con-flicts occur owing to indirect discrimination from both patients and colleagues. "You would expect to be supported when patients disre-gard the color of your skin, but this does not always directly happen," one of our respondents in nursing observed. A female cleaner from the Balkan area complained about racial harassment by the Moroccan minority in the hospital. In one nursing home, according to some em-ployees and the personnel manager, the codes, communication, and culture of the Surinamese working population dominated other eth-nic groups. In none of the eight cases, however, did a kind of diversity management exist. Nevertheless, the regional employers' association in Amsterdam has initiated a three-year joint project to develop a tool kit on this issue, and that project has been picked up by a large aca-demic hospital and a leading nursing organization.

JOB CREATION PROGRAMS

Subsidized hospital jobs existed in the late 1990s, but seldom for nursing positions. Since 2002, the government has ended all job cre-ation programs and has been encouraging hospitals to change subsi-dized jobs into permanent jobs. In our study, it appeared that some hospitals, as "good and trustful employers," were trying to retain the subsidized workers who already were employed in internal transport and in simple domestic and kitchen functions. In such cases, subsi-dized jobs had been made permanent.

A REPORTED EVALUATION OF JOB QUALITY

During our fieldwork, we interviewed more than fifty staff members in each of the three occupations and also administered a written questionnaire. The results show that the interviewed employees were often single and many were divorced women with children. The respondents mentioned a fast work pace, demanding physical working conditions, and a lack of training opportunities, but they still valued their job with a 7.5 on average (on a 10-point scale).

Our results fit with the conclusion of a sectoral survey on working conditions in the health care sector that the work pace in hospitals is relatively intense and the autonomy of employees in their jobs is lower than average in the care sector. Overall, 63 percent of hospital employees complained about hard physical work, and 44 percent complained about hard emotional work. Still, 90 percent of hospital employees thought they worked in a pleasant work environment, and 82 percent were (very) satisfied with their current job (Bekker et al. 2004).

In 2002, 69 percent of hospital employees were absent one or more days because of illness, and 25 percent were ill for more than six days. This rate of absenteeism due to illness is relatively moderate in comparison with the average in the health care sector. Sickness leave is primarily related to physical problems (95 percent) but also to mental problems (4 percent) or to a combination of mental and physical problems (1 percent) (Bekker et al. 2004).

It also appeared from our interviews that wage levels were not really an issue for nurses and management, who felt that employment conditions were fairly reasonable, especially when employees received a surplus for working irregular hours. Working conditions and working hours were considered to be fine, and participation in teamwork and self-organization were reported to be self-evident. Nevertheless, in hospital 1, a statement in the newspaper by the board director of the hospital suggesting that nurses should go home "sweating on their backs" was considered unacceptable, not only by nurses but also among middle management.

On the initiative of the government, the social partners in the health care sector have concluded various covenants on health and safety. For the hospital sector, a first covenant was reached in 2001 about sickness absenteeism and the reduction of occupational disability. In 2003 stipulations on physical strain, aggression, and the pace of work were added. It appears that after the covenant was signed, 60 percent of hospitals made an action plan to meet these objectives, which was less than the 75 percent target. Overall, a substantial reduction in sickness levels has been achieved. Not much progress was achieved, however, with regard to the goals of reducing physical strains, detecting problems with work pace, and providing care after traumas (Van Vree, van Petersen, and Knibbe 2005). According to our interviews with personnel managers, the key to reducing sickness levels is mutual effort and good communication between management and employees.

OUTLOOK: COSTS AND BENEFITS OF PROTECTIVE LABOR MARKET INSTITUTIONS

Among nurses in hospitals, low-paid employment hardly exists. In this chapter, we have shown that the Dutch concept of "integrated quality care" supported by strong labor market institutions is responsible for task enrichment and task integration on the hospital work floor. Nurses are assisted by caretakers, department assistants, and nutrition assistants, but the nurses, by far the largest category of employees, are responsible for the oil in the machine of a department.

The primary reason for low-wage employment is the relatively recent entry of employees at the lowest wage scales. A second reason is the prevalence of small part-time jobs whose hourly wages are not more moderated than for full-time jobs but in which the total monthly salary is meager. All surveys suggest that the possibility of working part-time is a strongly supported norm and the direct consequence of some employees' individual preference. In contrast to the United States, part-timers in the Netherlands are predominantly satisfied with their jobs and tend to stay in them for long tenures.

In the health care sector, the institutions of education, training, collective wage setting, and work organization are closely interconnected. Industrial relations are highly institutionalized, and working hours and working schedules are strictly planned. Collective labor agreements cover the entire workforce in the sector and prescribe annual wage developments, the system of working hours, and secondary benefits. Related to the CLA is the job classification scheme, which is used to grade jobs and also to reward the qualifications achieved through vocational training. All these institutions are being applied in line with the collective bargaining outcomes between employers' associations and trade unions. We also conclude that the minimum wage level, wage subsidies for low-wage workers, and governmental job creation programs do not substantially matter for the labor market allocation of nurses and their assistants. At this level, no jobs are being created.

Until now, the functioning of these labor market institutions vis-à-vis the hospital organization has not been evaluated in terms of the emerging discussion on cost-consciousness and efficiency improvement in the health care sector and in fact has seemed to be rather sheltered from this discussion. We therefore conclude that these labor market institutions are strongly protective in nature for employees. It is an open question for the future whether human resource practices in hospitals will stick to the direct "control" of its executives or will deliberately develop the skills and qualifications of staff members. Some hospitals informed us that they had thought about lowering the qualification levels of nurses, and thus their labor costs, but since job territories and wage grades in the CLA are broadly overlapping, no direct financial gains could be expected from this strategy.

Perhaps more benefits could be gained from innovative work organization and further flexibilization, which normally occur after deliberations between management, consultancy companies, and employee representatives. In the cleaning occupation, some jobs were outsourced, and new working techniques were introduced. Nutrition assistants, on the other hand, expected more value-added from their jobs in their attachment to the task of feeding the patients. The most important innovation was the introduction of "three-in-one," or the assist project. Such examples of enhanced work organization are predominantly the result of employers' initiatives to reshape the workforce and are not directly related to wage formation for low-wage employees.

———————————

I am grateful to Marieke van Essen for help with the hospital case studies; to Suzan Leydesdorff, who supported the visits to the nursing organizations; and to Judith Roosblad for joint work on gender and ethnicity in the health care sector.

NOTES

1. The board director of a hospital in Arnhem even estimated that the number of hospitals had decreased by 50 percent in ten years' time (*NRC-Handelsblad*, June 6, 2006).

2. A comparable financial accounting system has also been introduced in the United States, France, and Germany under the label diagnosis-related group (DRG). However, the Dutch system is different from those in other countries, and its financial benchmarks are hardly comparable: the DTC is coded after (not before) patient treatment; patients can be coded in more than one DTC; and the coding is conducted by the medical specialist. In 2006 only 10 percent of all costs were calculated according to the new DTC system (Den Exter et al. 2004, 116–7).

REFERENCES

Appelbaum, Eileen, Annette Bernhardt, and Richard J. Murnane, editors. 2003. *Low-Wage America: How Employers Are Reshaping Opportunity in the Workplace.* New York: Russell Sage Foundation.

Bekker, Sonja, Gerard van Essen, Edith Josten, and Hanne Meihuizen. 2004. *Trendrapport aanbod van arbeid in zorg en welzijn 2003. Een onderzoek onder verpleegkundigen, verzorgenden en agogisch werkenden* [2003 Labor Supply in Health Care and Welfare Trend Report: A Study of Nurses, Caregivers, and Social Workers]. Tilburg, Netherlands: OSA.

Den Boer, Paul, Ben Hövels, and Andrea Klaeijsen. 2004. *Ruimte maken en benutten. De aansluiting tussen beschikbare en vereiste competenties bij gediplomeerden van het nieuwe opleidingsstelsel verpleging en verzorging* [Making and Using Space: The Link Between Available and Required Competencies in Graduates of the New Education System for Nursing and Caregiving]. Tilburg, Netherlands: OSA.

Den Exter, Andre, Herbert Hermans, Milena Dosljak, and Reinhard Busse. 2004. *Health Care Systems in Transition: The Netherlands.* Copenhagen: WHO Regional Office for Europe on behalf of the European Observatory on Health Systems and Policies.

Ministry of Health, Welfare, and Sports. 2002. *A Question of Demand: Outlines of the Reform of the Health Care System in the Netherlands.* International Publication Series 14E. The Hague: Ministry of Health, Welfare, and Sports.

Van der Grinten, Ton, and Peter Vos. 2004. "Gezondheidszorg" ["Health Care"]. In *Maatschappelijke dienstverlening-een onderzoek naar vijf sectoren* [Social Services Provision: A Study of Five Sectors], edited by Huub Dijstelbloem, Pauline L. Meurs, and Erik K. Schrijvers. Amsterdam: Amsterdam University Press.

Van der Meer, Marc, and Judith Roosblad. 2004. *Overcoming Marginalization: Gender and Ethnic Segregation in the Construction, Health, IT, and Printing Industries in the Netherlands.* Working paper 29. Amsterdam: AIAS.

Van der Windt, Willem, and Henriette Talma. 2006. *De arbeidsmarkt van verpleegkundigen, verzorgenden en sociaalagogen 2006-2010*. [*The Labor Market for Nursing Staff, Caregivers, and Social Workers, 2006-2010*]. Utrecht: Prismant.

Van der Windt, Willem, Hilly Calsbeek, Henriette Talma, and Lammert Hingstman. 2004. *Feiten over verpleegkundige en verzorgende beroepen in Nederland 2003* [*Facts About Nursing and Care Professions in the Netherlands, 2003*]. Utrecht: Elsevier.

Van Til, Cita, Henk W. Kanters, Ineke Bloemendaal, and Evelien van der Schee. 2001. *Arbeidsdeelname van allochtone medewerkers in de zorgsector* [*Labor Market Participation of Ethnic Minorities in the Health Care Sector*]. The Hague: Servicecentrum Uitgevers.

Van Vree, Félice, Arnoud van Petersen, and Nico Knibbe. 2005. *Monitor Arbocovenant Ziekenhuizen: Eindrapport* [*Monitor for the Health and Safety Covenant for Hospitals: Final Report*]. Leiden, Netherlands: Research voor Beleid, nr.B2964.

Vandermeulen, Leo J. R., Adriaan Hoogendoorn, and Gijsbert van Lomwel. 2003. *Beloning ziekenhuis- en marktsector. Een vergelijking van de lonen in de ziekenhuissector met de lonen in de markt anno 1997 en 2002* [*Wages in the Hospital and Market Sector: A Comparison of Wages in the Hospital Sector and Wages in the Market in 1997 and 2002*]. Utrecht: Prismant.

Visser, Johan. 2002. *Incidentele loonontwikkeling in de algemene en categorale ziekenhuizen 1997-2001* [*Incidental Pay Development in the General and Specialist Hospitals, 1997-2001*]. Utrecht: Prismant.

World Health Organization (WHO). 2005. *World Health Report 2005*. Geneva: WHO.

CHAPTER 8

Call Center Employment: Diverging Jobs and Wages

Maarten van Klaveren and Wim Sprenger

We are at a multinational finance company. It owns five call centers "in-house" all over the country, with agents available to customers by phone. The firm has decided to offer customer care by phone twenty-four hours a day, seven days a week. The centers are located in different regions and operate in different regional labor markets. Each of them specializes in a particular kind of service. However, they are part of one company planning and logistic system for customer care; this system connects customers automatically with the agents qualified to deliver the kind of service they need.

Advanced technology clearly dominates the agents' jobs, from work organization and planning to job content. The large electronic screen on the wall, visible to all the agents in the room, shows the number of clients phoning, the number waiting, the number being served, and so on. The screens in front of the agents provide all of the necessary information about the client calling. All incoming calls are recorded and thus provide random material for supervisors to use in evaluating the performance and skills of the agents.

The company planning and guiding system covers more than just the five call centers of the financial giant itself. As the umbrella system for one "independent" call center and a number of temporary work agencies (TWAs), it also organizes the workload and job content of agents both in-house and at the independent centers. Extreme numerical flexibility can be realized by using temp agency workers in all centers. Parts of the more regular tasks are performed by one independent center, providing long-term flexibility for the firms' managers and supervisors. Thus, the in-house agents can be offered a fairly secure employment contract, even if the future brings a decrease in the number of agents (because of growing use of the Internet, falling market shares, change to product segments, or other reasons the company might need less telephone customer care).

CALL CENTER AGENTS: SAME JOB, DIFFERENT CONDITIONS

A visitor would not be able to see many differences between the employees behind the screen, answering phone calls. They share the same job environment, wear the same headsets, and depend on the same planning and guiding system. Their jobs, however, are based on a variety of contracts. A small majority of the agents have permanent contracts with the finance company or the independent call center. Others have fixed-term contracts that might become permanent after continuous positive evaluations, but they have no guarantee that this will happen. Groups of temp workers are employed on permanent contracts with their TWA, which is legally obliged to offer permanent contracts to employees to whom it has offered a series of temporary contracts.

The agents are covered by at least three collective labor agreements (CLAs): the CLA of the financial firm for the permanent in-house agents, the independent call center CLA for the permanent employees, and the temp work agency CLA for the temp workers—the latter two industry agreements having mandatory extension. With three different CLAs, this workplace is characterized by different hourly wages, different working times, different pension schemes, and large variations in schedules and work planning. The permanent employees are allowed to choose their working time preferences in a three-month scheme that handles the company's flexibility needs by requiring employees to work one "flex-week" within the 168-hour weekly schedules. TWA agents, on the other hand, are confronted with a flex-week once every three weeks. Permanent employees can earn bonuses based on their sales performance; their flexible colleagues usually have to stick to their CLA wages.

TEMP AGENCIES AND CALL CENTER WORK

TWAs play an important role in Dutch call center activities, and not only by providing flexible workers to produce numerical and time flexibility or to fill in for absent employees. In our case studies, we focused on the role of TWAs in shaping call center work. Using their growing recognition (also by the unions) and expertise, they have become more permanent partners in many call centers, based on a series of basic rights for temp workers that have originated from legislation and CLAs. Temp workers who work for the "better" TWAs can claim permanent contracts after a series of temporary contracts and have pension rights and training rights as well. In call center work, this permanent involvement of TWAs has become structural as TWAs looking for a stronger market position have expanded their service levels and expertise into various aspects of human resource management: selection, training, supervising, coaching, and (administration of) personnel policy.

For larger firms, TWAs concentrate on hiring new temp agents. They train and coach agents in the first half-year of their employment relation with the TWA and select agents for transfer to the call center staff after this initial period. These services are performed within the policy framework of the client firm, most of the time even on location. For smaller firms, this TWA service is often expanded to cover all human resource activities during the first half or full year. The expansion of this TWA service reflects one of the weaknesses of smaller independent centers—their lack of human resource skills and facilities. Personnel managers in in-house finance and utility firms admitted that they used TWAs to create long-term flexibility among new agents, because TWAs selected applicants for agent work who were willing to work nonstandard working hours and shifts, for which they would not receive extra pay while working for the TWA. When they later opted for a permanent contract with the center, supposedly they would not object to flexible hours and schedules.

These new human resource activities of the temp agencies pose problems for unions trying to mobilize temp workers in the centers. More than once workers commented that since TWAs provided training facilities and other services, what could unions add to such services?

A VARIETY OF TASKS AND WAGE LEVELS

Call center work is a form of customer service that especially in the last decade has found its place in the heart of a permanent flexibility challenge for all kinds of employers as they implement new technology, new logistic concepts, and new services. The original core function of agents—answering incoming telephone calls and phoning potential clients with special offers—made their jobs vulnerable to concentration in call centers and, later, to outsourcing and eventually offshoring. Nowadays the industry includes parts of firms that are dedicated to frontline customer care (in-house call centers) as well as independent companies (also synonymous with facilitating, outsourced, or subcontracting centers) that provide call center services for a range of clients across industries.

Call centers are extremely flat organizations. According to the Dutch Global Call Center (GCC) survey, agents (operators) make up 88 percent of all call center staff. Initially call centers received a bad press: early coverage presented them as "electronic sweatshops." Call center agents, it was suggested, were subject to "total" managerial control and occupied low-wage, "dead-end" jobs. Recent studies, however, acknowledge that call center jobs have evolved and actually vary considerably in terms of industry, market segment, job complexity, and skills and discretion required. Call center work ranges from answering simple questions—such as checking bills or providing public transport times—to providing information on complex mortgage loans or solving intricate IT problems. In an early stage of the research, the international call center team decided to concentrate on mid-complexity jobs, and evidence from neighboring countries made it clear that customer service for finance and utilities includes a wide range of such jobs (Belt et al. 1999; Johansen 2000).

Although job quality for call center staff in general seems to have improved, the available figures suggest that wages have been lagging behind. The share of those who work in independent centers and are "low-wage"—that is, who earn less than two-thirds of the median wage, the low-wage threshold used in our research—is considerable. Based on the 2002 Statistics Netherlands microdata, this share was 32 percent, and for women it was 54 percent, even though these data indicated a higher average hourly wage level (€12.72 [US$18.72] gross) than later sources.

The in-house CLAs in finance and utilities are mostly negotiated at the company level, and have considerably longer and higher wage scales than the industry CLAs for independents and temp agencies. Low-wage agents are found mostly among independent and TWA agents since independent call centers and TWAs offer lower wage levels, hire agents who are younger and tend to have shorter careers, and offer fewer bonuses based on sales performance. Indeed, for 2004 the Dutch GCC survey produced a mean gross hourly wage for agents with permanent contracts working in in-house call centers of €13.80 (US$20.30); the hourly wage for those in independent centers was €11.40 (US$16.77)—a 17 percent difference. According to this source, temp agents working in in-house call centers earned less, but on average still earned €13.40 (US$19.71), against those in this category working in independent centers who earned €10.30 (US$15.15)—a 23 percent difference (De Grip, Sieben, and van Jaarsveld 2005, 33). These outcomes are consistent with those of the WageIndicator from September 2004 to September 2006. According to this source, the mean gross hourly wage of agents working in in-house centers indexed for 2006 was €14.20 (US$20.89), and for those in independent centers it was €11.56 (US$17.01)—19 percent lower. This source also allows us to calculate the incidence of low wages: 45 percent of the agents in independent centers remained under the low-wage threshold, as did 38 percent of their colleagues in in-house centers. Projecting these shares onto the estimated call center workforce suggests that in the period 2004 to 2006 about 63,000 agents were paid under the low-wage threshold. This share would be lower in finance and, to a lesser degree, in utilities as well.

THE METHODOLOGY

The international call center team agreed to select both independent and in-house call centers whose activities and contracts served financial and utilities companies. As far as such call centers are in-house, they are "hidden" in the official statistics within the finance or utilities industries. The official call center industry is made up of the independent centers, but this industry is only just beginning to develop industry institutions, which produce only fragmentary statistics. Fortunately, we were able to include the results of the Dutch GCC research project, which provides an overview for both in-house and independent centers on a number of issues. Nevertheless, these limitations explain why the title of this chapter is "Call Center Employment," not "The Call Center Industry."

The decision to select call centers that serve the finance and utilities industries was based on the assumed contrast in ownership structure (private versus more publicly owned or recently privatized), in employment structure, in job complexity (assumed to be higher in finance), and in firm strategies. Finance and utilities are major principals for call center activities. The GCC research reports that 19 percent of all call centers (and 26 percent of all in-house centers) serve financial services and that 13 percent (18 percent of the in-house centers) serve public services and utilities (De Grip, Sieben, and van Jaarsveld 2005, 7). Thus, our selection covers about one-third of the call center workforce. Independents serving financial companies can work for other sectors too, as they tend to spread their portfolios over more than one client.

Getting access to companies and locations was far from easy, primarily because we drew fire from an ongoing conflict in collective bargaining. In 2005 the employers' association for independent call centers pushed out the large unions affiliated with the national confederations in favor of a small company-based union. Quite a few independents refused to let us in, especially since one of the key themes in the conflict was low wages. At the same time, many customer complaints about bad service in utilities came to the surface, and management first and foremost wanted to restore customer trust. Finally, however, we did get access to a sufficient number of firms.

In finance we investigated two "couples": one financial company with an in-house center and one of the independent centers that worked (partly) for this company. Both in-house centers owned several locations and split up the work according to customer categories, services, and sometimes inbound or outbound calls. In one of these locations, we gained detailed insights into work organization, human resource policies, and job quality. In utilities we managed to get access to four locations, two of which were independents servicing the same utilities provider. In total, we interviewed twenty-six people, including four trade union officials who dealt with the sectors involved.

Table 8.1 provides an overview of the main characteristics of the Dutch call center cases.

THE ECONOMIC AND INSTITUTIONAL CONTEXT

The Emergence of an Industry

Jointly with the United Kingdom and Ireland, the Netherlands has been in the forefront of the boom in call center work in Europe (Belt et al. 1999). The call center market in these three countries is often described as "mature." The first call centers in the Netherlands were small telemarketing facilities, and the second wave contained the call centers of a few large mail-order companies. The third wave was much broader. Between 1995 and 1999, the number of call centers

Table 8.1 The Case Study Call Centers

	In-House Call Centers				Outsourced Call Centers			
	IN A	IN B	IN C	IN D	OUT A	OUT B	OUT C	OUT D
Sector	Financial	Financial	Utility	Utility	Financial	Financial	Utility	Utility
Ownership	Dutch	Dutch	Dutch	Dutch	U.S.	Dutch	Dutch	Dutch
Service-level strategy	Mid/high	Mid, self-service client as leading principal	Mid	Low/mid	Low/mid, long-term relations with three to four clients	Mid, serving clients in call center sector by hiring, training, and supervising	Low/mid serving series of clients from various sectors	Low/mid serving series of clients in many sectors, partly specializing in call center agent activities
Number of call center locations	5	3	1	4	1	None: delivers staff and HR services	4	1
Complexity of jobs	Mid/high	Low/mid/high	Low/mid	Low/mid	Mid	Low/mid	Low/mid	Low/mid
Workforce (head-count)	1,200	2,300[a]	25	1,750	300	?[b]	2,200	?[c]
Number of agent seats	600	1,500	20	1,100	175	300	1,700	?
Share part-time	20%	85%	25%	30%	35%	?	65%	80%
Share women	45	50	80	65	45	60	65	55?
Share under age thirty	25	30	15	23	30	55	28	45

Source: Authors' compilation from case studies by the researchers.

[a] Of which about 30 percent are temps and other flexible workers.

[b] For finance, 0: employees are located/working at the in-house call center seats.

[c] Temp agency, recruiting, (temp) employing, and partly training agents.

and agents tripled—an annual growth rate of over 35 percent. Although growth slowed to 20 percent from 2000 to 2005, the industry's expansion was still respectable. After the turn of the century, and driven by globalization, privatization, heavy competition, and shorter product life cycles, all kinds of firms and institutions centralized their frontline customer contacts into dedicated call centers. In the last decade, most of the growth of the call center workforce has been in in-house centers that belong to banks, insurance companies, IT companies, utilities, publishing companies, government bodies, and travel agencies. The recent growth of the independents was lower: their numbers were estimated at 200 in 1998 and at 250 in 2004 (see www.datamonitor.com). Most evidence confirms that the market share for independents is gradually diminishing. Union sources maintain that they already account for no more than 15 to 20 percent of the total call center workforce (see Von Pickartz and van Stigt 2001).

Table 8.2 presents an overview of the estimated growth in the number of call centers, both in-house and independent, and the number of employees. In 2004 call center agents accounted for 2.6 percent of all wage earners. Statistics often end up in confusion if the number of employees (head-count) have not been distinguished from the number of jobs (full-time equivalents, or FTEs—in this industry called positions or seats). Based on various sources, we may assume that the average FTE-to-head-count ratio is 45 to 55 percent.

The maturity of the industry also relates to its use of technology. Already in the 1980s call centers were using automatic call distribution (ACD) as a key technology for processing and distributing incoming calls to agents. A second step was the integration of telecommunication and computer software technologies in computer telephony integration (CTI). In the 1990s these systems reached maturity with interactive voice response (IVR) or voice response units (VRUs), the integration of telephone, software, and data retrieval: customers use touch-tone telephones or their voices to interact with databases, and the center is able to obtain basic information from a customer before he or she speaks to an agent. According to the Dutch GCC report, 80 percent of centers used IVR or VRU systems in 2004, although only 12 percent of all calls were handled with such systems (De Grip, Sieben, and van Jaarsveld 2005, 15–16). One of the finance firms we researched reported, however, that 75 percent of all incoming calls were handled by IVR or VRU, without agents' interference.

Table 8.2 Call Centers and Employees, 1992 to 2004

Year (End)	Number of Call Centers	Number of Employees (est.)	Average Number of Employees
1992	150	12,000	80
1995	320	30,000	94
2000	1,020	110,000	108
2001	1,260	130,000	103
2002	1,400	150,000	107
2003	1,520	165,000	109
2004	1,750	180,000	103

Source: Authors' compilation from various estimates, such as Datamonitor.

Customer relationship management (CRM) applications allow call centers to communicate in standardized ways with customers. These applications have major effects on agents' autonomy. The use of scripted texts had become rather dominant. A contradiction was growing here: agents had a greater need for autonomy in dealing with the newest technologies, especially web-enabling tools, in order to fully utilize the available information and react quickly to customer preferences. In finance we did not find too many scripts because the industry had switched to using agents as salespersons and their client contacts as selling contacts. Yet as we will see, new regulations may lead to the return of scripting. In utilities the share of scripted phone contacts is higher, reflecting the less interactive job content in billing or reporting disturbances. Growing competition between utility firms, however, makes it viable to move to increasingly scriptless jobs. It should be stressed here, however, that a low use of scripts does not necessarily translate into high levels of autonomy (De Grip, Sieben, and van Jaarsveld 2005, 17).

RECENT CHANGES AT THE INDUSTRY LEVEL

Fewer Simple Jobs? A number of call center activities tend to develop into core services, reflecting the dynamics of "service intensity" competition in finance and utilities. Recently, forms of (standardized) specialization have been evolving, with call center facilities becoming centers that offer broader forms of customer service, including many forms of customer contact, and use a variety of technical platforms, such as business-to-business (B2B) and business-to-customer (B2C).

This development may diminish the number of simple jobs, but here we lack wider evidence. An illustrative case, however, may well be that of one of the independent centers under study. This center partly services a financial multinational and offers more complex jobs to agents who work for the bank than it does to their coworkers who give information to (potential) clients of an international telephone company entering the Dutch market. The job of the latter group entails less on-the-job training, calls of shorter length, and a wider use of scripts, and the job is performed by a higher share of temp workers. The gap between the two categories is quite structural (also at the location level), and there are few occasions to move from servicing one client to servicing the other—unless the service contract is changed or ended.

A Decline in Outbound Contacts The share of outbound calls is declining. Various sources estimated that already in the period 1998 to 2000 fewer than one-fifth of all call center activities were outbound, and those were mostly telemarketing (Braaksma 1998; Eimers and Thomas 2000). Since then, telemarketing has become more and more unpopular with the general public and made subject to strict regulation by the telecom supervisor Opta. Telemarketers are now required to ask for the customer's consent to phone him or her the next time. New regulations enable customers to register themselves as "non-phonable" for outbound calls (*NRC-Handelsblad*, May 18, 2006). Lately the Internet has developed into an ever-growing competitor.

The Dutch GCC report states that in 2004 86 percent of all in-house call centers identified customer service as their main activity and only 13 percent identified sales as their main activity. According to GCC, as many as 94 percent of the in-house centers mainly dealt with inbound calls. This is contrary to the breakdown with independents, 59 percent of which focused on sales while only 38 percent focused on customer services (De Grip, Sieben, and van Jaarsveld 2005, 6–7). Our cases showed that in in-house centers the distinction between customer service and sales was growing blurred. In particular, in finance the market seemed to be saturated, and firm strategies were focusing on intensifying the number of services *per customer*. Thus, customer service was developing into a core activity: every customer contact was regarded as a potential selling moment.

Recent Process Innovations Most process innovations recently implemented in call centers involve expert systems and integration with
Internet-based communication and web-enabling tools (voice-over
Internet protocol, or VOIP, text chat, and so on). Forerunners are to
be found among the independent centers: in 2004, 42 percent of
them used expert systems (26 percent of in-house centers), and 27
percent of the independents used VOIP (14 percent of in-house centers) (De Grip, Sieben, and van Jaarsveld 2005, 16). A human resource manager revealed one of the mechanisms behind these figures
when he told us that working with an independent servicer was
partly meant to keep the firm on track with process innovations and
that this would have been difficult to achieve if services were kept totally in-house. In spite of their intensive IT use, call centers remain
highly labor-intensive and prone to competition on labor costs. The
GCC research found that in 2004 the average in-house center used 74
percent of its budget for wage costs, against 72 percent for the average independent (De Grip, Sieben, and van Jaarsveld 2005, 19).

Demand Fluctuations: "Secure Insecurities" How vulnerable is the call
center industry to fluctuations in demand? In most of our cases,
management regarded such fluctuations as a permanent condition
for performance. Planning and scheduling were based on the expected peaks and troughs. Peaks are partly the result of consumer behavior, but they can also stem from outside events, such as the initiatives of competitors, and explicit firm policies, such as offering new
services. Such permanent "secure insecurities" shape the rationale
for the growing flexibility in hours of servicing. They also tend to
lead to independent call centers and temp work agencies cooperating
ever more intricately in a value chain with in-house customer services. That value chain includes:

- A mix of price and product competition (the use of different wage
  systems and CLAs, more or fewer temp agency workers, operation in one sector or—for some independents—in various sectors)

- Intensive cooperation within the chain (partly because of the regulation of customer contacts and service provision)

- Risk prevention concerning job quality that adds to the cost of independents (in finance and utilities) or of temp agency workers (in finance and in independent centers)

One human resource manager explained his risk prevention policy to cope with heavy market fluctuations:

> Our contracts and terms of employment are better than at the independent working with us. Therefore, we are prepared to protect our call center employees in the long run by collaborating with one or more independents. In case of a dramatic loss of customer contacts, we can change the contract and avoid expensive and painful layoffs and reorganizations within our own organization.

The planning and guiding systems that call centers use are quite sophisticated and include historical data on factors such as the frequency of calls, the introduction of new products and the expected impact on the number of calls, the influence of weather conditions, and expectations about client wishes and long-term behavior. These systems produce the playing field for long-term human resource and innovation programs.

One bank manager outlined the effects of his firm's long-term human resource policy on the number of employees: "To focus our long-term human resource strategy, we start from a series of expected innovations and changes, which are partly interdependent, sometimes counterbalancing:

- A movement to the Internet (fewer agents needed)

- Substantial investments in process innovation, resulting in fewer 'complaints' traffic (fewer agents needed)

- Rationalization of non-used working hours (except normal pauses) by improved floor management (fewer agents needed)

- Customer 'self-service' as a guiding principle, though with agents on hand to lend assistance if customers cannot find tracks and answers (more agents needed)

- New legislation may lead to higher standardization and script-driven calls, and thus longer calls (more agents needed)"

"All in all these changes could lead to a decrease in employment of about thirty to forty percent over five years. The 'flex-factor' [the share of workers who have contracts with an independent or a TWA] may well increase from fifty to sixty percent in order to avoid costly social plans within the company."

Recent changes in EU and national regulations concerning banking, insurance, and utilities have been instrumental in promoting the independent call center "industry." They stimulated international mergers and takeovers in finance. In utilities they opened up opportunities for privatization and deregulation, starting in the telecom sector and followed by energy. Moreover, in 2006 the new Identification for Servicing Act and the Financial Services Act gradually came into force. These laws oblige financial institutions to record orders of certain products and services according to more detailed formats that include a "care obligation" toward the customer. Initially the new regulatory frameworks enlarged the pressure to (partially) outsource activities. On the other hand, our case study interviews suggest that outsourcing has tended to stabilize (and sometimes reverse), although it remains difficult to interpret the outcomes yet. In one of the finance firms, all in-house agents had a contract with the bank except for newcomers delivered by TWAs. On the contrary, in the other financial company almost half of all employees had (mostly permanent) contracts with an independent or a TWA: they were managed by the TWA but working from seats and locations at the bank, as well as under conditions and procedures controlled by bank management.

Financial markets, dominated by multinational firms, emphasize more and more shareholder value. Our case studies show that this priority can be an incentive to outsource services, even if cost advantages seem to be marginal. Large conglomerates use outsourcing to lower the share of fixed costs, and thus enlarge shareholder value, while keeping the number of employees constant.

RECENT CHANGES IN FIRM STRATEGIES

We can analyze firm strategies within the call center industry at three levels: the strategies of finance and utility firms (global in finance, more regional or national in utilities, which still have features of government-granted monopolies); the strategies of independent call centers as they compete and cooperate in the customer service market; and the strategies of TWAs.

Roughly speaking, firm strategies are influenced by these elements: changes in competitive conditions; changes in institutions; higher-order firm or holding company strategies; and lower-order management, union, and staff choices. Concerning the third element, it is interesting to note that there was no division between the global companies in finance and utilities, on the one hand, and the national and local-based firms among independents and TWAs, on the other hand. The two finance firms were global players, if Dutch-based. For them, the Netherlands was just one region. Utilities usually compete within national borders and sometimes (as with water services) act as if they are still a public monopoly. Among the independents and TWAs we investigated were two multinationals: one Dutch-based, one American-based.

Competitive Conditions in Finance and Utilities   After a boom of non-sheltered competition, most finance markets seem saturated; growth can be obtained only by launching new products and niches. This is the background for the broad trend to position customer services as a core business. Leading firms also promote "self-service" by clients in order to target those clients who really need information and guidance. New strategies of customer care and sales are emerging in which call centers and their agents play central roles by detecting and using "selling moments" (then sending "leads" to back-office salespersons) and providing special groups of customers with targeted information and offers.

In utilities the main firms are still able to operate under more sheltered conditions. Their former local or central government owners are still heavily involved in policymaking, but they can no longer refrain from dealing with the stiffened competition on the energy markets. Even if some utility providers are still dependent on the government and sheltered monopolists in local markets—as is the case with water providers—they have to sell additional services and information. As the merging of water providers and public water administrators accelerates, managers are aware that offering extra services will make the difference in less sheltered water markets, and the first market-oriented shifts in firm strategies can already be noted. Here too the role of call centers will be more pronounced.

For independent call centers, the main choice is between finding and exploring niches and the opportunities they offer for standardization and cost cutting by process innovation and opting for broad portfolios, with their higher perspectives on sustainability. Actually, in independents and TWAs segmentation in agent work is at stake. A major issue for in-house centers is integration with other parts of customer service; this issue is urgent for the insurance divisions of the financial conglomerates, and somewhat less so for their banking divisions. In utilities this kind of integration is just evolving as an option.

A number of the services provided by utilities are still low-quality, and the industry continues to maintain low-complex jobs (billing, measuring, answering questions). However, public dissatisfaction with the poor service levels of one of the utility firms has recently resulted in higher levels of permanent contracts and extra training of agents. Management became aware that customers experience a lack of service if they cannot reach agents or if agents do not help them in the way the company suggests in its ads. One agent at the customer care center of a major utility firm described what can happen next: "We all went to extra training courses, to be able to answer more questions directly instead of connecting customers with back offices. Since then, the number of complaints has gone down considerably. Finally management recognizes the importance of our job for the image and performance of the firm in the long run."

LABOR RELATIONS

Employee Representation The labor relations that are relevant for the in-house call centers of financial and utilities firms follow those of the parent industries, including compliance with CLAs; patterns of unionization do as well. Consequently, labor relations vary considerably in these call centers: some are union strongholds, and others are marked by the virtual absence of union members and weak employee representation. Variation in employee representation can also be observed within large organizations. In 1995 ABN-AMRO bank and its works council ran into conflict over the issue of outsourcing call center work. In the judgment of the Labor Court, the need for cost reduction that the bank management emphasized was arbitrary: the bank had to withdraw its decision. This case set a standard for decent outsourcing by large companies (Gerechtshof Amsterdam 1996).

In the independent call center industry the identification and development of coherent institutional structures to serve as a basis for sound labor relations has met with many difficulties. From the viewpoint of employee representation, structured labor relations are crucial, as union density in independents remains low—about 14 percent. A typical Dutch deal seemed at hand when in 1998, stimulated by the national employers' federation VNO-NCW, the FNV Bondgenoten union, and the CNV union confederation, founded an association of independent call center employers, Werkgeversvereniging voor Facilitaire Call Centers (WGCC) (Eimers and Thomas 2000, 56).

Formal employee representation remains a weak point in call centers. Though in most of our cases a works council was active, in many call centers compliance with the Works Council Act remains low. Research undertaken in 2000 showed that employees of inhouse centers were mostly represented in the works council of the parent firm, although more than half of all respondents did not know. In the independent centers, 9 percent answered that they were represented by the works council, 54 percent thought the firm had no such council, and 35 percent did not know (Keizer 2001). Four years later, the Dutch GCC survey reported that 76 percent of the subcontracting centers had a works council, but the report confirmed the union impression that call center agents were often not represented, or weakly represented, in the councils (De Grip, Sieben, and van Jaarsveld 2005, 55; Von Pickartz and van Stigt 2001).

A member of the central works council at one of the banks described the difficulties of call center agents relying on such councils for representation:

> It is not easy to represent the students and temp workers at remote locations, as they tend to quit the job rather quickly. Moreover, we have one center employing a lot of students for three hours a day, mostly performing outbound calls. Relations between them and the core agents at other locations are remote, also because they perform specialized tasks and do not participate in regular training sessions. As a works councilor, I seldom have contacts with these colleagues.

A CLA for Independent Call Centers In 1999 the independent firm SNT agreed upon a CLA with four unions. Although rudimentary, this was the first CLA in the call center industry. Union efforts to negotiate more company CLAs failed until, in 2003, the WGCC association and FNV Bondgenoten reached an industry agreement that was declared mandatorily extended (meaning that all independent centers had to comply). In April 2005, however, WGCC agreed upon a CLA with only the small BTP union. Both parties stated that they were striving for a "modern CLA" with more flexible terms of employment. The FNV unions questioned whether BTP represented a substantial number of employees. In spite of their protests, the Minister of Social Affairs and Employment declared this CLA mandatorily extended. In 2006 WGCC radically changed its policies and reinvited the large unions—in particular FNV Bondgenoten—to negotiate a new CLA. Soon a new CLA came out, and the crack in the CLA coverage system that had announced itself a year earlier was thereby filled. According to the union officers involved, a crucial factor in this about-face was the need of employers to be respected and to have recognized terms of employment to offer. The tightening of (regional) labor markets may have done the rest.

After the 2006 CLA was signed, a new FNV Bondgenoten representative stated:

> Our first target was to reestablish contacts and trust with the employers' association for the independents. Alas, our colleagues from the official public workers' union, a sister FNV union, were no longer allowed to participate, as the employers would accept only one union from the FNV ranks. Next year we will push further, based on discussions with members that we hope to realize at some scale.

Other Institutional Changes Besides the results of collective bargaining, two other institutions that have an impact on firm strategies are the minimum youth wage and student grants. Both types of call centers employ groups of young people and students for special agent tasks and for specific working time schemes. In one of the independent centers they provided some of the coverage during flexible hours (evenings and weekends) so that the employer could avoid paying special rates for working unsocial hours. In our cases we observed that:

- Specialized centers were located in labor markets with an overrepresentation of part-time working students. Based on their general skills, they were judged to be qualified for this special job;

they might have worked on permanent contracts but did not yet belong to the core labor force, and they received substantially less on-the-job-training than other groups.

- The regional labor market was a decisive factor. Independent centers in tighter regional markets sometimes competed with in-house centers to keep experienced and well-performing workers on permanent contracts. One independent center offered permanent employees a firm pension scheme (not included in the industry CLA) in order to prevent them from leaving to work at the local Tax Ministry center.

The recent TWA industry CLA has enlarged opportunities for managerial flexibility in using temps. An example is the arrangement that entitles temp workers to payment according to the conditions of the user firm after twenty-six weeks of work. This is in line with a TWA policy of covering the first half-year of an employee's contract with a call center, providing human resource services and comparably low-wage costs.

Vocational Training   Since 2000, various reports have criticized the chaotic situation in education and training for agents' jobs, an area that had no broadly accepted end terms and no accepted certification system (Eimers and Thomas 2000; Keizer 2001). Employers, unions, and education providers separately took steps to fill the gap. In 2002 the WGCC association initiated the Foundation for Call Center Exams (SECC) with the goal of establishing a uniform system of occupational titles. This initiative was not very successful. The better chance was for the OOCC Foundation, formed on the initiative of the unions, which succeeded in interesting the Ministry of Social Affairs and Employment in an industry training (so-called O&O) foundation. The foundation remains rather small, and unlike other such efforts, it cannot rely on an industry wage levy. Finally, ECABO, the national vocational training system for clerical jobs, took the lead. Earlier, ECABO had commissioned research on occupational profiles that showed a growing demand for integrating customer demand with more conventional tasks; responding to this demand would lead to broader tasks at the mid-complexity level or higher. A conflict of interest arose, however: in-house centers promoted such broadening of tasks and differentiating the skill structure, but most independents gambled on retaining narrow jobs and limited training to the initial programs (Eimers and Thomas 2000, 39–40). Finally, in 2004, at the request of ECABO and with the support of OOCC, a committee of experts succeeded in developing a profile for a "call center professional," the basis for a new educational stream at the intermediate level in the vocational training system, and two sets of end terms linked with certificates.

CASES IN CONTEXT

EMPLOYMENT, WORK ORGANIZATION, AND JOB QUALITY

Gender and Age A characteristic call center employee is a young, female part-timer. We deal with the part-time issue in the next section; here we concentrate on gender and age.

Recently the call center workforce seems to have become even more "feminized." The Dutch GCC report concluded that overall 70 percent of call center employees are female, with a lower share (61 percent) in independent centers (De Grip, Sieben, and van Jaarsveld 2005, 23). The WageIndicator survey for 2004 to 2006 concludes that 80 percent of this workforce is female, with a slightly lower female share in independents (76 percent). Yet the share of women in our cases was substantially lower, varying from 45 to 80 percent (and here too their share in independents was a bit below that of the in-house cases).

All evidence points to a rather young call center workforce, although the available figures vary. The Dutch GCC report reported the youngest age structure, especially in independent centers, with 39 percent of employees below age twenty-five and only 8 percent over fifty, suggesting that in-house centers employ a larger share of older employees (14 percent over age fifty) (De Grip, Sieben, and van Jaarsveld 2005, 21–22). The WageIndicator data for 2004 to 2006 indicates that the percentage of men and women under age twenty-five employed by call centers is exactly 30 percent for both, with a somewhat larger share (9 percent) for women age fifty and older (6 percent for men this age). Also according to this source, men employed in the independents are slightly younger than those in in-house centers, and women are slightly older.

Based on the recent WageIndicator data, we also calculated shares of employees under age thirty in order to be on a par with the yard-stick derived from the low-wage studies in other countries and the indications derived from our cases. These shares were 54 percent for the independents and 44 percent for the in-house centers. Again, the shares in our cases varied widely, but with 15 to 30 percent in the independents, they were much lower than this general picture; the shares in the in-house centers (28 to 55 percent) are a closer match. In-house centers in finance seem to hire substantially older workers, and in that respect one of our financial cases may be typical. This in-house center reported a growing segment of older agents, but management complained that this could lead to a slowdown in innovation, since these workers might resist the new combinations of servicing and sales. One such older agent at a finance in-house call center, for instance, had this to say:

> Recently management changed job contents for all agents. It was kind of a restructuring operation without dismissals. Personally, I felt uncomfortable with the new targets: I have to try to sell as many products as possible during calls, using selling moments. We lost our thirteenth month of salary and have to "earn it back" by sale-related bonuses, with all administrative fuzz connected. We never did those things before, and it makes you feel guilty toward customers who did not ask for any offer when phoning. However, the younger colleagues do not seem to be that bothered.

Educational and Job Levels In line with our case observations, recent research points out that the large majority of call center operators are rather high-skilled. According to the WageIndicator, during the period 2004 to 2006, 78 percent of the agents working for independents and 81 percent of those working for in-house centers had completed secondary education, while the GCC report cited 70 percent as the figure for both categories (De Grip, Sieben, and van Jaarsveld 2005, 24). The WageIndicator data indicate that 25 percent of the independent agent workforce has completed (!) higher general or university education, as against 18 percent of the in-house agents.

These figures do not exclude the possibility, considering the lack of a mature vocational education system until recently, that many call center agents feel they are missing skills. For example, in the region Arnhem/Nijmegen many agents who were surveyed recently perceived themselves as lacking in general skills (39 percent), sector-specific skills (35 percent), or firm-specific skills (20   percent) (Sieben and De Grip 2004). The Dutch GCC report reveals that agents dealing with inbound calls receive on average 72 hours of initial training, with the agents in financial services receiving the most, at 105 hours. The initial inbound training in independent centers (33 hours) and the training for outbound services (46 hours) are on average much shorter (De Grip, Sieben, and van Jaarsveld 2005, 25). Parent firms sometimes control the on-the-job training of the independents working for them. In one of our cases, the parent firm provided the training sessions for independent agents in mixed groups with its own employees.

The CLA for independents distinguishes five job levels as a base for agents' wages, though the corresponding wage scales are highly overlapping. These job levels seem to reflect the required skills and autonomy levels. Within in-house centers, which have their own firm CLA, job levels are mostly further differentiated based on job descriptions for specific tasks and responsibilities.

Health Risks: Monotony, Workload, and Lack of Autonomy Work stress from production targets and "telephone lines" has been identified as a substantial risk for call center operators. The repetitive nature of the job, the static and sitting work position, and the dominance of onscreen work also put the agent at risk of RSI. Employees cited as negative aspects of call center work (in this order): many hours behind the screen; high workload; bad image of call center work; and lack of career perspectives (Keizer 2001). The GCC report indicated that in 2004 94 percent of the in-house call centers and 78 percent of the subcontracting centers formally complied with the regulations of the Working Conditions Act (De Grip, Sieben, and van Jaarsveld 2005, 37). Nevertheless, two years earlier an inventory of the Labor Inspectorate at seventy-six call centers showed a less rosy picture by detailing several health risks of call center work: RSI, voice problems, problems from working in too small or unsafe a workplace, and stress from a high workload (Arbeidsinspectie 2003). Other physical risks are those related to the use of headsets: infection, "acoustic shock" (which risks deafness), eyestrain, and headaches (TNO Arbeid 2002). The call centers we investigated had implemented a range of measures to counterbalance these risks, especially rest times.

A recent union-initiated survey of agents revealed striking differences between in-house and independent agents in their evaluations

Table 8.3 Job Levels in the Call Center Industry Collective Labor Agreement (CLA), 2005

	Level 1	Level 2	Level 3	Level 4	Level 5
Character of contacts with clients	Mostly inbound contacts	Inbound or outbound contacts	Inbound and outbound contacts	Inbound and outbound contacts	Inbound and outbound contacts
Autonomy	Very low discretion: scripts or systems dictate way of performing task	Low discretion: scripts or systems determine task performance; limited possibility for deviation	Medium to low discretion: conditions for task performance determined by script or directives; deviation allowed	Medium to high discretion: limited or no determination by scripts or systems; agent needs competence to perform without; freedom of approach within directives and system requirements	Higher discretion: analyzing questions/problems and taking proper actions; high degree of freedom within rough directives

Source: Call center industry CLA, 2005.

Table 8.4 Evaluation of Elements of Job Quality by Call-Center Agents, 2006

	In-house Agents	Independent Agents
Chair and table OK	72%	33%
Desktop and monitor OK	82	33
Climate control OK	39	17
Noise level OK	54	21
Work stress (very) high	56	48
Physical complaints	32	37
Monotony no problem	60	31

Source: FHKN (2006).

of job quality. As table 8.4 shows, these differences had mainly to do with physical working conditions; even the lowest-scoring items in the survey worked out to a substantial level of complaint.

Autonomy is a core job quality problem in call center work. Managers often perceive that call center workers have quite a lot of autonomy. According to the GCC research, three-quarters of the managers in the Dutch sample believed that it is important to allow agents more authority at work. The authors suggest that overall the level of standardization in Dutch call centers is comparatively low (De Grip, Sieben, and van Jaarsveld 2005, 17–18). Other surveys, including that of the Labor Inspectorate, emphasize that especially at lower complexity levels health risks are related to job content—notably the short-cycle character of the work, the lack of autonomy for agents, the variations in incoming calls, and the use of scripts. Some related health risks arise from the monitoring and control in the "regular" work situation. Quite a lot of evidence shows that continuous monitoring increases job-related stress. The GCC survey reports that almost all call centers monitor their agents, although managers maintain that monitoring is used for agent feedback purposes only. *Continuous* monitoring is virtually absent, the researchers suggest, because of the Dutch Personnel Data Protection Act (De Grip, Sieben, and van Jaarsveld 2005, 18–19).

Our cases show that most (financial) in-house agents work without scripts and have a call time of about five minutes to answer questions, do cross-selling, and reinforce the relationship with the customer. In utilities and at independents serving other industries, scripting is more dominant and leaves less room for autonomy. Yet new forms of regulation tend to put limitations on the autonomy of all agents. Self-monitoring as a new form of internalization of the monitoring concept deserves special mention here. We found out that, in order to gain extra bonuses, agents were asked to monitor and document the number of their successful "leads" themselves.

Working Hours and Contracts

Part-time work is for many agents the only realistic option—not only because it reconciles work with family life and study obligations, but also because the workload itself might be unmanageable as a full-time job. Some call center managers explained that they did not hire full-time agents because this type of work was too demanding to do full-time (De Grip, Sieben, and van Jaarsveld 2005, 25; for the same opinion, see Arbeidsinspectie 2003, 11). For the period 2004 to 2006, the WageIndicator survey measured a part-time rate of 50 percent—51 percent in independents, 49 percent in in-house centers—and the GCC report found an even higher share: 60 percent in in-house call centers and 77 percent in independents, leading to an average working week of twenty-six hours (thirty hours in the in-house financial services, twenty-one hours in independent call centers) (De Grip, Sieben, and van Jaarsveld 2005, 38).

A temp worker at an in-house center had this to say:

> I'm still employed by a temp agency, the one that hired me nearly a year ago. Of course, you hope to be evaluated positively, in order to get a permanent contract. Not so much for the money, though the secondary benefits make a difference. Important are the schedules. As a permanent worker, I will be able to have twelve weeks with schedules fitting most of my preferences, and [that will] ease the combination with my hobbies [band playing]. Only every thirteenth week is flexible in the way that you work all sorts of nonstandard times. Actually, I get such a "flex-week" every third week. In fact, we temps provide for a lot of the flexibility in scheduling, compared to the colleagues with normal contracts. Yet you have no choice if you want to be one of them in the future.

Most in-house agents covered by the relevant CLAs have standard working weeks of thirty-six hours, while those covered by the call center CLA or the TWA CLA have a forty-hour week. Independents and TWAs are institutionally designed to offer and impose flexible hours on their agents. Since 2005, the CLA for independents does not provide extra pay for work on Saturdays or at night before 10:00 P.M. Moreover, TWAs are hiring workers for certain nonstandard working periods, thus discharging call center management to schedule their own workers in nonstandard schedules.

In our cases, we traced a large variety of opening hours and schedules, from 8:00 A.M. to 7:00 P.M. during working days to schedules of seven days a week, twenty-four hours a day. We found that a general tendency to make call center services available during more hours per week was connected to client firms' behavior and firm strategy considerations. When their management decided to keep the center open continuously, agents working at an in-house finance center in high-complexity jobs had to indicate their willingness to work on 24/7 schedules. Here, according to line management and an employee representative, about 85 percent of the nonstandard working hours were divided voluntarily among permanent workers; the rest were obligatory for them to work. This arrangement was made at the expense of temps and fixed-term workers, who would usually work substantially more flexible hours than the core workforce.

The use of flexible contracts for call center agents seems to still be growing. Whereas the 1988 to 2000 surveys found 33 to 35 percent flexible contracts, both the Dutch GCC report and the 2004 to 2006 WageIndicator survey reported 40 percent. In this last survey, the independents had the highest score on contractual flexibility: 46 percent, against 33 percent for the in-house centers. Fixed-term contracts were most important among the flexible contracts with independents (50 percent), followed by contracts with temp agencies (33 percent), zero-hours contracts (7 percent), and on-call contracts (3 percent). Within in-house center flexible contracts, fixed-term contracts were even more important (58 percent), but contracts with TWAs were somewhat less so (20 percent), as were zero-hours contracts (6 percent) and on-call contracts (2 percent).

WAGES AND COMPENSATIONS

Our case evidence confirms that in-house agents with permanent contracts earn considerably higher wages than their colleagues at independent call centers or TWAs, especially if we include the usually shorter standard working week of the first group. Table 8.5 provides

Table 8.5 Comparison of Applicable Collective Labor Agreements (CLAs) for Call Center Agents at Monthly Entry Wage and Maximum Wage and in Steps in First Six Grades, Mid-2006

Grade	Entry Wage			Maximum Wage			Steps		
	CC	TWA	FIN	CC	TWA	FIN	CC	TWA	FIN
0	€1,381	€1,388	—	€1,381	€1,388	—	1	1	—
1	1,442	1,498	€661[a]	1,576	1,892	€1,738	7	ca. 9	13
2	1,489	1,541	809[a]	1,651	2,009	1,927	8	ca. 10	13
3	1,535	1,599	1,124[a]	1,831	2,141	2,081	10	ca. 11	13
4	1,581	1,672	1,445[a]	1,977	2,308	2,397	12	ca. 12	13
5	1,619	1,748	1,880	2,125	2,487	2,430	13	ca. 13	13

Source: Authors' compilation from various CLAs.
Note: Monthly wages above the low-wage threshold are printed in italics.
CC: Industry CLA for independent call centers, January 1, 2006, wages, based on forty hours per week.
TWA: Industry CLA for TWAs (ABU), July 3, 2006, wages, based on forty hours per week, agents in grade 1, 2, or 3.
FIN: Company CLA for financial group A, including in-house call center jobs, January 1, 2006, wages, based on thirty-six hours per week.
[a] Youth scales.

an overview of CLA wages and scales for these three agent categories. The monthly wages above the low-wage threshold are printed in *italics*.

The relevant CLAs not only diverge in wage levels, job grades, and number of steps within one grade, but they also vary in compensation rights for nonstandard hours. The GCC survey shows that all in-house centers offer their agents pension schemes, whereas only 39 percent of the independents do so. The shift in control concepts that we traced in finance call centers—away from standardization and the use of scripts—implies a greater share of flexible pay elements, such as bonuses. Indeed, following GCC, more than half of the in-house centers in finance mention performance rates for agents, a much higher share than in the rest of the call centers (De Grip, Sieben, and van Jaarsveld 2005, 34–37). Our case evidence points in the same direction, although larger pay flexibility advances slowly.

RECRUITMENT, TRAINING, AND CAREER DEVELOPMENT

In the recent recession, the labor turnover of agents fell substantially. The average churning rate went down from 22 percent in in-house centers and 36 percent in independents in 2000 to 11 and 19 percent, respectively, in 2004—a decline of 11 to 17 percent (De Grip, Sieben, and van Jaarsveld 2005, 40–42; Keizer 2001). A majority of the case study call center managers judged it important to reduce labor turnover. Yet some notable exceptions can be found. In one of our cases, the yearly turnover rate was just 3 percent, and the human resource manager saw this low rate as a potential problem for innovation in the firm and for job development.

We emphasized the role of TWAs in reshaping employment relations in call centers. At the peak of the tight labor market, in 2002, TWAs claimed that each day fifteen thousand employees worked in a call center through a TWA. In 2004 the GCC team found that two-thirds of call centers worked with temp agents. Most centers had contacts with one or two dedicated temp agencies, but some used more than that to take advantage of their mutual competition. According to the GCC, 19 percent of all agents are employed by a TWA (16 percent of the workforce in in-house centers, 25 percent in independents) (De Grip, Sieben, and van Jaarsveld 2005, 42). In our cases, we found a significant trend toward outsourcing some human resource management activities to TWAs or to staff human resource service providers. Selection and hiring mainly took place beyond the direct control of call center management. Introduction on-site, initial training, coaching, and on-the-job training, and job evaluation and monitoring were less widely outsourced, since they were usually embedded in the centers' management and planning systems.

One manager explained how new government regulation had changed quality concepts and agents' autonomy: "We train and evaluate our agents at four dimensions of quality:

1. Are you providing the right answer to the question?

2. Are you showing sufficient empathy toward the client?

3. Are you optimally utilizing selling chances?

4. Are you operating 100 percent according to legal and other regulations?"

CONCLUSIONS

A major conclusion to be drawn from our cases may well be that the simple dichotomy between in-house call centers and independent call centers is no longer adequate to analyze trends in employment and job quality in call centers. Management strategies, using changes in regulations, are heading toward integrated value chains of customer care services—first and foremost in finance, but such practices are also emerging in utilities. These chains are characterized by:

• Patterns of cooperation and communication between in-house centers, independents, and TWAs specializing in human resource servicing

• A combination of strategies in which agent work approaches the core business and, at the same time, peripheral agents work at a "flex-rate"

• The use of "flex-rates" as a form of risk reduction, in order to cope with decreases in employment and peaks in scheduling

Earlier analyses of the segmentation of call center work stressed the importance of IT in allowing management to create various segments (Batt 2000, 2001). The value chains developing in the Netherlands seem to combine segmentation and integration tendencies. Segmentation is primarily based on product market and (internal) labor market differentiation: variety in contracts with user firms, applicable CLAs, job characteristics, and labor supply characteristics, and differentiation in working time arrangements—between but also within centers. Under these conditions, IT is only one factor, and definitely not the most prominent. The changing profile of call center–oriented TWAs is one of the catalysts for the emergence of new forms of "integrated segmentation." They remain as important as ever in reshaping traditional employment relations and seem poised for permanent accessibility according to client demands.

Call center agent job quality is moving in various directions as well. In finance, scriptless calls of five minutes' duration have replaced monotonous jobs, partly by erasing short-cycle tasks with the help of new technologies—although new financial regulations promote the return of scripting. On the other hand, to some groups of employees the change toward cross-selling and intense customer contacts creates more work-related stress. In agent jobs (primarily) working for utilities, trends are more diverse, with both low job quality and high levels of customer service developing. Obviously, centers vary widely in their ability to find sustainable solutions to the omnipresent tension between low-cost servicing and customized approaches.

Thus, in Dutch call center work, high-road and low-road strategies coexist—interconnected and at the same time layered in various segments. Trade unions and other institutions may have quite a few reasons to question the idea of there being "one call center industry" as a starting point for efforts to enhance job quality and improve job perspectives for the various groups of employees concerned. A thorough analysis of the mechanisms of segmentation along the lines suggested here may be more rewarding.

REFERENCES

Arbeidsinspectie (Labor Inspectorate). 2003. *Projectverslag Inspectieproject Callcenters 2001–2002* [*Project Report of the Call Center Inspection Project 2001/2002*]. The Hague: Department of Social Affairs and Employment.
Batt, Rosemary. 2000. "Strategic Segmentation in Frontline Services: Match-

ing Customers, Employees, and Human Resource Systems." *International Journal of Human Resource Management* 11(3): 540–61.

———. 2001. "Explaining Wage Inequality in Telecommunications Services: Customer Segmentation, Human Resources Practices, and Union Decline." *Industrial and Labor Relations Review* 54(2A): 425–49.

Belt, Vicki, Maarten van Klaveren, Ranald Richardson, Juliet Webster, and Kea Tijdens. 1999. *Work Opportunities in the Information Society: Call Center Teleworking (WOWIS): Final Report*. Newcastle, London, U.K., and Eindhoven, Netherlands: CURDS, University of Newcastle upon Tyne, Tavistock Institute, STZ advies & onderzoek.

Braaksma, Ro. 1998. *Bedrijfsleven in beeld: Callcenters [Business in View: Call Centres]*. Zoetermeer, Netherlands: EIM.

De Grip, Andries, Inge Sieben, and Danielle van Jaarsveld. 2005. *Employment and Industrial Relations in the Dutch Call Center Sector*. Maastricht, Netherlands: ROA.

Eimers, Ton, and Eveline Thomas. 2000. *Onderwijs callcenterpersoneel vraagt nieuwe aanpak. Beroepenstructuur en kwalificeringsvraag in callcenters [Education of Call Center Personnel Requires New Approach: Occupational Structure and Qualification Demand in Call Centers]*. Nijmegen: ITS.

FHKN Partner in opleiding en examen. 2006. *Resultaten FHKN enquete onder call center medewerkers [Survey Among Call Center Agents]*. Amersfoort, Netherlands: FHKN.

Gerechtshof Amsterdam. 1996. 5 december 1996, nr 690/96 OK, Ondernemingsraad Nederland van ABN AMRO Bank NV tegen ABN AMRO Bank NV, ROR 1997, nr. 13 / art 25, 26 WOR. [Judgment of Labor Court (OK), published in *ROR*. Deventer, Netherlands: Kluwer.]

Johansen, Aslaug. 2000. *Tableau comparatif des plates-formes téléphoniques d'un échantillon de banques francaises [Comparison of Call Centers from a Selection of French Banks]*. Paris: ARETE.

Keizer, Margo. 2001. *Arbeid in callcenters. Eindrapport [Work in Call Centers: Final Report]*. The Hague: Research voor Beleid and Department of Social Affairs and Employment.

Sieben, Inge, and Andries de Grip. 2004. "Training and Expectations on Job Mobility in the Call Center Sector." *Journal of European Industrial Training* 28(2/3/4): 257–71.

TNO Arbeid. 2002. *Arbeidsrisico's in de branche Callcenters [Occupational Risks in the Call Center Branch]*. Hoofddorp, Netherlands: TNO Arbeid.

Von Pickartz, Ine, and Jacqie van Stigt. 2001. "De wereld is klant, de klant is de wereld" ["The World is the Customer, the Customer is the World"]. *Zeggenschap* 12(1): 26–28.

CHAPTER 9

The Food Industry: Meat Processing and Confectionary

Arjen van Halem

In this research project, the manufacturing industry is represented by the food industry. This industry consists of many subsectors, from small craft-based companies, such as local bakeries, to high-tech processing plants—for example, whey processing. Against this backdrop, the international food industry research group chose to focus on two subsectors in which a substantial number of low-wage jobs could be expected: the meat processing industry and the confectionary industry. The target occupation is the lower processing (and packaging) job. Both subsectors are traditionally low-skill industries with comparatively poor working conditions, but these features do not necessarily imply "low-wage." In confectionary the entry wage in the lower CLA scales is even above our low-wage threshold. The WageIndicator data for January 2004 to September 2006 indicates mean gross hourly wages (level 2006) in these subsectors that were 15 to 25 percent above the wage level of supermarkets and hotel cleaning.

Although the two subsectors have extensive but different institutions at the branch level, only small variations are found at the company and plant levels regarding wages and working hours. After providing a short overview of the food industry and the case selection, we present the two economic and institutional contexts separately in the next two sections. An analysis of job quality follows. In the final section we evaluate the outcomes.

TWO SMALL BUT INTERESTING SUBSECTORS

The food industry in the Netherlands is an integral part of the agribusiness value chain, which includes agriculture, manufacturing, supply, and distribution. Total employment (head-count) in food manufacturing has declined, from 146,600 in 1999, the top level in the last decade, to 124,400 at the end of 2005, a fall of 15 percent. Important subsectors are bread (32,100 employees in 2004), meat (20,400), and dairy products (10,700). The overall share of females is 32 percent, but it varies widely, from 52 percent in bread to 19 percent in dairy (CBS/Statline). The pressure on agriculture in the Netherlands, investments in new EU countries, and the implementation of the World Trade Organization (WTO) agreements may cut the food industry's ties to agribusiness in the future. The knowledge infrastructure, seen as an important asset of the Netherlands, will continue to play an important role.

Exports are important: 55 percent of food sales are exported. The trade cycle has little influence on industry performance, but competition is fierce; new opportunities may be in adding more value to food products. Multinational companies such as Unilever, Nestlé, Sara Lee, Heineken, and Masterfoods play important roles in the export-oriented subsectors. Playing a smaller—but in the Dutch context still quite large—role are the farmers' cooperatives in dairy (Friesland Foods), sugar (CSM), and meat (Vion Food). In Dutch manufacturing, food is relatively capital-intensive and process-oriented, and labor productivity is above average (EIM 2004).

Important trends in the food industry are the development of new products (such as functional foods and fresh food), new processes (mainly to improve conservation), and supply-chain management (aimed at quality control). The recent price war in grocery retailing, increasing international competition by pan-European players, and the introduction by the EU of a vast number of regulations and guidelines on food safety and health are also relevant factors. Jointly these developments hamper competition for small and medium-sized enterprises.

The case study research has been conducted in the subsectors of meat processing (excluding poultry processing) and confectionary (excluding cocoa processing). Both subsectors process semimanufactured products delivered by other food subsectors (sugar, cocoa, meat). They are comparatively labor-intensive and, with 5,000 to 5,500 employees each, about the same size. The estimated share of the lower processing jobs, our target occupation, in the total workforce is 50 to 60 percent. Historically the female share in these subsectors is relatively high, and in the last decade it remained stable.

Women workers can mainly be found in the packaging departments. Because our subsectors contribute only 8 percent to total employment in the food industry, our results cannot be regarded as representative for food manufacturing at large, but they may be indicative for related industries, such as pastry and biscuits and fish processing.

Their position in the value chain places both subsectors in a squeeze between the producers of raw materials and the retail industry. The recent supermarket price war put pressure on all manufacturers of consumer products, especially those that depend on the domestic market or the supply of private-label products. Their dominant market strategy is to remain cheap, flexible, and reliable. Reliability entails frequent just-in-time deliveries as well as compliance with the legal and retail quality standards. Only a few international A-brands are able to invest in innovative products, and even among them the success rate is low.

How do companies cope with the squeeze by the retail industry on costs, quality, reliability, and flexibility? How has this pressure influenced the position and prospects of our target occupation? One of the most important issues here is determining how firms deal with numerical flexibility.

THE METHODOLOGY

Chapter 4 dealt with the general methodology of the industry studies; here we go into the contrasts used in the food industry. The first contrast emerged from the choice of two subsectors that vary in product markets and technologies. Meat processing is mainly based on batch processes, while flow processes predominate in confectionary. Differences in technologies are assumed to be reflected in variations in job content and work organization. Institutional differences could not serve as a contrast: both subsectors have developed extensive social infrastructures with only limited variations in union density at the establishment level. With only a few large plants (three in confectionary and none in meat processing), the dominance of international ownership in confectionary, and only modest variations in technologies and labor markets, we opted for firm strategies as the second contrast. In confectionary some firms are fully focusing on private-label (retail brand) products, reacting quickly to retail's increasing quality and logistics requirements. Yet for meat processing this contrast appeared to be less relevant.

Access to case establishments went rather smoothly after we managed to cooperate with the employers' associations for confectionary (Vereniging voor de Bakkerij [VBZ]) and meat processing (Vereniging voor de Nederlandse [VNV]), as well as with the unions. In both industries this cooperation resulted in supportive letters from the employers' associations. Although we were still faced with some denials, we ended up with eight cases—in line with the agreed scope of the subsectors and the chosen contrasts. Within the chosen contrasts, we succeeded in getting access to two sweets manufacturers and two chocolate manufacturers. The selected establishments belong to the (small) category of larger companies. They are representative of the category of firms with more than one hundred employees and proved to give a good picture of developments at the subsector level.

It has to be noted that the choice of two small subsectors caused quite a few difficulties in gathering statistical data. An important source for meat processing is the Product Board (Productschappen Vee, Vlees en Eieren [PVE]); no comparable institution, however, exists for confectionary. Thus, the available data vary widely for the two subsectors. Official statistics at this level are hardly available and, if available, compare badly with the data of PVE and other industry institutions. As a result, this chapter is mainly based on the case studies. Tables 9.1 and 9.2 provide overviews of the "hard" characteristics of the food industry cases.

CONFECTIONARY: THE ECONOMIC AND INSTITUTIONAL CONTEXT

THE ECONOMIC CONTEXT AND FIRM STRATEGIES

The confectionary subsector is closely related to the biscuits subsector, not only with respect to raw materials (sugar) and position in the value chain but also in its social infrastructure. Some companies are involved in both product markets or sell combined products, but over the years processes of specialization can be traced. This kind of comanufacturing has become more common in confectionary, where multinational firms such as Nestlé and Cadbury sell production facilities to management or investment companies and change ownership into supplier-customer relations.

Confectionary consists of about one hundred firms, of which ten

Table 9.1 The Case Study Confectionary Establishments

	CON A	CON B	CON C	CON D
Sector	Sweets	Sweets	Chocolate	Chocolate
Contrast	Private label	Brand	Private label	Brand/niche
Ownership	Belgian	Italian	Belgian	German
Firm structure	Family	Multinational company	Family	Family
Number of production sites	3, 2 in the Netherlands	More than 10 in Europe, 4 in the Nether-lands	2, 1 in the Netherlands	10
Plant work-force	160	105	90	100
Plant work-force in man-ufacturing	100	85	50	62
Product range	Gums, licorices	Candies, mainly cara-mels, toffees	Chocolates, tablets, seasonal prod-ucts	Pastilles, tab-lets, seasonal products
Target jobs	Grade A: empty	Grade A: empty	Grades 1–4: 40% (mainly packaging)	Grades 1–4:
	Processing: 40% in grades B and C	Processing: 80% in grades B and C		Processing: none
	Packaging: 80% in grades B and C	Packaging: 100% in grades B and C		Packaging: 90% (mainly in grade 3)
Collective Labor Agree-ment	Branch (candy	Branch (candy)	Branch (biscuit)	Branch (biscuit)

Source: Author's compilation from case studies.

have fifty to one hundred employees and ten have more than one hundred employees (CBS/Statline). Mars (Masterfoods), Leaf (Leaf Holland), and Perfetti van Melle, important players on the European market and owners of the international brands Mars, Sportlife, and Mentos, can be found in the latter category.

After a series of acquisitions, it has been rather quiet recently, with

Table 9.2 The Case Study Meat Processing Establishments

	MEA A	MEA B	MEA C	MEA D
Contrast	Brand/Private label	Private label	Private label	Brand/private label
Ownership	Dutch	Dutch	Dutch	Dutch
Firm structure	Investment company	Multinational company	Family	Multinational company
Number of production sites	3, 1 in the Netherlands	Many, 1 in the Netherlands	2	12, 10 in the Netherlands
Plant work-force	73	95	115 (excluding 45 TAWs)	50 (excluding TAWs)
Plant work-force in man-ufacturing	60	60	100	40
Product range	Mainly "singular composed" meat products, smoked and cooked, ham, bacon, convenience meat comp's	Liver sausages, cooked ham, dry sausage, cooked sausage	Bacon products and sausages	Dry sausages
Target jobs	Grade A: 6 Grades B, C: 34	Grade A: 2 Grade B: 17 Grade C: 25	Grade A: 40 Grade B: 40 Grade C: 20	Grades B, C: 4
Collective labor agreement	Branch (meat products)	Branch (meat products), company job, classification, wage structure	Branch (meat products), company job classification	Branch (meat products), company job classification

Source: Author's compilation from case studies.

the exception of the disinvestment of the confectionary group CSM to CVC Capital Partners. The divesting strategies of the international players gave way to a larger role of such investment companies: family-dominated investors own three of the case firms. With respect to outsourcing, only in chocolate production can major changes be noted. In the 1970s and 1980s, manufacturers of chocolate products outsourced cocoa processing to industries in the Zaan region, near the port of Amsterdam (a move that played a major role in international cocoa logistics), but recently most firms have outsourced chocolate manufacturing completely to international companies such as Barry Callebaut.

Along with some international brand and private-label manufacturers, a number of small niche players with mainly domestic products remain active. Their investment strategies are based on reinstalling "mothball" production lines in order to make a relatively low-cost start with new products. Both retailers' strategies and food laws increasingly prevent small firms from entering the market. With 3 percent of retail sales and gross margins much higher than average, confectionary is very important for retailing (Hemmes 2004). The share of retail in sales has been stabilized at 67 percent for chocolate and 54 percent for sweets. Export figures are high for brand as well as private-label producers: about 75 percent of the output in the cases investigated. Overall sales have recently been stable. Both chocolate and confectionary sales had a peak in 2004 and declined slightly over 2005, when chocolate sales were €571 million (US$835 million) and confectionary (sweets) sales amounted to €702 million (US$1.03 billion) (Studiecentrum Snacks en Zoetwaren Benelux 2006).

In most confectionary manufacturing plants, technology is quite traditional. Innovation is mostly found in process control devices and in the mechanization of packaging. To reduce labor costs and the risks of sickness and disablement, robots are gradually being introduced into product handling and packaging, mainly the filling and palletizing of boxes. One of the case establishments had invested in a packaging robot to handle luxury chocolate boxes that had been hand-packed before. This robot was partially self-developed and replaced twenty (temp) workers, although the level of machine use was still too low to cover costs. Indeed, most plants are too small to make such investments feasible.

Product innovations may result in a greater variety of already existing products; they also include the production of organic, sugar-free, and functional food products, though still only for small niche markets. International market leaders, however, are always looking for new concepts and trying to anticipate demographic and health trends.

Seasonal production has major influences on work organization in confectionary, especially in chocolate processing. In peak periods such as December, production volume easily triples. This is regular business, but the way manufacturers organize their numerical flexibility is changing. Flexibility needs are also expanding with new product variations, including packaging, food legislation, and tracing and tracking. An increase in smaller batches or runs is one result, as well as increases in operational and numerical flexibility, higher complexity, and higher costs in both manufacturing and physical distribution. Firms also try to reduce costs and improve flexibility by combining automation and human resource policies.

Relationships between suppliers and customers have fundamentally changed. Nowadays long-term cooperation is exceptional, short-term contracts are the rule, and spot market relations are normal. However, the recent grocery price war has had limited effects on the confectionary industry, thanks to its export orientation and the importance of seasonal products with attractive margins for both manufacturing and retail. Although outsourcing of parts of confectionary manufacturing is not likely in the near future, job security is not necessarily high. The establishments we researched are performing relatively well, but their facilities and equipment are rather old. Owners will consider other options if reinvestment is inevitable; the fact that the owners already have modern facilities in Belgium and Germany may well be reason for serious concern on the employees' side.

EMPLOYMENT

Detailed figures about the size and composition of employment at the subsector level are not available, but combining various sources leads to the following picture. Head-count employment has declined, from 6,500 in 1999 to 5,500 in 2005. The workforce is relatively old: fewer than one-fifth are below age thirty (UWV 2004). Thirty-one percent have secondary vocational education, and 53 percent do not. Almost three-fifths are working in the manufacturing departments, equally divided between processing and packaging (Research voor Beleid 2003). These figures are about the same in the four cases, including the 50 percent share of employees in the manufacturing departments who are female. Women workers can mainly be found in packaging. The incidence of part-time jobs proved to be less than expected: in only one case did we find a substantial share (30 percent) of part-timers, and the firm was trying to reduce that number. In the past the confectionary industry employed many women in manual packaging jobs, but their share has decreased substantially owing to the combination of increases in shift work in packaging departments and the mechanization of packaging.

INSTITUTIONS AND LABOR RELATIONS

Labor relations in confectionary are grounded in the CLA for the confectionary and chocolate industry, which, except for four chocolate firms covered by the CLA for the sugar-processing industry, has 100 percent coverage owing to mandatory extension. Three unions (FNV Bondgenoten, CNV Bedrijvenbond, and De Unie) and the VBZ employers' association signed the CLA. In the current CLA, they have agreed to invest in technology and vocational training in order to improve job quality and the labor market position of the subsector, resulting in initiatives at both the branch and company levels. In the biscuit industry we found comparable structures, with the same actors. The employers' associations and unions are currently discussing integrating the two CLAs; the main obstacle is differences in pension rights. Company CLAs do not exist in this industry.

The employers' association represents 47 percent of the companies, which employ 93 percent of the total workforce (figures provided by VBZ). Union density is estimated to be 20 percent; FNV Bondgenoten is by far the largest union. The stronger position of the unions in companies employing more than one hundred workers is reflected in the case studies: we found densities between 30 and 95 percent in those companies. Both parties describe labor relations at the subsector level as "good." In recent collective bargaining negotiations, the effects of the changes in the national social security system made up the main issue. The employers sought more flexible working hours and reduction of compensations for working unsocial hours. In the last five years, flexible elements for both employers and employees have been introduced in the CLA, such as the replacement of seniority rights with performance-related bonuses. Labor relations within firms are, except in the ten larger firms, very traditional. Many companies with more than fifty employees do not comply with the Works Council Act. In the larger firms, compliance with the CLA is good, yet compliance may be questionable in small and medium-sized enterprises, particularly concerning in their use of the CLA grades and compensations for overtime and unsocial hours.

The job classification scheme is integrated into the CLA and is the basis of the wage structure. The classification system is based on the ORBA method, which is widely used in manufacturing. The jobs mentioned in the manual are used as references for grading. Companies do use various names for jobs and have various wage structures, but wages are based on these job grades.

The employers' associations and unions recently agreed on a separate pension CLA. Ninety percent of the average salary will be paid at the official pension age of sixty-five, and flexible pensioning is possible between ages fifty-five and seventy. The employer pays 75 percent of the pension premium. Moreover, a separate CLA social fund has been negotiated, with the object of improving labor relations and working conditions, including education. Firms are funding this initiative, as well as the RSI (repetitive strain injury) Covenant and vocational training.

Physical working conditions are extremely important in this subsector. In 2003 the social partners and the government signed a covenant to take measures to reduce RSI for the confectionary and biscuit industries, also in the form of a CLA. The social partners developed tools for risk analysis, a manual with technical solutions based on best practices, a branch competence center, a website, and dedicated contracts with service providers (Arbodiensten). An important part of the covenant is the employer's commitment to implement this plan at the company level, in discussion with the company's works council. In addition to this covenant, agreement was reached on a CLA on work and health in which employers have been asked to improve working conditions. One of the measures is job rotation: employers are obliged to offer a variety of tasks, which workers are obliged to perform.

VOCATIONAL TRAINING

Vocational training is integrated into the educational system, but dedicated vocational training institutes have not yet been established in the subsector. Vocational training facilities for process operators (VAPRO) and packaging functions (Nederlands Verpakkingscentrum [NVC]) are used only incidentally. In the 2004 CLA a small sum was reserved for subsector vocational training structures, the first project being Internet-based training for cocoa and chocolate manufacturing. In combination with an on-the-job training module, employees can get a Recognition of Acquired Competencies (EVC) certificate.

Recently a project was started to develop training facilities at the lowest level of secondary vocational education. The development of the teaching materials is encountering problems, however, with product and technology diversification and with the fact that large firms already have in-company training programs.

MEAT PROCESSING: THE ECONOMIC AND INSTITUTIONAL CONTEXT

THE ECONOMIC CONTEXT AND FIRM STRATEGIES

The meat-processing workforce decreased between 1995 and 2004, from 5,500 to 4,700 (head-count) (PVE 2005a). One of the reasons for the decrease has been further specialization, notably through disinvestment in slaughterhouses. This is just one of several recent changes in the value chain:

- Mergers of traders with slaughterers

- The forward integration of slaughtering

- The specialization of meat-processing companies

- The withdrawal of cooperatives (Cebeco) and retailers (Ahold) from meat processing

The result is an industry of about one hundred companies, of which four are market leaders: Zwanenberg, Meester Stegeman, Compaxo, and Vion Food. Compaxo and Vion Food are exceptions with respect to specialization; Vion even reviewed its strategic orientation toward the value chain after it acquired major companies in Germany and the Netherlands. The firm strategies of the "big four" indicate how highly internationalized marketing and manufacturing in this subsector have become. Internationalization includes an increasing number of meat imports from outside the EU, stimulated by GATT agreements, and improved packaging technology. Moreover, our case establishments mentioned strong competition from Germany, which has much lower labor costs. The market leaders are followed by a group of ten midsized family companies with 50 to 150 employees.

Meat markets in the Netherlands are generally perceived as saturated. The consumption of meat and meat products remains fairly constant, while the consumption of snacks is growing; thus, most examples of product innovation are found in snacks. Meat and meat products are traditional products with hardly any branding. With some exceptions, meat processing is oriented toward the domestic market; import and export figures are balanced. The main products are liver products, ham, and cooked and dried sausages; 86 percent of these products are prepacked, and 89 percent are sold in supermarkets. With the development of prepacking or slicing as a new element, slicing plants can now be found in various parts of the value chain. In two cases we found in-house slicing departments; the other firms had outsourced slicing—though one had outsourced to an in-company department.

All in all, saturated domestic markets, consumers' focus on price, and the dominant position of supermarkets have put strong pressure on meat processing. In 2004 the share of the supermarket channel in meat product sales increased to 90 percent (PVE 2005b). Retail pressure is both a threat and a challenge to innovation in meat processing: short-term contracts and low margins carry high risks, but internationalization, product innovation to add more value, and cost reductions offer various ways out. Such reductions can be found in restructurings at the group level, in specialization at the plant level, in the increasing use of temp workers (30 to 50 percent in the case study plants), and in the introduction of shift work and work on Saturdays.

Most plants house combinations of craft (deboning departments) and batch processes. Against the backdrop of batch processing and the necessary technical flexibility, leaps in automation and process integration are unlikely to happen; the possibility that integration may lead to food safety risks also inhibits innovation (Paardekooper 2005). One of the case plants underwent a complete renovation in 2005, but management was still studying further automation and integration of processes.

In recent years, the Dutch meat industry has gone through some major crises (cow, pig, and chicken diseases), resulting in a reduction of livestock and sales of meat. Yet the influence of these crises on the consumption and production of meat products was marginal owing to imports of (frozen) meat. The crises did have the indirect effect of inspiring new EU regulations on food safety (the General Food Act) and retail certificates. Sometime in the near future the ISO 22000 standard will be available for the food safety management system. Initially it was suggested that this standard would lead to problems for smaller companies, but insiders in fact regard it as an opportunity to improve quality. Large firms such as Encebe have used the obligations in the General Food Act to implement integrated enterprise resource planning (ERP) and traceability systems (Busser 2005). The implementation of regulations in the meat industry is directed by the tripartite Product Board, which does not play a direct role in labor relations.

EMPLOYMENT

Employment in meat processing is relatively stable over the year compared to the more seasonal pattern in confectionary. Twenty-five percent of the workforce is female. Seniority is very high, with only 21 percent of the workforce under the age of forty. Educational levels are quite low: 78 percent have no primary vocational education, or only very little (PVE 2005a). The composition of the workforce in the case studies was roughly in line with these figures.

INSTITUTIONS AND LABOR RELATIONS

Again, CLA coverage in these two subsectors is 100 percent, owing to mandatory extension; the CLA is signed by three unions (FNV Bondgenoten, CNV Bedrijvenbond, and De Unie) and two employers' associations, VNV and VNB. These structures are related to the meat and butchers' subsectors, which have separate CLAs. The unions are partners in all three CLAs. On the employers' side, with the integration of the human resource departments of large firms, cooperation is growing. Some firms have meat-processing activities but follow the CLA for the meat subsector, as well as the other way around. Unox (Unilever Bestfood) and Encebe (Vion Food) are covered by company CLAs yet follow the subsector CLA.

The two employers' associations organize about 15 percent of all companies, representing 60 percent of the workforce. The FNV Bondgenoten union represents about 35 percent of employees, while the other unions jointly represent 5 percent. Union density in larger firms is over 40 percent and is concentrated in the ranks of the semi-skilled.

Labor relations at the subsector level are described as "high trust" and "reasonable." Employers and unions have established quite a few institutions: the CLA, the pension CLA, the Foundation for Collective Interests, the Covenant on Working Conditions, and the SVO vocational training institute. Yet disagreement remains on the level of collectivism in regulations. Employers are seeking more flexibility on working times and less compensation for unusual working hours; they like to call these "tailor-made" arrangements. Within companies the picture varies. The larger companies have works councils and human resource departments, but the smaller ones either lack a works council or the council's position is weak. Labor relations in the smaller companies are very traditional. Against this background, FNV Bondgenoten is satisfied with the level of collectivism in the present CLA. All in all, compliance with the CLA is good, discounting incidental problems with working hours and job grading. Because of tight labor market conditions, most companies pay wages that are 5 to 10 percent above the CLA wage scales.

Job classification has recently been integrated into the CLA and is now being implemented in the companies. The job manual, containing an overview of the usual jobs (description and grading), is based on the ORBA method. Companies are supposed to make company-specific job descriptions and compare these with the manual.

Vocational Training

In this subsector, vocational training is integrated into the educational system. At the secondary vocational education level, students can combine work (four days a week) and school (one day a week). A minority of younger, talented workers follow the branch vocational training courses of the SVO vocational training institute. Secondary vocational education graduates are overskilled for production worker jobs, and thus companies recruit mainly unskilled workers or those with only primary vocational education. Lack of competencies is perceived as a problem in the industry. However, even with institutions and funding in place, firms hesitate to invest in vocational training.

In June 2002, employers' associations, unions, and the government agreed on a covenant to reduce RSIs; that agreement was followed in 2003 by the adoption of an action program at the meat industry level. RSI is a major problem in the meat industry: research concluded in 2001 that no fewer than 84 percent of production workers run an increased RSI risk (TNO Arbeid 2002). Consequently, one of the targets of this covenant was to reduce sick leave rates due to RSI by 30 percent by June 2006. The program developed a set of tools to support the companies, including checks, best practices, a website, and funding. It is too early to evaluate its results; the start has been slow because of problems with a union brochure about the liability of employers, delayed materials, and management-union debates about risky jobs and targets.

In the adjacent subsector of slaughterhouses and fresh meat, the use of contractor labor is so widespread that the CLA for the meat industry also covers dedicated temp agencies. Yet after the implementation of the Flexicurity Act (1998), problems with fraud and illegal workers have increased. Against this background, in 2002 the employers' associations and unions in the meat branch signed the Covenant on a Flexible Workforce, obliging companies to use only recognized temp work agencies. Interestingly, this covenant has appeared to be so successful that mala-fide agencies tended to shift their operations to meat processing, but in 2005 employers and unions in the latter industry integrated the covenant into their CLA too.

JOB QUALITY

JOB DESIGN AND WORK ORGANIZATION

Classification in the job classification system reflects the job structure in both subsectors. The confectionary structure is shown in table 9.3. We consider the categories A, B, and C the lower processing jobs: these employees perform mainly manual tasks or operate stand-alone machinery.

Basically the production structure of confectionary plants consists of three departments: preparation of raw material; forming; and packaging, integrated with forming in one processing line (such as manufacturing chocolates) or separated by cooling or drying. The few key jobs are located in the first two departments; most employees can be found in handling jobs: filling and emptying machines, internal transport, and packaging. In most plants, category A is almost empty: it is mostly used to pay temp workers after twenty-six weeks of work.

The work organization can be described as traditional hierarchical, though rather flat: plant manager, production manager, group leader, operator. A span of control including fifty employees is no exception. New forms of teamwork have not been implemented, but job rotation within a department is standard; in some plants even job rotation be-

Table 9.3 Job Classification in the Confectionary Subsector

Category	Processing Department	Packaging Department
A	Manual work, not product-related	Manual packaging
B	Manual, product-related work, unskilled	Operating packaging machine
C	Manual operation of stand-alone batch processes	Operating packaging equipment
D	Operation of integrated mechanized batch processes or craft-based operations	operating automated packaging line
E	Process operators (continuous processes)	operating high-performance automated packaging line
F	Supervisor	Supervisor
G	Management	Management
H	Management	Management

Source: Functieboek voor de suikerverwerkende industrie [Job Classification in the Confectionary Industry], CLA partners, 2002.

tween departments can be found. Operational responsibility over packing lines has been given to machine leaders in category D and sometimes E, including registration and inspection tasks related to quality systems. In some cases, we heard comments on debates between management and employees over the scheduling of senior packaging operators: the employees involved lost their case when management restricted their responsibility to one production line. Operational flexibility has its price in the wage system, which is based on competencies and task flexibility, not educational levels.

As a heritage from the past, the boundaries between processing and packaging departments are quite strong, owing to differences in climate, technology, tasks, physical demands, and workforce composition. In packaging departments, women make up the majority, even after mechanization. In chocolate processing, however, we found an interesting experiment aimed at changing this. Together with the mechanization and even automation of internal transport (the first robots have been introduced and others are foreseen), the traditional division of labor between men and women may well change in the near future. Horizontal mobility could offer opportunities for the target job.

In one experiment, female packaging operators underwent a short on-the-job training and then worked on a new production line for a seasonal product during the season. This was necessary because of a shortage of process operators during the temporary three-shift period; after the season, the female operators returned to the packaging department. The works council and management evaluated this experiment differently: management regarded it as a step toward multi-tasking, while the works council saw it as the solution to a short-term problem. Yet they agreed to develop this experiment in the future.

In the confectionary subsector, a difference can be traced between sugar confectionary and chocolate when it comes to job levels: processing jobs in chocolate are all to be found in category D and higher, but partly because of differences in technology, sugar confectionary includes a substantial number of lower processing jobs, up to 80 percent.

The job classification structure of meat processing is comparable to that of confectionary. The lower processing jobs are those with just manual tasks or responsibility for operating stand-alone batch equipment, the standard in meat processing. The outsourcing of slicing and direct supply to wholesale and retail outlets combine to make packaging departments in this industry much smaller, but we did witness in deboning departments (in two out of the four plants) the very labor-intensive processing of changing raw materials.

Traditionally, deboning was craft-based, but more and more often now it is being downgraded into a single skill-job that gives the operator no opportunities to develop into a skilled butcher. At one establishment, for instance, deboning had been outsourced to two teams of ten to twelve employees each, the majority of them Polish, by a secondment contract at piece rates. Management had decided to outsource this work because of the high health and safety risks.

Production structures and work organizations in meat processing, however, are quite different. Here the variety of batch processes leads to a variety of tasks, with increasing opportunities for multiskilling through on-the-job training.

WORKING CONDITIONS

Working conditions in both subsectors are traditionally very poor. A 2003 report on working conditions in the sugar-processing industry concluded that the averages in the industry remained below (national) critical values, but that specific occupations ran higher risks on work pressure, work-related stress, physical workload, and RSI-related complaints. The report concluded that the female packaging employees with no formal education made up the main risk group, following from their short-cycle and machine-bound tasks. It also stated that 70 percent of sick leave was caused by flu and cold and that over one-third of workers' complaints in confectionary were work-related. Including office jobs, 45 percent of these complaints were connected with physical strain (such as lifting), 38 percent with work pressure and stress, and 28 percent with RSI (Research voor Beleid 2003). Another ergonomic report concluded that extra risks were emanating from noise and dust (because of maize flour), as well as from working with inexperienced employees, many of them temps (VHP Ergonomie 2003).

We gathered many comments confirming the results of these reports:

> "Work pressure has increased because of the use of temps and tight schedules."
> "Schedules are tight owing to more frequent switching of equipment [smaller runs]. We cannot adjust the schedules."
> "There's a lot of pressure in case of equipment breakdowns."
> "More than half of the temps drop out within a week."
> "Job rotation helps to reduce the effects of work pressure, but not everyone wants to rotate."
> "A lot of people with physical work-related problems (such as a painful shoulder) stay at work."

As these quotations indicate, we found in the case studies quite a few reasons for increased attention to working conditions. Although the Covenant on Health and Safety may have improved employers' awareness of health and safety issues, the main stimulus probably came from the new national legal framework on sickness and disablement. In addition to the implementation of technical improvements, a set of policies is now used to reduce the costs resulting from this legislation: tight control on absenteeism and reintegration, outsourcing of high-risk jobs to temps, strict job rotation, and the robotizing of handling and palletizing. These policies have had a significant impact on the position of those in the target occupation. The lower processing jobs are increasingly exposed to high health and safety risks. In some cases, these jobs are "outsourced" through TWAs to temp workers, except during periods of smaller production volumes, when permanent employees are distributed along the various production lines.

Recently sick leave rates in confectionary have been substantially lowered. We estimate, based on the four case studies, an average reduction over four years from 10 percent down to 5 percent. Employees reported a reduction of physical risks but at the same time an increase in work pressure. Labor turnover in confectionary, however, is almost zero.

The meat-processing industry too is notorious for its poor working conditions. The report on which the RSI covenant was based concluded that 72 percent of the jobs and 39 percent of the production workers bore a high RSI risk and that a medium RSI risk applied to 14 percent of the jobs and 45 percent of the workers (TNO Arbeid 2002). Other major health risks include temperature, noise, and machine safety; the latter two were recently the subject of a report by the Labor Inspectorate (Arbeidsinspectie 2004). Its report also concluded that awareness of the risk was low and that employers lack policies for dealing with it. Another report identified the use of unskilled workers and insufficient training as problems (TNO Arbeid 2003). These risks are confirmed in our four case studies, although one had recently renovated a plant and thus made many improvements in floors, tools, and internal transport. Sick leave rates in the case establishments varied between 4 and 10 percent. Labor turnover in meat processing is higher than in confectionary, but at 5 to 10 percent, it is still rather modest.

WAGES

Wages are regulated by industry CLAs and established for each function following the job classification scheme (see figures 9.1 and 9.2).

Employees are classified in one of the functions at step 0 and will reach the maximum wage related to the function by yearly steps: six steps in wage group A and ten steps in group H. Compensations for poor working conditions are integrated into the job classification system. What is striking are the small differences between the job levels.

There are additional pay elements at the firm level, such as extra holidays, higher compensation for shift work, and a thirteenth month. Most companies have tried to abolish these elements, but do-

Figure 9.1 Monthly Wages in the Confectionary Industry per CLA, 2005–2006

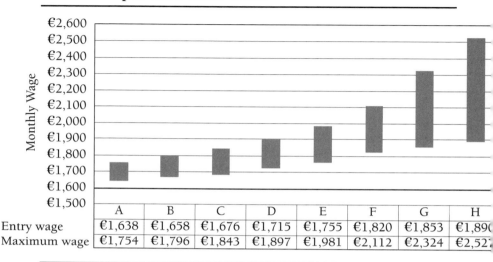

	A	B	C	D	E	F	G	H
Entry wage	€1,638	€1,658	€1,676	€1,715	€1,755	€1,820	€1,853	€1,89(
Maximum wage	€1,754	€1,796	€1,843	€1,897	€1,981	€2,112	€2,324	€2,52;

Source: Collective Labor Agreement, confectionary industry 2005–2006, CLA-partners, 2005.

ing so is rather complicated, since they are part of individual contracts; newcomers are offered contracts without such extras. With the introduction in 2002 of a new job classification system, some employees have enjoyed personal bonuses after being classified in a lower job grade. What is new is the more flexible application of the CLA rules, especially in the direction of performance pay. Yet steps and bonuses can be related to individual performance only if the employer and the works council agree on an assessment system.

Figure 9.2 shows the CLA wage structure for the meat processing industry. Under this CLA, the minor differences between the job levels are obvious. All entry wages are below the low-wage threshold. Yet all maximum wages—to be reached in nine or ten yearly steps—are above the threshold. Group A is only used for employees in their probation period, and group B is used for apprentices and packaging workers. Group A proved to be empty in the cases we researched, with one exception: the firm used group A to reduce labor costs, arguing that the workers had little mastery of the Dutch language. Skilled employees can be found in groups E and up.

Other compensations and bonuses under the CLA relate to shift

Figure 9.2 Monthly Wages in the Meat-Processing Industry per Collective Labor Agreement, July 7, 2005

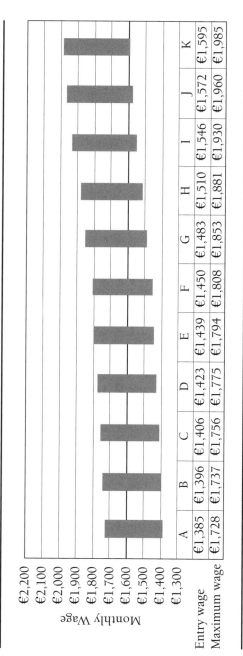

	A	B	C	D	E	F	G	H	I	J	K
Entry wage	€1,385	€1,396	€1,406	€1,423	€1,439	€1,450	€1,483	€1,510	€1,546	€1,572	€1,595
Maximum wage	€1,728	€1,737	€1,756	€1,775	€1,794	€1,808	€1,853	€1,881	€1,930	€1,960	€1,985

Source: Collective Labor Agreement, meat processing industry 2005–2006, CLA-partners, 2005.

work, the holiday allowance (8 percent), health insurance (50 percent of the premium is paid by the employer), child care, the annual bonus (2 percent, or a profit-related maximum of 4 percent), the pension premium (85 percent is paid by the employer), and compensation for working in cold areas. Some workers receive personal bonuses because of past reorganizations or because of the introduction in 2005 of the new job classification system. Examples of firm-specific bonuses are gifts at Christmas or birthdays, bonuses for being present (not being sick), and bonuses for operational flexibility.

To trace the real low-wage jobs under both CLAs, we have to consider the youth scales, almost all of which are (far) below the low-wage threshold, and the inflow scale, which is at SMW level plus 10 percent. Inflow scales are meant for employees who need extra coaching, for a maximum of two years. In the cases we have not yet found any examples of such scales, a fact that can be explained by the use of TWAs to recruit new (temp) employees. In both subsectors, the substantial group of temps make up the primary low-wage category. They are usually paid according to the CLA for TWAs, but their wage level is just above the SMW. After twenty-six weeks, they are paid according to the industry CLA (without a pension premium or company extras), but most temps have been classified as grade A, which keeps them in the low-wage range.

Wages in meat processing are lower than in confectionary. Skilled operators in meat processing have a rating of a maximum of seventy-two points (grade F), but multi-skilled in confectionary are rated at a maximum of ninety-six points, a difference reflected in their respective wages. Moreover, in confectionary the gap between entry and end wages is much smaller, and there are fewer steps. Finally, the much smaller differences between grades in meat processing have a substantial impact on the wages of the skilled.

These and other differences between the subsectors have a long history and cannot simply be explained by differences in labor productivity or union density; the position in the value chain is important too. Meat processing has, after years of restructuring, developed as a separate industry out of wholesale and retail, while confectionary has a long tradition as a manufacturing industry with strong brands. Unions in confectionary have used their presence in major firms—such as Mars and, in the past, Verkade—to negotiate a "quality CLA" at the branch level, and these firms have been motivated to go along, since such a CLA levels the playing field.

CHANGES IN EMPLOYMENT RELATED TO NUMERICAL FLEXIBILITY

The standard working week in both industries is thirty-six hours. Working hours in meat processing are normally Monday to Friday, somewhere between 7:00 A.M. and 4:15 P.M. Some smaller departments, such as brining, salting, and the smokehouse, may work in shifts. Managers stated that they wanted to implement more shift work so as to reduce fixed costs and ease Saturday deliveries.

In the confectionary subsector, shift work is the rule. Processing departments usually work in three-shifts and packaging in two-shifts (sugar confectionary) and three-shifts (chocolate). In the past, five-shift systems were not unusual, but most companies went back to three. Weekly cleaning operations made five-shift systems financially unattractive. At the same time, the flexibility in shift systems increased; these systems change with the seasonal product flow. Firms have long-term contracts (two to three years) with TWAs that supply temps based on the production planning, and sometimes these agencies have a coordinator on-site. During peak periods, temps are integrated into the work organization and rotate jobs as long as their skills allow them to do so. Some temps return each year, and others need a (short) period of on-the-job training.

External and internal numerical flexibility are to some extent functional equivalents. In confectionary variation in shifts is the main form of internal numerical flexibility. Here the use of overtime is marginal and takes place only when there are technical problems. Also, the use of the so-called CLA à la carte and the extent of part-time work is limited. The cases in the meat processing industry showed somewhat more (but still not structural) overtime, except in one case firm where 80 percent of the employees worked forty hours and extra hours were paid as overtime. In that case, including overtime on Saturdays for cleaning purposes, the limits of the Working Hours Act were reached.

Over the years the role of TWAs in confectionary has changed. While in the past TWAs supplied workers mainly for unpredictable shortages, they now are used for various reasons, such as during periods of high-volume manufacturing or manufacturing without long-term contracts. In one case the parent company invested in a new plant in eastern Europe to produce for the local market. Between the decision and the opening, production was done in the Netherlands with the assistance of temps. Another case firm reused equipment for a private-label contract that was not a long-term contract, and temps staffed the related production line. Another reason a firm might use temps would be in anticipation of investing in packaging and handling robots. If labor turnover allows, temps can occupy the posts to be automated. This practice is related to another reason for temp use that is also found in the other industries we investigated: to avoid high sick leave rates of permanent staff and related costs.

TWAs strengthened their position in the period before 2002 when labor markets were tight and firms struggled to recruit enough temps, or even enough permanent employees. TWAs were asked to recruit employees from all over Europe. During the research period, Polish workers were not commonly used in confectionary, but in meat processing larger numbers of these workers could be found. Meat-processing jobs are physically demanding, labor turnover is about 10 percent, and the domestic workforce is not attracted to these jobs. In all eight case establishments, the recruitment of new employees has been completely outsourced to TWAs. Newcomers start as temps, switch to a fixed-term contract, and then finally are offered a permanent contract. A final argument in favor of the ascendancy of TWAs is that temps are cheaper, not only because of the reduction in sick leave costs, which are included in the management fee, but also because, with temp wages at group A level and no industry pension premium or company extras to pay out, the direct labor costs are lower.

It is not an exaggeration to state that the unions and the Labor Inspectorate will need to keep a sharp eye on suppliers of workers at the fringes of the industry unless the Covenant on a Flexible Workforce is extended to meat processing. Clause 25 in the confectionary CLA states that the (average) use of temp employees should be restricted to 7.5 percent above the sick leave rate of the year before; otherwise, consultation with the unions is required. However, temp use is often much higher, and the unions are rarely consulted. Works councils are supposed to monitor this arrangement, but they do not want to cause problems because they feel that the use of temps reduces the employment risks of restructuring, a position that shows some understanding of employers' recruitment problems. In the short run, management is generally satisfied with this recruitment strategy and with the quality of temps in terms of skills and attitudes, though Eastern European workers in particular are not inclined to learn Dutch and show high churning rates. This strategy therefore cannot solve the long-term problems related to the aging of the workforce and to the skill formation of key operators.

OPPORTUNITIES FOR INTERNAL MOBILITY: WHICH PERSPECTIVES?

The general picture in both confectionary and meat processing is that of an aging workforce with average tenures between ten and twenty years. Most employees are recruited without secondary vocational education, and some even lack primary vocational education. Industry institutions for vocational training do exist in meat processing, but not in confectionary. In both subsectors, students who have completed vocational training, especially at levels 3 and 4, prove to be overskilled and usually leave within a couple of years. As a result, higher-level production jobs (grades E and higher) are occupied by employees who entered as unskilled and subsequently seized opportunities to pursue internal careers through combinations of on-the-job training and sometimes external education.

With the recruitment of new employees almost totally outsourced to TWAs, vocational education or skills are not required, only good attitudes, good hygiene, and a facility with the Dutch language. In tight labor markets, even the language requirement is dropped. On-the-job training for the simpler tasks is a matter of hours, and learning to work with (packaging) machines takes one to three or four weeks. The only classroom training provided is a basic hygiene course.

Two packaging employees illustrate the severely limited opportunities in confectionary processing. "I thought about another job in the firm, but there are very few opportunities for a position as 'belt-leader.' A job in the processing department is not possible because of the necessary heavy lifting." Another employee with RSI problems tried to find a job in health care, cleaning, or horticulture, "but I was told, even by the temp agency, that I am too old."

In confectionary most low-wage jobs are in the packaging departments. Packaging workers and operators are nearly all female. Mechanics and internal transport jobs are traditionally male. Opportunities for internal careers can only be found in packaging. In most plants senior packaging operators are graded D or E and are working with just operational management tasks. As in most firms, hierarchy is reduced to the absolute minimum; the next step in confectionary would be packaging manager. Horizontal careers are no option, owing to the classic distinction between processing and packaging departments. The experiments mentioned earlier may change this, and physical problems (as with heavy lifting) will be less important in the future too. Interviews with employees gave us the impression that their motivation to develop internal careers is limited. Senior employees must bear a lot more responsibility in exchange for only slightly higher wages, while further internal careers are lacking.

Yet labor turnover in this subsector remains very low, suggesting that those in the target occupation regard work in the confectionary industry as well paid. Management is prepared to pay senior employees higher wages, but it has to operate within the constraints of the CLA, which limits the scope for bonuses, as well as within headquarters' policies putting budgetary limits on bonuses.

Opportunities for upward mobility in the meat-processing industry look better because of the larger variety of tasks and the managerial desire for operational flexibility. The findings in the case studies indicate that firms will have problems in the near future recruiting skilled operators and qualified team leaders. Some companies are anticipating these problems already and have encouraged employees to participate in vocational education programs; they are also considering becoming certified work-learn companies. Employees, however, are not always motivated and sometimes regard the offer of such opportunities as criticism. Other firms hesitate to invest in their employees.

Although CLAs promote vocational education and funding is in place, both management and works councils told us that the impact of these measures on human resource policies is limited. An exception was one of the two chocolate companies, where a vocational education program had been implemented for all workers at levels 1, 2, and 3. Management here aimed to upgrade the quality of the workforce (being a supplier of quality products) and to improve external mobility; the works council had not been involved. Another confectionary firm tried to improve the quality of (semi-)skilled employees by facilitating their participation in an education program for process operators (VAPRO, the standard for such operators in food and chemicals), but the educational backgrounds of most of these employees had not prepared them for a program as challenging as this one.

CONCLUSIONS

The confectionary and meat-processing industries are both under pressure from heightened competition. Both are confronted with more stringent quality requirements, more and more requirements in the field of reliability and flexibility, increasing raw material costs, saturated markets, changing demographics in Europe, and rising demands for healthier food. Management has to cope with substantial challenges. Yet for most companies, especially those that are more private label–oriented, the only option is a survival strategy—one that focuses on cost reduction and, if possible, investment in new products and technology.

International confectionary companies have already invested in eastern Europe, mainly to serve local markets. However, large-scale offshoring to eastern Europe is not yet planned, for a number of reasons, such as the need for operational and logistical flexibility, difficulties with maintaining quality standards, the challenges of production technology (small batches), a focus on the domestic market, and branding (Belgian chocolate). In the meat-processing industry, all these reasons may well change in five years' time because of the growing internationalization of this subsector in sales as well as in sourcing; for instance, the importing of frozen meat from Asia and Latin America is just one indication of the increasing globalization of the agricultural supply chain.

Both confectionary and meat processing are traditionally low-skill (but not always low-wage) industries with limited opportunities for internal career development. Firms recognize the necessity to improve the quality of the workforce, but the large-scale use of temp workers gives rise to stagnating qualification processes, while job content, working conditions, and wages are not attractive to employees who have completed secondary vocational education. If the labor market tightens again, these firms may meet real recruitment problems.

Vocational education in meat processing offers a wide range of training, but it is predominantly used for basic hygiene training or for training lower and middle management. Comparing this situation with confectionary, we have to conclude that the presence of industry-level vocational training institutions is not a sufficient precondition to create a sustainable skilled workforce. High-road product market strategies need to be translated into high-road human resource strategies; improved market conditions may be of help here. Yet employment is falling slightly each year, and further declines are expected. We did not trace firms' plans for offshoring, but employment might be at stake when companies with out-of-date facilities are compelled to invest.

For quite a few reasons, human resource policies tend to shift low-skilled jobs with a high degree of numerical flexibility to TWAs: the desire to avoid high costs for sick leave and disability has a greater impact than job protection legislation. Job protection is hardly an issue for management after the enactment of the Flexicurity Act and subsequent implementation of TWA CLAs. The conclusion seems justified that these institutions are used to escape legally from the ties of their own CLA in order to reduce labor costs. Recent changes in CLAs can be regarded as the results of the social dialogue at the industry level and reflect to some extent the socioeconomic context: lower inflow scales, growing attention to health and safety, vocational training and TWAs, and more room for flexible wages and flexible working hours. In both subsectors, a new job classification system was implemented during our research. This new system is being used to redefine jobs at the plant level and to help develop training programs. If jobs are downgraded, the wages of actual employees are protected. In the long run, however, labor costs will decrease. According to management, the new system has had no influence on work organization. Yet in one case we found some examples of registration tasks and responsibilities being formally concentrated in the job of senior packaging operator so as to keep the operator job at a lower scale. In another case we witnessed a reduction of the number of multi-skill operators to reduce labor costs.

We have to be careful in drawing conclusions with respect to the chosen contrasts: confectionary versus meat industry, brand versus private label. First, two cases per cell is quite a limited sample. Second, the contrast of brand versus private label is not absolute: firms with brands also use their capacity for private-label manufacturing, and private-label firms supply brand firms. Reduction of manufacturing costs and compliance with quality standards are of equal importance to all the plants we investigated. Multinational firms and firms with strong brands are more likely to risk investing in new products and manufacturing capacity, but they may also opt for co-manufacturing. These companies tend to score better on measures of vocational training and employability. Maybe we should conclude that the contrast of private label versus brand does not matter much for job quality. Both firm categories try to meet the enforced standards of quality, efficiency, and flexibility, while the CLA strongly limits the ability to reduce labor costs. This reflects the changing industry structure: major brands are withdrawing from manufacturing and selling their manufacturing facilities. Product market strategies may vary at the company level but not at the plant level, and that is where low-wage jobs tend to be concentrated in temp agency work.

REFERENCES

Arbeidsinspectie (Labor Inspectorate). 2004. *Slachtvaardig, Verslag van het inspectieproject op het gebied van Arbobeleid, Veiligheid en Geluid in de vlees(verwerkende)industrie* [*Skillful Slaughtering: Report of the Inspection Project for Occupational Health, Safety, and Noise in the Meat(packing) Industry*]. The Hague: Department of Social Affairs and Employment.

Busser, Wim. 2005. "NAWI Europe S&D implementeert GPMS bij Encebe vleeswaren" ["NAWI Europe S&D Implements GPMS at Encebe Vleeswaren"]. *Vleesindustrie* (March): 6.

EIM. 2004. *Sectorscoop, ondernemen in de industrie* [*Sectorscope: Doing Business in the Industry*]. Zoetermeer, Netherlands: EIM.

Hemmes, Erik. 2004. "Lustrumcongres SSZ gehuld in magische sferen" ["SSZ Anniversary Conference Shrouded in Magical Atmosphere"]. *Consudel* 26(4): 15.

Paardekooper, Ernst, editor. 2005. *Fabriek van de toekomst* [*Factory of the Future*]. Arnhem, Netherlands: Proca.

Productschappen Vee, Vlees en Eieren (PVE). 2005a. *Sectorprofiel 2002/2003/2004* [*Sector Profile 2002/2003/2004*]. Zoetermeer, Netherlands: PVE.

———. 2005b. *Het jaar 2004 voorlopig* [*The Year 2004, Preliminary*]. Zoetermeer, Netherlands: PVE.

Research voor Beleid. 2003. *Arbeidsomstandigheden in de sectoren koek en snoep* [*Working Conditions in the Pastry and Candy Sectors*]. Leyden, Netherlands: Research voor Beleid.

Studiecentrum Snacks en Zoetwaren Benelux. 2006. *Markt van snacks en zoetwaren Nederland 2003–2005* [*Market of Snacks and Sweets, the Netherlands 2003-2005*]. Zeist, Netherlands: Studiecentrum Snacks en Zoetwaren.

TNO Arbeid. 2002. *RSI in de Vleessectoren* [*RSI in the Meat Industry*]. Hoofddorp, Netherlands: TNO Arbeid.

———. 2003. *Arborisico's in de branche Slachterijen en Vleesverwerkende in-*

dustrie [*Occupational Health and Safety Risks in the Slaughterhouse and Meatpacking Idustry*]. Hoofddorp, Netherlands: TNO Arbeid.

VHP Ergonomie. 2003. *Arboconvenant Koek en Snoep, Stand der techniek* [*Occupational Health and Safety Covenant in Pastry and Candy: State of the Art of Technology*]. The Hague: VHP Ergonomie.

CHAPTER 10

Labor Market Institutions and Firm Strategies that Matter for the Low-Paid

Wiemer Salverda, Maarten van Klaveren,
Marc van der Meer, Wim Sprenger, Kea Tijdens,
Arjen van Halem, and Ria Hermanussen

Over recent decades, the Netherlands has witnessed a record growth of head-count employment and a low level of unemployment. Currently, labor markets are tightening, in significant contrast with the stagnation and decline in the preceding years, when we carried out the case study fieldwork reported in this volume. The present employment-to-population ratio is at the top of the euro zone, and the unemployment rate is at the bottom. Virtually all job growth has been in part-time jobs, leading to a 46 percent share of part-time jobs in employment that is unique in the world. As a result, the current *full-time-equivalent* employment rate is no different from that of 1979, implying zero net growth on balance.

At the same time, low-wage employment has increased significantly, particularly over the last ten years, from 11 percent to 18 percent of all employees, and from 11 percent to 16 percent of all employee hours worked. The low-wage head-count employment-to-population ratio almost doubled, from 5.9 percent to 11.5 percent. On a full-time equivalent basis, the same ratio grew by two and a half percentage points, suggesting a decline in the better-paid ratio. Employees are working fewer hours that are paid above the low-wage threshold nowadays than they did at the end of the 1970s. For demographic reasons—a declining youth population—the composition of low-wage employment shifted significantly toward adult women and men—meaning that more people are earning low pay at a later stage in their labor market career. With a high incidence of low-paid youths, immigrant minorities and adult women play very important roles. Low pay shows a strong relation to the explosive growth of (small) part-time jobs. Today these jobs make up 70 percent of all low-paid jobs, up from 25 percent in 1979, and conversely, low-paid part-time jobs account for around 27 percent of all part-time jobs, up from 17 percent in 1979. A steady 10 percent of full-time jobs, however, are low-paid. Employment at the lowest skill level has remained largely unchanged over the prolonged period, but many more of the low-skilled are now in small part-time jobs. Increasingly, better-educated employees are found in low-wage and low-level jobs, and we need to distinguish between low-pay, low-educated persons and low-level jobs. We found substantial mobility of employees out of low pay—to higher levels of pay, but also to inactivity, especially for women in low-wage part-time jobs, and the possibility of a "low pay, no pay" cycle is nontrivial and may be increasing.

This concluding chapter offers an interpretation of the national overview and the industry case studies. The first section returns to the subject of economic governance at the national level. The next section evaluates firm strategies regarding job quality. That is followed by a discussion of six institutional preconditions that affect the volume and quality of low-wage employment. Each precondition covers an "organizational" field (Scott 2004) that combines institutions, firm strategies, and job quality; together they affect the conditions for, or constraints on, healthy and innovative work processes at the lower end of the labor market:

- Tax and income policy
- Collective labor agreements
- Employment contracts and dismissal protection
- Education and training
- Job quality (regulation)
- Employee representation

We end the chapter with some observations about the sustainability of what we think can be termed the Dutch model of low-wage employment.

THE DELIBERATIVE INSTITUTIONS

The deliberative institutions of the consultation economy are the essential point of departure for establishing and changing labor market institutions. Their specific nature defines the "Polder model," which in turn is thought by many to determine the social and economic evolution of the country. The fundamental setup, including that of various individual labor market institutions, dates back to the immediate postwar period. Each of the three institutional parties has something to offer in negotiations: peace at the workplace can be had from the unions, employers can offer the cooperation of firms, and the level and composition of public spending is determined by the government. Virtually every imaginable issue of policymaking that relates to the labor market and the economy at large is subject to the deliberations of these parties.

The central institutions have survived basically unscathed during this period, though their roles have changed. During the first fifteen to twenty postwar years, the government had the last word in wage developments; then, after a brief non-regulatory interlude, a period of coordinated decentralization followed, leaving for the representative actors of the consultation economy a more limited role in policy preparation. The role of the government in the labor market has become more focused on ensuring optimal market conditions for an economy that is fully part of the European internal market. Market regulation is gradually being adapted to enable the future growth of labor market participation. The government defines a "floor" in the market, provides social assistance at a minimum level, and briefly intervenes in wage formation when external conditions are extreme. Conversely, the social partners negotiate wages without direct state intervention, but separately or jointly, they also put demands on the government—for example, concerning education, employment stability, and job quality. The deliberations about these and related issues result in a gradual adaptation and revision of labor market institutions.

Our case studies reveal particular patterns of decisionmaking between governmental agencies, employers' associations, unions, and companies in each industry. In some industries, old corporatist boards are still in place, though their role is slowly eroding. In health care, the government, professional associations, new regulatory bodies, and private insurance companies compete in rule setting. This contrasts with other industries where various competitive market pressures matter for regulation.

We first evaluate how firms respond to the changes in their competitive and institutional environment with respect to job quality.

FIRM STRATEGIES

All industries are under strong pressure from international competition and market liberalization—naturally with specific differences. This pressure is institutionally sanctioned: national and European Union market regulators keep a keen eye on fair competition and impose heavy financial sanctions in cases of noncompliance. We summarize the competitive and institutional pressures with which the case study firms are coping and evaluate the strategies they are developing in relation to job quality vis-à-vis these pressures.

Competitive Pressures

Competitive pressures derive from internationalization, new technologies, market saturation, and specific market strategies of leading multinational companies. The effects of internationalization have become most manifest in supermarkets, consumer electronics retailing, hotels, call centers, and meat and confectionary manufacturing. Those effects are intertwined with the growth of value chains where supply-chain management directly affects the work organization and job quality of the target groups. The effects work most strongly through the deployment of (international) financial and personnel benchmarking, the clearest examples being found in the supermarket and hotel cases. The development of new value chains also often stimulates market segmentation. This was observed in hospitals, call centers, meat processing, and confectionary, nearly always in conjunction with specialization and upscaling. Yet seemingly contradictory trends were also observed, notably in call centers, where the job boundaries of sales and phone agents are increasingly blurred.

The advance of new technologies is the second competitive driver in all five industries, varying from self-scanning in supermarkets and robotization in food manufacturing to the use of advanced medical equipment in hospitals. Providing customer service through call centers would not have matured without the integration of ACD, CTI, and IVR/VRU technologies, perfected with CRM applications. It is in call centers that technology shows its most direct influence on work organization and on crucial elements of job quality, especially the agents' autonomy. In other industries, the effects of technology are more indirect, mediated by human resource strategies and labor relations in the firm and on the shop floor. Nevertheless, the immense transparency and spread of one particular technology—the Internet—is already having major effects on the competitive position and profitability of hotels and hotel chains and on their work organization. In the coming years, technological innovation, especially the maturing of RFID technology, will become more closely related to the development of value chains, particularly in retail and food processing.

Third, the effects of market saturation and declining disposable consumer incomes from 2002 to 2005 could be observed in supermarkets, consumer electronics retail, meat, confectionary, and financial call centers. The market strategies of leading retail firms were concentrated on price wars and the reduction of labor and supply costs, thus affecting the profitability, employment, and work organization of supermarkets, consumer electronics stores, suppliers in meat processing, and, to a lesser extent, confectionary.

Fourth, specific strategies of multinational firms are often changing the relations in value chains—the divesting policies of multinationals in confectionary providing a clear example. Though not yet very convincingly, the retail case shows signs that growing consumer spending may lead to a shift toward high-road market strategies. It remains to be seen whether the leading retail firms will also incorporate high-road human resource policies into their strategies, let alone whether this will result in enhanced work organizations and improvements in job quality.

INSTITUTIONAL PRESSURES

Specific institutional pressures with which firms are dealing strategically were found in both the labor market and the product market:

- Collective bargaining with mandatory extension and linked to equal treatment: all industries

- Statutory minimum (youth) wages: most relevant for supermarkets, hotels, and independent call centers

- Flexicurity labor market regulations: mainly supermarkets, hotels, and independent call centers

- Disability (Gatekeeper Improvement Act) and sick leave regulation, leading firms to develop risk prevention strategies: hotels, call centers, meat, and confectionary

- Liberalization of zoning regulations and opening hours: relevant for supermarkets and consumer electronics retail

- New financial incentives model in health care: hospitals

- Legal restrictions on telemarketing: call centers

- Legal (EU) regulation of food safety: meat and confectionary

- Industrial and product boards: a modest role for supermarkets, consumer electronics retail, hotels, and meat processing

Product Market and Human Resource Strategies

In retail the effects of market saturation and declining disposable incomes seem to have reinforced existing low-road strategies focused on lowering consumer prices. Yet this is clearer in supermarkets than in consumer electronics, while low-road elements are more evident in the human resource strategies of supermarkets. Market strategies in supermarkets and in the meat and confectionary industries include the introduction of labor-saving technology, but this cannot simply be attributed to low-road firm behavior. We witnessed high-road elements in the market strategies of hotels, hospitals, and confectionary firms, characterized by investment in upgrading and innovation. In confectionary, segmentation in product market strategies was visible, with choices depending on the strategic perspectives of the parent firms. The pressure of hotel-chain formation led to branding and standardization, which affected rather directly cleaning standards and the job quality of room attendants. We also found strategies aimed at realizing economies of scale and cooperation in hotels and hospitals. A mixture of price and product competition, with related market strategies, was observed for call centers, meat, and confectionary. Parent firms are using segmented-market approaches for their call center activities, partly by more intricate outsourcing, especially to temp work agencies.

It is obvious that there is strong pressure in most firms to have human resource strategies supporting an operation with a minimal core workforce and surrounding layers of numerical flexibility. Human resource management no longer acts as a countervailing power. To the contrary, personnel benchmarking, often linked with optimal staffing software, is now a powerful human resource instrument in supermarkets and consumer electronics chains, hotel chains, and call centers. It typically operates top-down, significantly reducing the discretionary power of lower-level personnel and line management for setting priorities in everyday personnel matters, including the possible creation of a more or less sheltered environment for low-skilled workers. Numerical flexibilization is the most important human resource strategy for adapting to variable market conditions—or to product variation, as in confectionary, where it combines with automation. We traced the alternative—functional flexibility of normally contracted employees—in a minority of cases only: in supermarkets mostly as an informal practice, in hospitals and some confectionary firms as a formalized but still experimental practice, and in consumer electronics stores in its most mature form. Functional flexibility among the low-paid is not a popular management issue because the job classifications of virtually all CLAs, which are based on competencies and task flexibility, would dictate higher wages.

Numerical flexibility takes various forms: use of flexible contracts, hiring of temp workers, and outsourcing. The flexibilization of employment contracts, mostly fixed-term and less often on-call, is a trend in hotels, call centers (both in-house and independent), and confectionary. In 2003–2004 supermarkets provided a strong example of flexible hiring and firing policies when they "bullied away" older women and concentrated on recruiting younger people. These policies, however, generated bad press and accusations of age discrimination. Hotels, hospitals, and in-house call centers structurally outsource some of their jobs to specialized companies, but retail stores and hospitals, by contrast, hardly ever use temps from TWAs or other kinds of temps. TWAs have become a substantial supply structure for human resource services as risk selection develops into an important driver of human resource practices. Contracting with TWAs to provide human resource activities such as recruitment has become a rather widespread practice in call centers, meat processing, and confectionary. The agencies offer specialization and value-added in recruitment and selection, and they can take over the health risks that are becoming increasingly important to firms because of changing provisions on sickness and disability insurance, which has made the employer responsible for income during the first two years of sickness. Such specialization may well be an unintended positive aspect of outsourcing: it has led in some cases to higher added-value and consequently more job security for the temp workers. Temp work may function as a stepping-stone to regular work, though it is doubtful whether this happens for many of the low-skilled; moreover, most temp agency work is low-paid and has little to offer to step up to.

In general, the human resource strategies in the target industries do not seem to open up promising prospects for the low-wage workers involved. It is rare to find truly enhanced work organizations or improved job quality for low-paid workers. We can, with some goodwill, consider one supermarket, two hotels, some food industry cases, and a single hospital as positive exceptions. Nevertheless, it is important to note that individual firm behavior can differ within the same institutional environment and is not fully determined by it. We found a number of agreements on improving working conditions, sometimes with implications for job content, but implementation and compliance were usually uncertain, as were the benefits for the low-paid and low-skilled. Most of our field research was done in rather slack labor markets, although in some supermarket, hotel, and call center cases the tightening of labor markets was already being felt. What was striking, however, was the low responsiveness of human resource strategies to this tightening and the ensuing potential labor supply problems. In the two industries with the highest shares of low-paid workers, supermarkets and hotels, most human resource and line managers seemed to bet on a continuing supply of staff with (just) enough general skills to work in the target jobs; some of them admitted, however, that this strategy might well be a dead-end street.

INSTITUTIONAL PRECONDITIONS THAT MATTER FOR THE LOW-PAID?

Work organizations do respond strategically to their changing competitive and institutional environment, and now we turn to the latter, distinguishing six institutional preconditions that may help to raise job quality for low-wage employees, ranging from income policies to education to worker representation.

INCOMES AND TAX POLICY FOR THE LOW-PAID

The Dutch policy debate on low pay goes back all the way to the late 1940s, but it underwent fundamental change during the unemployment crisis of the early 1980s. Until then, low pay had followed the general trend and was first based directly on government-approved collective agreements and later partly mediated by the statutory minimum wage, the evolution of which depended on the trend of wages. Since 1980, however, minimum wages and social benefits have been lowered considerably in nominal and real terms (by 25 percent) and relative to average earnings (by twenty percentage points); this decline matched the decline in the U.S. federal minimum wage.

The change opened the door to the growth of low-wage employment that occurred especially after the mid-1990s. At that time, the minimum wage itself and its employment incidence had largely stopped falling, illustrating that the institutional change may have created room for maneuver that firms did not necessarily need and may have started to use only later. Measures taken by the European Union to promote equal treatment have improved pay and entitlements for women workers. They have not, however, made the Netherlands first in Europe with respect to equal pay. Equal treatment helped to decrease the part-time pay gap as, for example, it led to the abolishment of the exemption of small part-time jobs from the statutory minimum wage in the early 1990s. However, this change has not reduced the extremely high incidence of low pay (50 percent) among the smallest jobs.

There is no tradition in the Netherlands of an earned income tax credit, but tax progression and the recent introduction of tax credits—as well as the possibility of receiving the public old-age pension without ever having made financial contributions—help to explain the enormous popularity of part-time employment. These tax policies also serve as a caveat against linking low wages directly to income inequality.

The strong recent social insurance reform follows the paradigm of "work first." Benefit levels and entitlements were further reduced, with the aim of activating the (non-)receivers. The role of benefits as a possible constraint on the low-wage labor supply significantly diminished as the replacement ratio fell as a result of the reforms. Also, re-entrant women sharing a household with an earning partner are normally not entitled to unemployment benefits, and entitlements for school-leavers and many other youths, whether working or unemployed, were virtually abolished. The reform also put increasing demands on firm behavior. The firm has to seek a solution itself for sickness, disability, or unemployment before an employee can be accepted for benefits, and in the meantime firms are obliged to maintain the employment relationship. This potentially benefits incumbent workers and may make new entries more difficult and selective.

Other changes particularly affected the potential labor supply of young people. The youth minimum wages were drastically lowered, youth wage rates in collective agreements lagged considerably behind, and the incidence of temporary and flexible contracts or small part-time jobs held by young people is now way above that of adults. At the same time, the position of students was much improved by means of student grants that can also be combined with substantial net earnings from paid labor. This gives students a competitive edge in the low-wage labor market and has contributed to the strongly increased part-timing of low-wage jobs. As a result, high numbers of Dutch students work and go to school at the same time, and this overlap leads to a substantial low-paid, part-time segment of the labor market. All this serves to make the youth labor market more and more unlike the adult market. Today only 43 percent of young people are not employed in a flexible job, not working in a small job, or not working in a low-paying industry, compared with 74 percent in 1979.

Collective Labor Agreements

Collective labor agreements are the most essential institution regarding low-wage work in the Netherlands. CLAs cover all target occupations in this study and are the main vector not only for the trade-off between wages and working hours but also for job grading and training of employees. The system applies to all workers and offers no premium for union members. Mandatory extension affects only a small percentage of employees (4 percent), but many of them are low-paid. Perhaps unexpectedly, the high coverage of employees crucially depends on the high rate of membership of employers' associations, which far exceeds union density. Each time the principle of collective agreements is threatened, employers' associations come to its defense as a safeguard of labor peace and stability in industrial relations. The CLA for temp agencies obtained mandatory extension so as to cover all temp workers, including those employed in conditions of outsourcing and external flexibilization.

The pay and grading systems laid down in nearly all agreements are based on broadly recognized systems of job classification, cover 90 to 95 percent of employees, keep wage developments within a narrow band, and offer the prospect of annual wage increases to all workers, including low-wage workers. Admittedly, the magnitude of the wage increases implied by the range of annual steps within a grade is the least for the lowest wages.

Since the early 1980s, in exchange for an almost steady moderation of wage growth relative to productivity growth, the agenda of collective bargaining has substantially broadened to include a growing list of other issues, such as the promotion of the employability of employees or the activation of groups targeted by labor market policies. This approach has enjoyed the full backing of the government and provides an example that is being followed in other European countries.

The government's role in wage setting is restricted to monitoring, which usually remains limited to the formal adoption by the social partners of a measure but does little to check if firms follow it in practice. This is particularly true for the government's drive to close the gap between the lowest wage scales of the agreements and the minimum wage.

In some industries—the independent call centers, hotels, and catering in particular—two competing collective agreements exist. This allows employers to "shop" between different wage regimes and to push down the lowest (agreed) wages. These practices are unfavorable to those workers in the target jobs, especially room attendants and call center agents in independent centers. We also note that collective agreements in some industries are densely regulated, with high coverage, comparatively high wage levels, and many procedural requisites. This may encourage employers to outsource activities and to seek to profit from cheaper collective agreements. These result in a particular type of flexibilization of the workforce, especially since some temp agencies, such as those employed by hotels and the food industry, negotiate the terms of labor contracts with unions other than those of the industry where these employees work.

Employers can also try to evade collective agreements and the statutory minimum wage entirely, but for the large majority of Dutch employers this is not a popular option, as our case studies underline. Only in small-scale services and manufacturing, among self-employed persons, and in the illegal economy is there no collective wage setting.

Employment Contracts and Dismissal Protection

Dutch employment contracts are strongly regulated by law and fall under the scope of collective agreements, which do have the status of law. Employment contracts define the terms and conditions that legally subordinate the employee to the employer in exchange for pay. The contract can be permanent or temporary. The termination of the contract before the agreed termination occurs with mutual agreement or through termination with notice by one of the two parties involved.

The introduction of the Flexibility and Security Act (1999) is best considered as a revision of contract law and the start of a discussion on the relaxation of dismissal protection, an unchanged social right since 1945. It created a new regime of temporary contracts aimed at better protecting long-run temp workers against layoff, lack of pension rights, and so on. Contract law is strengthened by equal treatment regulation, which grants equal access to full-time and part-time jobs, vocational training, and social security. According to the OECD, the Netherlands has relatively strict rules for individual protection and collective dismissal, but less so for temporary contracts. However, in spite of the fact that the dual institutions for dismissal—either through an administrative body or in court—remain unchanged, we found a significant shift in firm behavior toward the court option and an increased responsiveness of dismissals to the unemployment situation. For some employers, the administrative route of the dual system is a thorn in the side, but others prefer this route because it offers no compensation to the employee.

Trade unions defend the employment protection system as a necessity and a benefit to low-wage employees. Deliberative talks since 2003 in the Social and Economic Council on relaxing dismissal protection have ended in a stalemate. The Scientific Council for Government Policy (WRR 2007) very recently suggested diminishing contract protection for those employers who have truly invested in the employability of their workers, adding that employers who do not sufficiently invest in skills shall be penalized with substantial indemnity payments if they end a contract. The approach may be relevant for low-paid employees. Though we do not find a clear insider-outsider gap between younger and older cohorts in the labor market and many young employees use temporary contracts as a stepping-stone to start their career, our case studies confirm that many companies do not sufficiently invest in the vocational education and training of the low-qualified, the issue to which we now turn.

EDUCATION AND TRAINING

General education is a public provision. During the unemployment crisis of the 1980s, many of the larger companies closed their company training schools, and after several rounds of reorganization the contours of a public-private structure in vocational education have become visible. Vocational certification is under the government's authority, with the social partners in an advisory role. The government and the social partners have been in a standoff, however, when it comes to the effectiveness of the educational system. At first sight, education and training is an essential institution that influences the position and perspectives of workers in low-wage jobs, since higher educational attainment and longer training can lead to higher job grades and wage scales. However, some of the target industries, food processing in particular, have relatively high numbers of lower-educated workers in their (aging) workforces, but not high shares of low-wage jobs. Call centers and hospitals, on the other hand, employ better-educated workers than the other industries but differ substantially in their use of low pay—there are more low-paid jobs in call centers than in hospitals. Moreover, for many of the occupational groups in our sample no formal educational requirements were defined.

The transition of pupils from vocational education and training in schools to firms is a bone of contention in the Netherlands. The vocational training system is very modest compared to Germany's, and there are not nearly as many apprenticeships and internships. The educational system, especially its vocational part, continues to "produce" a very sizable output of low-skilled workers by international standards. For incumbent workers, the social partners have established about one hundred large industrial funds for workforce training, but they are restricted to narrowly defined industries whose needs are not met by the educational system, and they usually refuse to support interindustry job mobility. In addition, there is a substantial and growing divergence between the low-skilled and the better-skilled with respect to post-initial education.

We also found institutional segmentation effects. For example, in-house call centers in financial services and utilities are connected to such training facilities, but the independents lack any industrial funding. Also, there are no training facilities for hospital cleaners, and many hospitals cut back the training options for low-wage workers in periods of economic decline. The importance of training for hiring varied between our target occupations. Retail (in particular supermarkets), hotel cleaning, independent call centers, and temp agencies recruit mostly on the basis of general skills and some specific competencies. They invest more in job-related training only when the relevant "general" labor supply dries up and vacancies are no longer easily filled. Hospitals, food firms, and consumer electronics stores recruit nearly all their staff from specific labor markets and build internal educational structures and on-the-job training procedures into their organizations. These are strongly embedded in job evaluation and wage schemes that also cover lower-level jobs. In hotel cleaning and independent call centers no such schemes were developed until just recently.

This may explain why a (formal) low educational level is not always correlated with low pay. However, we should also mention some of the weaker features of the Dutch education and vocational training infrastructure, in particular with regard to low pay. First, many low-wage jobs have been outsourced over the last decades and have lost their direct connection with the company, the company's human resource policy, and industrial training funds. Second, industries with a high share of low-wage jobs produce at best "poor" training funds, since these are filled by a percentage of the wage sum. Third, where training funds exist, they are mostly used by larger firms and to the advantage of full-timers, whereas low pay is concentrated among part-timers and smaller firms. Finally, some workers, such as long-term disabled or ethnic minorities who face language problems or discrimination, are unable or unwilling to obtain new educational credentials. Others drop out from training because of long-term unemployment, psycho-social problems, or disability. This makes education a potentially disruptive dossier, especially in an aging labor market.

JOB QUALITY

Unlike the American case (Appelbaum et al. 2000; Ehrenreich 2001), we have not come across a substantial dehumanization of work in the Netherlands. Objective measures of job quality, legal protections, and the substantial role of the Labor Inspectorate seem to prevent that. Nevertheless, health and safety risks are concentrated among the low-educated who hold low-level jobs, and more generally among youths. For them, labor market flexibility is also very substantial and dismissal protection relatively loose. Men perform heavy physical work, use force, are exposed to vibration and noise, and carry out dangerous work, while women at low job levels are much more frequently involved in low-autonomy jobs, subject to external aggression, or liable to have their skin exposed to dangerous substances. There is also clear evidence that these concentrations of physical health and safety risks are persistent in low-wage industries, especially the hotel industry and to a more limited degree in health care and parts of manufacturing, such as meat processing.

Tackling the risks, which are mostly physical, is the main goal of health and safety regulation, 90 percent of which is based on EU rules and ILO treaties. A typical Dutch element is the so-called health and safety covenant, which is initiated by the government and aims to stimulate unions and employers to take preventive measures at the firm level. Many of these initiatives have resulted in lengthy debates and monitoring studies but then failed to see significant implementation or follow-up. Often insufficient attention is paid to the health risks implied in job content (job latitude, task variety, and autonomy) and work pressure. The latest regulatory framework has adopted less ambitious goals than were proposed a decade ago, and EU initiatives to stimulate the development of new forms of work organization (such as high-performance work systems, or HPWS) were wrecked.

It is worrying that low-autonomy jobs remain widespread, especially, again, among the low-skilled and youths. In recent surveys, the retail, hotel, and health care industries in particular showed above-average scores on combinations of work and time pressure as majorities of workers reported that they worked "regularly at very high speed." Our case study observations, together with the statistical evidence, allow the conclusion that for many low-skilled workers work intensity remains quite high (Parent-Thirion et al. 2007; van Klaveren and Tijdens 2008). As a focus group of checkout operators in one of our retail cases concluded: "Our working hours are packed." Most likely, the intensive character of much low-wage work has to do with the widespread occurrence of (informal) forms of functional flexibility. Workers' assessments of this are often ambivalent: on the one hand, such work is experienced as mentally rewarding, but on the other hand, there is a fear that, with no clear limits, work pressure and eventually work stress will mount. This danger is the more realistic in light of the fact that unions and works councils have done very little to develop ways to monitor activities on the shop floor.

THE REPRESENTATION OF LOW-WAGE WORKERS

Compliance with collective labor agreements by firms and on the shop floor is the flaw of Dutch workers' representation. Unions are hardly present at the shop-floor level, and there is no legislation covering their representation in companies. The responsibility for monitoring whether employers actually implement the clauses of collective agreements has been shifted largely to the works councils, and that responsibility contributes strongly to their feelings of being overburdened and lacking expertise.

The position of low-wage workers in the Netherlands seems better protected by legal institutions, such as mandatory extension of collective labor agreements and the statutory minimum wage, than by genuine workers' representation and voicing. Low-wage workers are formally included in pay and job classification systems, but they remain largely outside unions' policy preparations and the monitoring of the implementation of CLAs. Union membership and the meetings preparing for new collective agreements are dominated by skilled employees with permanent contracts within the larger firms. This is the general picture that finds confirmation in our case studies. Union density is comparatively high in industries and firms where low-wage jobs are few (for example, hospitals and food). Unions affiliated with the two major confederations FNV and CNV, which organize retail firms, hotels, and independent call centers, represent only small shares of the workforce and have to compete with small unions that aim to obtain a position in collective bargaining. Moreover, outsourcing brings low-wage work outside the reach of unions, partly because workers move to other, less organized industries.

Works councils face similar problems of representation that are sometimes even more pronounced than for the unions. In the council membership, medium-wage and higher-wage earners are overrepresented, and our target groups are underrepresented. There are two implications of low-wage earners' lack of visibility within unions and works councils: low wage–related problems are often perceived as "external problems" that do not directly affect the policymaking of workers' representatives at the industry and firm levels; and among low-wage workers there is a widespread and deep-rooted lack of recognition of the necessity and added value of membership in unions and works councils. These problems can be seen clearly in workplaces with many low-wage migrant workers, as some of our supermarket and hotel cases show.

To curb these processes, unions should stop focusing primarily on large firms and existing institutions and start concentrating on industries where they are traditionally weak by investing in organizing low-wage workers and establishing a power base outside the dominant employment patterns. The national unions have attempted such an approach rather successfully in the temp agency and cleaning industries (outside the hotel industry) but with less clear-cut results in independent call centers and supermarkets. Worker representatives obviously encounter considerable problems in convincing both their constituencies and their colleagues in related industries of the effectiveness of such an approach. Even when the results of improved organizing and improved job quality can be shown, disbelief continues to reign, especially in the lower ranks. This may partly reflect problems of employee representation as well as of organizational learning, and it may also be an inherent weakness of the approach: when the union is not clearly visible as "the workers' shield," low-wage workers cannot help but be concerned about the personal consequences for them of major trends such as globalization, offshoring, outsourcing, and rapid technological change. The obvious fallback option for the unions in such conditions is to negotiate at the national level the need for additional regulatory measures for the target groups.

THE OUTLOOK

At the end of this study, we can confirm that a "Dutch model" of low-wage employment does indeed exist. It is part and parcel of the Dutch model in general, both in terms of its deliberative institutions and in its labor market outcomes. Collective agreements, however imperfect they may be, also cover the low-paid, and rates of part-time employment and youth employment are high. The low-wage model not only derives from the Dutch model but also contributes to reinforce it, as the model's special features apply more strongly to low-wage employment. For the low-paid, job growth and wage moderation have been stronger, the rate of part-time employment is much higher (and more concentrated in small jobs), and its rates of youth employment, female employment, and minority employment are high as well. As a result, a noticeable segment of the labor market has developed that is increasingly dissimilar to the rest of the labor market, with far lower pay, far more small jobs, far more flexible contracts, far more immigrants, youths, and women, worse working conditions, and vanishing union membership. This segment is also increasingly penetrating the economy as a whole, reaching firms that before would have had their "own" low-skilled labor but now hire from a temp work agency. These agencies have matured as a new branch of the economy and are servicing this segment less and less on a casual basis. They may not necessarily provide a bad route for professionalizing the low-wage segment, assuming that the agencies with a massive low-wage presence on staff have more of an interest in caring for the low-skilled than the many firms that each have only a few such employees. That is, in a nutshell, the "national story" of low pay in the Netherlands.

We might ask: So what? Is low pay a problem? Does it not operate as a kind of "conscription" that helps to spread the nuisance jobs over many more persons, for a shorter period of their lives, and thus mitigates the individual nuisance? If that were true, yes, low pay would not be a problem. But increasingly more adults are found on low pay, and fewer of them are low-skilled—because they can neither get a living wage from a part-time job nor compete with the over-schooled supply of students and married women. Even if they could match the functional flexibility offered by the latter supply, it is clear that the growth of that flexibility has not been matched by better pay. Unsurprisingly, Dutch household worklessness remains high. The growth of low-wage employment in the presence of a downward trend in the prospects for the population of better-paid employment is not a promising trend for a country that is intent on cultivating the "knowledge economy." Measures that stimulate low-wage growth risk taking away employers' and employees' incentives to improve the quality of the low-wage segment.

A possible high road to low-skill employment cannot be considered in isolation from the rest of the economy. Equally, the question of whether the Dutch model of low-wage employment is sustainable should be considered in conjunction with the overall model. Part-time employment has already reached such high levels that its future growth is likely to be slower. The policy debate is already starting to aim at increasing the working hours of part-time employees, but if people stick to their preferences for small jobs or easily accessible, geographically widespread jobs, they will find these primarily in the low-wage segment. More generally, the gross (head-count) labor force participation rate has reached such high levels that a significant further increase is not self-evident. Its slight fall in recent years—as in the United States, where it is more pronounced—may be pointing in that direction. In addition, net emigration has replaced immigration, and the growth of the minority population, though still high, is slowing quickly. However, increasing labor supply from Eastern Europe, which has a momentum of its own since EU enlargement, may mitigate this effect. Political pressure is building for a radical improvement of the educational system, which could have a lowering effect on the still ample supply of unskilled labor and might in due course also restrict the competition of students in the low-wage segment.

The outlook for the Dutch model of low-wage employment hinges on these market developments in labor supply. Only if these developments limit supply, reduce turnover, and make the low-wage segment less volatile will unions be able to make a comeback. For now, their promotion of the interests of workers in low-level employment is hampered by the sheer flexibility of these jobs and remains threatened by a number of factors: the possible abolition of mandatory extension of collective agreements; the political pressure to align low pay with the minimum wage, in decline because of its role in social expenditure; the growing significance of market regulators with virtually no democratic control; and last but not least, the downward pressures stemming from European unification on existing national rules concerning health, safety, and working conditions. In the meantime, unions could focus on learning from their achievements, however modest, in organizing and bargaining for particular groups in the low-wage segment, and they could also try to improve the quality of this segment by supporting the professionalization of the flexible arrangements that temp agencies could offer to low-wage workers—which they have already done with some success.

REFERENCES

Appelbaum, Eileen, Thomas Bailey, Peter Berg, and Arne L. Kalleberg. 2000. *Manufacturing Advantage: Why High Performance Work Systems Pay Off.* Ithaca, N.Y.: Cornell University Press.

Ehrenreich, Barbara. 2001. *Nickel and Dimed: On (Not) Getting By in America.* New York: Metropolitan Books.

Parent-Thirion, Agnes, Enrique Fernandez-Macias, John Hurley, and Greet Vermeylen. 2007. *Fourth European Working Conditions Survey.* Dublin: European Foundation for the Improvement of Living and Working Conditions.

Scott, W. Richard. 2004. "Reflections on a Half-Century of Organization Sociology." *Annual Review of Sociology* 30: 1–21.

Van Klaveren, Maarten, and Kea Tijdens, editors. 2008. *Bargaining Issues in Europe: Comparing Countries and Industries.* Brussels: European Trade Union Institute for Research, Education and Health and Safety (ETUI-REHS).

WRR. 2007. *Investeren in werkzekerheid [Investing in Job Security].* Amsterdam: Amsterdam University Press.

Index

Boldface numbers refer to figures and tables

ABN-AMRO, 73, 251
Accor, **181**
active labor market policies, 25, 90–92
age analysis: call center agents, 255–6;
  employment rates, **33**; health care
  sector, **213**; low-wage work incidence, 14, 50–52; meat processing
  employees, 279; mobility out of low-
  wage work, 58–59; part-time workers, **33**; retail employees, 153–5;
  union membership, **71**
age discrimination, 101–2
agriculture, **42**
Ahold, 156–58
Albert Heijn (AH), 148, 160, 161, 164
Aldi, 157, 164
Amsterdam hotel industry, 178, 187–8,
  193, 194, 203
Antillean immigrants, 230–31
Appelbaum, E., 2, 17, 142, 222–3
apprenticeships, 215
assistant nurses, 214–15, 227–8
assistants, in hospitals, 227–8, 234
Association of Grocery Multiple Stores
  (VGL), 161–2
automatic call distribution (ACD), 244
autonomy, of employees, 167, 193, 245,
  259–60

banking. *See* financial and business ser-
  vices industry
Barry Callebaut, 273
batch processes, 269, 278
Bauer, T., 141
BBA. *See* Buitengewoon Besluit Arbei-
  dsverhoudingen (BBA)
BCC, 159

"Because Everybody is Needed," 29
benchmarking, 211, 303
Bernhardt, A., 2, 142
Best Western, **181**
boards, hospital, 222
bonuses, 149, 171, **196**, 286, 288
boutique hotels, 181–2
branded products, 294–5
bread industry, 268
BTP, 253
Buitengewoon Besluit Arbeidsverhoudingen (BBA), 100

Cadbury, 270
call centers: case study data, **243**; collective labor agreements, 238, 252–3,
  257, **258**, 261–3; competitive conditions, 250–1; data sources, 133; demand fluctuations, 247–9; emergence
  and growth of industry, 242, 244;
  employee characteristics, 255–6; employee evaluation, 264; employee
  representation, 251–2; employee
  turnover, 263; employers' associations, 252; employment contracts,
  238; employment flexibility, 247–9,
  261; employment statistics, 133, **134,**
  135, **245**; female employees, 255; industry trends, 245–9; job design and
  responsibilities, 237, 239–40, 245–6;
  job levels, 257, **258**; job quality, 240,
  257, 259–60, 265; job skills and qualifications, 256–7; labor intensity, 247;
  labor relations, 251–3; low-wage
  work, **135**, 240–1; monitoring of employees, 259–60; outbound calls,
  246; outsourcing, 249, 251; part-time

call centers (*continued*)
work, 260; process innovations, 247; regulations, 249; research considerations, 132; research methodology, 241–2; sales activity, 246; student employees, 253–4; technology, 237, 244–5, 247; temporary agency work and workers, 238–9, 241, 249, 254, 260–1, **262**, 263–4; training, 239, 257; unions and unionization, 242, 252–3; vocational training, 254–5; wages, 136, **137**, 138, **139**, 240–1, 261–3; work hours and schedules, 260–1; working conditions and organization, 237, 257. *See also* independent call centers; in-house call centers
candy. *See* confectionary industry
career advancement opportunities: confectionary industry, 291–2; hospitals, 215, 227; hotel industry, 185; hotel room attendants, 195, 197; meat processing industry, 292; nurses, 215; supermarket industry, 172
case studies: call centers, **243**; confectionary industry, **271**; consumer electronics industry, **151**; hospitals, **224**; hotel industry, 178–9, **180**; meat processing, **272**; overview of, 145, 146; supermarket industry, **151**
CBS (Statistics Netherlands). *See* Statistics Netherlands (CBS)
Center for Work and Income, 101
Central Planning Bureau (CPB), 13–14, 19, 23, 61n4
chain hotels, 179, 181–2, 192
checkout operators: job design and responsibilities, 167; shelf-stackers as, 148, 166; wages, 170; women as, 153; working conditions, 168. *See also* supermarkets
child care, 34
chocolate, 273, 282–3, 292. *See also* confectionary industry
CLAs (collective labor agreements). *See* collective labor agreements (CLAs)
cleaners, in hospitals, 226, 227–8

cleaners, in hotels. *See* hotel room attendants
cleaning companies, 189–90, 192, **196**, 197, 226
cleaning industry, **87**, **139**, 195
CNV, 185, 252
CNV Bedrijvenbond, 275, 279
CNV Dienstenbond, 162, 163
collective labor agreements (CLAs): call centers, 238, 252–3, 257, **258**, 261–3; confectionary industry, 275–6; consumer electronics industry, 171; coverage, 57–58, 75, 118, **139**; cross-country studies, 8–9; disabled workers, 117; economic impact, 76; employers' role, 74–75; employment contracts, 102; gender differences and issues, 70, 76, 84–85; government control over, 20–22, 23, 27, 299, 307; health care sector, 216–20, 221, 233; hotel industry, 185–6, 187, 195, **196**; industry analysis, **139**; job classification schemes, 75–76, 142–3; job dismissals, 101; legal framework for, 18, 74; and low-wage workers, 57–58, 78–80, 306–8, 312; mandatory extension, 75, 78, 301, 306–7; meat processing industry, 279–80, 281, 285–8; model of, **69**; moderation trend, 120–1; "New Course Accord" (1993), 72; outcomes, 75–76; part-time work, 72; retail industry, 161; role of, 118–9; sickness benefits, 113; supermarket industry, 162, 170; temporary agency workers, 103; vocational education and training, 98–99; and wages, 76–78, 136, **137**; wage scales, 76, 78–80; and Wassenaar Accord, 23, 72; work hours, 86, 113, 169; working conditions, 115
college education, 14
communication industry, 41, **42**
compensation. *See* wages and earnings
competitive conditions: call centers, 250–1; confectionary industry, 293; consumer electronics industry,

158–9; financial services industry, 250; Germany's impact on, 14–15; hotel industry, 7, 201–2; meat processing industry, 293; retail industry, 155–61; sources of, 300–301; supermarket industry, 7; utilities industry, 250

computer telephony integration (CTI), 244

confectionary industry: career advancement opportunities, 291–2; case study data, **271**; characteristics of, 268–9, 270–1; collective labor agreements, 275–6; competitive conditions, 293; data sources, 270; employee characteristics, 291; employee turnover, 285; employers' associations, 270, 275; employment flexibility, 274, 289–91; employment statistics, 133–4, 274–5; female employees, 274–5; firm strategies, 270–4; job classification, 275–6; job skills and qualifications, 274, 291; labor relations, 275–6; low wages, 135; manufacturing process, 269, 273; offshoring, 293; outsourcing, 272–3; pensions, 276; product innovation, 273; relationship with customers, 274; research methodology, 269–70; sales trends, 273; seasonal production, 273–4; temporary agency workers, 289–90; training, 276–7, 291; unions and unionization, 275, 288; vocational training, 276–7, 292, 293; wages, 136, **137**, 138, **139**, 267, 288; work hours and schedules, 289; working conditions and organization, 276

consumer electronics industry: case study data, **151**; collective labor agreements, 171; competitive conditions, 158–9; employee recruitment, 173; employers' association, 162; employment flexibility, 148–9, 166; employment statistics, 134, 152–3; job design and responsibilities, 167; job tenure, 155; low-wage work, **135**,

171; number of, 156; part-time employment, 153; research methodology, 149–50; sales trends, 156; training, 172; wages, 136, **137**, **139**, 149, 171; work hours and schedules, 169; working conditions and organization, 149, 168–9; work organization, 149; young employees, 155

consumer spending, 156

consumption per capita, 40

contract law, 308

contracts, employment. *See* employment contracts

corporate governance, 222

Corus, 73

cost-cutting strategies: health care sector, 210–1, 223; hotel industry, 184; and low-wage workers, 7–8; meat processing industry, 278; supermarket industry, 157

Covenant on a Flexible Workforce, 281, 290

CPB. *See* Central Planning Bureau (CPB)

cross-country studies: advantages of, 3; collective bargaining agreements, 8–9; institutions, 65; labor market, 9–12; "natural" variations, 8; overview of, 4–13; research considerations, 4–5

CSM, 272

CTI. *See* computer telephony integration (CTI)

customer relationship management (CRM), 245

customer reviews, 202–3

customer service, 149, 158, 245–6, 251. *See also* call centers

CVC Capital Partners, 272

dairy industry, 268

data sources: call centers, 133; confectionary industry, 270; low-pay probability, 56; meat processing industry, 270; wages and earnings, 136

deboning, 283

demographic analysis, 51–54

Denmark, 6, 10
department store cashiers, 168
De Unie, 185–6, 275, 279
diagnostic-treatment combinations (DTCs), 210–1
disability insurance, 22, 113, 115–7, 301–2
disabled workers, 113, 116, **117**
discrimination, 101–2, 231
dismissals, 101, 103–5, 308–9
diversity management, 231
doctors, 222
Dutch Executive Housekeepers Association, 178
Dutch language training, **98**
Dutch Personnel Data Protection Act, 259
Dutch Survey on Working Conditions, 168

early retirement, 110–1
earnings. *See* wages and earnings
ECABO, 254–55
ECHP. *See* European Community Household Panel (ECHP)
Economic and Monetary Union, 27
economy, 39–42, 72–73, 76
educational attainment: disincentives, 120; and employment rates, 36–38; and job training, 99–100; meat processing employees, 279; and mobility out of low-wage work, 59; and union membership, 70, **71**; vs. U.S., 14, **37**
education and training. *See* training, firm-based; vocational training
electrical goods retailers. *See* consumer electronics industry
electronic consumer response (ECR) systems, 160
electronics industry. *See* consumer electronics industry
employee involvement, 141
employee recruitment, 171–2, 173, 195
employee representation, 26, 163–4, 251–2, 312–3. *See also* unions and unionization

employee turnover: call center agents, 263; confectionary industry, 285; hospitality industry, 186; hospitals, 212; hotel room attendants, 197, 199; meat processing industry, 285, 290; supermarket industry, 171
employers' associations: call centers, 252; and collective labor agreements, 74–75, 119; confectionary industry, 270, 275; firm-based training, 98; hotel industry, 185; meat processing industry, 270, 279–80; retail industry, 161–2; role of, 68
employment contracts: call centers, 238; collective labor agreements, 102; coverage, 100, **139**; fixed-term contracts, 58, 102, 238, 261; flexible, 105–6, 261; hotel room attendants, 194, 195; industry analysis, **139**; low-wage workers, 308–9; and low-wage work probability, 58; and mobility out of low-wage work, 59; regulation of, 308; termination of, 308
employment protection legislation (EPL), 100–101, 103–4, 108, 308–9
employment rate: and educational attainment, 36–38; full-time equivalent approach, 35–36, 297; by industry, 41–42; of low-wage workers, 51; and minimum wage, 82–84; of older workers, 110, 111; and SPAK, 90; trends, 16, 43; vs. U.S., 32–34; women, 33, 34–35; of working-age population, 124*n*2
employment statistics: call centers, **134**, 135, **245**; confectionary industry, 133–4, 274–5; consumer electronics industry, 134, 152–3; food processing industry, 133–4, 267–68; hospitals, **134**, 135, 211; hotel industry, 134–5, 177, 184; manufacturing, 133; meat processing industry, 133, 277, 279; nurses, 212; nursing homes, 211; retail industry, 134, 150, 152; supermarket industry, 152
employment to population ratio (EPOP), 32–34, 36, **37**, **42**, 51. *See*

also head-count employment-population rates; hours-count employment-population rates
Encebe, 279
Engbersen, G., 25
enterprise resource planning (ERP), 279
EPL. *See* employment protection legislation
equal opportunity, 2
Equal Pay for Men and Women Act (1975), 85
equal treatment, 109–10, 305, 308
Equal Treatment Commission, 85, 86
ergonomics, 168, 192
ERP. *See* enterprise resource planning
European Commission, "Partnership for a New Organization of Work" green paper, 140
European Community Household Panel (ECHP), 56, 58, 62*n*12
European Union (EU): food safety regulations, 268, 278; gender wage gap, 85; labor market rules and regulations, 73; Posted Workers Directive, 103; Services Directive, 103; working conditions, 112
EVC (Recognition of Acquired Competencies) certificates, 276
Even, W., 124*n*9
exports, 268
externalization, 18

financial and business services industry: competitive conditions, 250; firm strategies, 249–50; gender wage gap, 87; growth of, 41; regulations, 249; research considerations, 241–2; scripted phone calls, 245; service intensity, 245. *See also* call centers
Financial Services Act (2006), 249
firm size: and flexible employment, 106; industry analysis, **139**; and low-wage work probability, 57; retail industry, 159
fixed-term contracts, 58, 102, 238, 261
flexibility: call centers, 247–9, 261; con-fectionary industry, 274, 289–91; consumer electronics industry, 148–9, 166; factors in, 27–28; growth of, 102–9; hospitals, 207, 229–30; hotel industry, 184, 194, 199, 202; meat processing industry, 289–91; need for, 8; and part-time work, 27–28; supermarket industry, 148, 165–7; unions' support of, 27; youth, **106**, 121–2. *See also* temporary agency work and workers
Flexibility and Security Act (1999), 102, 308
Flexicurity Act (1999), 86, 281
flexicurity system, 10, 301
flow processes, 269
FNV Bondgenoten: call centers, 252, 253; food processing industry, 275, 279, 280; retail industry, 162, 163, 164, 171
FNV (Dutch Trade Union Federation), 112, 157, 161, 185
food-processing industry: employment statistics, 133–4, 267–8; exports, 268; female employees, 268; gender wage gap, 87; research considerations, 132; subsectors, 267, 268; trends, 268; wages, **139**, 267. *See also* confectionary industry; meat processing
food retailers. *See* supermarkets
food safety, 268, 278–9, 302
foreign-born workers. *See* immigrants and immigration
Foundation for Call Center Excellence (SECC), 254
Foundation of Labor (STAR): CLA wage scale recommendations, 79; collective bargaining role, 73; creation of, 19; employment protection, 102; equal employment representation, 109; minimum wage, 21; pensions, 111; role and agenda of, 27, 68, **69**
France, 6, 10–11
freelance workers, 107–8
Freeman, R., 74, 124*n*1, 141

full-time equivalents: definition of, 35; employment rate, 297; low wages, 46, 48, **49**, 298; wages, **45**, 46

Functiewaardering Gezondheidszorg (FWG), 216–20, 225

functional flexibility, 148, 166, 303

The Future of Work, 2–3

Gatekeeper Improvement Act (2002), 113, 186

GCC (Global Call Center) survey. *See* Global Call Center (GCC) survey

GDP. *See* gross domestic product (GDP)

gender analysis: disabled workers, **117**; flexible employment, **106**; health care employment, 212; hotel room attendants, 188, 203; low-wage work incidence, 14, **50**; mobility out of low-wage work, 58. *See also* men; women

gender wage gap, 84–87

General Food Act, 279

generational transference, 2

Germany, 6, 9–10, 14–15

Global Call Center (GCC) survey: call center activities, 241, 246; employee autonomy, 259; employees, 240, 255; flexible contracts, 261; labor costs, 247; part-time work, 260; technology, 244; temporary agency workers, 263; training, 257; wages, 263; works councils, 252

globalization, 8, 179, 277, 293, 300

Glyn, A., 120

Golden Tulip, **181**

governance, corporate, 222

government regulation. *See* regulation

government spending, 68

grants, for students, 92, **93**, 306

Great Britain, 6, 11, 140–1

Gregg, P., 34

grocery stores. *See* supermarkets

gross domestic product (GDP), 24, 39–40, **41**, 76

guest workers, 21, 109. *See also* immigrants and immigration

Hall, P., 64

Hartog, J., 74

HBD. *See* Industrial Board for Retail Trades (HBD)

head-count employment-population rates: by industry, **42**; for low vs. better-paid workers, **52**, 60; low-wage employment, **47**, 297; trends, **36**, 51; by work hours, **49**; for youth, **53**

health and safety. *See* occupational health and safety

health care: collective labor agreements, 216–20, 221, 233; demand for, 206, 211; employment outlook, 212; financial incentives model, 209–10. *See also* hospitals; nursing homes

health care costs, 209

Health Care Inspectorate, 208

Health Care Quality for Health Care Institutions Act (1996), 208

health insurance, 22, 61n9, 209–10

High Council of Labor, 29n1

high-performance work systems (HPWS), 141–2

high-road organizations, 3, 140–4, 199–202, 293–4

holiday pay, 61n9, 80–81

home care organizations, 209, 211, 230

hospitality industry, 177, 185–7. *See also* hotel industry

hospitals: assist role, 227–8, 234; budget allocation, 206, 209–11; career advancement opportunities, 215, 227; case study data, **224**; cleaning, 226, 227–8; collective labor agreements, 216–20, 221; diagnostic-treatment combinations, 210–1; duration of stay, 209; employee characteristics, 212–3, 230–1; employee turnover, 212; employment flexibility, 207, 229–30; employment statistics, **134**, 135, 211; gender wage gap, 87; governance and supervision boards, 222;

immigrant workers, 230–1; internal labor pools, 230; job classification, 216–20, 225; job quality, 231–33; low-wage work, **135**, 206–7, 220, 223, 225, 233; number of, 209; nursing assistants, 214–5, 227–8; outsourcing, 230; part-time work and workers, 233; regulation of, 208; research considerations, 132, 206–8; specialization, 208–9; student workers, 229; subsidized workers, 231; temporary agency work, 230; training, 213–16; unions and unionization, 220, 221, 222; in U.S., 222–3; vocational training, 213–6; volunteers, 228–9; wages, **137**, 138, **139**, 216–20; work hours and schedules, 220–2; working conditions and organization, 206, 222–3, 227, 229–30, 232–3, 234. *See also* nurses

hotel industry: in Amsterdam, 178, 187–8, 193, 194, 203; career advancement opportunities, 185; case study data, 178–9, **180**; chain formation and internationalization, 179, 181–2; collective labor agreements, 185–6, 187, 195, **196**; competitive conditions, 7, 201–2; cost-saving strategies, 184; customer reviews, 202–3; employee categories, 184–85; employee recruitment, 195; employers' associations, 185; employment flexibility, 184, 194, 199, 202; employment statistics, 134–5, 177, 184; gender wage gap, **87**; high-road strategy, 199–202; housekeeping departments, **191**; innovation, 183–4; labor market, 184, 186–7, 188; labor relations, 185–6; low-wage work, **135**; occupational health and safety, 186, 192–3; outsourcing, 178, 186, 188–90, 199–200; research considerations, 132; research methodology, 177–8; sales and profitability, 182–3; statistics, 179, **181**, **183**; structural changes, 179, 202; training, 185;

trends, 177, 179–84; unions and unionization, 185, 191; working conditions and organization, 186, 192–4

hotel room attendants: career development opportunities, 195, 197; characteristics of, 187–88; employment contracts, 194, 195; immigrants, 178, 188, 203; job design and responsibilities, 190–2, 197–9; job quality, 197–9, 202–3; outsourcing tasks of, 178, 186, 188–90, 199–200; as percentage of hotel staff, 177; recruitment of, 195; supervisors or forewomen, 190, **191**, 197; turnover rate, 197, 199; wages, 136, **137**, 195, **196**; work hours and schedules, 184, 194; working conditions and organization, 186, 192–4

hourly wages, 43

hours-count employment-population rates: for low vs. better-paid workers, **52**; low-wage employment, **47**; trends, **36**, 51; by work hours, **49**

hours of work. *See* work hours and schedules

household income, 40

housekeeping, in hospitals, 226, 227–8

housekeeping, in hotels. *See* hotel room attendants

HPWS. *See* high-performance work systems (HPWS)

human capital, 8

human resource strategies: call centers, 239, 264; food processing industry, 293–4; high vs. low-road, 143; hotel industry, 200–201; and labor supply issues, 304; numerical vs. functional flexibility, 303–4; personnel benchmarking, 161, 303; retail industry, 161, 173; supermarket industry, 149

hypermarkets, 159

Identification for Servicing Act (2006), 249

IKEA, 70

illegal workers, 189, 281

ILO. *See* International Labor Organization (ILO)

immigrants and immigration: hospital workers, 230–1; hotel room attendants, 178, 188, 203; in lower-level jobs, 39; low-wage work, 14, 53–54, 109–10; minimum wage, 103; policy, 110, 201; retail employment, 154; temporary agency work, 103; trends, 110; unemployment, 61n7

Incomes Policy Act, 21–22

independent call centers: case study data, **243**; collective labor agreements, 238, 252–3; competitive conditions, 250–1; employee characteristics, 255–6; employee turnover, 263; growth of, 244; job design and responsibilities, 246; job levels, 257; job skills and qualifications, 256; labor relations, 251–2; part-time work, 260; regulations, 249; research limitations, 241, 242; training, 257; VOIP (voice-over Internet protocol), 247; wages, 240–1, **262**; working conditions and organization, 257

Individual Health Care Provisions Act, 208

Industrial Board for Retail Trades (HBD), 153, 163, 174

industrialization, 133

industrial relations. *See* labor relations

industry analysis: employment, 133–5; head-count employment-population rate, **42**; low-wage incidence, 54–56, 57, 135–40; research design, 132; research methodology, 144–6

Industry Board for Retail, 152

industry boards, 68

in-house call centers: case study data, **243**; collective labor agreements, 238; competitive conditions, 251; employee characteristics, 256; employee representation, 252; employee turnover, 263; growth of, 244; job levels, 257; part-time work, 260; research limitations, 241; wages,

240–1, **262**; working conditions and organization, 257

innovation, 140–1, 183–4, 247, 273

inspections, of workplace, 112, 114

institutional analysis, 17, 63–66, 117–8

Integration Act (2006), 110

interactive voice response (IVR), 244

internalization, 18

internal labor pools, 230

internationalization, 8, 179, 277, 293, 300

International Labor Organization (ILO), 112

Internet, 202–3, 301

interviews, 144–6, 150, 177–8, 231–2

invalidity provisions, 18, 22

IT (information technology), 160, 202–3, 247

job classification: collective labor agreements, 75–76, 142–3; confectionary industry, 275–6; hospitals, 216–20, 225; meat processing industry, 280, 281, 283; Statistics Netherlands, 38; supermarket industry, 170

job creation, 91–92, 231

job design and responsibilities: call centers, 237, 239–40, 245–6; consumer electronics sales clerks, 167; hospital cleaners, 226; hotel room attendants, 190–2, 197–9; nurses, 226; nursing assistants, 227; nutrition assistants, 226–7; supermarket checkout operators, 167. *See also* working conditions and organization

job dismissals, 101, 103–5, 308–9

job enlargement, 26

job ladders. *See* job classification

job mobility, 6, 58–59, 78–79. *See also* career advancement opportunities

job quality: call centers, 240, 257, 259–60, 265; components of, 66; definition of, 3; high vs. low-road strategy, 143–4; hospitals, 231–3; hotel room attendants, 197–9, 202–3; institutions relevant to, 65, 67; low-wage

workers, 311–2; research considerations, 18; retail industry, 167–9. *See also specific components*
job rotation, 141, 168, 281–2
job security, 100–102, 141, 142, 195
job segregation, 85, 86
job skills and qualifications: call centers, 256–7; confectionary industry, 274, 291; meat processing industry, 291; nurses, 225–6
job tenure: consumer electronics industry, 155; health care sector, 212, **213**; by industry, **139**; and low-wage probability, 57, 58; and mobility out of low-wage work, 59
job training. *See* training, firm-based; vocational training
Jones, D., 142

Kalleberg, A., 142
Knegt, R., 125*n*17
Kok, W., 72
Koninklijke Horeca Nederland (KHN), 185
Kuylaars, L., 26

labor contracts. *See* employment contracts
Labor Inspectorate: CLA wage scale use, 79; health and safety regulation enforcement, 114, 257, 259; low-wage probability, 57; minimum wage violations, 81, 195; occupational segregation by gender, 85
labor market: cross-country comparison, 9–12; EU rules and regulations, 73; hotel industry, 184, 186–7, 188; low-wage workers, 315; Polder model, 12, 13–14, 66–74, 100, 299; regulation, 299; research considerations, 16; retail industry, 172, 173–4; supply constraints, 109–11
labor relations: after WWII, 18–20; call centers, 251–53; confectionary industry, 275–6; dual system of, 68, 70; hotel industry, 185–6; meat processing industry, 279–80; retail industry,

161–5; supermarket industry, 164. *See also* collective labor agreements (CLAs); employers' associations; unions and unionization
labor supply, 109–11, 172–3, 184, 186–7
Labor Tax Credit, 88, 90
labor turnover. *See* employee turnover
Laurus, 158
layoffs, 101, 103–5, 308–9
lean retailing, 160
legislation, 8–9. *See also* regulation
Lidl, 157, 164
literacy, 125*n*14
low-level jobs, 38
low-road organizations, 3, 140–4, 156, 173–4
low-skill workers: employers' organization of, 3; employment rates, 95; gender wage gap, 86; groups of, 95–96; job dismissals, 105; low-wage work incidence, 50; as percentage of working-age population, 95; in U.S., 36, 95; working conditions, 115
Low-Wage America: How Employers Are Reshaping Opportunity in the Workplace (Appelbaum, Bernhardt, and Murnane), 2–3, 17, 142
low-wage work and workers: concentration of, 7; definition of, 5–6, 44–45; Dutch model, 314–6; employment rate, 51; human capital, 8; incidence of, 5, 6, 13, 14, 45–46, 48, 50–51, **55**, 297–8; vs. poverty, 1; probability of, 56–58; and productivity, 1–2; in U.S., 1, 5. *See also specific entries*
Lubbers I coalition, 23

MacPherson, D., 124*n*9
manufacturing, 23, 42, 133, 267. *See also* food-processing industry
marginal income tax, 10, 88–90
market saturation, 301
market segmentation, 300
married women, lower-level jobs, 38–39

meat processing: career advancement opportunities, 292; case study data, 272; characteristics of, 268–9, 277; collective labor agreements, 279–80, 281, 285–8; competitive conditions, 293; cost-cutting strategies, 278; data sources, 270; deboning, 283; employee characteristics, 279, 291; employee turnover, 285, 290; employers' associations, 270, 279–80; employment flexibility, 289–91; employment statistics, 133, 277, 279; female employees, 279, 282–3; firm strategies, 277–9; illegal workers, 281; internationalization, 277, 293; job classification, 280, 281, 283; job skills and qualifications, 291; labor relations, 279–80; low wages, 135, 286, 288; manufacturing process, 269, 278; prepacking, 278; product innovation, 278; regulations, 279; research methodology, 269–70; retail price pressures, 278; safety crises, 278–9; specialization, 277; temporary agency workers, 281, 288, 290; unions and unionization, 279–80; vocational training, 280–1, 292, 293; wages, 136, 137, 138, 139, 280, 285–8; work hours and schedules, 280, 289; working conditions and organization, 281–85; young workers, 288
MediaMarkt, 159
median wage, 44, 45, 46
Melkert, A., 91
men: disabled workers, 117; employment rates, 33–34, 52; flexible employment, 106; health care employment, 212; hotel room attendants, 188, 203; low-wage work incidence, 14, 50, 52–53; mobility out of low-wage work, 58; part-time work, 59; union membership, 71
methodology: call centers, 241–2; confectionary industry, 269–70; consumer electronics industry, 149–50; food processing, 269–70; hotel industry, 177–8; industry analysis, 144–6; supermarket industry, 149–50
migrant workers. *See* immigrants and immigration
mini-jobs, 9–10
minimum wage: and CLA wage scales, 79–80; definition of, 81; enforcement of, 81, 195; establishment of, 21; for foreign temporary workers, 103; in France, 11; freezing of, 25, 81–82; industry analysis, 136, 137; level of, 23, 44, 64, 80, 81–84, 305; and low-wage employment, 82–84, 85; part-time work, 81; real vs. relative, 83; social insurance benefits linkage, 22, 82; and taxation, 88, 90; in U.K., 11; for young people, 12, 81, 84, 122, 306
Ministry of Health Care, Welfare, and Sports, 208
Ministry of Social Affairs and Employment, 81, 253, 254
minorities, 39, 97–98, 109, 230–1
mobility, out of low-wage work, 6, 58–59, 78–79. *See also* career advancement opportunities
modern socio-technical (MST) approach, 26
Moroccan immigrants, 231
Mühlau, P., 90–91
multinational corporations, 268, 270, 294, 301
multiskilling, 283
Murnane, R., 2, 142

Nestlé, 270
Netherlands Association of Hospitals (NVZ), 216, 221–2
NH-Hotels, 181
niche markets, 273
nurses: career advancement opportunities, 215; characteristics of, 207; CLA job levels, 215; employment statistics, 212; job design and responsibilities, 226; job skills and qualifications, 225–6; Nurses Advisory Council, 222; as percentage of health care

workers, 211; vocational training, 213
Nurses Advisory Council, 222
nursing assistants, 214–5, 227–8
nursing homes: budget allocation, 210; collective labor agreements, 216–20, 221; employee characteristics, 212, 230; employment statistics, 211; gender wage gap, **87**; research considerations, 207–8; volunteers, 228–9; wages, 216–20
nutrition assistants, 226–8
NVZ. *See* Netherlands Association of Hospitals (NVZ)

occupational classification, 38
occupational health and safety: call centers, 257; confectionary industry, 276; and high-performance work systems, 141–2; hospitals, 232–33; hotel industry, 186, 192–3; low-wage workers, 311–2; meat processing industry, 280–1, 284–5; regulation, 111–7, 311; retail industry, 168–9
occupational segregation, 85, 86
OECD (Organization for Economic Co-operation and Development). *See* Organization for Economic Cooperation and Development (OECD)
Oelen, U., 105
offshoring, 293
older workers, 110–1
on-call work, 108, 261
on-the-job training, 57, 59, 257, 276
OOCC Foundation, 254, 255
Opta, 246
ORBA method, 276, 280
organizational structure and change, 41, 179, 202. *See also* strategies, of firms
Organization for Economic Cooperation and Development (OECD): employment protection legislation, 103, 104, 108; institutions, 64; store opening hours, 160; Structural Analysis Indicators Database, 61*n*4
outsourcing: call centers, 249, 251; con-

fectionary industry, 272–3; data limitations, 107–8; hospitals, 230; hotel industry, 178, 186, 188–90, 199–200
overtime, 108, 166, 221, 289

packaging, 269, 274–5, 282, 284
part-time work and workers: call centers, 260; collective labor agreement coverage, 72; consumer electronics industry, 153; and flexibility strategy, 27–28; growth of, 13, 14, 34, 121, 297; health care sector, 212; hospitals, 233; hours worked, 48; and institutional change, 121, **122**; laws regulating, 86; low wages, 6, 48, 57, 60, 297–8; men, 59; minimum wage, 81; mobility out of low-wage work, 59; policy issues, 315; retail industry, 152–3; share of total employment, **33**, **34**; supermarket industry, 152, 165; taxation, 88, 90; and Wassenaar Accord, 24; women, **33**, **34**, 86
pensions, 276
Personnel Data Protection Act, 259
piece rates, 199
Polder model, 12, 13–14, 66–74, 100, 299
policy issues: collective labor agreements, 119; immigration, 110, 201; low-wage work, 28–29, 305–6; part-time work, 315; phases after WWII, 19–20
Polish workers, 103, 283, 290
Posted Workers Directive (EU), 103
poverty, 1, 2, 5, 25
PPP. *See* purchasing power parity (PPP)
preventive medicine, 208–9
price wars, 156–8, 173, 268, 269, 274
private label products, 157, 294–5
probability, of low-wage work, 56–58
Product Board (PVE), 270, 279
productivity, 1–2, 3, 120
product-market strategies, 143, 295, 302
promotion opportunities. *See* career advancement opportunities

public sector, 23–24, 91–92
purchasing power parity (PPP), 45, 82

qualifications. *See* job skills and qualifications
quality, job. *See* job quality

radio frequency identification (RFID) technology, 160, 301
real wages, 6, 23
recessions, 16, 21, 40, 184
Recognition of Acquired Competencies (EVC) certificates, 276
recruitment, of employees, 171–2, 173, 195
regulation: call centers, 249; collective wage agreements, 20–22, 23, 27, 299, 307; employment contracts, 308; financial services industry, 249; food safety, 268, 278; hospitals, 208; industry boards' power over, 68; labor market, 73, 299; sick leave, 301–2; temporary agency work and workers, 103; utilities industry, 249; vocational education, 309; work hours and schedules, 86, 111–2, 113; working conditions and organization, 26, 111–2, 115
repetitive strain injury (RSI), 257, 276, 280–1, 284, 285
research considerations: call centers, 132; cross-country studies, 4–5; financial services industry, 241–2; hospitals, 132, 206–8; hotel industry, 132; industry analysis, 132; institutions, 17, 63–66; job quality, 18; labor market, 16; nursing homes, 207–8; organizational structure, 17–18; retail industry, 132; utilities industry, 241–2
research methodology. *See* methodology
retail industry: collective labor agreements, 161; competitive pressures, 155–61; confectionary, 273; employers' associations, 161–2; employment statistics, 134, 150, 152; female workers, 153; gender wage gap, 87; industrial relations, 161–5; job quality, 167–69; low-wage work in, 55, 56; overtime, 166; part-time employment, 152–3; research considerations, 132; sales trends, 152; staffing, 161; supply-chain management, 160–1; underemployment, 167; unions and unionization, 162, 163–4; vocational training, 162; wages, 136, 155. *See also* consumer electronics industry; supermarkets
retirement, 110
RFID. *See* radio frequency identification (RFID) technology
RND (Council for Netherlands Retail), 161
room attendants. *See* hotel room attendants
RPB. *See* Spatial Planning Bureau (RPB)
RSI. *See* repetitive strain injury (RSI)

sales activity, of call centers, 246
sales clerks, 149, 166–7, 167, 168–9, 171. *See also* consumer electronics industry
Salverda, W., 90–91
scheduling, of work. *See* work hours and schedules
Schils, T., 119
schooling. *See* educational attainment
Scientific Council for Government Policy, 109, 308
SCP. *See* Social and Cultural Planning Office (SCP)
seasonal production, 273–4
SECC. *See* Foundation for Call Center Excellence (SECC)
second-generation immigrants, 154
security, job, 100–102, 141, 142, 195
segregation, occupational, 85, 86
self-employment, 32, 107–8
self-regulation, 68
self-service, 161, 168, 250, 300
SER (Social and Economic Council). *See* Social and Economic Council (SER)
Services Directive (EU), 103

service sector, 14, 41, 55–56. *See also* retail industry
severance pay, 101
sheltered workplaces, 91
shift work, 221, 289
Shop Closing Act (1996), 160, 165
sick leave: confectionary industry, 284, 285; hospital sector, 212, 232–3; hotel industry, 186; hotel room attendants, 197; meat processing industry, 280, 285; and privatization of sickness insurance, 117; regulations, 301–2; and working conditions, 115
Sickness Benefits Act (1930), 113
sickness insurance, 18, 22, 111, 113, 117
single parents, **35**
single women, **35**
Sitter, Ulbo de, 26
skills. *See* job skills and qualifications
slaughterhouses, 133, 277. *See also* meat processing
SMIC (minimum inter-branch growth wage), 11
SNT, 252
Social and Cultural Planning Office (SCP), 96
Social and Economic Council (SER): CLA wage scale recommendations, 79; creation of, 19; employee participation, 26; employment protection legislation, 308; equal employment representation, 109; role and agenda of, 27, 68, **69**; temporary agency work, 103; vocational education, 97
social insurance: establishment of, 22; link to minimum wage benefits, 22; phases of, 20; reform, 305–6; since 1980, 24–25; taxation, 87–88; work first principles, 25, 305; before WWII, 18
social security, 87–88, 124–5n10
social welfare model, 10
Soskice, D., 64
SPAK (specific tax rebate), 90–91
Spatial Planning Bureau (RPB), 159
specialization, 277, 303–4

staffing. *See* work hours and schedules
STAR (Foundation of Labor). *See* Foundation of Labor (STAR)
Statistics Netherlands (CBS): call center employment, 133, 240; job classification, 38; low-wage threshold, 61n9; wages, 135, 136, **137**
Storrie, D., 107
strategies, of firms: call centers, 249–50; confectionary industry, 270–4; food processing industry, 293–5; hotel industry, 199–202; internalization vs. externalization, 17–18; low vs. high-road strategy, 3, 140–4, 156, 173–4, 199–202, 293–4; meat processing industry, 277–9; supermarket industry, 156, 173–4
stress, employee, 142, 168–9, 186, 259
strikes, 70, **71**
students: call center employment, 253–4; grants, 92, **93**, 306; hospital sector, 229; labor market participation, 92; lower-level jobs, 38; retail employment, 154
subsidies, 90–92, 231
supermarkets: career advancement opportunities, 172; case study data, **151**; collective labor agreements, 162, 170; competitive conditions, 7; cost-cutting strategies, 157; employee recruitment, 171–2; employee turnover, 171; employers' association, 161–2; employment flexibility, 148, 165–7; employment statistics, 152; female employees, 152, 153; job levels, 170; labor relations, 164; low-wage work, **135**; meat products, 278; number of, 156; opening hours, 160; part-time employment, 152, 165; price wars, 156–8, 173, 268, 269, 274; research methodology, 149–50; sales trends, 156; store size, 159; supply-chain management, 160–1; unions and unionization, 163–4; wages, **137**, **139**, 154–5, 170–1; work hours and schedules, 165–6, 169, 173; working conditions and orga-

supermarkets (*continued*)
nization, 148–9, 165–6, 168; work organization, 148–9, 165–6; young employees, 154–5
supply-chain management, 160–1, 173, 268
Surinamese immigrants, 109, 230–1

taxation, 87–90, 305
tax credits, 88, 90
Taylorism, 26, 211
teamwork, 148, 193
technology, 27, 237, 244–5, 247, 300–301
telemarketing, 246, 302. *See also* call centers
temporary agency work and workers: call centers, 238–9, 241, 249, 254, 260–61, **262**, 263–4; collective labor agreements, 103; confectionary industry, 289–90; employment protection, 102–3; and flexibility strategy, 27–28, 316; gender wage gap, **87**; hospitals, 230; immigrants, 103; low wages, 58, 107; meat processing industry, 281, 288, 290; regulation of, 103; specialization, 303–4; trends, **107**; young workers, 107
tenure, job. *See* job tenure
Teulings, C., 74
Tinbergen, J., 19
trade, 39
trade unions. *See* unions and unionization
training, firm-based: call centers, 239, 257; confectionary industry, 276–7, 291; consumer electronics industry, 172; Dutch language training, **98**; funding, 98–99; hospitals, 213–6; hotel industry, 185; importance of, 99–100; industry analysis, **139**; industry-level agreements, 98–99; on-the-job programs, 57, 59, 257, 276. *See also* vocational training
transportation industry, 41, **42**
tripartite institutions, 12, 13, 19, 66–74
Turkish immigrants, 231

turnover, employee. *See* employee turnover

Uitvoering Werknemers Verzekeringen (UWV), 184
underemployment, 167
unemployment: and earnings growth, 77; of foreign-born population, 61n7; and low-wage work probability, 57; probability of, 59; trends, 12, 16, 21, 22; vs. U.S., 32, **33**
unemployment insurance, 22, 92–95, 102
UNETO-VNI, 162
Unie, 185–6, 275, 279
Unilever Bestfood, 279
unions and unionization: call centers, 242, 252–3; confectionary industry, 275, 288; density, 70, **139**; and flexibility, 27; in France, 11; hospital sector, 220, 221, 222; hotel industry, 185, 191; industry analysis, **139**; influence of, 70; job dismissals, 101; low-wage workers, 312–3, 316; meat processing industry, 279–80; membership statistics, **71**; minimum wage changes, 81; priorities, 19, 28; retail industry, 162, 163–4; role of, 74; shop-floor representation, 26; strikes, 70, **71**; supermarket industry, 163–4; training, 98; working conditions, 28, 112; work organization, 26–27. *See also* collective labor agreements (CLAs); *specific unions*
United Kingdom, 6, 11, 140–1
United States: educational attainment, 14, **37**; employment protection legislation, **104**; employment to population ratio, 32–33, **37**; high-performance work systems, 141; hospitals, 222–3; low-skilled workers, 36; low-wage work in, 1, 5, 6
Unox, 279
unskilled workers, employers' organization of, 3. *See also* low-skill workers
utilities industry: competitive conditions, 250; customer service, 251;

firm strategies, 249–50; gender wage gap, **87**; regulations, 249; research considerations, 241–2; scripted phone calls, 245. *See also* call centers

UWV. *See* Uitvoering Werknemers Verzekeringen (UWV)

VAD. *See* Verordening Arbeidsvoorwaarden Detailhandel (VAD)

Vakcentrum, 162

value-added per hour worked, 174*n*3

value-added per retail worker, 159

value chains, 247–8, 264–5, 269, 300–301

van der Meer, M., 92

Van der Valk, **181**

van de Westelaken, A., 174*n*4

van Doorn, E., 126*n*29

van Horssen, C., 126*n*29

van Zevenbergen, R., 105

Vereniging voor de Bakkerij (VBZ), 270, 275

Vereniging voor de Nederlandse (VNV), 270

Verordening Arbeidsvoorwaarden Detailhandel (VAD), 163

VET (secondary-level vocational education). *See* vocational training

VGL (Association fo Grocery Multiple Stores), 161–2

Vion Food, 268, 279

VNO-NCW, 252

VNV. *See* Vereniging voor de Nederlandse (VNV)

vocational training: call centers, 254–5; collective labor agreements, 98–99; confectionary industry, 276–7, 292, 293; consequences of, 14; health care sector, 213–6; meat processing industry, 280–1, 292, 293; minority youth, 97–98; nurses, 213; problems of, 96–98, 309–11; regulation, 309; retail industry, 162

voice response units (VRUs), 244

VOIP (voice-over Internet protocol), 247

volunteers, 228–9

Voss-Dahm, D., 174*n*4

Wadsworth, J., 34

wage bargaining. *See* collective labor agreements (CLAs)

wage distribution, 5–6, **44**, 46, 73, 82

wage gap: based on gender, 84–87; by industry, 136, 138

WageIndicator: call centers, 241, 255–6, 260, 261; food processing industry, 267; industry analysis, 136, **137**; retail industry, 170, 171

wages and earnings: call center agents, 136, **137**, 138, **139**, 240–1, 261–3; and collective labor agreement coverage, 78, 136, **137**; confectionary industry, 136, **137**, 138, **139**, 267, 288; consumer electronics industry, 136, **137**, **139**, 149, 171; cross-country comparisons, 6; data sources, 136; food processing industry, **139**, 267; health care sector, 216–20; hospital sector, **137**, 138, **139**, 216–20; hotel room attendants, 136, **137**, 195, **196**; hourly pay, 43; industry analysis, 135–40; meat processing industry, 136, **137**, 138, **139**, 280, 285–8; median wage, **44**, 45, 46; moderation trend, 120–21; part-time workers, 6, 48, 57, 60, 297–8; real wage growth, 23; retail industry, 136, 155; supermarket industry, **137**, **139**, 154–5, 170–1; temporary agency workers, 58, 107; vs. U.S., **45**. *See also* minimum wage

Wal-Mart, 160

Wassenaar Accord, 23, 24, 70, 71

Werkgeversvereniging voor Facilitaire Call Centers (WGCC), 252–3, 254

Wielers, R., 92

women: call center employment, 255; confectionary industry employment, 274–5; disabled workers, **117**; employment by industry, **139**; employment rates, 33, 34–35, 43; flexible employment, **106**; food processing

women (*continued*)
    employment, 268–9; health care employment, 212, **213**; hotel room attendants, 188, 203; low-wage work incidence, 50–51, 52, **135**; low-wage work probability, 56; meat processing employment, 279, 282–3; mobility out of low-wage work, 58; occupational segregation, 85, 86; part-time work, **33**, 34, 86; retail employment, 153; supermarket employment, 152, 153; taxation, 90; union membership, 70, **71**; wage gap, 84–87
work hours and schedules: benchmarking or staff optimization, 184, 211, 303; call centers, 260–1; collective labor agreements, 86, 113, 169; confectionary industry, 289; consumer electronics industry, 169; flexible strategies, 108; health care sector, **213**; hospital sector, 220–2; hotel industry, 184, 194; meat processing industry, 280, 289; on-call work, 108; part-time workers, 48; regulation of, 86, 111–2, 113; supermarket industry, 165–6, 169, 173; and union membership, **71**; and Wassenaar Accord, 72
Working Conditions Act, 26, 112, 114, 257
working conditions and organization: call centers, 237, 257; collective labor agreements, 115; confectionary industry, 276; consumer electronics industry, 149, 168–9; high vs. low-road strategy, 143; hospitals, 206, 222–3, 227, 229–30, 232–3, 234; hotel industry, 186, 192–4; low-skill workers, 115; low-wage workers, 311–2; meat processing industry, 281–5; regulation of, 26, 111–2, 115; supermarket industry, 148–9, 165–6, 168; Taylorism, 26; types of, **115**; unions' priorities, 28, 112
Working Conditions Covenant, 186
Working Hours Act (1996), 113, 114
working week, 24
work organization. *See* working conditions and organization
works councils: call centers, 252; hospital sector, 222; legal basis for, 19, 26–27; low-wage worker representation, 313; meat processing industry, 280; retail industry, 164; role of, 68; working conditions, 112
Works Councils Act (1950), 19, 164, 275
World Trade Organization (WTO), 268

young workers: call center employees, 255; disabled workers, **117**; employment rates, 43; flexible employment, **106**, 121–2; hotel employment, 187; job characteristics, **53**; job creation, 91; low-wage work incidence, 50–52, **53**, 122–3; low-wage work probability, 56–57; meat processing industry, 288; minimum wage, 12, 81, **84**, 122, 306; mobility out of low-wage work, 58–59; retail employment, 153–5; supermarket employees, 157; temporary agency work, 107; unemployment insurance, 93–94. *See also* students
Youth Guarantee Fund, 25

zero-hours contracts, 261